Who Stole Feminism?

How Women Have Betrayed Women

Christina Hoff Sommers

A Touchstone Book
Published by Simon & Schuster
New York   London   Toronto
Sydney   Tokyo   Singapore

 TOUCHSTONE
Rockefeller Center
1230 Avenue of the Americas
New York, New York 10020

First Touchstone Edition 1995
TOUCHSTONE and colophon are registered trademarks of Simon & Schuster Inc.

Designed by Levavi & Levavi

Manufactured in the United States of America

10 9 8 7 6 5 4 3 2 1

Library of Congress Cataloging in Publication Data
Sommers, Christina Hoff.
  Who stole feminism? : how women have betrayed women / Christina Hoff Sommers.
    p. cm.
  Includes bibliographical references and index.
  1. Feminism—Philosophy. 2. Feminism—United States—History. I. Title.
HQ1154.S613 1994
305.42′0973—dc20   94-4734
                                                                        CIP

ISBN: 0-671-79424-8
ISBN: 0-684-80156-6 (Pbk)

The charts that appear on pages 246 and 247 are reprinted by permission of The Commonwealth Fund, a New York–based national philanthropic organization.

Acknowledgments

Of the many friends who helped me I single out those who read and criticized the manuscript at various stages: Martin Boer, Robert Costrell, Barbara Ellis, John Ellis, Ronni Gordon, Don Klein, Erika Kors, Evelyn Rich, Gail Savitz, David Stillman, Abigail Thernstrom, and Stephan Thernstrom.

I am grateful to Dawn Baker, an undergraduate at Boston University, Peter Welsh, a political science graduate student at Boston College, and Alex Stillman, an undergraduate at Johns Hopkins. They checked facts and looked for primary sources, which were more often than not difficult to trace. Special thanks also to Hilary Olsen for her many hours of proof-reading, editing, and retyping.

I am obliged to Lynn Chu and Glen Hartley for having urged me to undertake this book. My editor, Rebecca Saletan, has been superb throughout the two years I took in writing it. Denise Roy and Jay Schweitzer ably shepherded the book through the editorial and production processes.

Louise Hoff, my sister, traveled with me to many feminist conferences, into the very dens of the lionesses, providing much needed moral support. Our mother, Dolores Hoff, has shown us both that being a feminist has nothing to do with resenting men.

It is easy enough to get grants for feminist research aimed at showing how women are being shortchanged and "silenced" by the male establishment. It is not so easy to receive grants for a study that criticizes the feminist establishment for its errors and excesses. The Lynde and Harry Bradley Foundation, the Carthage Foundation, and the John M. Olin Foundation believed that what I had to say was important, and I thank them for their gracious and generous support for this project. I could not have written this book without their aid and cooperation, nor without the support of Clark University, which allowed me a two-year leave and awarded me a Mellon Faculty Development Grant and a Higgins Research Grant.

Numerous others—too numerous to identify here—supported me morally and intellectually. They know well who they are and know as well how thankful I am. I apologize for not acknowledging them by name.

A great deal of what is valuable and right about *Who Stole Feminism?* is due to the wisdom, encouragement, and unfailing assistance of my husband, Fred Sommers. My views on feminism are controversial, and when those who do not take well to criticism react by maligning me rather than my argument, Fred helps me stay calm and clear.

I am grateful to my stepson, Tamler Sommers, whose twenty-three-year-old perspective saved me more than once from what he assured me were misguided efforts at humor.

This book is dedicated to Fred, to Tamler, and to my nine-year-old son, David Sommers, who is, I suspect, delighted to see the last of its writing.

Contents

Preface

ễ

In *Revolution from Within*, Gloria Steinem informs her readers that "in this country alone . . . about 150,000 females die of anorexia each year."[1] That is more than three times the annual number of fatalities from car accidents for the total population. Steinem refers readers to another feminist best-seller, Naomi Wolf's *The Beauty Myth*. And in Ms. Wolf's book one again finds the statistic, along with the author's outrage. "How," she asks, "would America react to the mass self-immolation by hunger of its favorite sons?"[2] Although "nothing justifies comparison with the Holocaust," she cannot refrain from making one anyway. "When confronted with a vast number of emaciated bodies starved not by nature but by men, one must notice a certain resemblance."[3]

Where did Ms. Wolf get her figures? Her source is *Fasting Girls: The Emergence of Anorexia Nervosa as a Modern Disease*[4] by Joan Brumberg, a historian and former director of women's studies at Cornell University. Brumberg, too, is fully aware of the political significance of the startling statistic. She points out that the women who study eating problems "seek to demonstrate that these disorders are an inevitable consequence of a misogynistic society that demeans women . . . by objectifying their bodies."[5] Professor Brumberg, in turn, attributes the figure to the American Anorexia and Bulimia Association.

I called the American Anorexia and Bulimia Association and spoke to Dr. Diane Mickley, its president. "We were misquoted," she said. In a 1985 newsletter the association had referred to 150,000 to 200,000 *sufferers* (not *fatalities*) of anorexia nervosa.

What is the correct mortality rate? Most experts are reluctant to give exact figures. Reasonable estimates range from 100 to as many as 400 deaths per year. The National Center for Health Statistics reported 101 deaths from anorexia nervosa in 1983 and 67 deaths in 1988.[6] Thomas Dunn of the Division of Vital Statistics at the National Center for Health Statistics (NCHS) reports that in 1991 there were 54 deaths from anorexia nervosa. For 1990, NCHS data show 70 deaths. The deaths of these young women are a tragedy, certainly, but in a country of one hundred million adult females, such numbers are hardly evidence of a "holocaust."

Yet now the false figure, supporting the view that our "sexist society" demeans women by objectifying their bodies, is widely accepted as true. Ann Landers repeated it in her syndicated column in April 1992: "Every year, 150,000 American women die from complications associated with anorexia and bulimia."[7]

I sent Naomi Wolf a letter pointing out that Dr. Mickley had said she was mistaken. Wolf sent me word on February 3, 1993, that she intends to revise her figures on anorexia in a later edition of *The Beauty Myth*.[8] Will she actually state that the correct figure may be less than one or two hundred per year? And will she correct the implications she drew from the false report? For example, will she revise her thesis that masses of young women are being "starved not by nature but by men" and her declaration that "women must claim anorexia as political damage done to us by a social order that considers our destruction insignificant . . . as Jews identify the death camps"?[9]

Will Ms. Steinem advise her readers of the egregious statistical error? Will Ms. Landers? Will it even matter? By now, the 150,000 figure has made it into college textbooks. A recent women's studies text, aptly titled *The Knowledge Explosion,* contains the erroneous figure in its preface.[10]

The anorexia "crisis" is only one sample of the kind of provocative but inaccurate information being purveyed by women about "women's issues" these days. On November 4, 1992, Deborah Louis, president of the National Women's Studies Association, sent a message to the Women's Studies Electronic Bulletin Board: "According to [the] last March of Dimes report, domestic violence (vs. pregnant women) is now responsible for more birth defects than all other causes combined. Personally [this] strikes me as the most disgusting piece of data I've seen in a long while."[11] This was, indeed, unsettling news. But it seemed implausible. I asked my neighbor, a pediatric neurologist at Boston's Children's Hospital, about the report. He told me that although severe battery may occasionally cause miscarriage, he had never heard of battery as a significant cause of birth defects. Yet on February 23, 1993, Patricia Ireland, president of the National Organization of Women, made a similar claim during a PBS interview with Charlie Rose: "Battery of pregnant women is the number one cause of birth defects in this country."

I called the March of Dimes to get a copy of the report. Maureen Corry, director of the March's Education and Health Promotion Program, denied any knowledge of it. "We have never seen this research before," she said.

I did a search and found that—study or no study—journalists around the country were citing it.

Domestic violence is the leading cause of birth defects, more than all other medical causes combined, according to a March of Dimes study. (*Boston Globe*, September 2, 1991)

Especially grotesque is the brutality reserved for pregnant women: the March of Dimes has concluded that the battering of women during pregnancy causes more birth defects than all the diseases put together for which children are usually immunized. (*Time* magazine, January 18, 1993)

The March of Dimes has concluded that the battering of women during pregnancy causes more birth defects than all the diseases put together for which children are usually immunized. (*Dallas Morning News*, February 7, 1993)

The March of Dimes says battering during pregnancy causes more birth defects than all diseases for which children are immunized. (*Arizona Republic*, March 21, 1993)

The March of Dimes estimates that domestic violence is the largest single cause of birth defects. (*Chicago Tribune*, April 18, 1993)

I called the March of Dimes again. Andrea Ziltzer of their media relations department told me that the rumor was spinning out of control. Governors' offices, state health departments, and Washington politicians had flooded the office with phone calls. Even the office of Senator Edward Kennedy had requested a copy of the "report." The March of Dimes had asked *Time* for a retraction. For some reason, *Time* was stalling.

When I finally reached Jeanne McDowell, who had written the *Time* article, the first thing she said was "That was an error." She sounded genuinely sorry and embarrassed. She explained that she is always careful about checking sources, but this time, for some reason, she had not. *Time* was supposed to have printed a retraction in the letters column, but because of a mixup, it had failed to do so. *Time* has since called the March of Dimes' media relations department to apologize. An official retraction finally appeared in the magazine on December 6, 1993, under the heading "Inaccurate Information." [12]

I asked Ms. McDowell about her source. She had relied on information given her by the San Francisco Family Violence Prevention Fund, which in turn had obtained it from Sarah Buel, a founder of the domestic violence advocacy project at Harvard Law School who now heads a domestic abuse project in Massachusetts. [13] Ms. Buel had obtained it from Caroline Whitehead, a maternal nurse and child care specialist in Raleigh, North Carolina. I called Ms. Whitehead.

"It blows my mind. *It is not true,*" she said. The whole mixup began, she explained, when she introduced Sarah Buel as a speaker at a 1989 conference for nurses and social workers. In presenting her, Ms. Whitehead mentioned that according to some March of Dimes research she had seen, more women are screened for birth defects than are ever screened for domestic battery. "In other words, what I said was, 'We screen for battery far less than we screen for birth defects.'" Ms. Whitehead had said nothing at all about battery *causing* birth defects. "Sarah misunderstood me," she said. Buel went on to put the erroneous information into an unpublished manuscript, which was then circulated among family violence professionals. They saw no reason to doubt its authority and repeated the claim to others. [14]

I called Sarah Buel and told her that it seemed she had misheard Ms. Whitehead. She was surprised. "Oh, I must have misunderstood her. I'll have to give her a call. She is my source." She thanked me for having informed her of the error, pointing out that she had been about to repeat it yet again in a new article she was writing.

Why was everybody so credulous? Battery responsible for more birth defects than *all* other causes combined? More than genetic disorders such as spina bifida, Down syndrome, Tay-Sachs, sickle-cell anemia? More than congenital heart disorders? More than alcohol, crack, or AIDS—

more than all these things *combined?* Where were the fact-checkers, the editors, the skeptical journalists?

Unfortunately, the anorexia statistic and the March of Dimes "study" are typical of the quality of information we are getting on many women's issues from feminist researchers, women's advocates, and journalists. More often than not, a closer look at the supporting evidence—the studies and statistics on eating disorders, domestic battery, rape, sexual harassment, bias against girls in school, wage differentials, or the demise of the nuclear family—will raise grave questions about credibility, not to speak of objectivity.

When they engage in exaggeration, oversimplification, and obfuscation, the feminist researchers may be no different from such other advocacy groups as the National Rifle Association or the tobacco industry. But when the NRA does a "study that shows . . . ," or the tobacco industry finds "data that suggest . . . ," journalists are on their guard. They check sources and seek dissenting opinions.

In January 1993 newspapers and television networks reported an alarming finding: incidence of domestic battery tended to rise by 40 percent on Super Bowl Sunday. NBC, which was broadcasting the game that year, made special pleas to men to stay calm. Feminists called for emergency preparations in anticipation of the expected increase in violence on January 31. They also used the occasion to drive home the message that maleness and violence against women are synonymous. Nancy Isaac, a Harvard School of Public Health research associate who specializes in domestic violence, told the *Boston Globe:* "It's a day for men to revel in their maleness and unfortunately, for a lot of men that includes being violent toward women if they want to be." [15]

Journalists across the country accepted the 40 percent figure at face value and duly reported the bleak tidings. The sole exception was Ken Ringle, a reporter at the *Washington Post,* who decided to check on the sources. As we shall see later in this book, he quickly found that the story had no basis in fact. [16] No study shows that Super Bowl Sunday is in any way different from other days in the amount of domestic violence. Though Ringle exposed the rumor, it had done its work: millions of American women who heard about it are completely unaware that it is not true. What they do "know" is that American males, especially the sports fans among them, are a dangerous and violent species.

To the question "Why is everyone so credulous?" we must add another: "Why are certain feminists so eager to put men in a bad light?" I shall try to answer both these questions and to show how the implications affect us all.

American feminism is currently dominated by a group of women who seek to persuade the public that American women are not the free creatures we think we are. The leaders and theorists of the women's movement believe that our society is best described as a patriarchy, a "male hegemony," a "sex/gender system" in which the dominant gender works to keep women cowering and submissive. The feminists who hold this divisive view of our social and political reality believe we are in a gender war, and they are eager to disseminate stories of atrocity that are designed to alert women to their plight. The "gender feminists" (as I shall call them) believe that all our institutions, from the state to the family to the grade schools, perpetuate male dominance. Believing that women are virtually under siege, gender feminists naturally seek recruits to their side of the gender war. They seek support. They seek vindication. They seek ammunition.

Not everyone, including many women who consider themselves feminists, is convinced that contemporary American women live in an oppressive "male hegemony." To confound the skeptics and persuade the undecided, the gender feminists are constantly on the lookout for proof, for the smoking gun, the telling fact that will drive home to the public how profoundly the system is rigged against women. To rally women to their cause, it is not enough to remind us that many brutal and selfish men harm women. They must persuade us that the system itself sanctions male brutality. They must convince us that the oppression of women, sustained from generation to generation, is a structural feature of our society.

Well-funded, prestigious organizations as well as individuals are engaged in this enterprise. In 1992, for example, the American Association of University Women and the Wellesley College Center for Research on Women announced findings that our schools systematically favor boys and are contributing to a dramatic drop in girls' self-esteem. In another study, the Commonwealth Fund, relying on polls taken by Louis Harris and Associates, spread the news that 37 percent of American women are psychologically abused by their husbands or partners every year and that "40 percent of women . . . experience severe depression in a given week." [17] As we shall see, these alarming reports have little more basis in fact than did the Super Bowl hoax.

I recently told a friend that I was coming across a lot of mistakes and misleading data in feminist studies. "It's a mess," I said. "Are you sure you want to write about it?" she asked. "The far right will use what you find to attack all women. It will harm the women who are working in such problem areas as battery and wage discrimination. Why do anything to endanger our fragile gains?" My friend's questions were sobering, and I want to underscore at the outset that I do not mean to confuse the women who work in the trenches to help the victims of true abuse and discrimination with the gender feminists whose falsehoods and exaggerations are muddying the waters of American feminism. These feminist ideologues are helping no one; on the contrary, their divisive and resentful philosophy adds to the woes of our society and hurts legitimate feminism. Not only are women who suffer real abuse not helped by untruths, they are in fact harmed by inaccuracies and exaggerations.

For example, as Ms. Whitehead noted, more women are screened for birth defects than for battery. She was touching on a terribly important problem. Battery is still not taken seriously enough as a medical problem. Most hospitals have procedures to avoid discharging patients at high risk of suffering a relapse of the condition for which they are being treated. Yet few hospitals have procedures that would put women likely to suffer further abuse in touch with the professional services that could help them avoid it, a real and shocking problem. That battery is the chief cause of birth defects is perhaps more shocking, but it is untrue. The March of Dimes has developed an excellent hospital "Protocol of Care for the Battered Woman." Wouldn't it have been more effective to publicize the problem that Ms. Whitehead had actually talked about and promoted the March of Dimes' solution? True, the alleged findings had great value as gender feminist propaganda. But, being incorrect, they could lead to nothing constructive in the way of alleviating the actual suffering of women.

American women owe an incalculable debt to the classically liberal feminists who came before us and fought long and hard, and ultimately with spectacular success, to gain for women the rights that the men of this country had taken for granted for over two hundred years. Exposing the hypocrisy of the gender feminists will not jeopardize those achievements. Battered women don't need untruths to make their case before a fair-minded public that hates and despises bullies; there is enough tragic truth to go around.

With that in mind, I shall evaluate here the views of such feminists as Gloria Steinem, Patricia Ireland, Susan Faludi, Marilyn French, Naomi Wolf, and Catharine MacKinnon and the findings that inform them. I shall take a look at the feminist institutions that now control large areas of information about women. I shall take note of overly trusting journalists and the many politicians who are eager to show that they "get it."

Above all, I shall examine the philosophy, the beliefs, and the passions of the feminist theorists and researchers—the ones who do the "studies that show . . ." and who provide the movement its intellectual leadership. These articulate, energetic, and determined women are training a generation of young activists. All indications are that the new crop of young feminist ideologues coming out of our nation's colleges are even angrier, more resentful, and more indifferent to the truth than their mentors.

The large majority of women, including the majority of college women, are distancing themselves from this anger and resentfulness. Unfortunately, they associate these attitudes with feminism, and so they conclude that they are not really feminists. According to a 1992 *Time*/CNN poll, although 57 percent of the women responding said they believed there was a need for a strong women's movement, 63 percent said they do not consider themselves feminists.[18] Another poll conducted by R. H. Brushkin reported that only 16 percent of college women "definitely" considered themselves to be feminists.[19]

In effect, the gender feminists lack a grass roots constituency. They blame a media "backlash" for the defection of the majority of women. But what happened is clear enough: the gender feminists have stolen "feminism" from a mainstream that had never acknowledged their leadership.

The women currently manning—womanning—the feminist ramparts do not take well to criticism. How could they? As they see it, they are dealing with a massive epidemic of male atrocity and a constituency of benighted women who have yet to comprehend the seriousness of their predicament. Hence, male critics must be "sexist" and "reactionary," and female critics "traitors," "collaborators," or "backlashers." This kind of reaction has had a powerful inhibiting effect. It has alienated and silenced women and men alike.

I have been moved to write this book because I am a feminist who does not like what feminism has become. The new gender feminism is badly in need of scrutiny. Only forthright appraisals can diminish its inordinate and divisive influence. If others join in a frank and honest critique, before long a more representative and less doctrinaire feminism will again pick up the reins. But that is not likely to happen without a fight.

Chapter 1

Women Under Siege

The New Feminism emphasizes the importance of the "women's point of view," the Old Feminism believes in the primary importance of the human being.
—WINIFRED HOLTBY, 1926 [1]

A surprising number of clever and powerful feminists share the conviction that American women still live in a patriarchy where men collectively keep women down. It is customary for these feminists to assemble to exchange stories and to talk about the "anger issues" that vex them.

One such conference—"Out of the Academy and Into the World with Carolyn Heilbrun"—took place at the Graduate Center of City University of New York in October 1992. The morning sessions were devoted to honoring the feminist scholar and mystery writer Carolyn Heilbrun on the occasion of her voluntary retirement from Columbia University after thirty-two years of tenure. I had just then been reading Marilyn French's *The War Against Women,* which Ms. Heilbrun touts on the cover as a book that "lays out women's state in this world—and it is a state of siege." [2]

Intelligent women who sincerely believe that American women are in a gender war intrigue me, so a day with Ms. Heilbrun and her admirers promised to be rewarding. I arrived early, but so did an overflow crowd of more than five hundred women. I was lucky to get a seat.

Though she had long held a prestigious chair in Columbia's English department, Heilbrun made it clear that she felt beleaguered there. But she had survived. "In life, as in fiction," she told the *New York Times,* "women who speak out usually end up punished or dead. I'm lucky to escape with my pension and a year of leave."[3] Thirty-two years ago, there were no tenured female professors in Columbia's English department. Now eight of its thirty-two tenured professors are women, and a majority of its junior professors are women. According to the *Times,* such facts do not impress Heilbrun. "Female doesn't mean feminist," she snapped.[4]

As if to underscore that Columbia was intent on slighting her, Professor Heilbrun accused the male and female members of the Columbia English department of deliberately scheduling their own feminist conference on the same day as the conference honoring her. The *Chronicle of Higher Education* later reported that Ms. Heilbrun was mistaken: the rival conference, "Women at the Turn of the Century: 1890–1910," had been planned many months before this one.[5]

Heilbrun's theme of "siege" set the tone for the rest of the conference. As the *Chronicle* put it, "If someone as prominent as Ms. Heilbrun could feel so 'isolated and powerless' . . . where did that leave other feminists?"[6] One admirer of Ms. Heilbrun, Professor Pauline Bart of the University of Illinois, spoke of Heilbrun and herself as victims of mass persecution: "Carolyn [Heilbrun] and people like us will survive, from the outside if need be. One of my male students, a Chilean refugee, and his wife just had a baby. They named him Paolo, after me, because his father fought back and was tortured under Pinochet, and he sees me carrying on in that tradition."[7]

Throughout the day, speakers recited tales of outrage and warned of impending male backlash. Sarah Ruddick, a New School for Social Research feminist known for "valorizing" women as the gentle nurturers of our species, paid tribute to Heilbrun's "politicized anger": "Our anger, as Carolyn puts it so well, arouses the patriarchy to disgust." The historian Blanche Wiesen Cook (who had just released a book in which she claimed that Eleanor Roosevelt was really a lesbian) spoke of the vital stake women had in the impending 1992 presidential election: "It is a cross-road that will lead to a Fourth Reich or a real opportunity."

Jane Marcus, of the City University of New York, called the afternoon "Anger Session" to order, introducing herself as "an expert on anger" and thanking Heilbrun for teaching her "to use my rage in my writing." She introduced the other panelists as angry in one way or another: Alice Jardine of Harvard University's French department was "angry and struggling." Brenda Silver of Dartmouth had been "struggling and angry since 1972." Catharine Stimpson, a former vice-provost at Rutgers and recently selected to head the distinguished MacArthur Fellows Program, was introduced as "an enraged and engaged intellectual."[8]

Gloria Steinem took the microphone and explained why *she* was enraged: "I have become even more angry . . . the alternative is depression." To deal with patriarchal schools, she recommended an "underground system of education," a bartering system in which a midwife could exchange her services "in return for Latin American history." Steinem believes things are so bad for contemporary American women that we might have to consider setting up centers for training political organizers.

For someone like me, who does not believe that American women are in a state of siege (and so lacks the basis for the kind of anger that drives out depression), the conference was depressing. It was clear that these well-favored women sincerely felt aggrieved. It was equally clear to me that the bitter spirits they were dispensing to the American public were unwholesome and divisive.

For whom do these "engaged and enraged" women at the conference speak? Who is their constituency? It might be said that as academics and intellectuals they speak for no one but themselves. But that would be to mistake their mission. They see themselves as the second wave of the feminist movement, as the moral vanguard fighting a war to save women. But do American women need to be saved by anyone?

The women at the Heilbrun conference are the New Feminists: articulate, prone to self-dramatization, and chronically offended. Many of the women on the "Anger" panel were tenured professors at prestigious universities. All had fine and expensive educations. Yet, listening to them one would never guess that they live in a country whose women are legally as free as the men and whose institutions of higher learning now have more female than male students.

It was inevitable that such single-minded and energetic women would find their way into leadership positions. It is unfortunate for American feminism that their ideology and attitude are diverting the women's movement from its true purposes.

The presumption that men are collectively engaged in keeping women down invites feminist bonding in a resentful community. When a Heilbrun or a Steinem advises us that men are not about to relinquish their hegemony, the implicit moral is that women must form self-protective enclaves. In such enclaves women can speak out safely and help one another to recover from the indignities they suffer under patriarchy. In such enclaves they can think of how to change or provide alternatives to the "androcentric" institutions that have always prevailed in education and the workplace. The message is that women must be "gynocentric," that they must join with and be loyal only to women.

The traditional, classically liberal, humanistic feminism that was initiated more than 150 years ago was very different. It had a specific agenda, demanding for women the same rights before the law that men enjoyed. The suffrage had to be won, and the laws regarding property, marriage, divorce, and child custody had to be made equitable. More recently, abortion rights had to be protected. The old mainstream feminism concentrated on legal reforms. In seeking specific and achievable ends, it did not promote a gynocentric stance; self-segregation of women had no part in an agenda that sought equality and equal access for women.

Most American women subscribe philosophically to that older "First Wave" kind of feminism whose main goal is equity, especially in politics and education. A First Wave, "mainstream," or "equity" feminist wants for women what she wants for everyone: fair treatment, without discrimination. "We ask no better laws than those you have made for yourselves. We need no other protection than that which your present laws secure to you," said Elizabeth Cady Stanton, perhaps the ablest exponent of equity feminism, addressing the New York State Legislature in 1854.[9] The equity agenda may not yet be fully achieved, but by any reasonable measure, equity feminism has turned out to be a great American success story.

Heilbrun, Steinem, and other current feminist notables ride this First Wave for its popularity and its moral authority, but most of them adhere to a new, more radical, "Second Wave" doctrine: that women, even modern American women, are in thrall to "a system of male dominance" variously referred to as "heteropatriarchy" or the sex/gender system. According to one feminist theorist, the sex/gender system is "that complex process whereby bi-sexual infants are transformed into male and female gender personalities, the one destined to command, the other to obey."[10] Sex/gender feminism ("gender feminism" for short) is the prevailing ideology among contemporary feminist philosophers and leaders. But it lacks a grass roots constituency.

The New Feminists claim continuity with the likes of the eighteenth-century feminist Mary Wollstonecraft or later feminists like the Grimké sisters, Elizabeth Cady Stanton, Susan B. Anthony, and Harriet Taylor. But those giants of the women's movement grounded their feminist demands on Enlightenment principles of individual justice. By contrast, the New Feminists have little faith in the Enlightenment principles that influenced the founders of America's political order and that inspired the great classical feminists to wage their fight for women's rights.

The idea that women are in a gender war originated in the midsixties, when the antiwar and antigovernment mood revivified and redirected the women's movement away from its Enlightenment liberal philosophy to a more radical, antiestablishment philosophy. The decisive battles of the sexual revolution had been won, and students here and on the Continent were reading Herbert Marcuse, Karl Marx, Franz Fanon, and Jean-Paul Sartre and learning how to critique their culture and institutions in heady new ways. They began to see the university, the military, and the government as merely different parts of a defective status quo.

Betty Friedan and Germaine Greer would continue to offer women a liberal version of consciousness raising whose aim was to awaken them to new possibilities of individual self-fulfillment. But by the midseventies, faith in liberal solutions to social problems had waned, and the old style of consciousness raising that encouraged women to seek avenues of self-fulfillment rapidly gave way to one that initiated women into an appreciation of their subordinate situation in the patriarchy and the joys and comforts of group solidarity.

Having "transcended" the liberalism of Friedan and the fierce individualism of Greer, feminists began to work seriously on getting women to become aware of the political dimension of their lives. Kate Millett's *Sexual Politics* was critical in moving feminism in this new direction. It taught women that politics was essentially sexual and that even the so-called democracies were male hegemonies: "However muted its present appearance may be, sexual dominion obtains nevertheless as perhaps the most pervasive ideology of our culture and provides its most fundamental concept of power."[11]

The New Feminists began to direct their energies toward getting women to join in the common struggle against patriarchy, to view society through the sex/gender prism. When a woman's feminist consciousness is thus "raised," she learns to identify her personal self with her gender. She sees her relations to men in political terms ("the personal is the political"). This "insight" into the nature of male/female relations makes the gender feminist impatient with piecemeal liberal reformist solutions and leads her to strive for a more radical transformation of our society than earlier feminists had envisioned.

It is now commonplace for feminist philosophers to reject the Enlightenment ideals of the old feminism. According to the University of Colorado feminist theorist Alison Jaggar, "Radical and socialist feminists have shown that the old ideals of freedom, equality and democracy are insufficient." [12] Iris Young, of the University of Pittsburgh, echoes the contemporary feminist disillusionment with the classically liberal feminism of yesteryear, claiming that "after two centuries of faith . . . the ideal of equality and fraternity" no longer prevails: [13]

> Most feminists of the nineteenth and twentieth century, including feminists of the early second wave, have been humanist feminists. In recent years, a different account of women's oppression has gained influence, however, partly growing from a critique of humanist feminism. Gynocentric feminism defines women's oppression as the devaluation and repression of women's experience by a masculinist culture that exalts violence and individualism. [14]

The University of Wisconsin philosopher Andrea Nye acknowledges that the liberal agenda had been successful in gaining women *legal* freedoms, but she insists that this means very little, because "the liberated enfranchised woman might complain that democratic society has only returned her to a more profound subordination." [15]

The loss of faith in classically liberal solutions, coupled with the conviction that women remain besieged and subject to a relentless and vicious male backlash, has turned the movement inward. We hear very little today about how women can join with men on equal terms to contribute to a universal human culture. Instead, feminist ideology has taken a divisive, gynocentric turn, and the emphasis now is on women as a political class whose interests are at odds with the interests of men. Women must be loyal to women, united in principled hostility to the males who seek to hold fast to their patriarchal privileges and powers.

This clash of "old" and "new" feminism is itself nothing new. Here is the British feminist and novelist Winifred Holtby writing in 1926: "The New Feminism emphasizes the importance of the 'women's point of view,' the Old Feminism believes in the primary importance of the human being. . . . Personally I am . . . an Old Feminist." [16] The old feminism has had many exponents, from Elizabeth Cady Stanton and Susan B. Anthony in the middle of the nineteenth century to Betty Friedan and Germaine Greer in our own day. It demanded that women be allowed to live as freely as men. To most Americans, that was a fair demand. The old feminism was neither defeatist nor gender-divisive, and it is even now the philosophy of the feminist "mainstream."

The New Feminists, many of them privileged, all of them legally protected and free, are preoccupied with their own sense of hurt and their own feelings of embattlement and "siege." When they speak of their personal plight they use words appropriate to the tragic plight of many American women of a bygone day and of millions of contemporary, truly oppressed women in other countries. But their resentful rhetoric discredits the American women's movement today and seriously distorts its priorities.

Indeed, one of the main hallmarks of the New Feminism is its degree of self-preoccupation. Feminists like Elizabeth Stanton and Susan B. Anthony were keenly aware of themselves as privileged, middle-class, protected women. They understood how inappropriate it would be to equate their struggles with those of less fortunate women, and it never occurred to them to air their personal grievances before the public.

During the Clarence Thomas–Anita Hill hearings, Catharine MacKinnon, the influential feminist theorist and professor of law at the University of Michigan, seized the opportunity for a "national teach-in" on feminist perspectives. Calling the Senate's treatment of Ms. Hill "a public hanging," she was quick to promote it as an example of how women suffer when other women are mistreated. She was similarly affected by Patricia Bowman's ordeal in the trial of William Kennedy Smith:

> Watching the second public hanging of a woman who accused a powerful man of sexual violation reflects the way in which sexual assault in the United States today resembles lynching in times not long past. One is lynched and raped as a member of a socially subordinated group. Each is an act of torture, a violent sexual humiliation ritual in which victims are often killed. When it happens, the target population cringes, withdraws, identifies and disidentifies in terror.[17]

That the ordeals of Ms. Hill and Ms. Bowman were comparable to lynchings is debatable. Although the dire effect they had on Ms. MacKinnon and other New Feminists may not be debatable, the alleged ramified effect on all women, the so-called "target population," is. In fact, there is no evidence that most women, including those who believed that the truth lay more with Ms. Hill or Ms. Bowman, felt terrorized or "targeted"; or that they "cringed" or thought of themselves as members of a "socially subordinated group."

Alice Jardine ("angry and struggling" at the Heilbrun conference) told the *Harvard Crimson* how she reacted to the report that a crazed misogynist male had just shot and killed fourteen women students at the University of Montreal: "What I saw in the incident in Montreal was the acting out of what I experience discursively every day of my life and particularly at this institution."[18] Ms. Jardine's claim sets a standard of sisterly empathy that not many can hope to match, but her exquisite sensibility is paradigmatic for the New Feminist.

Popular books advertising motifs of humiliation, subordination, and male backlash bolster the doctrine of a bifurcated society in which women are trapped in the sex/gender system. The feminists who write these books speak of the sex/gender system as a "lens" that reveals the world in a new way, giving them a new perspective on society and making them authorities on what facts to "see," to stress, and to deplore.

Virginia Held, a philosophy professor at the City University of New York, reported on the feminist conviction that feminist philosophers are the initiators of an intellectual revolution comparable to those of "Copernicus, Darwin, and Freud."[19] Indeed, as Held points out, "some feminists think the latest revolution will be even more profound." According to Held, the sex/gender system is the controlling insight of this feminist revolution. Ms. Held tells us of the impact that the discovery of the sex/gender system has had on feminist theory: "Now that the sex/gender system has become visible to us, we can see it everywhere."[20]

Indeed, most feminist philosophers are "sex/gender feminists," and most do "see it everywhere." Held describes the "intellectually gripping" effect of the new perspective. I confess I sometimes envy Held and her sister gender feminists for the excitement they experience from seeing the world through the lens of sexual politics. On the other hand, I believe that how these feminist theorists regard American society is more a matter of temperament than a matter of insight into social reality. The belief that American women are living in thrall to men seems to suit some women more than others. I have found that it does not suit me.

Anyone reading contemporary feminist literature will find a genre of writing concerned with personal outrage. Professor Kathryn Allen Rabuzzi of Syracuse University opens her book *Motherself* by recounting this incident:

As I was walking down a sleazy section of Second Avenue in New York City a few years ago, a voice suddenly intruded on my consciousness: "Hey Mama, spare change?" The words outraged me. . . . Although I had by then been a mother for many years, never till that moment had I seen myself as "Mama" in such an impersonal, external context. In the man's speaking I beheld myself anew. "I" disappeared, as though turned inside out, and "Mama" took my place.[21]

Ms. Rabuzzi informs us that the panhandler's term caused in her a "shocking dislocation of self." Similarly, University of Illinois feminist theorist Sandra Lee Bartky recounts:

It is a fine spring day, and with an utter lack of self-consciousness, I am bouncing down the street. Suddenly . . . catcalls and whistles fill the air. These noises are clearly sexual in intent and they are meant for me; they come from across the street. I freeze. As Sartre would say, I have been petrified by the gaze of the Other. My face flushes and my motions become stiff and self-conscious. The body which only a moment before I inhabited with such ease now floods my consciousness. I have been made into an object. . . . Blissfully unaware, breasts bouncing, eyes on the birds in the trees, I could have passed by without having been turned to stone. But I must be *made* to know that I am a "nice piece of ass": I must be made to see myself as they see me. There is an element of compulsion in . . . this being-made-to-be-aware of one's own flesh: like being made to apologize, it is humiliating. . . . What I describe seems less the spontaneous expression of a healthy eroticism than a ritual of subjugation.[22]

Marilyn French, the author of *The War Against Women,* finds herself vulnerable in museums:

Artists appropriate the female body as their subject, their possession . . . assaulting female reality and autonomy. . . . Visiting galleries and museums (especially the Pompidou Center in Paris) I feel assaulted by twentieth-century abstract sculpture that resembles exaggerated female body parts, mainly breasts.[23]

Janet Radcliffe Richards has pointed to some significant similarities between modern feminism and religion.[24] I think she is right, but there is an interesting difference in the public testimony of the adherents. The devout tend to confess their sins. By contrast, the feminist ideologue testifies relentlessly to how she has been sinned *against.* Moreover, she sees revelations of monstrosity in the most familiar and seemingly innocuous phenomena. Her experience of the world may be compared to that of the Dutch naturalist Antonin Van Leeuwenhoek when he looked for the first time at a drop of water through the microscope he had invented and saw there a teeming predatory jungle.

This, for example, is what Professor Susan McClary, a musicologist at the University of Minnesota, tells us to listen for in Beethoven's Ninth Symphony: "The point of recapitulation in the first movement of the Ninth is one of the most horrifying moments in music, as the carefully prepared cadence is frustrated, damming up energy which finally exexplodes in the throttling, murderous rage of a rapist incapable of attaining release."[25] McClary also directs us to be alert to themes of male masturbation in the music of Richard Strauss and Gustav Mahler.

The "gender war" requires a constant flow of horror stories showing women that male perfidy and female humiliation are everywhere. The gender feminists who expose these evils for us often argue that what appears innocent to the untrained perception is in fact degrading to women. They highlight the pain this causes to those feminists who are sufficiently aware of what is really going on.

Addressing the Scripps College graduating class of 1992, Naomi Wolf told of an incident from her own commencement exercises when she was graduated from Yale eight years before. Dick Cavett, the speaker, had made the experience a "graduation from hell."[26] Cavett, himself a Yale alumnus, had opened his address with an anecdote about his undergraduate days: "When I was an undergraduate . . . the women went to Vassar. At Vassar they had nude photographs taken of the women in gym class to check their posture. One year the photos were stolen, and turned up for sale in New Haven's red light district. . . . The photos found no buyers." According to Ms. Wolf, the moment was devastating. "There we were, silent in our black gowns, our tassels, our brand-new shoes. We dared not break the silence. . . . That afternoon, several hundred men were confirmed in the power of a powerful institution. But many of the women felt the shame of the powerless: the choking silence, the complicity, the helplessness."[27] Never mind that Ms. Wolf was addressing some of the most privileged young women in the country. The remainder of her speech was devoted to giving them suggestions for the "survival kit" they would need in the hostile male world they were about to enter.

Is it possible that the Yale women were so stricken by Cavett's tasteless joke? Did the Scripps women really need a survival kit? If these privileged young women are really so fragile, what could Wolf's survival kit do for them anyway? (It seems that Cavett discombobulated Wolf even more than she realized. In a letter to the *Times,* Cavett pointed out that though Wolf had called him "the speaker" at her commencement, he spoke not at commencement but on Class Day, "a separate, more lighthearted event."[28])

Wolf herself was showing the Scripps graduating class how *she* survives, but though her methods were different, her general approach was old-fashioned indeed. Earlier in this century, many households still had smelling salts on hand in the event that "delicate" women reacted to displays of male vulgarity by fainting. Today, women of delicacy have a new way to demonstrate their exquisitely fragile sensibilities: by explaining to anyone who will listen how they have been blighted and violated by some male's offensive coarseness. If nothing of a telling nature has recently happened to us, we can tell about how we felt on hearing what happened to others. We faint, "discursively" and publicly, at our humiliations at the hands of men.

The Hyatt Regency in Austin, Texas, is a pleasant hotel, but not all of the five hundred participants of the 1992 National Women's Studies Association Conference were happy with it. One woman, a professor of women's studies from a well-known southern college, complained to me about the weddings being held there throughout the weekend. "Why have they put us in a setting where *that* sort of thing is going on?"

The conference participants represented a cross section of the New Feminist leadership in all areas of the women's movement. Some head urban women's centers. Others work in the offices of important politicians. Many of the women who attended the conference are in the academy in one capacity or another, either as teachers or as administrators.

Being aggrieved was a conference motif. The keynote speaker, Annette Kolodny, a feminist literary scholar and former dean of the humanities faculty at the University of Arizona, opened the proceedings with a brief history of the "narratives of pain" within the NWSA. She reported that ten years ago, the organization "almost came apart over outcries by our lesbian sisters that we had failed adequately to listen to their many voices." Five years ago, sisters in the Jewish caucus had wept at their own "sense of invisibility." Three years later the Disability caucus threatened to quit, and the following year the women of color walked out. A pernicious bigotry, Kolodny confessed, persisted in the NWSA. "Our litanies of outrage . . . overcame our fragile consensus of shared commitment and the center would no longer hold."[29]

At past conferences, oppressed women had accused other women of oppressing them. Participants met in groups defined by their grievances and healing needs: Jewish women, Jewish lesbians, Asian-American women, African-American women, old women, disabled women, fat women, women whose sexuality is in transition. None of the groups proved stable. The fat group polarized into gay and straight factions, and the Jewish women discovered they were deeply divided: some accepted being Jewish; others were seeking to recover from it.[30] This year, concern extended to "marginalized" allergy groups. Participants were sent advance notice not to bring perfumes, dry-cleaned clothing, hairspray, or other irritants to the conference out of concern for allergic sisters. Hyperconcern is now the norm: at the first National Lesbian Convention in Atlanta, flash cameras were outlawed—on grounds that they might bring on epileptic fits.

Eleanor Smeal, the former president of NOW, was scheduled to be the first speaker on the NWSA "empowerment panel," but her plane had been delayed in Memphis. To pass the time, we were introduced to an array of panelists who were touted as being experienced in conflict resolution. One woman was introduced as a member of the Mohawk nation who "facilitates antibias training." Another, an erstwhile dancer, was described as a black lesbian activist who was "doing an amazing, miraculous job on campuses building coalitions." A third, who had training as a holistic health practitioner, headed workshops that "creatively optimize human capacity."

The moderator told us that "these women have agreed to come to us as a team and work together to help us figure out how we might begin to deal much more effectively . . . with issues of inclusion, empowerment, diversity." To keep our spirits high, we were taught the words to a round, which we dutifully sang:

> We have come this far by strength,
> Leaning on each other.
> Trusting in each other's words.
> We never failed each other yet.
> Singing, oh, oh, oh. Can't turn around.
> We have come this far by strength.

After several minutes of singing and still no Smeal, panelist Angela (the former dancer) took the mike to tell about "ouch experiences." An "ouch" is when you experience racism, sexism, classism, homophobia, ableism, ageism, or lookism. One of Angela's biggest ouches came after her lesbian support group splintered into two factions, black and white. Tension then developed in her black group between those whose lovers were black and those whose lovers were white. "Those of us in the group who had white lovers were immediately targeted. . . . It turned into a horrible mess. . . . I ended up leaving that group for self-protection."

A weary Eleanor Smeal finally arrived and was pressed into immediate service. She confided that she was feeling discouraged about the feminist movement. "We need totally new concepts. . . . In many ways it's not working. . . . It is so depressing. We are leaving . . . the next generation [in a] mess." Smeal's liveliest moment came when she attacked "liberal males on the campus," saying, "they have kept us apart. They have marginalized our programs. We need fighting madness."

Despite the call to arms, Smeal's talk was a downer, and the moderator acted quickly to raise our spirits: "What we want to do now is to dwell for a minute on success. . . . Think about the fact that we have been so successful in transforming the curriculum." It was soon time for another song.

> We are sisters in a circle.
> We are sisters in a struggle.
> Sisters one and all.
> We are colors of the rainbow,
> Sisters one and all.

As it happened, I did have a real sister (in the unexciting biological sense) with me at the conference. Louise and I were frankly relieved to have the singing interrupted by a coffee break. Cream was available, but perhaps not for long. The ecofeminist caucus had been pushing to eliminate all meat, fish, eggs, and dairy products at NWSA events. As the break ended, Phyllis, the panelist from the Mohawk nation, came around with two little puppets, a dog and a teddy bear, to inform us, "Teddy and his friend say it's time to go back inside." Louise, who is a psychologist, was beginning to find the conference professionally intriguing.

Phyllis, who told us that in addition to her Mohawk ancestry she is French and Irish with traces of Algonquin, asked us to "take a moment to give ourselves a big hug. Let me remind us that the person we're hugging is the most important person we have in our life." She continued:

> Let's do it again! Each and every one of you is my relative . . . we are interconnected. We are interdependent. And we have respect. Those are principles. So, what would I need from you in a loving relationship, the reminder that I have gotten away from my principles here; and to help me get back to my principles. Even if I have to say "ouch" and hug my puppets—or whatever I have to do.

To conclude the empowerment panel session, a "feminist facilitator" led us in a "participatory experience." She told us to turn to our neighbor and tell her what we liked most about the NWSA.

After the morning session, Louise and I visited the exhibition hall. There, dozens of booths offered women's studies books and paraphernalia. Witchcraft and goddess worship supplies were in aisle one. Adjoining aisles featured handmade jewelry, leather crafts, ponchos, and other peasant apparel. One booth offered videos on do-it-yourself menstrual extractions and home abortions for those who want to avoid "patriarchal medicine." Though weak on scholarship, the conference was strong on workshops and film screenings. We were idly thinking of looking in on one of two movies: *Sex and the Sandinistas* and *We're Talking Vulva*.

A feminist philosopher, Paula Rothenberg, spotted me and approached. She knew I was a skeptic. "I am very uncomfortable having you here. I saw you taking notes. We are in the middle of working through our problems. I feel as if you have come into the middle of my dysfunctional family, and you are seeing us at the worst possible moment."

But Professor Rothenberg's "dysfunctional family" has had many such moments. Ouchings and mass therapy are more the norm than the exception. The year before, at a meeting of women's studies program directors, everyone joined hands to form a "healing circle." They also assumed the posture of trees experiencing rootedness and tranquility. Victim testimonials and healing rituals crowd out the reading of academic papers at NWSA conferences. I told Ms. Rothenberg that this was supposed to be an open conference and that I had every right to attend. But I did feel a bit sorry for her. As a philosopher she was trained to think analytically. Now she finds herself in a "dysfunctional family" whose faddish therapies even she must find fatuous. Still, she has her consolations. She is director of the "New Jersey Project: Integrating the Scholarship on Gender," a state-funded educational reform movement to make the New Jersey curriculum more "women-centered." Later that day, she would be boasting to fellow workshoppers about how sympathetic the New Jersey chancellor of education, Edward Goldberg, was to her goals.

Ms. Rothenberg and the other Austin conferees run the largest growth area in the academy. Though their conferences may be untidy, they are politically astute on their campuses. They have strong influence in key areas, in English departments (especially freshman writing courses), French and Spanish departments, history departments, law schools, and divinity schools. They are disproportionately represented in dean of students' offices, in dormitory administration, in harassment offices, in offices of multicultural affairs, and in various counseling centers. They are quietly engaged in hundreds of well-funded projects to transform a curriculum that they regard as unacceptably "androcentric." These consciousness-raisers are driving out the scholars on many campuses. Their moral authority comes from a widespread belief that they represent "women." In fact, their gynocentric version of feminism falls far short of being representative.

The conference received a warm letter from Governor Ann Richards welcoming us to the great state of Texas. The governor called the assembled feminists "the vanguard of the latest incarnation of the women's movement" and praised them for their crucial leadership role. The NWSA audience broke into thunderous applause as the letter was read aloud. It is, however, unlikely that Governor Richards was aware of the witchcraft booths, the menstrual extraction videos, the teddy bear puppets, or the paranoid exposés of "phallocentric discourse"—let alone the implacable hostility to all exact thinking as "male."

Many foundations and government agencies are involved in making it financially possible for a lot of resentful and angry women to spread their divisive philosophy and influence. If I had my way, those who make the decisions to support them with generous grants would be required to view the tapes of the meetings they fund, and then asked to hug themselves until they "ouch."

To understand how the women's movement has changed, we must look back to its beginnings. On July 14, 1848, the following notice appeared in the Seneca County Courier: "A convention to discuss the social, civil, and religious condition and rights of women will be held in the Wesleyan Chapel, at Seneca Falls, N.Y., on Wednesday and Thursday, the 19th and 20th of July current; commencing at 10 o'clock A.M."[31] The unsigned announcement had been drafted by four women meeting in the home of Richard Hunt, a wealthy reformer who had offered to help them organize the convention. Two of the women, Lucretia Mott and Elizabeth Cady Stanton, were to become famous. The tea table on which they wrote the announcement is now on exhibit at the Smithsonian as a relic of the moment when American women began the political struggle to win such elementary rights as the right to divorce without losing property and children and the right to be educated, culminating in the right to vote and the attainment of full legal equality.

The press immediately called them "sour old maids," "childless women," and "divorced wives" and implied that they would be ineffectual. These criticisms would always be made of feminists. In fact, the organizers of the Seneca Falls convention were exceptionally well-favored, well-adjusted, morally advanced women—and they were making social and political history. As for being old maids, that too was inaccurate. Stanton, the movement's principal organizer and scribe, would have eight children. Nor was there anything sour about them. Referring to the women who participated in the Seneca Falls convention, Elizabeth Cady Stanton and Susan B. Anthony later wrote that "they had not in their own experience endured the coarser forms of tyranny resulting from unjust laws, or association with immoral and unscrupulous men, but they had souls large enough to feel the wrongs of others without being scarified in their own flesh." [32]

The small notice brought more than three hundred women to Seneca Falls. The organizers were not quite certain how to go about putting together a convention, so they "resigned themselves to a faithful perusal of various masculine productions." [33] They reviewed the procedures of temperance and abolitionist conventions to see how they had been managed, and with the help of several sympathetic and experienced men, they went ahead with their history-making program.

The convention voted to adopt a "Declaration of Sentiments" written by Elizabeth Cady Stanton, who adapted the words of Jefferson's "Declaration of Independence" but specified that the liberties demanded were for women as well as men. It opened thus:

> When, in the course of human events, it becomes necessary for one portion of the family of man to assume among the people of the earth a position different from that which they have hitherto occupied, but one to which the laws of nature and of nature's God entitle them, a decent respect to the opinions of mankind requires that they should declare the causes that impel them to such a course. [34]

And she went on to speak of the truth we all hold to be self-evident, that "all men and women are created equal."

The organizers presented a list of grievances, detailing injuries that women suffer at the hands of men. Among them:

> He has never permitted her to exercise her inalienable right to the elective franchise. . . . He has compelled her to submit to laws, in the formation of which she had no voice . . . thereby leaving her without representation in the halls of legislation. . . . He has made her, if married, in the eye of the law, civilly dead. . . . In the cove-

nant of marriage, she is compelled to promise obedience to her husband, he becoming, to all intents and purposes, her master— the law giving him power to deprive her of her liberty, and to administer chastisement.[35]

Seneca Falls focused on specific injustices of the kind that social policy could repair by making the laws equitable. In thinking about that first women's conference, it is helpful to remember the state of the average American woman in the mid–nineteenth century. Consider the story of Hester Vaughan. In 1869, at the age of twenty, she had been deserted by her husband. She found work in a wealthy Philadelphia home where the man of the house seduced her and, when she became pregnant, fired her. In a state of terrible indigence, she gave birth alone in an unheated rented room, collapsing minutes afterward. By the time she was discovered, the baby had died. She was charged with murder. No lawyer represented her at her trial, and she was not permitted to testify. An all-male jury found her guilty, and the judge sentenced her to death.

Elizabeth Cady Stanton and Susan B. Anthony learned of her plight and organized a campaign to help her. One protest meeting drew nearly a thousand women. Here is how the historian Elisabeth Griffith describes it: "They demanded a pardon for Vaughan, an end to the double standard of morality, the right of women to serve as jurors, and the admission of women to law schools. . . . According to Stanton, Vaughan's trial by a jury of men . . . illustrated the indignity and injustice of women's legal status."[36]

Vaughan was pardoned. More crucially, her champions and their successors went on to win for American women in general full equality before the law, including the right to vote, the right to hold property even in marriage, the right to divorce, and the right to equal education.

The aims of the Seneca Falls activists were clearly stated, finite, and practicable. They would eventually be realized because they were grounded in principles—recognized constitutional principles—that were squarely in the tradition of equity, fairness, and individual liberty. Stanton's reliance on the Declaration of Independence was not a ploy; it was a direct expression of her own sincere creed, and it was the creed of the assembled men and women. Indeed, it is worth remembering that Seneca Falls was organized by both men and women and that men actively participated in it and were welcomed.[37] Misandrism (hostility to men, the counterpart to misogyny) was not a notable feature of the women's movement until our own times.

A 1992 meeting of the American Association of University Women held at Mills College in Oakland, California, shows how far modern feminism has come—or gone.[38] Mills had been much in the news two years before, when its board announced its decision to go the way of colleges like Vassar and Bennington in admitting male students. Televised film footage showed sobbing, hysterical young women protesting. So distraught were they at the prospect of allowing men into Mills that the trustees revoked the decision. When the reversal was announced, the cameras rolled again, this time showing students sobbing with joy and relief. Mills on the West Coast, like Smith on the East Coast, remains exclusively female.

As at most gender feminist gatherings, the Mills College meeting had almost no men. One man, however, did figure prominently in a panel discussion called "The Perils and Pleasures of Feminist Teaching." Raphael Atlas, professor of music at Smith College, had come to talk about what it is like to be a male feminist at a women's college. His fellow panelists were Candice Taylor Hogan, assistant professor of history at Wheaton College in Massachusetts, and Faye Crosby, a psychology professor, also from Smith. Professor Hogan spoke first, reading a paper in which she described her trauma when Wheaton College went coed. "I was aghast, saddened, appalled, and angered. . . . The transition was brutal, painful, and demoralizing." Before it could be made clear what her remarks had to do with the conference's theme, "Balancing the Educational Equation," Raphael Atlas spoke.

Raphael (as all the participants called him) was earnest and nonthreatening. He, too, read his paper because, he explained, its contents were too emotional for a more informal delivery. He told us that being a male feminist at Smith College filled his life with "great anxiety." The course he gave last spring on women composers made him feel like "an imposter." He asked, "Is it honest to identify my project as feminist? . . . Am I just one of those social and cultural forces trying to police women's voices?"

As we pondered these questions, Raphael told us about the many colleagues and students who believe that the few males at Smith "poisoned" the atmosphere. He said in anguished tones, "What do these women's voices say to me? I am alien. I do not belong. *I believe them.*" I felt a bit less sorry for Raphael when he finished his confession by telling us that he finds it all "exciting."

It was Professor Crosby's turn. "In feminist pedagogy," she explained, "you do not just theorize, but take action." For homework, she had instructed her introductory psychology students at Smith to buy three condoms, making eye contact with the vendor. She thought the assignment had been successful until several students pointed out that it was "heterosexist." It marginalized lesbians. They told her about dental dams —condomlike devices useful for safe lesbian oral sex.

Professor Crosby told us that during Parents' Weekend, she had invited her students and their parents to a small interactive lecture. Condoms were again a theme. The class played a "condom relay race," in which parents and students raced each other to see which group of five could put five condoms on an unpeeled banana without breaking the banana. Said Professor Crosby, referring to the condom, "They had to own it and enjoy it."

Once again Ms. Crosby thought all had gone well. She had been careful to make mention of the dental dams. But angry students pointed out to her that though she had *shown* the parents the dental dams, she hadn't used them in the relay races. They'd complained, she said, that "it was as if you said, oh, well, here are the dental dams—boring, insignificant lesbian sex . . . now let's get to the really great and fun heterosexual sex." Professor Crosby ended by telling us about her guilt over having been "exclusionary." "I felt terrible!" Like Raphael, she was clearly exhilarated by how terrible she felt.

The workshop had been a bit unconventional, but until that point all had been decorous. Decorum was irreparably shattered by "Rita" from the City College of San Francisco, who spoke loudly and angrily from the rear of the room. Addressing Raphael, she said, "First of all, why did you read your paper? As a poet and someone who cares about language, I found it extremely dull to have to sit though all of that." But then Rita went on to say she was so upset that she too preferred to read her statement: "Raphael said he was a male feminist: that is an oxymoron. My deep belief is that men cannot be feminists. They have no place in women-centered spheres. Raphael is a womb envier and a feminist wannabe—a poseur in our midst. Let him take his voice into an all-male forum."

Terry, a day care provider from Oakland, was very moved by Rita's declaration. "I agree with Rita. I did not come to a workshop to hear *that*," she said, referring to the male voice.

Ms. Crosby, who was also the moderator, looked a bit nervous. It seemed clear that she should come to the defense of her beleaguered Smith colleague. But she was patently intrigued by what she described as an "affectively charged exchange." "Rita, your attack on Raphael was extremely rude," she said. "You are breaking norms by attacking our speaker like that. And that is wrong. But," she continued, "as a feminist, I believe in breaking norms."

Then Raphael spoke up, although he looked at the floor as he spoke. "It is a dilemma. Little parts of me agree with Rita," he said. "Men do not belong at Smith. So why am I there? In addition to nitty-gritty issues of job market and my modest research projects—I still ask: do I belong there? It saddens me, demoralizes me, and depresses me. Yet I feel anger toward you, Rita. I feel you have typed me. I wonder if it is possible for us to have a dialogue? On the flight home I will be thinking about what I might have said."

Ms. Crosby was now in her element: "One aspect of the patriarchy is that we have to keep to schedules. But before breaking up, let us go around the room and see if anyone wants to share their feelings." She moved about, Phil Donahue–style, soliciting comments. Her first taker was a woman who said, "My heart is pounding with Rita and Terry. . . . I was upset to see a man on the panel. I thought there would be only women; I was not expecting this sort of—difference."

My sister Louise spoke up. "I *like* differences between people. I try to heighten differences between people. I like individuals." Ms. Crosby moved along hastily to another speaker. "My name is Anthea; I am the daughter of Beatrice, who is the daughter of her mother, who was a vegan and a suffragette. Let's clap for everybody." Most people did clap. Then Raphael called out, "Rita and I inhabit different spheres. I am a white male, age 30–34. That is difficult for me."

A gray-haired woman in the back, an AAUW member and an old-school feminist, ventured meekly: "I am in favor of educating our young people, girls and boys, to accept one another as equals." But before anyone could pounce on that particular heresy, it was time to go.

The workshoppers filed out to attend the next event. Raphael disappeared completely. At the next workshop all the panelists were women, which Rita's faction would undoubtedly find more comfortable. As my sister and I were leaving the seminar room, we passed a jubilant Professor Crosby speaking to a Smith College student and her visiting parents. The parents had attended the workshop and were looking a little bemused. "I consider that session a great success," said Crosby, "because it was the most like a Smith College class than any of the other events so far!"

Gender feminists do not relish criticism, and there are no forums where old and new feminists meet for a free exchange of competing ideas. I did learn of one such encounter that occurred spontaneously in the spring of 1991 at a conference called "Glasnost in Two Cultures: Soviet Russian/North American Women's Writing," sponsored by feminist scholars at the New York Institute for the Humanities at New York University. The episode was recounted by the Russian-American writer David Gurevich, who attended the conference as a translator.[39]

A small group of talented and outspoken Russian women poets and novelists had been invited to attend the conference, which began, inauspiciously, with the American author Grace Paley taking the visitors on a tour of the Lower East Side for a close-up look at America's slums, complete with panhandlers and junkies. The visitors, who had since childhood seen Soviet propaganda films highlighting American misery, were not duly appreciative.

At the meeting itself, the ideological gulf between the Russian and American feminists became more obvious. The literary critic Natalya Adzhikhina championed the idea of throwing out the canon, an idea that was well received all around until it slowly dawned on the gender feminists that Ms. Adzhikhina was referring to the official Communist Party canon. She and most of the other Russian writers wanted to *return* to the canon of masterworks that American feminists consider "masculinist."

When the other Russian writers spoke, they too uttered blasphemies, such as "There is only good and bad literature—not male and female." It became shockingly clear that the Russians were seeking to liberate art from politics, including sexual politics. Professor Linda Kauffman of the University of Maryland was alarmed and offended: "I don't want to sound like I am from California—which actually I am—but this is, like, heavy-duty denial." Ms. Kauffman went on to deliver an impromptu sermon on the evils of the FBI, Jesse Helms, and censorship at the NEA. She pointed out that the "MacNeil/Lehrer News Hour" was funded by AT&T and spoke of a women's gulag.[40] As she continued in this familiar vein, several of the Russian women slowly made their way to the ladies' room, the only place where they were free to smoke.

When it was again the Russian women's turn to speak, the blasphemies poured forth once more. Olesya Nikolayeva, the Moscow poet, told the American feminists how socialism had denied women their femininity, how it broke the tradition of moral and spiritual women in Russian literature, and how it broke the Christian tradition without which Russian literature after Pushkin was unthinkable. She insisted that the attack on religion had been fatal to literature, since religion had always been such a sustaining force for writers. She concluded by citing disturbing statistics about juvenile crime in Moscow and encouraging all the women in the audience to pay more attention to their traditional role as "keepers of the hearth."

Catharine Stimpson, a program director at the MacArthur Foundation and one of the founding mothers of the New Feminism, could no longer contain herself. She warned of a "new totalitarianism" and said that working mothers could not be blamed for runaways and delinquency: the state should find a solution. Domna Stanton, a Michigan women's studies professor who had organized the conference, warned of the perils of "white male morality."

A young novelist, Valerya Narbikova, took the microphone and spoke about her writers' group, the New Amazons. The American feminists were beginning to hope they could finally make contact when Ms. Narbikova announced, "It is just a name. We have nothing to do with feminism."

"Nothing at all?" the disbelieving critic Hortense Spiller asked. Gurevich describes the scene: "Wine glass in hand, Valerya was pure *artiste*. 'Nope.' . . . Ladylike pretenses were dropped. The women were tearing the mike from each other's hand. . . . Stanton was soon left alone—her faction, including Stimpson, had fled quietly—and she was actually wringing her hands." (Stimpson has objected to being classified as part of a "faction" and described as having "fled quietly.") Tatyana Tolstaya, a writer whose short stories had been recently acclaimed by American critics, thundered: "You . . . keep coming to Russia and we keep telling you these things! Why do you never listen to us? Why do you think you know more about our life than we do?"

Undoubtedly, the gender feminists left the conference pitying the benighted Russian writers for being so retrograde in their attitudes to gender. To me, those Russian women are the hope of feminism—a new avant-garde. I wish they would all emigrate to the United States. They know firsthand about the terrible consequences of group loyalty based on groupthink; they are utterly immune to ideological blandishments.

Since reading Gurevich's account of the New York University encounter, I have been attending feminist meetings in a more hopeful frame of mind. When some gender feminist is in the middle of yet another mind-numbing exposé of the evils of male culture, I find myself looking about for some innocent or intrepid soul who looks as if she might speak up and say what I, as an observer, must often refrain from saying. It hasn't happened yet, but now I know it is not out of the question.

Chapter 2

Indignation, Resentment, and Collective Guilt

❧

Every day the public is witness to feminist outrage at how badly women are treated: in the workplace, in the courts, on dates, in marriages, in the schools—by men mostly, but sometimes by other women. Much of what is reported is true, and some of it is very disturbing.

Of course, the abuse or slighting of women must be made known and should arouse indignation. Plato himself recognized the role of righteous indignation as a mainspring of moral action. In his metaphor, indignation is the good steed helping the charioteer to stay on the path of virtue by controlling the vicious, wayward steed straining to go its own brutish way. It is the "spirited element" in the soul that supplies the wise person with the emotional energy, the horsepower, to curb the appetites so that he or she may act virtuously.

But most of those who publicly bemoan the plight of women in America are moved by more dubious passions and interests. Theirs is a feminism of resentment that rationalizes and fosters a wholesale rancor in women that has little to do with moral indignation. Resentment may begin in and include indignation, but it is by far the more abiding passion. Resentment is "harbored" or "nurtured"; it "takes root" in a subject (the victim) and remains directed at another (the culprit). It can be vicarious—you need not have harmed me personally, but if I identify with someone you *have* harmed, I may resent you. Such resentment is very common and may easily be as strong and intense as resentment occasioned by direct injury. In a way it is stronger, for by enlarging the class of victims to include others, it magnifies the villainy as well.

Having demarcated a victimized "us" with whom I now feel solidarity, I can point to one victim and say, "In wronging her, he has betrayed his contempt for us all," or "Anyone who harms a woman harms us all," or simply "What he did to her, he did to all of us." The next step is to regard the individual who wronged "us" as himself representative of a group, giving our animus a larger target. This I may do quite "reasonably" by adopting a position from which people *like* the perpetrator (male, rich, etc.) are regarded as "the kind of people" who exploit people like "us." My social reality has now been dichotomized into two groups politically at odds, one of whom dominates and exploits the other.

Susan Faludi, author of *Backlash* and one of the more popular resenters of our time, reminds us of the feminist truism that feminist anger comes when women construe their individual experiences in a political framework: "When you're not able to see your experience as political, you're not able to be angry about it."[1] Sandra Bartky, who is an expert on something she calls the "phenomenology of feminist consciousness," puts it succinctly: "Feminist consciousness is consciousness of *victimization* . . . to come to see oneself as a victim" (her emphasis).[2]

Once I get into the habit of regarding women as a subjugated gender, I'm primed to be alarmed, angry, and resentful of men as oppressors of women. I am also prepared to believe the worst about them and the harm they cause to women. I may even be ready to fabricate atrocities. Eleanor Smeal spoke in Austin of the need to get women fighting mad. Neither she nor any of the other feminist leaders and thinkers who promote the sexual politics of resentment and anger seem to be aware of how injuriously divisive their version of feminism is—or if they are, they seem not to care.

Consider how Patricia Ireland, the president of NOW, speaks of her seven years as a flight attendant for Pan Am: "I thought of myself as a professional. But what I really did was go down the aisle and take people's garbage and thank them for it. That's what women have been doing. We've been taking their garbage and thanking them for it. We've got to stop."[3] Ms. Ireland is telling us how easy it is (in a society that routinely humiliates women) for women to deceive themselves into thinking they are doing something dignified when they are "really" doing something demeaning. She speaks of "their garbage," meaning "men's," though probably half the passengers were women. She asks us to note the shame of taking their garbage and having to thank "them" for it. Would she be in favor of having the airlines phase out women flight attendants, replacing them with men? But Ireland knows what she is doing. By so construing male/female relations, she is doing what any political leader does in time of war: get potential allies angry and unified behind the effort to defeat the enemy.

Resentment is not a wholesome passion. Unlike indignation, it is not an ethical passion. But because it often originates in moral outrage at real injustice (from wife battering to job discrimination), resentment can be made to sound like a commendable passion for social justice. The idea that men are generally culpable has the status of a first principle among some establishment feminists.

According to Marilyn French, "The entire system of female oppression rests on ordinary men, who maintain it with a fervor and dedication to duty that any secret police force might envy. What other system can depend on almost half the population to enforce a policy daily, publicly and privately, with utter reliability?"[4] It is a system that uses threat as well as force to exploit and humiliate women.

> As long as some men use physical force to subjugate females, *all* men need not. The knowledge that some men do suffices to threaten all women. Beyond that, it is not necessary to beat up a woman to beat her down. A man can simply refuse to hire women in well-paid jobs, extract as much or more work from women than men but pay them less, or treat women disrespectfully at work or at home. He can fail to support a child he has engendered, demand the woman he lives with wait on him like a servant. He can beat or kill the woman he claims to love; he can rape women, whether mate, acquaintance, or stranger; he can rape or sexually molest his daughters, nieces, stepchildren, or the children of a woman he claims to love. *The vast majority of men in the world do one or more of the above* [her emphasis].[5]

In French's view, male atrocity and criminal abuse are pandemic. We must, however, insist that the burden of proof for so broad a claim be on her. Even if we accept the premise that men and women are at odds, the factual question of guilt cannot be begged—at least not in this country.

Moreover, we cannot help noticing that French's contempt for men is accompanied by a strong bias in favor of women: "While men strut and fret their hour upon the stage, shout in bars and sports arenas, thump their chests or show their profiles in the legislatures, and explode incredible weapons in an endless contest for status, an obsessive quest for symbolic 'proof' of their superiority, women quietly keep the world going."[6]

Resenter feminists are convinced that men generally take every opportunity to exploit women and that they often delight in humiliating them physically and mentally. "Given the prevalence of rape and given the socio-cultural supports for sexual aggression and violence against women in this society, perhaps we should be asking men who don't rape, why not! In other words, we should be asking what factors prevent men from abusing women in rape-supportive societies."[7] That is the view of Diana Scully, author of *Understanding Sexual Violence*.

Recently several male students at Vassar were falsely accused of date rape. After their innocence was established, the assistant dean of students, Catherine Comins, said of their ordeal: "They have a lot of pain, but it is not a pain that I would necessarily have spared them. I think it ideally initiates a process of self-exploration. 'How do I see women?' 'If I did not violate her, could I have?' 'Do I have the potential to do to her what they say I did?' These are good questions."[8] Dean Comins clearly feels justified in trumping the common law principle "presumed innocent until proven guilty" by a new feminist principle, "guilty even if proven innocent." Indeed, she believes that the students are not really innocent after all. How so? Because, being male and being brought up in the patriarchal culture, they *could easily have done* what they were falsely accused of having done, even though they didn't *actually* do it. Where men are concerned, Comins quite sincerely believes in collective guilt. Moreover, she feels she can rely on her audience to be in general agreement with her on this.

The idea of collective guilt may sound like the theological doctrine of original sin, but in Christianity, at least, it applies equally to all human beings. Racists and gender feminists are more "discriminating."

In the spring of 1993, nine women students, who were taking a course called "Contemporary Issues in Feminist Art" at the University of Maryland, distributed posters and fliers all over the campus with the names of dozens of male students under the heading "Notice: These Men Are Potential Rapists." The women knew nothing whatever about the bearers of the names; they had simply chosen them at random from the university directory to use in their class project. The instructor, Josephine Withers, would not comment to the press.[9]

The New Feminists are a powerful source of mischief because their leaders are not good at seeing things as they are. Resenter feminists like Faludi, French, Heilbrun and MacKinnon speak of backlash, siege, and an undeclared war against women. But the condition they describe is mythic—with no foundation in the facts of contemporary American life. Real-life men have no war offices, no situation rooms, no battle plans against women. There is no radical militant wing of a masculinist movement. To the extent one can speak at all of a gender war, it is the New Feminists themselves who are waging it.

Gender feminists are fond of telling men who don't realize the depth of women's anger and resentment that "they just don't get it." Feminist leaders immediately rallied to the side of Lorena Bobbitt, the Virginia woman accused of having severed her sleeping husband's penis but who in turn accused him of having raped her. The Virginia chapter of NOW set up a support line for Ms. Bobbitt headed by Virginia's NOW coordinator, Denise Lee.[10] In *Vanity Fair,* Kim Masters reported on "Lorena supporters who have transformed the V-for-Victory sign into a symbol of solidarity by making scissorlike motions with their fingers."[11] Kim Gandy, executive vice president of NOW, talked of the many women "who have gone through this and probably wish they had a chance to get their own revenge."[12]

The journalist Daniel Wattenberg rightly saw in all this the presumption of John Wayne Bobbitt's guilt long before the case had gone to trial. "It is assumed that he routinely beat his wife over a period of years. It is assumed that he raped her the night she castrated him." It hardly matters that Mr. Bobbitt has since been found not guilty by the courts. Commenting on the castration on "20/20," Patricia Ireland said, "The depth of anger that was plumbed by this and the response of support that comes for Lorena Bobbitt comes from the depth of anger, of feeling there has not been adequate resources and recourse and redress of the terrible violence that women face." But, sticking to what facts we have, all we can say is that Lorena was enraged to the point of violence. The personal tragedy of this unhappy couple has been appropriated as a symbol of righteous feminist revenge. The in-joke among Lorena's feminist admirers is that Lorena has since been greeting John by saying, "*Now* do you get it?"

When collective guilt is assigned (to males, to Germans, to Moslems, etc.), children are usually included. Explaining why Minnesota has adopted strict sexual harassment policies for children as young as five, Sue Sattel, the "sex equity specialist" for the Minnesota Department of Education, points out that "serial killers tell interviewers they started sexually harassing at age 10, and got away with it."[13]

Nan Stein, a project director at the Wellesley College Center for Research on Women who specializes in sexual harassment by juveniles, is angry with Montana school officials and teachers for ignoring the "gendered terrorism" in their schoolyards.

> Friday "Flip-Up Day" is a weekly occurrence at many elementary schools in Montana. Every Friday, boys chase girls around the school playgrounds; those girls who have worn skirts are fair game —their skirts will be flipped up, not once, but as many times as possible by as many boys as can get them. School administrators . . . have seen no reason to intervene or to punish the perpetrators. Their silence has allowed this gendered terrorism on the playground to continue.[14]

Boys who tease girls by flipping up their skirts should be dealt with decisively and perhaps severely. But only women who view the world through "sex/gender" lenses would see in children's schoolyard rudeness the making of serial killers and gender terrorists.

Should the rudeness even be regarded in sexual terms? The gender monitors believe it should be and that girls should be made aware of its true nature. One of the goals of the sex equity experts is to teach little girls to be resentful of boys' pranks by pointing out that what they are doing is sexual harassment and against the law. Bernice Sandler, a gender relations specialist at Washington's Center for Women Policy Studies, offers harassment workshops to elementary school children. At one workshop, a little girl told about a classmate who had pushed her down and tickled her. Ms. Sandler made sure to put the boy's act in perspective: "Now, you have to ask, what is this boy doing, throwing girls to the ground? This happens to be a sexual offense in New York, and in most states."[15]

The presumption of sexual guilt continues as children grow up. In more and more public schools and colleges, we find a dynamic group of feminist reformers—harassment officers, women's studies professors, resident hall staff, assorted deans and assistant deans, and sex equity experts —who regard male sexuality with alarm and seek ways to control it. The Rutgers University anthropologist Lionel Tiger has described the contemporary sexual environment with its hysteria over harassment and date rape as a reversal of the one described in *The Scarlet Letter*: "It's the male who now bears the stigma of alleged sexual violation." [16]

If they do, not many notice it. The gender feminist ideology affects women far more deeply. Many are "converted" to a view of the society they inhabit as a patriarchal system of oppression. For most, this happens in college. Laurie Martinka, a women's studies graduate from Vassar, talked to me about her personal transformation. "You're never the same again. Sometimes I even bemoan the fact that so much has changed. I am tired of always ripping things apart because they exclude the perspective of women. . . . You become so aware of things. And it is hard. My mother cannot accept it. It is hard for her because I have changed so completely." Anne Package, a student at the University of Pennsylvania, told me that students talk among themselves about this keen new awareness: "We call it 'being on the verge' or 'bottoming out.' You are down on everything. Nothing is funny anymore. It hits you like a ton of bricks. You hit rock bottom and ask: how can I live my life?" When I suggested to her that many would count her and her classmates among the world's more fortunate young women, she bristled. "We still suffer psychological oppression. If you feel like the whole world is on top of you, then it is."

I was intrigued, though, by her expression "being on the verge." On the verge of what? Though the expression suggests a transitory experience, being on the verge is construed as the permanent condition of women who feel they have achieved a realistic awareness of their plight in male-dominated society. Such women sometimes organize into small but powerful groups within institutions they regard as masculinist bastions and where they make their presence felt in no uncertain terms.

The *Boston Globe* is New England's largest and most prestigious newspaper. In 1991, some two dozen women editors, managers, and columnists (including Ellen Goodman) formed a group called "Women on the Verge" to counter what senior education editor Muriel Cohen called the "macho newsroom." [17] The "vergies," as they have come to be known, have some traditional equity feminist concerns about salaries and promotions; but they have also taken up arms against such things as the use of sports metaphors in news stories and the traditional lunchtime basketball game, which symbolizes to them the once-powerful and exclusionary old-boy network (though that complaint is unfounded because women are welcome to play, and some do). Defending the basketball games, editor Ben Bradlee, Jr., says: "All it is really is a bunch of people who want to get exercise and play a game. In the current conspiracy that's abroad, it's me and the other editors perhaps cutting secret deals and giving the boys the best stories."[18] Ms. Cohen expressed concern to editor Jack Driscoll over the "hormones that are running around here."[19] Vergies are also irritated by "the strutting zone"—a corridor where some of the managerial males like to pace before deciding on the day's lead stories. The Women on the Verge at the *Globe* are feared but not loved. Since their advent, the newspaper has known no internal peace.

David Nyhan, a senior editor and syndicated columnist, has been on the paper for more than twenty years and is part of what is known as its liberal "Irish mafia." He is an old-style newspaperman who wears his sleeves rolled up and has a booming voice and a penchant for bawdy humor. It was just a matter of time before he got into trouble with the Women on the Verge. On April 20, 1993, he was on his way to play in the infamous noontime basketball match when he spotted a fellow reporter, Brian McGrory, and invited him to join the game. Brian was on assignment and had a bad knee that day, so he declined. Nyhan persisted, but when it was clear that McGrory was not going to play, Nyhan jeered him as "pussy-whipped."

Betsy Lehman, a vergie, overheard the remark in passing and made it clear that she was very offended. Nyhan, who hadn't realized anyone was listening, immediately apologized. Sensing he was in trouble, he placed a memo on his door restating his remorse. He went around the newsroom and again apologized to any woman he could find. But he was about to be made an example of, and nothing could stop it. Already several Women on the Verge had interpreted his statement as an insult to a woman editor who, they assumed, had given Brian McGrory his assignment. McGrory denies it was a woman.

The *Globe* management had just spent thousands of dollars on sensitivity workshops. Senior editor Matt Storin drew the moral: "Coming off of that experience [the workshops], I for one am all the more saddened by today's experience."[20] Storin warned the staff that "remarks that are racially and sexually offensive to co-workers will not be tolerated here. Those who utter such remarks will be subject to disciplinary procedures." The publisher fined Nyhan $1,250 and suggested he donate that sum to a charity of Ms. Lehman's choice.

The vergies had made their point, but the men of the *Globe* (and some women reporters who sympathized with them) had been alerted to the climate of resentment they lived in. They began to react. A price list was circulated: "babe" cost $350, "bitch" went for $900, "pussy-whipped," $1,250. Someone started a David Nyhan relief fund. (The fine was eventually rescinded.) Even some of the vergies were uncomfortable. Ellen Goodman said that she disapproved of the fine: "You do not want to get

to the point where everybody feels every sentence is being monitored."
But that is just the point the *Globe* had gotten to.[21]

The *Globe* incident is emblematic of the "achievements" of the New
Feminists elsewhere. They have achieved visibility and influence, but they
have not succeeded in winning the hearts of American women. Most
American feminists, unwilling to be identified as part of a cause they find
alien, have renounced the label and have left the field to the resenters.
The harmful consequences of giving unchallenged rein to the ideologues
are nowhere more evident than in the universities.

Chapter 3

Transforming the Academy

I am grateful . . . to the students of my women's studies
ovular at Washington University in the spring semester of
1982.[1]

This little acknowledgment, in the preface of a book by the feminist philosopher Joyce Trebilcot, is one of the more amusing examples of the feminist effort to purge language of sexist bias. Trebilcot considers "seminar" offensively "masculinist," so she has replaced it by "ovular," which she regards as its feminist equivalent. Linguistic reform is one characteristic activity of feminist academics, and biological coinages are very much in favor. Feminist literary critics and feminist theologians (who call themselves thealogians) may refer to their style of interpreting texts as "gynocriticism" or "clitoral hermeneutics," rejecting more traditional approaches as inadmissibly "phallocentric."

Does it matter that academic feminists speak of replacing seminars with "ovulars," history with "herstory," and theology with "thealogy"? Should it concern us that most teachers of women's studies think of knowledge as a "patriarchal construction"? It should, because twenty years ago the nation's academies offered fewer than twenty courses in women's studies; today such courses number in the tens of thousands. Such rapid growth, which even now shows little signs of abating, is unprecedented in the annals of higher education. The feminist colonization of the American academy warrants study. What is driving it? Is it a good thing?

Women's studies, though officially an academic discipline, is consciously an arm of the women's movement, dedicated to a utopian ideal of social transformation. In the words of the preamble to the National Women's Studies Association constitution, "Women's Studies owes its existence to the movement for the liberation of women; the feminist movement exists because women are oppressed. . . . Women's Studies, then, is equipping women . . . to transform the world to one that will be free of all oppression."[2]

The goal may be salutary, but equipping students to "transform the world" is not quite the same as equipping them with the knowledge they need for getting on in the world. Much of what students learn in women's studies classes is not disciplined scholarship but feminist ideology. They learn that the traditional curriculum is largely a male construction and not to be trusted. They learn that in order to rid society of sexism and racism one must first realign the goals of education, purging the curriculum of its white male bias and "reconceptualizing" its subject matter.

The majority of women in the academy are not feminist activists. They are mainstream equity feminists: they embrace no special feminist doctrines; they merely want for women what they want for everyone—a "fair field and no favors." Equity feminists, regarding themselves as engaged on equal terms in contributing to a universal culture of humanity, do not represent themselves as speaking for Women. They make no dubious claims to unmask a social reality that most women fail to perceive. Their moderate, unpretentious posture has put them in the shadow of the less humble and more vocal gender feminists.

The gender feminists are convinced they are in the vanguard of a conceptual revolution of historic proportions, and their perspective, predicated on the "discovery" of the sex/gender system, is a beguiling one. Carolyn Heilbrun exults in the conviction that the New Feminist thought is comparable to the intellectual revolutions produced by Copernicus, Darwin, and Freud.[3] Gerda Lerner, professor of history at the University of Wisconsin and author of the influential book *The Creation of Patriarchy*, warns that attempts to describe what is now going on in women's scholarship "would be like trying to describe the Renaissance—ten years after it began."[4] Sociologist Jessie Bernard compares the feminist scholars to the *philosophes* of the French Enlightenment, characterizing the explosion of research in women's scholarship as "the storming of the Bastille" or "the shot heard round the world." "Academia will never be the same again," she claims.[5] Alison Jaggar, director of women's studies at the

University of Colorado, says, "We're developing a whole reconstruction of the world from the perspective of women, with the keyword being 'womencenteredness.' "[6]

The gender feminists are exuberantly confident that they are qualified to overhaul the American educational system. Unlike other, more modest reformers, these women are convinced that their insights into social reality uniquely equip them to understand the educational needs of American women. Their revolution is thus not confined to "feminist theory." On the contrary, it is essentially practical, pedagogical, and bureaucratic.

Not all gender feminist academics teach women's studies. Many are in administration. Some direct harassment centers. Others have controlling positions in such para-academic organizations as the Association of American Colleges (AAC) or the American Association of University Women (AAUW). Some head women's centers that do research on women. Still others head "curriculum transformation projects."

"The goal of feminist teaching," says University of Massachusetts feminist philosopher Ann Ferguson, "is not only to raise consciousness about . . . male domination system but also to create women and men who are agents of social change."[7] That motivation, powerfully enhanced by the gender feminists' faith that they are privy to revolutionary insights into the nature of knowledge and society, inspires them with a missionary fervor unmatched by any other group in the contemporary academy. Not only do they pursue their mission in their classrooms, they are also involved in "transforming the academy" to render it more women-centered. Gender feminists are at work in hundreds of transformation projects for changing university curricula that they regard as inadmissibly "masculinist." The bias of the traditional "white male curriculum" must be eliminated, and new programs that include women must replace those in which women are "absent," "silent," "invisible." The whole "knowledge base" must be transformed.

Gender feminists have been influential in the academy far beyond their numbers partly because their high zeal and single-mindedness brook no opposition; or rather, because they treat opposition to their exotic standpoint as opposition to the cause of women. University trustees, administrators, foundation officers, and government officials tend generally to be sympathetic to women's causes. Apart from an unwillingness to be considered insensitive and retrograde, they are aware that women have been discriminated against and may still need special protections. So they want to do what is right. But when future historians go back to find out what happened to American universities at the end of the twentieth century that so weakened them, politicized them, and rendered them illiberal, anti-intellectual, and humorless places, they will find that among the principal causes of the decline was the failure of intelligent, powerful, and well-intentioned officials to distinguish between the reasonable and just cause of equity feminism and its unreasonable, unjust, ideological sister —gender feminism.

At the 1992 National Women's Studies Conference in Austin, Texas, that I described in chapter 1, the moderator urged us to "dwell for a moment on success. . . . Think about the fact that we have been so successful in transforming the curriculum." My sister Louise, who attended the conference with me, has two sons in college and a daughter starting junior high, and this remark alarmed her. Having spent several hours with the Austin conferees, she had doubts about their competence and reasonableness. "What exactly did she mean?" she asked me. She did well to ask; for she had stumbled on an area of feminist activism that has gone virtually unnoticed by the public. What began as a reasonable attempt to redress the neglect of women in the curriculum has quietly become a potent force affecting the American classroom at every level, from the primary grades to graduate school.

A nationwide feminist campaign to change the curriculum of the American academy is receiving support from the highest strata of education and government. The Ford Foundation recently helped launch a National Clearinghouse for Curriculum Transformation Resources at Towson State University in Maryland, to give the growing number of transformation consultants in our nation's schools quick access to resources. The Towson center provides consultants and project directors with readings on feminist pedagogy, samples of women-centered syllabi, lists of womencentered textbooks, and suggestions for women-centered audiovisual materials. It provides aspiring transformationists with manuals on how to start their own projects, as well as a list of resources to help them to "counter resistance."[8] The transformation projects receive generous funding from major foundations and from federal agencies such as the Women's Education Equity Act Program and the Fund for the Improvement of Postsecondary Education (FIPSE), as well as from the state governments of New Jersey, Tennessee, Montana, Pennsylvania, Maryland, and California.

In a recent book chronicling the triumphs of "the transformation movement," Caryn McTighe Musil reports on the success of the "hundreds of curriculum transformation projects around the country since 1980."[9] In fact, the transformationists have been at it for longer than that, but they are only now coming into their own. On April 16, 1993, more than eight hundred teachers, college professors, school administrators, and state officials gathered at the Hilton Hotel in Parsippany, New Jersey, for a three-day "national" conference on curriculum transformation. The official program gives the overview: "A celebration of twenty years of curriculum transformation, this conference will bring together teachers, scholars, activists, and cultural leaders to share insights, knowledge, and strategies to assess our accomplishments and to imagine together a curriculum for the 21st century."

The conference was sponsored by a variety of state and federal agencies such as the National Endowment for the Humanities, the Pennsylvania Humanities Council, and the New Jersey Committee for the Humanities. The keynoter, New Jersey chancellor of education Edward Goldberg, pointed out with great pride that New Jersey had invested "millions" in the curriculum transformation project. "The rest of America cannot be far behind."

Most of the eight hundred transformationists at the Parsippany Hilton had their expenses paid by their employers—mainly state governments, public schools, and public colleges and universities. Yet very few people know what transformationists do, why they do it, or why it might matter.

Ms. magazine used to run a feature called "The Click Experience," in which a woman would write in to tell about the moment when a light went on in her head and she had her first blazing realization of how women had been cheated and silenced. The "click" is a quantum leap in feminist awareness—"the sudden coming to critical consciousness about one's oppression." Gender feminist academics have their own particular version of the click experience: it happens at the moment one "sees" that the entire college curriculum has, with very few exceptions, been wrought and written by men, about men, and for men. History is "his story," men telling about men. Social science research, usually conducted by men and about men, holds up men as the norm; women are the Other. The great thoughts we study, the great art we revere, the literature we learn to love are largely male achievements. Men wrote the books, and they concocted the theories: knowledge is a male creation. In a single "click," a woman realizes that the culture and science men have created are not only wrong but self-serving and dangerous for women. The experience often has a depressing and alienating effect on a woman; the culture she had revered is suddenly not hers, and she may feel like a child of indifferent parents who discovers at a late age that she has been adopted.

Sooner or later, most women, gender feminist or not, have something like a click experience. Men, except for the more myopic and hidebound among them, have it too. Just about everything bears the impress of patriarchy: high culture is largely a male achievement. As women have attained parity in economic status and access to higher learning and culture, the disparities, injustices, and exclusions of the past have been brought home to them as never before.

The evidence that women have been excluded, and their abilities as thinkers and writers demeaned, is everywhere. But once a woman appreciates the extent to which culture and civilization have been male-dominated, two roads lie before her. She can learn what can be learned about women's past achievements, and learn as well the reasons that their contributions to the larger enterprise were not greater; and she can then avail herself of the freedom she now has to accept the challenge to join with men on equal terms in the making of a new and richer culture. Or she can react to the cultural and scientific heritage as "androcentric" and move consciously to reconstruct the "knowledge base." It is at this juncture that equity and gender feminist academics begin to go their separate ways. The former stay within the bounds of traditional scholarship and join in its enterprise. The latter seek to transform scholarship to make it "women-centered."

Geraldine Ruthchild, a professor of English at Albion College, typifies the gender feminist reaction to the keen awareness that so much of culture has been made by men. Her click sounded when she came across these remarks by Louise Bernikow: "Which writers have survived their time and which have not depends upon who noticed them and chose to record the notice. . . . Such power, in England and America, has always belonged to white men." [10] Professor Ruthchild writes, "After reading Louise Bernikow . . . I was never again the same person, for her words abruptly crystallized random ideas I had had into a gem of revelation." [11]

The historian Gerda Lerner's revelation illuminates what for her is an ongoing atrocity. She asserts that men have been teaching women that sound thinking must exclude feeling. "Thus they [women] have learned to mistrust their own experience and devalue it. What wisdom can there be in menses? What source of knowledge in the milk-filled breast?" [12] The cognitive abuse of women fills Lerner with anger: "We have long known that rape has been a way of terrorizing us and keeping us in subjection. Now we also know that we have participated, although unwittingly, in the rape of our minds." [13]

The gender feminist "re-vision" has been described in more sober terms in a brochure distributed by the prestigious American Association of Colleges:

In the last two decades, educators have begun to recognize that the experiences and perspectives of women are almost totally absent from the traditional curriculum. Surveys in the 1970s revealed, for example, that history textbooks devoted less than 1 percent of their coverage to women; that the most widely used textbook in art history did not include a single woman artist; and that literature courses contained, on average, only 8 percent women authors. Such discoveries have led many people to question the validity of the version of human experience offered by the liberal arts.[14]

It is possible to come to such an awareness without deciding that the rational response is to overhaul the entire canon of Western experience. Many scholars have begun to take pains to give women the recognition that was often denied them in past accounts. Women scholars of anthropology, psychology, and sociology have discovered that much previous research, which tended to concentrate on men, generalized to conclusions that did not necessarily apply to women. For the past ten or fifteen years social scientists have been working to correct this neglect. Feminist literary scholars have discovered and rescued many gifted women writers from undeserved oblivion. Textbook publishers now take pains to see that women are duly represented and that they are not demeaningly stereotyped. Such achievements stay well within the bounds of the kind of equitable adjustment that a mainstream feminism has rightly demanded. But the gender feminists are not content with them. They want transformation; a mere correction of the record won't do.

There are, most people are aware, two meanings to the word *history*. On the one hand, history refers to a series of events that actually happened. On the other hand, there is History, an *account* of what happened. The gender feminists claim that History (written by men and focusing almost exclusively on men) has systematically distorted history.

It is undeniable that scholars often failed to recognize the role and importance of many gifted and historically important women. These neglected women deserve their place in History, and historians have a professional obligation to give it to them. Nevertheless, the paucity of women in History is, in the main, due *not* to the bias of male historians but rather to their concentration on politics, war, and conceptual change. Such History inevitably reflects the fact that women have not been allowed to make history in the way that men—and relatively few men at that—have been allowed to make it. It is a pervasive fact of history that men have rarely permitted women to participate in military and political affairs and that they have kept them away from learning and the high arts. Any History that is faithful to the facts must acknowledge that in the past women were simply not permitted the degree of freedom commensurate with their talents. As Virginia Woolf pointed out, even the most gifted sister of Shakespeare would, tragically, never have been given the opportunities to make use of her genius. Lamentable as this may be, there is simply no honest way of writing women back into the historical narrative in a way that depicts them as movers and shakers of equal importance to men.

To be sure, giving women only 1 percent of the narrative is too little, but 30 percent would be too much, and giving women *half* the space in a conventional History would blatantly falsify the narrative. Nor can historians do much about the "common people" whom God made so numerous. The vast majority of people, including *most* men and almost *all* women, have had a disproportionately small share in the history-making decisions about war, politics, and culture that historians count as momentous. But what is any historian of integrity supposed to do about that?

It is a standard feminist objection to traditional History that it focuses too much on male-dominated activities such as politics, war, and, more recently, science. A more balanced History would focus on areas of life that would give women greater visibility and importance. In effect, the complaint is that women figure importantly in social history but that political history has been given pride of place. This was a reasonable grievance twenty years ago, and the trend in high school and college history books since then has been toward social history. Even a strongly feminist report on the curriculum by the Wellesley College Center for Research on Women points this out: "An informal survey of twenty U.S. history textbooks compiled each year from 1984 to 1989 found a gradual but steady shift away from an overwhelming emphasis on law, wars, and control over territory and public policy, toward an emphasis on people's daily lives in many kinds of circumstances."[15]

In fact, both political and social history are important. By itself, social history, too, is insufficient. Even an exhaustive survey of daily life cannot substitute for the traditional kind of political history. Students need a reliable account of the events, philosophies, and cultural developments that have made a difference in the fates of nations and peoples, rendering some more successful and prosperous than others. Sooner or later the responsible teacher of history must get down to the history of politics, war, and social change.

But the gender feminists have far more ambitious goals than the redressing of historical neglect and bias. If history cannot be changed, History can be. Better yet, why not insist that all we *ever* have of history is the History we write, and *that* depends on who writes it? Heretofore, men have written History, giving us a masculinist account of the past; now women are free to change that version of History to make it more women-centered.

It is now common practice in high school textbooks to revise History in ways that attribute to women a political and cultural importance they simply did not have. Overt revisionism is rare. More often, history is distorted and the importance of women is falsely inflated without directly tampering with the facts. High school history texts now lavish attention on minor female figures. Sixteen-year-old Sybil Ludington, who alerted colonial soldiers in a failed attempt to cut off the escape of a British raiding party, gets more space in *America: Its People and Its Values* than Paul Revere. In the same textbook, Maria Mitchell, a nineteenth-century astronomer who discovered a comet, gets far more attention than Albert Einstein. In another popular high school text, there are three pictures of Civil War nurses but none of General Sherman or General Grant.[16]

One of the ways human agents transform the course of history is by making war. The preeminence of men in war seems inescapable. But the feminist philosopher and transformationist Elizabeth Minnich maintains that women have played important roles in decisions about war and in war itself.

> Women have been part of and actively opposed to war throughout the ages and across cultures. Women have fought; women have tried to stop the fighting; women have been on the front lines as suppliers, as nurses, as spies; and have worked behind the lines as cooks, secretaries, seamstresses, drivers, experts in language; to keep the country going. . . . Without women . . . no war could ever have been fought.[17]

Minnich does not give examples, but where historians have overlooked or airbrushed women out of significant roles they played in war, she is right to demand a truer and more complete picture. However, she also implies that a fuller picture would reveal that women's role in warfare has been pivotal. In fact it would not; no amount of supplementation can change the fact that women's roles in war have been relatively minor and their occasional protests against war have generally been unavailing. Nor would it be right to deprecate the importance of war as a factor in historical change; it remains true that war—conducted almost exclusively by men—has been the agent of cataclysmic historical upheavals, and any adequate History must reflect that fact, even if it means "leaving women out."

The idea that men have awarded themselves a dominance in history that they did not actually possess is becoming increasingly popular. I recently gave a public lecture on feminism and education before an audience that included several transformationists. In the lecture I defended traditional ideals of striving for objectivity and historical veracity. An annoyed man in the audience asked, "But how do we know that Mrs. Washington did not give her husband all his ideas?" I replied that we had no evidence for that. "Yes," said my interlocutor, now very excited, "that is just the point. *There is no evidence!* There cannot be evidence. Because those writing history would have suppressed it: the fact that there is no history proves nothing. It's lost to us forever."

I answered that we have got to rely on the evidence we have until we have good reason to change our minds. I pointed out that it is most implausible that Martha Washington knew much about military campaigns or statecraft. It's also possible (and just as unlikely) that one of Washington's great-aunts was the brains behind his military prowess. We just can't do history that way.

I could see that some members of the audience were altogether unimpressed with my rejoinder and my "obtuse" insistence on a conventional historical reasonableness, and I knew why: transformationists want "Herstory." They are impatient with an approach to History that impedes the kind of revisionism so many gender feminists are demanding as part of a "transformed knowledge base."

The gender feminist "reconceptualization" of History is moving right along at the university level. But the curricular changes are even more dramatic in the secondary and elementary schools. Because local and state governments are closely involved in public school curricula, and because they are very sensitive and responsive to gender feminist pressures, these changes are being imposed by fiat on thousands of public schools.

Writers of contemporary history and social science texts, especially for the primary and secondary grades, make special efforts to provide "role models" for girls. Precollege texts usually have an abundance of pictures; these now typically show women working in factories or looking through microscopes. A "stereotypical" picture of a woman with a baby is a frowned-upon rarity. Instead, a kind of reverse stereotyping has become an informal requisite. Once Charles Lindbergh was a great role model for American boys; today, a textbook will make a point of informing students about Lindberg's World War II isolationism. In the same text, Anne

Morrow Lindbergh's very considerable achievements will be praised, but there will be no mention of her dalliance with fascism.[18]

The misplaced efforts to avoid slighting women lead quickly to extensive "re-visionings" of history, art, and the sciences. The Center for the Study of Social and Political Change at Smith College did a critical study of three of the most widely used new high school American history textbooks. Because of state mandates for gender equality, the authors of the new textbooks had to go out of their way to give women prominence. The Smith researchers were not happy with the results:

> There is one major problem . . . in writing nonsexist history textbooks. Most of America's history is male-dominated, in part because in most states women were not allowed to vote in federal elections or hold office until the twentieth century. This may be regrettable, but it is still a fact. What, then, is a nonsexist writer of the American history textbook to do? The answer is filler feminism.[19]

Filler feminism pads history with its own "facts" designed to drive home the lessons feminists wish to impart. The following passage from one of the most widely used high school American history texts, *American Voices,* is a good example of the sort of "feel good" feminist spin that has become the norm in our nation's textbooks.

> A typical [Indian] family thus consisted of an old woman, her daughters with their husbands and children, and her unmarried granddaughters and grandsons. . . . Politically, women's roles and status varied from culture to culture. Women were more likely to assume leadership roles among the agricultural peoples than among nomadic hunters. In addition, in many cases in which women did not become village chiefs, they still exercised substantial political power. For example, in Iroquois villages, when selected men sat in a circle to discuss and make decisions, the senior women of the village stood behind them, lobbying and instructing the men. In addition, the elder women named the male village chiefs to their positions.[20]

Though some of the information about the Iroquois is vaguely correct, the paragraph is blatantly designed to give high school students the impression that most Native American societies tended to be politically matriarchal. Since that is not true, the textbook "covers" itself by the formal disclaimer that "in many cases . . . the women did *not* become village chiefs." (In how many cases? A small minority? A large majority?) This is patronizing to both Indians and women, and there is no basis for it. There are more than 350 recognized Indian tribes—one can no more generalize about them than one can about "humanity." Here is what Gilbert Sewall of the American Textbook Council says about this passage: "Female-headed households? Bad old history may cede to bad new history. The presentist spin on Indian society found in the *American Voices* passage is less versed in evidence than aligned to contemporary feminist politics and perspectives."[21]

Social studies texts are full of such "filler feminism"; indeed, in some cases, feminist pressures determine what is excluded even more than they determine what is to be included. In an extensive survey of the new textbooks written under feminist guidelines, New York University psychologist Paul Vitz could find no positive portrayal of romance, marriage, or motherhood.[22]

> By far the most noticeable ideological position in the readers is a feminist one. . . . To begin with, certain themes just do not occur in these stories and articles. Hardly a story celebrates motherhood or marriage as a positive goal or as a rich and meaningful way of living. . . . Though great literature, from *Tristan and Isolde* to Shakespeare to Jane Austen to Louisa May Alcott, is filled with romance and the desire to marry, one finds very little of that in these texts.[23]

That American students are short on cultural literacy is well known. What is not known is that the transformationists are exacerbating the situation. A 1989 study entitled "What Do Our 17 Year Olds Know?" by Diane Ravitch and Chester Finn determined that more high school students recognized the name of Harriet Tubman (83 percent) than Winston Churchill (78 percent) or Joseph Stalin (53 percent); in fact, more knew about Ms. Tubman than knew that Abraham Lincoln issued the Emancipation Proclamation (68 percent) or that the Constitution divides powers between the states and the federal government (43 percent). Seventy-seven percent recognized that women worked in factories during World War II, but fewer could identify the Great Depression (75 percent) or find France on a map (65 percent) or knew that the Renaissance was characterized by cultural and technological advances (39 percent).[24] In the fall of 1992, Dr. Frank Lutz, a fellow at the Harvard University Institute of Politics, surveyed Ivy League students to find out how much history and civics they knew.[25] His survey of 3,119 of our nation's brightest and best-

educated students revealed that three out of four did not know that
Thomas Jefferson had authored the opening words of the Declaration of
Independence. Most (three out of four) were unable to name four Su-
preme Court justices, nor could they name the U.S. senators from their
home states. More than a third could not name the prime minister of
Great Britain. Such consequences are typical and predictable when teachers are distracted from the material they should be teaching by the effort
to be ideologically correct.

The problem of "filler feminism" will get worse. Transformationists are
well organized, and their influence is growing apace. Because of transformationist pressures, the law in some states now actually mandates "gen-
der-fair" history. The California State Department of Education has issued
guidelines called "Standards for Evaluation of Instructional Materials with
Respect to Social Content." According to Education Code section
60040(a) and 60044(a), "Whenever an instructional material presents
developments in history or current events, or achievements in art, science,
or any other field, the contributions of women and men should be represented in approximately equal number."[26] In effect, this law demands
that the historian be more attentive to the demands of "equal representation" than to the historical facts. Needless to say, histories and social
studies presented in this "fair" but factually skewed manner constitute an
unworthy and dishonest approach to learning.

In the history of the high arts the absence of women is deplorable but
largely irreparable. Few women in the past were allowed to train and
work in the major arts. Because of this, men have wrought most of the
works that are commonly recognized as masterpieces. But here, especially, the temptation to redress past wrongs through "reconceptualization" has proved irresistible.

The transformationists claim that works of art made by women have
been passed over because the standards have always been tilted to favor
men. Peggy McIntosh, a director at the Wellesley College Center for
Research on Women and a leader in the movement to transform the
curriculum, calls for measures to redress the historical wrong that wom-
en's art has suffered at the hands of male critics:

> The study of music, art and architecture is transformed if one goes
> beyond those works that were made for public use, display, or
> performance and were supported by the aristocratic or institutional
> patrons. One begins to study quilts, breadloaf shapes, clothing, pots,
> or songs and dances that people who had no musical literacy or
> training took for granted.[27]

Janis Bell, an art historian at Kenyon College, asks the question repeated in thousands of women's studies courses: "But is the traditional rectangle of a canvas any less limiting to the design than the rectangle of the quilt?"[28] Professor Bell calls for reconceptualizing "our courses to create a place for women that is no longer peripheral—but rather the center of our inquiry into the history of the visual arts."[29]

Professor Bell and Dr. McIntosh ask us to "go beyond" the great public works of art, such as cathedrals, to look at what women have done. And a quilt can have great aesthetic value. But the loveliest quilt is plainly inferior to the canvases of Titian and Rembrandt in subtlety, complexity, and power, and we should be able to acknowledge the neglect of women's art without claiming otherwise. It is in fact true that the study of women's contributions to art has been neglected and that this neglect must be— and is—addressed and repaired. On the other hand, revisionist proposals to rewrite the historical record or to change the standards of artistic excellence to put women's art on a par with the highest classic achievements must be rejected as unworthy of a feminism that reveres great art and respects truth.

Feminists who resent the "male culture" tend to load their courses with remedial materials emphasizing women. There is, to be sure, much interesting new scholarship on women, and it may be tempting for feminists to devote a disproportionate amount of class time to it. But teachers have an obligation to ensure that their students acquire some basic "cultural literacy." Those who deploy the new scholarship in an attempt to make up for the shortcomings of the "male-centered curriculum" almost inevitably shortchange their students.

In the summer of 1992, I attended a workshop given by Elizabeth Minnich when she and I were both speakers at the annual meetings of the Phi Kappa Phi Society in Charlotte, North Carolina. She outlined most of the arguments above—including the critiques of the notion of masterpiece in art and the "hegemony" of Greco-Euro-American standards. During the discussion I asked Dr. Minnich if she really believed there were quilts that rivaled or surpassed the ceiling of the Sistine Chapel. She admitted that such a judgment did indeed shock our sensibilities but pointedly asked me in turn, "Isn't that what the history of art is all about—shocked sensibilities?" Standards and tastes are *always* in flux, she said. What one society or group judges to be great another finds banal or offensive.

The audience appeared startled by my open disagreement with Dr.

Minnich. Their reaction, I am ashamed to say, made me restrain myself from asking her the questions I badly wanted to ask: Why should we women be playing an undignified game of one-upmanship that we are bound to lose? What motivates the revisionist efforts to rewrite History or to revise the standards of "greatness" in a manner calculated to give to women victories and triumphs they never had the opportunities to win? We now *have* those opportunities. Why can't we move on to the future and stop wasting energy on resenting (and "rewriting") the past?

Many of us who call ourselves feminists are very much aware of the past indignities and deprivations that have limited women in the arts. Although we deplore the past, we appreciate that the situation has changed: today, artistically gifted women do have their level playing field. So we reject the call to change the standards of greatness, and we are exploring the more constructive alternatives now open to us, where we judge our best prospects to lie.

Unfortunately, no one is consulting mainstream feminists about the value or wisdom of proposals to change standards in order to "valorize" women in the History of art or any other branch of History. If the transformationists continue to have their unchecked way in the academy, large numbers of American students will learn to view the great masterpieces in a doctrinally correct way—to their profound loss. Moreover, the women's movement loses by being associated with the partisan and resentful anti-intellectualism that is inspiring a gynocentric revisionism in art criticism.

In literature, as in the arts, gender feminists have made a sweeping attack on allegedly male conceptions of excellence. As Elaine Marks of the University of Wisconsin French department puts it, "We are contesting the canon and the very concept of canons and masterpieces."[30] Professor Marks reminds us once again that many gifted women in the past have not received due recognition. Good feminist scholarship addresses this problem and in many cases resurrects reputations that would otherwise remain overlooked. But gender feminists are not content to stop there. As transformationist activist Charlotte Bunch declares, "You can't just add women and stir."[31] According to Bunch, we must attack the problem at the roots "by transforming a male culture" and by "reconstructing the world from the standpoint of women." We must, in other words, reject the masculinist *standards* that have placed European males like Michelangelo and Shakespeare in the highest ranks and relegated their sisters to oblivion.

The gender feminists challenge the very idea of "great art," "great literature," and (as we shall presently see) "great science." Talk of "greatness" and "masterpieces" implies a ranking of artists and works, a "hierarchial" approach considered to be unacceptable because it implicitly denigrates those who are given lesser status. The very idea of "genius" is regarded with suspicion as elitist and "masculinist." Peggy McIntosh is among the proponents of this belief: "The study of literature usually involves a very few geniuses. . . . To be ordinary is a sin, in the world of most literature teachers. . . . Only those works which distance themselves from an audience, by setting themselves up in a genre separate from the reader and requiring no answer from the reader, are considered to be 'literary.' "[32] McIntosh does not explain why a work by a genius like Leo Tolstoy should be more "distancing" than a work by a twentieth-century feminist novelist like Margaret Atwood or Alice Walker.

The transformationist project has already strongly influenced American universities, and the scornful attitude it fosters toward traditional literary classics is becoming increasingly fashionable. The organizers of a literary conference on diversity and multiculturalism in Boston in June 1991 asked the two hundred–plus participating professors to list the five American authors they believed most necessary to a quality education. Mark Twain got thirty-six votes; Toni Morrison, thirty-four; Maya Angelou, twenty-six; Alice Walker, twenty-four; John Steinbeck, twenty-one; Malcolm X, eighteen; Richard Wright, thirteen; James Baldwin, thirteen; Langston Hughes, thirteen; William Faulkner, eleven; Nathaniel Hawthorne, ten; Ernest Hemingway, ten; Henry David Thoreau, nine; Willa Cather, eight; F. Scott Fitzgerald, seven; Dee Brown, seven; W.E.B. DuBois, seven; Emily Dickinson, six; Amy Tan, six; Harper Lee, five; and Walt Whitman, five.[33] Thomas Palmer, the *Boston Globe* reporter who covered the conference, stopped counting after Whitman. In any case, Herman Melville, whom most literary critics used to regard as the greatest American writer, did not make the list. Nor did Henry James. The conferees cheered the results of the poll. "This list makes me feel so much more connected," one participant told the *Globe*. I, on the other hand, was depressed by the results.

In their critique of the imperial male culture, the transformationist feminists do not confine themselves to impugning the history, art, and literature of the past. They also regard logic and rationality as "phallocentric." Elizabeth Minnich traces the cultural tradition to a "few privileged males . . . who are usually called 'The Greeks.' "[34] In common with many other transformationists, Minnich believes that the conceptions of rationality and intelligence are white, male creations: "At present . . . not only are students taught 'phallocentric' and 'colonial' notions of reason as *the* forms of rational expression, but the full possible range of expression of human intelligence also tends to be forced into a severely shrunken notion of intelligence."[35] Note the reference to a "colonial" rationality with its implication of deliberate subjugation. It is now common practice to use scare quotes to indicate the feminist suspicion of a "reality" peculiar to male ways of knowing. For example, the feminist philosopher Joyce Trebilcot speaks of "the apparatuses of 'truth,' 'knowledge,' 'science,' " that men use to "project their personalities as reality."[36]

The attack on traditional culture has thus escalated to an attack on the rational standards and methods that have been the hallmark of scientific progress. The New Jersey Project for reforming the public schools circulates a document entitled "Feminist Scholarship Guidelines." The first guideline is unexceptionable: "Feminist scholars seek to recover the lost work and thought of women in all areas of human endeavor."[37] But after that, the guidelines unravel: "Feminist scholarship begins with an awareness that much previous scholarship has offered a white, male, Eurocentric, heterosexist, and elite view of 'reality.' "

The guidelines elaborate on the attitude toward masculinist scholarship and methods by quoting the feminist theorist Elizabeth Fee: "Knowledge was created as an act of aggression—a passive nature had to be interrogated, unclothed, penetrated, and compelled by man to reveal her secrets." Fee's resentment and suspicion of male "ways of knowing" follows a path well trodden by such feminist thinkers as Mary Ellman, Catharine MacKinnon, and Sandra Harding, whose views of patriarchal knowledge and science have quickly become central gender feminist doctrine. Playing on the biblical double meaning of *knowing* to refer both to intercourse and to cognition, Ellman and MacKinnon claim that men approach nature as rapists approach a woman, taking joy in violating "her," in "penetrating" her secrets. Feminists, says MacKinnon, have finally realized that for men, "to know has meant to fuck."[38] In a similar mood, Sandra Harding suggests that Newton's Principles of Mechanics could just as aptly be called "Newton's Rape Manual."[39]

The New Jersey Project is inspired by such insights. As a teacher of philosophy, I suppose I should be happy to see profound issues in metaphysics and the theory of knowledge being discussed in government pamphlets on educational reform. But it is quite clear that this discussion is more political than philosophical. New Jersey gets its theory of knowledge from feminist activists like Paula Rothenberg and Catharine Stimpson. That the state should underwrite a condemnation of "phallocentric" conceptions of reality and scientific knowledge is far more a tribute to the energy and political influence of the feminist transformationists than to New Jersey's profound appreciation of contemporary epistemology.

. . .

Male scholars specializing in their masculinist academic disciplines (from chemistry to philosophy) are known to transformationists as "separate knowers." The authors of Women's Ways of Knowing, a text much cited by transformationists, define "separate knowing" as "the game of impersonal reason," a game that has "belonged traditionally to boys."[40] "Separate knowers are tough-minded. They are like doormen at exclusive clubs. They do not want to let anything in unless they are pretty sure it is good. . . . Presented with a proposition, separate knowers immediately look for something wrong—a loophole, a factual error, a logical contradiction, the omission of contrary evidence."[41]

Separate knowers—mainly men—play the "doubting game." The authors of Women's Ways of Knowing contrast separate knowing with a higher state of "connected knowing" that they view as the more feminine. In place of the "doubting game," connected knowers play the "believing game." This is more congenial for women because "many women find it easier to believe than to doubt."[42]

Peggy McIntosh has developed her own special variant of the connected-knower/separate-knower distinction. Why, she asks, should schools focus so much on the people at the top—on the "mountain strongholds of white men"—when what we need to study are the "valley values" of women and minorities?[43] McIntosh shifts between the mountain-valley metaphor and a distinction that sounds more technical (though it is in fact equally metaphorical) between the two ways of knowing: a narrow, patriarchal, male, "vertical" way and a richer, female, "lateral" way.

The male dominant elite—the "vertical thinkers," as Dr. McIntosh calls them—aim at "exact thinking, or decisiveness or mastery of something, or being able to make an argument and take on all comers, or turning in the perfect paper."[44] Vertical thinking is "triggered by words like excellence, accomplishment, success, and achievement." Lateral thinking is more spiritual, "relational, inclusive." Women and people of color tend to be lateral thinkers. For "laterals," the "aim is not to win, but to be in a decent relationship with the invisible elements of the universe."

McIntosh elaborates the vertical-lateral metaphor in proposing five stages in the development of an acceptable curriculum. Her "phase theory" is one of several popular typologies influencing the gender feminist mission to transform American schools. Stage theories lend themselves well to the workshop mode and provide administrators a useful means for evaluating faculty. McIntosh grades instructors by the level of the phases their courses exemplify.

In phase one, the instructor focuses on the mountain people, or "pinnacle people." A phase one history course "tends to emphasize laws, wars . . . and to tell the stories of winners, at the tops of the ladders of so-called success, accomplishment, achievement, and excellence."[45] Phase one thinkers take for granted such dogmas as "the quest for knowledge is a universal human undertaking."[46] Dr. McIntosh speaks of the "hidden ethos" hanging over the "phase one" curriculum, with its logic of "either or, right or wrong. . . . You win lest you lose: kill or be killed." At a 1990 workshop for public school teachers and staff in Brookline, Massachusetts, she reminded the audience of all the "young white males dangerous to themselves and the rest of us, especially in a nuclear age."[47] Their orientation toward logic and achievement is what makes them so threatening.

By phase two, instructors have noticed the absence of women and minorities, so they find a few exceptional cases to include. McIntosh calls this the "exceptional minority" phase.[48] She considers this "worse" than phase one in that "it pretends to show us 'women,' but really shows us only a famous few."[49]

In phase three, the instructor begins to get interested in the valley people and why so few have made it up the mountain. "Phase three curriculum work involves getting angry."[50] The emphasis now is on women as a victimized group. "Most teachers in the United States . . . were taught that the individual is the main unit of society and that the U.S. system is a meritocracy."[51] But at phase three, these naive beliefs get dropped. Phase three instructors become radical critics of the United States: they begin to see "how patterns of colonialism, imperialism and genocide outside the U.S. match patterns of domination, militarism and genocide at home."[52]

Phase four takes us beyond winning and losing. "It produces courses in which we are all seen to be in it together, all having ethnic and racial identity, all having culture . . . all with some power to say no, and yes, and 'This I create.' . . . Phase four classes can be wondrous in their healing power."[53]

McIntosh's description of phase four is allusive and poetic, but to hidebound "vertical" thinkers not very illuminating. She says even less about the fifth and highest phase in her ideal of knowledge. She admits that it is "as yet unthinkable" and writes of it in sentences with an abundance of capital letters that signify its apocalyptic character: "Phase five will give us Reconstructed Global and Biological History to Survive By."[54]

Discussing the fifth phase reminds McIntosh of a remark made by the feminist historian Gerda Lerner: "Don't worry . . . we were 6000 years carefully building a patriarchal structure of knowledge, and we've had only 12 years to try to correct it, and 12 years is nothing."[55]

Marilyn R. Schuster and Susan R. Van Dyne of Smith College "consult nationally" on feminist curriculum transformation. They have developed a six-stage theory of pedagogical levels that looks very much like McIntosh's five-phase theory. Theirs describes a feminist alternative to the masculinist curriculum that is to be pluralistic instead of hierarchical, attentive to difference rather than elitist, concrete rather than abstract. But they, too, are not keen to tell us where the transformations will lead:

> What would a curriculum that offers an inclusive vision of human experience and that attends as carefully to difference and genuine pluralism as to sameness and generalization actually look like? Although we possess the tools of analysis that allow us to conceive of such an education, we can't, as yet, point to any institution that has entered the millennium and adopted such a curriculum.[56]

But the problem is not that the "millennium" of a transformed academy has not yet arrived. Schuster and Van Dyne do not realize that they have no idea of the curriculum that is to replace the "androcentric" one now in place. Instead of submitting a comprehensive feminist curriculum for serious consideration and scrutiny, we are given a lot of loose and metaphorical talk about female epistemologies characterizing how women view the world from a female perspective.

Catharine Stimpson, one of the matron saints of transformationism, is a former president of the Modern Language Association and, until recently, was dean of the Graduate School and vice-provost at Rutgers University. We do get a fairly detailed description from her of a late-stage curriculum that she outlined in *Change* magazine in 1988.[57] Stimpson begins in conventional transformationist fashion by denouncing the traditional phase one curriculum for teaching students to recognize big (male) names from "Abraham and Isaac to Zola" as little more than a game that, "at its most innocent," appeals only to crossword puzzle or "Jeopardy" fans. Dean Stimpson has a more "coherent curriculum" in mind, and because she has been unusually specific, I shall quote her at some length:

> What might a coherent curriculum be like? Let me pass out some whiffs of a syllabus, which focuses on the humanities. . . . "My syl-

labus" desires to show . . . culture, not as a static and immobile structure, but as a kinetic series of processes, in which various forces often compete and clash. However, a student must have a certain security in order to appreciate diversity. . . . To help create that sense of stability and security for U.S. students . . . my . . . college curriculum starts with a linear narrative about America's own weird, complex history. . . . For example, when the narrative shuttles towards the seventeenth century, it could stop at four texts: Native American myths, legends and rituals; the 1637–38 trials of Anne Hutchinson; the poems of Anne Bradstreet . . . and finally, the narrative of Mary Rowlandson, issued in 1682, about her capture by Native Americans during the liberation struggle of 1676.[58]

Stimpson gives us an idea of how one could correct the standard masculinist narratives with their endless discussion of "explorers," "founding fathers," and the Constitution—none of which figure in Stimpson's version of American studies.

Among my novels would be *Stars in My Pocket like Grains of Sand.* . . . Like many contemporary speculative fictions, *Stars in My Pocket* finds conventional heterosexuality absurd. The central figures are two men, Rat Korga and Marq Dyeth, who have a complex, but ecstatic, affair. Marq is also the proud product of a rich "nurture stream." His ancestry includes both humans and aliens. His genetic heritage blends differences. In a sweet scene, he sees three of his mothers.

Stimpson knows her curriculum will be criticized. But she is lightheartedly defiant: "If my curriculum seems to yowl like a beast of relativism, I find this cause for cheer. . . . My reconstructive project affirms that relativism is no beast but a goon that will nurture a more democratic, a more culturally literate, and yes, a brainier university."

We can let Stimpson's talk of a "coherent curriculum" and "brainier university" fall of its own weight. Other transformationists have not been so forthcoming about where *they* are taking the academy—and we can see why. As it happens, I have met Ms. Stimpson at several recent conferences and found her to be more moderate and sensible than she appears to have been in 1988. Nevertheless, her views of the eighties cast light on the predicament of universities in the nineties. Many courses of the kind Stimpson dreamed of are now in place, and the campaign against "patriarchal" culture and scholarship is unabated.

It is understandable that the transformationists are more lyrical than informative about what the transformed academy will actually look like and what its curriculum will be. There is no lack of programmatic discussion about "subjectivity," "lateral thinking," "concreteness," "inclusiveness," "relatedness," and the importance of interdisciplinary studies as features of a feminist reconceptualization of higher learning. There is also lots of metaphorical talk about windows and mirrors and voices. But the description of the new curriculum is silent on crucial matters. What, for example, is supposed to be the fate of such suspect "first phase, vertical, male" subjects as math, logic, or analytical philosophy?

Linda Gardiner, editor of the *Women's Review of Books,* which is housed in the Wellesley College Center for Research on Women, wonders whether Western philosophy speaks for women at all. "We might begin to question the import of Descartes' stress on logic and mathematics as the ideal types of rationality, in a society in which only a tiny percentage of people could realistically spend time developing skills in those fields," she writes.[59] Noting that the philosophical elite is biased in favor of the abstract, methodical, and universal, Gardiner suggests that a feminist philosophy would be more concrete and more suspicious of logic and method. "What would a female logic be like?" she asks, and answers that this would be like asking what female astronomy or particle physics would be like. "We cannot imagine what it would mean to have a 'female version' of them."[60] For that, says Ms. Gardiner, we should first need to develop different epistemologies. Reading Gardiner's spirited arguments for the thesis that classical philosophy is essentially and inveterately male biased, one cannot avoid the impression that the feminist critic is more ingenious at finding male bias in a field than in proposing an intelligible alternative way to deal with its subject matter.

The gender feminist "critique" of the physical sciences, one of the busiest areas of feminist transformationist theory, is also rich in metaphor and poor in literal content. To be sure, science does present some genuine issues of concern to any feminist. Laboratories can be as unwelcoming to women as male locker rooms; a lot still needs to be done to make the *life* of science more hospitable to women. But equity feminists part company with those who hold that science itself—its methodology, its rules of evidence, its concern for empirical grounding, its ideal of objectivity—is an expression of a "masculinist" approach to knowledge. Indeed, the gender feminist doctrines are a distinct embarrassment and a threat to any woman with aspirations to do real science.

Inevitably, gender feminist philosophers seek to find their ideas confirmed by eminent women scientists. Evelyn Fox Keller argues that Nobel laureate Barbara McClintock's achievements in cell biology were made possible because of her outsider status, which gave scope to her uniquely feminine approach. As a woman of integrity, says Fox Keller, McClintock could not accept the "image of the scientist modeled on the patriarchal husband."[61] This, according to Fox Keller, led McClintock to creative and radical redefinitions: "Nature must be renamed as not female, or, at least, as not an alienated object. By the same token, the mind, if the female scientist is to have one, must be renamed as not necessarily male, and accordingly recast with a more inclusive subjectivity."[62] But Professor McClintock herself does not accept Fox Keller's interpretation of her work. As Fox Keller candidly acknowledges, "She [McClintock] would disclaim any analysis of her work as a woman's work, as well as any suggestion that her views represent a woman's perspective. To her, science is not a matter of gender, either male or female; it is, on the contrary, a place where (ideally at least) 'the matter of gender drops away.' "[63]

Feminist critics have looked at the metaphors of "male science" and found them sexist. I recently heard a feminist astronomer interviewed on CNN say in all seriousness that sexist terminology like "the Big Bang Theory" is "off-putting to young women" who might otherwise be interested in pursuing careers in her field.[64] It is hard to believe that anyone with an intelligent interest in astronomy would be put off by a graphic description of a cosmic event. Other critiques of science as masculinist are equally fatuous and scientifically fruitless. After asserting that "the warlike terminology of immunology which focuses on 'competition,' 'inhibition,' and 'invasion' as major theories of how cells interact reflects a militaristic view of the world," Sue Rosser, who offers workshops on how to transform the biology curriculum, concedes that "a feminist critique has not yet produced theoretical changes in the area of cell biology."[65] She does not tell us how the "feminist critique" *could* lead to advances in biology, but she considers it obvious that it must: "It becomes evident that the inclusion of a feminist perspective leads to changes in models, experimental subjects, and interpretations of the data. These changes entail more inclusive, enriched theories compared to the traditional, restrictive, unicausal theories."[66]

To some, just the promise of a female perspective in the sciences seems enough. To demand more seems churlish to them. Sandra Harding has made feminist philosophy of science her specialty. Harding makes it sound as if merely articulating a feminist critique of male science is equivalent to having broken through to a feminist alternative: "When we began theorizing our experiences . . . we knew our task would be a difficult though exciting one. But I doubt that in our wildest dreams we ever imagined we would have to reinvent both science and theorizing itself in order to make sense of women's social experience."[67] Unfortunately, we are not given even a vague idea of how her alleged breakthrough must now affect the study of the natural sciences; in particular, we remain in the dark on the question of what a feminist scientific curriculum would look like and how it would lead to "reinventing science." As philosopher of mathematics Margarita Levin dryly remarks, "One still wants to know whether feminists' airplanes would stay airborne for feminist engineers."[68]

Chapter 4

New Epistemologies

৯৯

Some gender feminists claim that because women have been oppressed they are better "knowers." Feeling more deeply, they see more clearly and understand reality better. They have an "epistemic" advantage over men.[1] Does being oppressed really make one more knowledgeable or perceptive? The idea that adversity confers special insight is familiar enough. Literary critics often ascribe creativity to suffering, including suffering of racial discrimination or homophobia. But feminist philosophers have carried this idea much further. They claim that oppressed groups enjoy privileged "epistemologies" or "different ways of knowing" that better enable them to understand the world, not only socially but scientifically.

According to "standpoint theory," as the theory of epistemic advantage is called, the oppressed may make better biologists, physicists, and philosophers than their oppressors. Thus we find the feminist theorist Hilary Rose saying that male scientists have been handicapped by being men. A better science would be based on women's domestic experience and practice.[2] Professor Virginia Held offers hope that "a feminist standpoint would give us a quite different understanding of even physical reality."[3] Conversely, those who are most socially favored, the proverbial white, middle-class males, are in the worst epistemic position.

What do mainstream philosophers make of the idea of "standpoint theories"? Professor Susan Haack of the University of Miami is one of the most respected epistemologists in the country. She is also an equity feminist. In December 1992 she participated in a symposium on feminist philosophy at meetings of the American Philosophical Association. It was a unique event. For once, someone outside the insular little world of gender feminism was asked to comment on gender feminist theories of knowledge. Watching Professor Haack critique the "standpoint theorists" was a little like watching a chess grandmaster defeat all opponents in a simultaneous exhibition, blindfolded.

Haack told the audience that she finds the idea of "female ways of knowing" as puzzling as the idea of a Republican epistemology or a senior citizens' epistemology.[4] Some of her arguments are too technical to review here. I cite only a few of her criticisms:

I am not convinced that there *are* any distinctively female "ways of knowing." All *any* human being has to go on, in figuring out how things are, is his or her sensory and introspective experience, and the explanatory theorizing he or she devises to accommodate it; and differences in cognitive style, like differences in handwriting, seem more individual than gender-determined.[5]

She pointed out that theories based on the idea that oppression or deprivation results in a privileged standpoint are especially implausible; if they were right, the most disadvantaged groups would produce the best scientists. In fact, the oppressed and socially marginalized often have little access to the information and education needed to excel in science, which on the whole puts them at a serious "epistemic *dis*advantage." Professor Haack also observed that the female theorists who argue that oppression confers an advantage are not themselves oppressed. She asks: if oppression and poverty are indeed so advantageous, why do so many highly advantaged, middle-class women consider themselves so well situated "epistemically"?

Ms. Haack identifies herself as an "Old Feminist" who opposes the attempt "of the New Feminists to colonize philosophy." Her reasons for rejecting feminist epistemologies were cogent and, to most of the professional audience, clearly convincing. Unfortunately, her cool, sensible admonitions are not likely to slow down the campaign to promote "women's ways of knowing."

The gender feminists' conviction, more ideological than scientific, that they belong to a radically insightful vanguard that compares favorably with the Copernicuses and Darwins of the past animates their revisionist theories of intellectual and artistic excellence and inspires their program to transform the knowledge base. Their exultation contrasts with the deep reluctance of most other academics to challenge the basic assumptions underlying feminist theories of knowledge and education. The confidence of the one and the trepidation of the other combine to make transformationism a powerfully effective movement that has so far proceeded unchecked in the academy.

Yolanda Moses is the newly appointed president of City University of New York. She was formerly the chair of women's studies and provost at California State University at Dominguez Hills. Her anti-intellectual ideas might seem surprising to anyone unfamiliar with the fashionable doctrine that extols the new "ways of knowing" while devaluing the traditional male European approach to "knowing": "Institutions of higher education in the United States are products of Western society in which masculine values like an orientation toward achievement and objectivity are valued over cooperation, connectedness, and subjectivity."[6] In President Moses' view, the masculine emphasis on achievement and objectivity is an obstacle to progress! She also finds it deplorable that faculty members' research has been valued above their community service. "That will have to change if cultural pluralism is to flourish."[7]

Despite its influence, the gender feminist project of "transforming the knowledge base" must in the end prove to be a deep embarrassment to the feminist movement. As Susan Haack has pointed out, the belief in female "ways of knowing" is reminiscent of male chauvinist denigrations of women. Those who promote it and cheer it on find themselves cheering alongside those who have always held that women think differently from men.

The transformationists are out to reconstruct our cultural and scientific heritage. Even if one believes that this badly needs doing (and I, for one, do not), there is little reason to be sanguine that the gender feminists are intellectually equipped to do it. Their belief in the superiority of "women's ways of knowing" fosters a sense of solidarity and cultural community that seems to have allowed them to overlook the fact that their doctrine tends to segregate women in a culture of their own, that it increases social divisiveness along gender lines, and that it may seriously weaken the American academy. Nor does it worry these feminists that their teaching allows insecure men once again to patronize and denigrate women as the naive sex that thinks with its heart, not with its head.

The early feminists of the First Wave, fighting for equity and equal opportunities in politics and education, rejected all theories of male superiority. However, they were not tempted to retaliate against sexism by making unfounded claims that women were superior to men. They knew all too well the dangers of promoting divisive dogmas about male and female ways of knowing. They were especially leery of being called more intuitive, hence less analytical, less "rational," than men.

An event in the life of Elizabeth Cady Stanton, the great foremother of American feminism, illustrates the attitude that the First Wave feminists had toward those who believed that women negotiated the world less with skeptical reason than with a trusting intuition. Stanton had discovered that her four-day-old baby had a bent collarbone. The doctor placed a bandage on the shoulder and secured it by tying it to the child's wrist. Soon after he left, Stanton noticed the child's hand was blue. She removed the bandage and summoned a second doctor. He did much the same thing. Again the baby's fingers turned blue soon after the doctor left. Over the protests of the nurse, Ms. Stanton removed the bandage a second time. She told the nurse, "What we want is a little pressure on that bone; that is what both of those men have aimed at. How can we get it without involving the arm, is the question."[8] Ms. Stanton then soaked strips of linen in a solution of water and arnica and wrapped them around the baby "like a pair of suspenders over the shoulder, crossing them both in front and behind, pinning the ends to the diaper." This provided the necessary pressure without stopping the child's circulation, and the baby soon recovered.

When the doctors returned, Ms. Stanton told them how inadequate their bandages had been and how she had solved the problem. They smiled knowingly at one another. "Well after all, a mother's instinct is better than a man's reason," one remarked. "Thank you, gentlemen," Stanton replied, "there was no instinct about it. I did some hard thinking before I saw how I could get pressure on the shoulder without impeding the circulation, as you did."[9]

. . .

Promoting a gynocentric critique of knowledge is unworthy of a dignified feminism. It is also educationally harmful. We hear a lot about how poorly our entering college students compare with American students of past decades or with their contemporaries in foreign countries. When respect for learning and academic achievement is at such a low point, why should feminist academics be contributing to it?

Creating a climate of gender mistrust of received knowledge only adds to the rampant anti-intellectualism of our troubled culture. There is a more constructive way, and it is the way of the classical equity feminist who asks for women "a fair field and no favors" in joining men to create the culture of the future. My own "equity feminist" creed is eloquently articulated by Iris Murdoch. Murdoch still believes in a "culture of humanity," and her warnings about the dangers of the divisive, mean-spirited alternative are timely.

> Men "created culture" because they were free to do so, and women were treated as inferior and made to believe that they were. Now free women must join in the human world of work and creation on an equal footing and be everywhere in art, science, business, politics, etc. . . . However, to lay claim, in this battle, to *female* ethics, *female* criticism, *female* knowledge . . . is to set up a new female ghetto. (Chauvinist males should be delighted by the move . . .) "Women's Studies" can mean that women are led to read mediocre or peripheral books by women rather than the great books of humanity in general. . . . It is a dead end, in danger of simply separating women from the mainstream thinking of the human race. Such cults can also *waste the time* of young people who may be reading all the latest books on feminism instead of studying the difficult and important things that belong to the culture of humanity [her emphases].[10]

Transformationism is galvanizing, and it has proved to be profitable. No one is offering money for a workshop that would teach its participants that men and women are not all that different, that the traditional standards are better left untransformed by the ideologues who believe in "women-centeredness," or that students are better off learning a universal curriculum that is not gender-divisive. The thoughts of Susan Haack, Iris Murdoch, and a handful of critics of transformationism do not lend themselves to the workshop mode: they cannot be expressed as a "five-phase theory" that lends itself so neatly to workshops and retreats. It is almost impossible to get funding to implement ideas that favor moderate reform rather than exciting Copernican transformations. By supporting and promoting transformationism, not only do school administrators build up their résumés, they get to feel they are participating in the educational equivalent of the storming of the Bastille. Equity feminists have nothing that exciting to offer.

Transformationists do not invite criticism or intellectual scrutiny of their assumptions, and it is not likely that the transformation movement will be checked by fair and open debate. Women's conferences tend to be rallies of the faithful. Critics who do venture doubts about the value of the transformationist movement are dismissed as "right-wing extremists," and their arguments are ignored. The usual system of checks and balances by means of peer review seems to have fallen apart.

Yet although the transformationists have every reason to celebrate their many successes, they have recently experienced a setback from an unexpected quarter. When McIntosh, Minnich, and their followers demanded that the oppressive European, white, male culture being taught in the schools be radically transformed, they had not imagined that anyone could look upon *them* as oppressors. The transformationist leaders are not men, but they *are* white, they are "European," they are middle-class. Minority women have begun to deny that the leaders of the women's movement have any right to speak for them. Most members of the women of color caucus boycotted the 1992 Austin National Women's Studies Conference I attended for its failure to recognize and respect *their* political identity. The slighted group sent the conferees an African-American women's quilt made from dashiki fabrics, as both a reprimand and a "healing gesture." The assembled white feminists sat before it in resentful but guilty silence. In the game of moral one-upmanship that gender feminists are so good at, they had been outquilted, as it were, by a more marginalized constituency. Clearly any number of minority groups can play the victimology game, and almost all could play it far more plausibly than the socially well-positioned Heilbruns, McIntoshes, and Minniches.

An obvious recourse is to deflect criticism by "confessing" at the outset one's privileged status. Two feminist editors of *Feminism,* a new women's studies textbook, introduce themselves as follows:

> "We" are Robyn and Diane; we speak as white middle-class heterosexual American feminist academics in our early thirties—to cover a number of the categories feminist criticism has lately been emphasizing as significant to one's reading and speaking position: race, class, sexual orientation, nationality, political positioning, education level, and age. Colleagues at the University of Vermont since

1989, we two have found that we share passionate interests in fiction, feminism, and quiltmaking.[11]

More and more frequently, the gender feminists who run the women's centers, the workshops, the transformationist projects, and the various women's conferences are finding themselves accused of being elitist and members of oppressor groups.

In the spring of 1993, twenty-five hundred women gathered in Albuquerque, New Mexico, for a spiritual conference organized by the Catholic feminist "Women-Church" movement. Feminist inclusiveness was the order of the day, and so all goddesses were honored equally—from Hera, Artemis, and Isis to Mary of the Christian tradition.[12] The participants had been told to bring drums, and all events were accompanied by drum beating. This thematic ritual was intended as a way of honoring Native Americans. But it was not well received. Peter Steinfels of the *New York Times* was there, and he reported that a "traditional American Indian Pipe Ceremony was nearly drowned out by the drumming of goddess worshipers who were 'raising power' not far away in the Albuquerque Convention Center."[13] Soon, word came that the drumming of the white women had offended the Native American women.

That practice [of drum-beating] was implicitly questioned when a general session on spirituality turned into a probing discussion of how religious voyagers from dominant cultures enhance their spiritual experience by expropriating exotic practices from the religions of minorities, just as well-to-do tourists decorate themselves and their houses with the crafts and art of indigenous people. . . . Amid growing complaints from several groups about latent racism in the conference—the organizers requested that, out of sympathy for those who had been offended, the drums not be played.

So the white women goddess worshipers could not beat their drums, and even their well-known predilection for peasant jewelry and ethnic clothing was put in question.

The leaders and theorists of academic feminism have prudently sought to ward off minority censure by placing women's issues under the broad and popular umbrella of multiculturalism. President Moses took that tack when she castigated males who value objectivity and achievement above community service, warning her City University faculty that such values were inconsistent with an emphasis on "cultural pluralism." But "cultural pluralism" has many sides, each with its own sharp edge. The well-educated, white, middle-class women who have for the past two decades been denouncing men for treating them as "the Other" now find themselves denounced for having marginalized and silenced Native American women, Hispanic women, disabled women, and other groups, all of whom claim to be victims in a complex ecology of domination and subjugation.

Even the beloved "click experience" has become a symbol of white, middle-class privilege. Two African-American feminists, Barbara Smith and Beverly Smith, have written an article unmasking the elitism of women who describe the "click" as "an experience that makes you realize your oppression as a woman."[14] They point out that clicks are for those who are relatively privileged. Minorities, whether male or female, do not experience them: "The day-to-day immediacy of violence and oppression" suffices well enough to remind them of their condition.

The feminist leaders and theorists are somewhat discomfited by these unexpected reproaches. But it would be a mistake to underestimate the self-assurance and resolve of the gender feminists. They are not about to relinquish their dominance, not even to other women whose bona fides as victims are greater than their own.

The typical gathering of gender feminist academics illustrates the uneasy and somewhat unstable compromise that has been struck. The audience consists largely of the white, middle-class women who are the mainstays of academic feminism. On the other hand, minority women are given strong representation in the panels and symposia, and the rhetoric of feminist transformation is given a multicultural cast.

The April 1993 Parsippany, New Jersey, conference on transforming the curriculum that I discussed in chapter 3 is a case in point. All the leading gender feminist transformationists were there: Catharine Stimpson, Annette Kolodny, the Schuster and Van Dyne team, Elizabeth Minnich, Beverly Guy-Sheftall, Sandra Harding, and, of course, the ubiquitous Peggy McIntosh.[15]

Professor Paula Rothenberg, the conference moderator and self-described "Marxist-feminist," welcomed us and invited us to join her "to imagine together a curriculum for the next century." The mood was generally upbeat, but one presenter after another warned of impending backlash. Rothenberg cautioned the audience to be suspicious of the Clinton administration's announced commitment to diversity; she called it an "ethnic foods and fiestas" version of inclusiveness.

Annette Kolodny explained how her position as dean of humanities at the University of Arizona had given her the means to promote transformationist changes there. Kolodny had been instrumental in introducing "new promotion and tenure" proposals that reward and protect transformationist work at the University of Arizona. Kolodny also reported on the transformation retreats where "outside facilitators" are brought in to help selected faculty and administrators "rethink how they teach." She hailed the New Jersey Project as the inspiration for Arizona. "Thank you, Paula!" she cried.

A discordant note was introduced by Beverly Guy-Sheftall, director of the Women's Research Center at Spelman College, who attacked Kolodny's charts. "What about those of us who are women and members of a minority? Which chart includes us?" Ms. Guy-Sheftall conceded that identifying a common black perspective presented difficulties. Some Afrocentrists, for example, hold views that conflict with those of the black lesbian movement. Whose point of view is to count as representative? Ms. Guy-Sheftall spoke of the issue of fragmented representation as a "problematized" area. Calling a subject "problematized" often serves to paper over the embarrassing and touchy questions it raises; this is especially true of questions about the politics of group identity.

Like several other speakers who touched on the future of curricular transformation, Guy-Sheftall confessed she is "still not sure we have a clue about what this really means as we approach the twenty-first century." But her doubts did not dampen her enthusiasm for the transformation movement or her determination to help it get more funding. Indeed, Guy-Sheftall, a consultant to the Ford Foundation, has been advising the foundation that support for women's studies and transformation work should *intensify* during this paradoxical period.[16]

Professor Rothenberg introduced the New Jersey chancellor of higher education, Edward Goldberg, as "the Fairy Godmother of the New Jersey Project." Middle-aged and balding, sporting a suit and tie and a paunch, Goldberg looked as though he would be more at home at a conference of Shriners or Legionnaires. He spoke pridefully of the millions of dollars that New Jersey had put into the Curriculum Transformation Project and expressed hope that other states would soon follow suit. For him, curriculum transformation is a matter of basic decency. Curriculum transformation, he announced, is "a vindication of the simple and honest concept that scholarship should reflect contributions of all." When I heard Mr. Goldberg say this, it confirmed my belief that many well-meaning government officials do not understand the implications of the feminist demand for a more woman-centered curriculum. Goldberg is not a "gynocrat"; he is probably an old-fashioned equity feminist who wants a fair deal for women in education. Apparently he did not see that beneath the charges of sexism and gender unfairness is an illiberal, irrational, and anti-intellectual program that is a threat to everything he probably believes in: American democracy, liberal education, academic freedom, and the kind of mainstream feminism that has gained women near-equality in American society.

Did Goldberg stay long enough to appreciate what an unusual gathering of academics this was? Was he surprised by an academic audience in which the atmosphere of mass agreement and self-congratulation was almost total? Did he count the number of times the leading transformationists admitted they had *no idea what they were doing*? Had he any idea of the number of workshops on thorny topics like "Resistance in the Classroom" or "Anti-Oppression Methods of Teaching"? I wondered what he would have made of the packed afternoon session on transforming the science curriculum in which Sandra Harding discussed how science was part of a discredited "bourgeois" Christian legacy practically indistinguishable from imperialism, its cognitive core "tainted by sexism and racism."

Richard Bernstein of the *New York Times* attended the Parsippany conference. When I asked him what he thought of Harding's presentation he said that her thesis was absurd: if Western science is repressive and elitist and part of a bourgeois Christian legacy, why are the Japanese and the Chinese so good at it? Bernstein, who had spent several years in China as *Time* magazine's bureau chief, and who has written a wonderful book on China, told me that throughout the twentieth century Chinese reformers have had great respect for Western science as a progressive force. "Science and Democracy" was the slogan of the celebrated May 4th Movement between 1915 and 1918. Chinese reformers saw Western science as a powerful weapon against the authoritarianism and superstition that were the bulwark of the imperial system. Neither Bernstein nor I ventured a criticism of Ms. Harding's views. We were both very much aware that it would have been exceedingly indecorous for anyone to raise objections. This was a gathering of "connected knowers": hard questions from "separate knowers" were decidedly unwelcome.

Ronald Takaki, the Berkeley expert on ethnic studies, was easily the most popular figure at the Parsippany gathering, and not least because his presence conferred on the feminist transformation projects the cachet of a multicultural movement. Gender feminists have found it is wise to ally themselves with men and women of non-European descent who are critical of Western culture for its "Eurocentrism." A more general offensive on Western "Eurocentric" culture (created by and controlled by "bourgeois white males of European descent") is then prosecuted under the banners of "cultural pluralism," "inclusiveness," and "diversity." Feminist leaders have eagerly embraced these causes partly to deflect attention from the largely white, middle-class character of their own movement and partly to camouflage the divisive misandrism that inspires them but is off-putting to others. The propitiatory strategy of placing their radical feminism under the banner of "inclusiveness" has also been successful in an internal respect: it has given many feminist activists the feeling that they are part of a wider struggle for social justice. Finally, the call for "inclusiveness" usefully diverts attention from the uncomfortable but undeniable fact that the feminists are the ones getting most of the money, the professorships, and the well-paid (but vaguely defined) jobs inside the burgeoning new victim/bias industry.

Takaki began by recognizing that no one seemed to know exactly what a transformed curriculum would look like. And he asked, "How do we do it?" "How do we conceptualize it?" He advised the assembled gender feminists to listen carefully to his lecture because he was going to show them what a transformationist lecture actually looks like. "I will do it! I will practice it," he said.

He told us about the misunderstood and alienated Chinese railroad workers in California, and about the exploited and denigrated Irish factory girls in Lowell, Massachusetts, in the nineteenth century, mixing his facts with remarks about British colonialism and the Opium War. He read us some telegrams sent by a young Chinese railroad worker to some male friends urging them to help him in his plans to marry a young Chinese woman. Takaki explained that he studied telegrams because the Chinese left few documents for study. The telegrams—which Takaki called "texts" —revealed the powerlessness of the prospective Chinese bride. (It seemed to me they revealed much about Chinese immigrant attitudes toward women that reflected on the status of women in China, a point Takaki neglected to make.) Takaki urged the audience to listen to the silences. The silence of the Irish factory workers, the silence of the Chinese immigrants. The silence of the bride. The silence of millions of aliens who are a part of American history yet rarely, if ever, figure in the narrative.

"Blame the historians!" he cried. He singled out Oscar Handlin and Arthur Schlesinger, Jr., both Pulitzer Prize historians, for special censure. Few in the crowd seemed to know much about Handlin's seminal writings on American history. More recognized Schlesinger, who is a liberal Democrat but a critic of much of what passes under the banner of multiculturalism, and they hissed and booed at the mention of his name. Takaki attacked Handlin's *The Uprooted* and Schlesinger's *The Age of Jack-*

son on the ground that both "completely ignored" the Chinese, the Cherokee Indians, and the African-Americans. Takaki did not tell the audience of nonhistorians that the books were written in 1941 and 1945, respectively.

The Harvard historian Stephan Thernstrom, editor of the award-winning *Harvard Encyclopedia of American Ethnic Groups* and the author of numerous books and articles on ethnic history, told me that at the time Handlin and Schlesinger wrote their books, few historians addressed race, class, or gender issues. In recent decades, research on immigrant groups —Chinese, Jewish, and especially Irish factory workers—has been very much in vogue. "Now we think of nothing else," said Thernstrom. Ethnic studies are thriving. African-American history and Native American history are now respected and established fields with recognized experts and classics. Takaki was attacking a straw man.

As a point of fact, Handlin's *The Uprooted* portrays the archetypal patterns and configurations of immigrant experience, and it is still a classic. Handlin is now in his late seventies, and many consider him to be among the greatest American historians of this century. I called him to get his reaction to Takaki's complaints.

"The whole attack is silly," he said. "And too bad he did not do his homework. In 1954 I wrote a book, *The American People*, which does give an account of the Asian immigrant experience . . . but what can you do?"

I had a look at *The American People* and found that Handlin does indeed give attention to the Asian experience at the turn of the century. He describes not only the loneliness of the Chinese but also their resourcefulness. He also considered the effects of the paucity of females on the immigrants and of the racism they were subject to, topics Takaki discussed as if for the first time in history.

I recently appeared with Mr. Takaki on a local (Boston) PBS discussion panel on multiculturalism.[17] He was charming and personable, and I joined the Parsippany crowd in liking him. While we were waiting for the show to begin, I asked him why he had not given Mr. Handlin credit for his treatment of Asian-Americans in the 1954 book. "What book is that?" he asked.

Takaki's New Jersey talk was billed as a transformationist lecture that was to show how the new inclusive learning handles the sensitive themes of the dispossessed. The success of the talk depended on the audience being completely unaware not only of Handlin's work but of thirty years of American social history. But success was assured. The conference had not invited a single person who could possibly be expected to challenge anything being said by any presenter.

Professor Thernstrom, for example, was very surprised to hear that Takaki spoke about the Irish factory girls of Lowell, Massachusetts, as "silenced": they are in fact among the most studied groups in American social history. But no one remotely like Professor Thernstrom had been invited.

The spring issue of the journal *Transformations* had been distributed at the registration desk. Inside, the editor, Sylvia Baer, compared the university curriculum to a dilapidated two-hundred-year-old house she was helping to renovate: "We can all help each other scrape and paint and design and build our curriculums. It's hard work, all this renovation, and sometimes the decisions are risky—but look at the glorious results. . . . Together we can do this. I invite you to help with the planning, the building, and the singing and dancing." [18]

The Parsippany audience, which consisted almost exclusively of white American middle-class females, was in fact thrilled by Takaki's "renovations." Paula Rothenberg and Annette Kolodny were beaming throughout the talk, and they applauded it wildly. Takaki was the topic of conversation for the next two days. By providing a vivid example of what a transformationist approach could do, he had helped them all "to imagine together a curriculum for the next century." He had said he would do it, and he did.

An exhilarating feeling of *momentousness* routinely surfaces at gender feminist gatherings. Elizabeth Minnich is among those who invoke Copernicus and Darwin to give us an idea of the vital importance of what the feminist theorists have discovered. She and several other transformationists took part in a panel discussion called "Transforming the Knowledge Base" in Washington, D.C., in February 1989. The Ford-funded National Council of Research on Women published the proceedings and reported the mood: "There was a palpable sense of making history in the room as we concluded our discussions." [19]

But making history and contributing to progress are not necessarily the same. It is in fact true that the transformationists are having a significant effect on American education. They are imposing a narrow political agenda, diluting traditional scholarly standards, and using up scarce resources. They are doing these things in the name of a transformation project they themselves do not seem fully to comprehend.

Chapter 5

The Feminist Classroom

The exhilaration of feeling themselves in the vanguard of a new consciousness infuses feminist pedagogues with a doctrinal fervor unique in the academy. Here is how five professors from the University of Massachusetts describe the feminist classroom:

> The feminist classroom is the place to use what we know as women to appropriate and transform, totally, a domain which has been men's. . . . Let us welcome the intrusion/infusion of emotionality—love, rage, anxiety, eroticism—into intellect as a step toward healing the fragmentation capitalism and patriarchy have demanded from us.[1]

Women: A Feminist Perspective is said to be the best-selling women's studies textbook of all time. The first selection, "Sexual Terrorism" by Carole J. Sheffield, is a good example of how the feminist classroom can "infuse" anxiety and rage. Ms. Sheffield describes an "ordinary" event that took place early one evening when she was alone in a Laundromat: "The laundromat was brightly lit; and my car was the only one in the lot. Anyone passing by could readily see that I was alone and isolated. Knowing that rape is a crime of opportunity, I became terrified." Ms. Sheffield left her laundry in the washer and dashed back to her car, sitting in it with the doors locked and the windows up. "When the wash was completed, I dashed in, threw the clothes into the drier, and ran back out to my car. When the clothes were dry, I tossed them recklessly into the basket and hurriedly drove away to fold them in the security of my home. Although I was not victimized in a direct, physical way or by objective or measurable standards, I felt victimized. It was, for me, a terrifying experience." At home, her terror subsides and turns to anger: "Mostly I was angry at being unfree: a hostage of a culture that, for the most part, encourages violence against females, instructs men in the methodology of sexual violence, and provides them with ready justification for their violence. . . . Following my experience at the Laundromat, I talked with my students about terrorization."[2]

Any course (be it on Baroque art, English composition, or French drama) can be taught in this "women-centered" way. Committed instructors speak of their "feminist classrooms" as "liberated zones" or "safe spaces" where "silenced women" will be free for the first time to speak out in a secure gynocentric ambience. This is a pedagogy that aims above all to teach the student to unmask the inimical workings of the patriarchy.

We get a good idea of what students experience in the feminist classroom by looking at a "model" introductory women's studies course developed by twelve Rutgers University professors.[3] One of the stated goals of the course is to "challenge and change the social institutions and practices that create and perpetuate systems of oppression." Forty percent of the student's grade is to come from:

1. performing some "outrageous" and "liberating" act outside of class and then sharing feelings and reactions with the class;
2. keeping a journal of "narratives of personal experience, expressions of emotion, dream accounts, poetry, doodles, etc."; and
3. forming small in-class consciousness-raising groups.

The professors in the Rutgers course hand out a list of mandatory classroom "ground rules." According to one of these rules, students agree to "create a safe atmosphere for open discussion. If members of the class wish to make comments that they do not want repeated outside the classroom, they can preface their remarks with a request and the class will agree not to repeat the remarks." This confidentiality rule is critical in classes in which the instructor encourages students to reveal whether a family member, boyfriend, or stranger has molested, raped, battered, or otherwise victimized them.

The general effect of feminist pedagogy is described in a 1990 "Report to the Professions" by five women's studies leaders:

> Women's studies students typically undergo a profound transformation as they claim more knowledge. They pass through an identifiable series of moments of recognition. . . . Such insights are followed by moments of empowerment in which patriarchal frameworks and perceptions are modified, redefined, or rejected altogether and replaced by a newly emerging view of the self and society. The difficulty and complexity of this process . . . cannot be overemphasized. . . . Breaking what feminist writer Tillie Olsen calls the "habits of a lifetime" is no trivial matter. It is accompanied by the full range of human resistance, by continual attraction and repulsion, denial and recognition.[4]

Professor Susan Arpad, who has been teaching women's studies courses at California State University at Fresno for almost fifteen years, describes the powerful effect the courses have on both student and teacher:

> It is a radical change, questioning the fundamental nature of everything they know. . . . At its worst, it can lead to a kind of psychological breakdown. At its best, it necessitates a period of adjustment. . . . On a daily basis, I talk to students and colleagues who are euphoric as a result of their change of consciousness. . . . I also talk to other students and colleagues who are stuck in a stage of anger or despair.[5]

There are some solid scholarly courses offered by women's studies programs, where the goal is simply to teach subjects like women's poetry or women's history in a nonrevisionist way. Unfortunately such courses are not the norm. In their report, the women's studies officers included thirty-seven sample syllabi, of which the Rutgers "model syllabus" was given pride of place. Buried among the thirty-seven syllabi were two that were relatively free of ideology and pedagogical gimmicks.

One of these was a course called "Southern Women: Black and White" given by Professors Susan Tush and Virginia Gould (the report does not say where they teach). The students read well-regarded historical and sociological texts, such as Elizabeth Fox-Genovese's *Within the Plantation Household,* Charles Joyner's *Down by the Riverside,* and Eugene Genovese's *Roll Jordan Roll.* V. S. Naipaul's *A Turn in the South* was on the list—as well as works by Kate Chopin, Ellen Glasgow, and August Evans Wilson. I was sorry not to find Eudora Welty or Flannery O'Connor, who are generally esteemed as two of the most outstanding southern women writers. All the same, it appears to be a solid course. Unfortunately, courses like this one are the exception. The Rutgers model is more the norm, not only for women's studies but for all "feminist classrooms."

For the past few years I have reviewed hundreds of syllabi from women's studies courses, attended more feminist conferences than I care to remember, studied the new "feminist pedagogy," reviewed dozens of texts, journals, newsletters, and done a lot of late-into-the-night reading of e-mail letters that thousands of "networked" women's studies teachers send to one another. I have taught feminist theory. I have debated gender feminists on college campuses around the country, and on national television and radio. My experience with academic feminism and my immersion in the ever-growing gender feminist literature have served to deepen my conviction that the majority of women's studies classes and other classes that teach a "reconceptualized" subject matter are unscholarly, intolerant of dissent, and full of gimmicks. In other words, they are a waste of time. And although they attract female students because of their social ambience, they attract almost no men. They divert the energies of students—especially young women—who sorely need to be learning how to live in a world that demands of them applicable talents and skills, not feminist fervor or ideological rectitude.

Journalist Karen Lehrman visited women's studies programs at Berkeley, the University of Iowa, Smith College, and Dartmouth, audited almost thirty classes, and interviewed many professors and students for a story in *Mother Jones*: "In many classes discussions alternate between the personal and the political, with mere pit stops at the academic. Sometimes they are filled with unintelligible post-structuralist jargon; sometimes they consist of consciousness-raising psychobabble, with the students' feelings and experiences valued as much as anything the professor or texts have to offer."[6] Ms. Lehrman considers this a betrayal: "A hundred years ago, women were fighting for the right to learn math, science, Latin—to be educated like men; today, many women are content to get their feelings heard, their personal problems aired, their instincts and intuition respected."[7]

The feminist classroom does little to prepare students to cope in the world of work and culture. It is an embarrassing scandal that, in the name of feminism, young women in our colleges and universities are taking courses in feminist classrooms that subject them to a lot of bad prose, psychobabble, and "new age" nonsense. What has real feminism to do with sitting around in circles and talking about our feelings on menstruation? To use a phrase much used by resenter feminists, the feminist classroom *shortchanges* women students. It wastes their time and gives them bad intellectual habits. It isolates them, socially and academically. While male students are off studying such "vertical" subjects as engineering and biology, women in feminist classrooms are sitting around being "safe" and "honoring" feelings. In this way, gender feminist pedagogy plays into old sexist stereotypes that extol women's capacity for intuition, emotion, and empathy while denigrating their capacity to think objectively and systematically in the way men can.

A parent should think very carefully before sending a daughter to one of the more gender-feminized colleges. Any school has the freedom to transform itself into a feminist bastion, but because the effect on the students is so powerful it ought to be honest about its attitude. I would like to see Wellesley College, Mount Holyoke, Smith, Mills, and the University of Minnesota—among the more extreme examples—print the following announcement on the first page of their bulletins:

> We will help your daughter discover the extent to which she has been in complicity with the patriarchy. We will encourage her to reconstruct herself through dialogue with us. She may become enraged and chronically offended. She will very likely reject the religious and moral codes you raised her with. She may well distance herself from family and friends. She may change her appearance, and even her sexual orientation. She may end up hating you (her father) and pitying you (her mother). After she has completed her reeducation with us, you will certainly be out tens of thousands of dollars and very possibly be out one daughter as well.

At the Austin conference, my sister and I attended a packed workshop called "White Male Hostility in the Feminist Classroom," led by two female assistant professors from the State University of New York at Plattsburgh. What to do about young men who refuse to use gender-neutral pronouns? Most agreed that the instructor should grade them down. One of the Plattsburghers told us about a male student who had "baited her" when she had defended a fifteen-year-old's right to have an abortion without parental consent. The student had asked, "What about a 15-year-old that wanted to marry a 30-year-old?" She referred to this as a "trap." In philosophy, it is known as a legitimate counterexample to be treated seriously and dealt with by counterargument. But she wanted to know what advice we had to offer.

The agreed-upon remedy was to say to this misguided young man, "I am trying to figure out why you are asking this kind of question." Someone noted that female students in the class can usually be relied upon to keep male students in check. One woman got a big laugh when she told of a feminist student who silenced an "obnoxious male" by screaming "Shut up, you fucker!"

The group was more perplexed about what to do with recalcitrant females. Now that women's courses are required on more and more campuses, the feminist pedagogues expect more resistance. As one participant triumphantly noted, "If the students are comfortable, we are not doing our job."

In the feminist classroom, students encounter committed teachers eager to interpret their lives, their societies, their intellectual heritage for them—in no uncertain terms. Here, for example, is how Professor Joyce Trebilcot of Washington University in St. Louis sees her primary pedagogical duty: "If the classroom situation is very heteropatriarchal—a large beginning class of 50 or 60 students, say, with few feminist students—I am likely to define my task as largely one of recruitment . . . of persuading students that women are oppressed."[8]

Persuading female students that they are oppressed is the first step in the arduous consciousness-raising process. Professor Ann Ferguson, a University of Massachusetts philosopher, uses her philosophy classes to help students uncover their feelings of "anger and oppression": "There are various techniques which aid such personal recovery of feelings, including personal journals, role playing . . . class and teacher collectively sharing personal experiences and feelings."[9] Students like strong-minded teachers who breathe commitment, and the feminist teacher has her appeal. But it is fair to say that most students are not "buying into" gender feminism. Many resent the attempt to recruit them. Even more resent the shift away from a traditional pedagogy whose *primary* objective is teaching students a subject matter that will be useful to them. Professor Ferguson has also had to work out techniques to deal with student resentment toward her. She admits she is routinely accused of being "narrow-minded and polemical."[10]

The Parsippany conference on curricular transformation included several workshops on student resistance: in "Resistance in the Classroom," Professor K. Edington from Towson State University referred to her male students as "Chips" and the females as "Buffys." Professor Edington was delighted by an "enormous federal grant" that Towson State had received for transformation work. But she did not give the impression of liking her students, and she certainly seems to have little regard for them morally or intellectually. Having told us about the Buffys and the Chips and about what "all the preppy clones believe," she went on, without a hint of irony, to say, "We have to teach them to confront stereotypes and bias directly."

Although they are themselves doctrinally immune to criticism—it's really "backlash" in disguise—transformationist teachers are far from indifferent to the dissidents in their classrooms. In a recent issue of *Thought and Action,* the journal on higher education put out by the National Education Association, two professors from Fresno State University, Marcia Bedard and Beth Hartung, report on a "crisis" in women's studies courses created by "hostile male students" and their "negative body language." [11] They single out members of "hypermasculine campus subcultures . . . fraternities, organized athletics, and military and police science" as especially disruptive. "They never miss a class."

What sort of behavior do the Fresno pedagogues consider examples of "classroom harassment"? Their list of offenses includes "challenging facts," stating the exceptions to every generalization, and leaping to an argument at the first pause in the teacher's lecture. Professor Hartung says students are harder on women's studies teachers than on teachers of other courses: "Male and female students evaluating their women's studies teacher . . . compared to teachers of other courses . . . were more likely to make negative and even cruel assessments, even in retrospect." [12]

Reading between the lines of Ms. Bedard and Ms. Hartung's report, and many others on the subject, we get a clear picture of students trying hard to manage all by themselves, with what must be a very frustrating classroom situation. The student who is unaware of the charged atmosphere in the feminist classroom quickly learns that humor is not a good idea. A University of Michigan sophomore, Shawn Brown, wrote a paper for a political science course in which he discussed the difficulties of getting reliable polls:

> Let's say Dave [the] Stud is entertaining three beautiful ladies in his penthouse when the phone rings. A pollster on the other end wants to know if we should eliminate the capital gains tax. Now Dave is a knowledgeable businessperson who cares a lot about this issue. But since Dave is "tied up" at the moment, he tells the pollster to "bother" someone else. [13]

Deborah Meizlish, a graduate teaching assistant who graded Mr. Brown's paper, was incensed. She wrote in the margins:

> Professor Rosenstone has encouraged me to interpret this comment as an example of sexual harassment and to take the appropriate formal steps. I have chosen not to do so in this instance. However, any future comments, in a paper, in a class or in any dealings [with me] will be interpreted as sexual harassment and formal steps will be taken. . . . YOU are forewarned!

The male professor who read Mr. Brown's paper had indeed advised teaching assistant Deborah Meizlish to file formal harassment charges. The chair, Professor Arlene Saxonhouse, backed Rosenstone's and Meizlish's censuring of Mr. Brown: "There is a difference between censorship and expressing concern over a student's mode of expression."[14] In a reply to Saxonhouse's letter, an undergraduate, Adam Devore, pointed out that "there is also a difference between 'expressing concern' and writing, 'You are forewarned!' "

In a case of this kind, faculty do not usually rally to the support of the student. However, the incident attracted the attention of Professor Carl Cohen, a well-known social philosopher and free speech defender. Professor Cohen wrote to the school newspaper, defending Shawn Brown and criticizing the chair of the department of political science, the dean, and the teaching assistant for their violation of Brown's right to write as he did. Professor Cohen's arguments were later cited by a member of the board of regents who voted against a highly restrictive behavior code being proposed for the university.

Shawn Brown had not meant to offend or even to criticize anyone. For the most part, students prudently tend to reserve critical comment until after final grades are in and student evaluations can be safely published. Dale M. Bauer, a professor of English who teaches composition and introductory literature courses at Miami University, reported that about half of the evaluation responses from two first-year composition and introduction to literature sections expressed objections to her feminist stance.[15] Ms. Bauer provides samples, "copied verbatim," of student complaints:

> I feel this course was dominated and overpowered by feminist doctrines and ideals. I feel the feminist movement is very interesting to look at, but I got extremely bored with it and it lost all its punch & meaning because it was so drilled into our brains.

I . . . think you shouldn't voice your "feminist" views because we don't need to know that—It's something that should be left outside class.

I found it very offensive that all of our readings focused on feminism.

Feminism is an important issue in society—but a very controversial one. It needs to be confronted on a personal basis, not in the classroom. I didn't appreciate feminist comments on papers or expressed about work. This is not the only instructor—others in the English Dept. have difficulties leaving personal opinions out of their comments.

Characteristically, Ms. Bauer and her colleagues profess not to be disconcerted by the negative evaluations. Instead they take them to show that renewed efforts are needed. As Ms. Bauer sees it, the question remains "How do we move ourselves out of this political impasse and resistance in order to get our students to identify with the political agenda of feminism?"[16] She regards her teaching as "a kind of counter-indoctrination." The need for "counter-indoctrination" was made clear to her when she saw the following negative evaluation of herself from a student who had taken one of her first-year composition courses: "[The teacher] consistently channels class discussions around feminism and does not spend time discussing the comments that oppose her beliefs. In fact, she usually twists them around to support her beliefs."[17]

In dealing with this kind of resistance, the feminist pedagogue tends to read student criticism as the expression of unacknowledged but deep-seated prejudice or fear. "Resistance" is "only to be expected." After all, students have been thoroughly "socialized" to their gender roles and class loyalties; only a painful process of reeducation can free them from those roles and loyalties. Their very resistance is dramatic evidence of their condition. Criticism may cause her to modify her tactics; it can never cause her to doubt her cause.

The gender feminist will usually acknowledge that her aims are indeed political and that she is seeking to persuade her students to become active in the cause. She justifies turning her classroom into a base in the struggle against patriarchy by arguing that *all* teaching is basically political, that all teachers indoctrinate their students, though often without being aware that they are doing so. As for the pedagogical ideal of disinterested scholarship and "objective truth," the gender feminists deny that these ideals are attainable.

The claim that all teaching is a form of indoctrination, usually in the service of those who are politically dominant, helps to justify the pedagogy of the feminist classroom. Feminist academics often say that apart from the enclave of women's studies, the university curriculum consists of "men's studies." They mean by this that most of what students normally learn is designed to maintain and reinforce the existing patriarchy. To anyone who actually believes this, combatting the standard indoctrination with a feminist "counter-indoctrination" seems only fair and sensible.

The British philosopher Roger Scruton, aided by two colleagues at the Education Research Center in England, has pointed to several prominent features that distinguish indoctrination from normal education.[18] In a competent, well-designed course, students learn methods for weighing evidence and critical methods for evaluating arguments for soundness. They learn how to arrive at reasoned conclusions from the best evidence at hand. By contrast, in cases of indoctrination, the conclusions are assumed beforehand. Scruton calls this feature of indoctrination the "Foregone Conclusion." According to Scruton, the adoption of a foregone conclusion is the most salient feature of indoctrination. In the case of gender feminism, the "foregone conclusion" is that American men strive to keep women subjugated.

The "Hidden Unity" is a second salient feature. The foregone conclusions are part of a "unified set of beliefs" that form the worldview or political program the indoctrinator wishes to impart to the students. In the case of the gender feminist, the "Hidden Unity" is the sex/gender interpretation of society, the belief that modern women are an oppressed class living "under patriarchy."

Indoctrinators also operate within a "Closed System" that is immune to criticism. In the case of gender feminism, the closed system interprets *all* data as confirming the theory of patriarchal oppression. In a term made popular by Sir Karl Popper, gender feminism is *nonfalsifiable,* making it more like a religious undertaking than an intellectual one. If, for example, some women point out that *they* are not oppressed, they only confirm the existence of a system of oppression, for they "show" how the system dupes women by socializing them to *believe* they are free, thereby keeping them docile and cooperative. As Smith College transformationists Marilyn Schuster and Susan Van Dyne note, "The number of female professors who still see no inequity or omissions in the male-defined curriculum . . . serves to underscore dramatically how thoroughly women students may be deceived in believing these values are congruent with their interests."[19]

But what these approaches dramatically underscore is how "effectively" doctrinaire feminists deal with any phenomenon that poses the remotest threat to their tight little mental island. Gender feminism is a closed system. It chews up and digests all counterevidence, transmuting it into confirming evidence. Nothing and no one can refute the hypothesis of the sex/gender system for those who "see it everywhere."

Every society teaches and highlights its own political history, and America is no exception. Recognizing this, however, is very different from admitting that a "normal education" is basically an indoctrination in the politics of the status quo. In fact, objectivity remains the ideal toward which fair-minded teachers aspire. One way they approximate it is by presenting both sides of a controversial subject. Of course, we recognize and acknowledge that what and how he or she teaches is very often affected by the biases of the teacher. It remains true, nevertheless, that some teachers and the courses they teach are more biased than others.

Consider how history is taught in totalitarian societies. Is a standard course in, say, ancient history, as typically taught by an American professor, ideological in the same sense as a state-monitored history of the USSR taught in Stalin's era? To hold that all teaching is ideological is to be blind to the cardinal distinction between education and indoctrination. If one believes that all knowledge is socially constructed to serve the powers that be, or, more specifically, if one holds that the science and culture we teach are basically a "patriarchal construction" designed to support a "male hegemony," then one denies, *as a matter of principle,* any important difference between knowledge and ideology, between truth and dogma, between reality and propaganda, between objective teaching and inculcating a set of beliefs. Many campus feminists do, in fact, reject these distinctions, and that is pedagogically and politically irresponsible and dangerous. For when the Big Brothers in an Orwellian world justify their cynical manipulation of the many by the tyrannical few, they, too, argue that reality is "socially constructed" by those in power and that indoctrination is all we can expect.

In *1984,* George Orwell's tragic hero, Winston Smith, tries to defy the torturer, O'Brien, by holding fast to the belief in an objective reality. O'Brien reminds Winston Smith that he will be paying the price for that old-fashioned belief: "You believe that reality is something objective, external, existing in its own right. . . . But I tell you, Winston, reality is not external. . . . It is impossible to see reality except by looking through the eyes of the Party."[20]

And Winston Smith is "persuaded" to change his mind.

Those who believe that all teaching is political have labeled everything in advance, and they brook no counter arguments. Critical philosophers are well acquainted with this move: first it labels everything, then it rides roughshod over fundamental differences. That happens when armchair psychologists come up with the startling doctrine that *all* human activity is motivated by selfishness, or when armchair metaphysicians announce that whatever happens is *bound* to happen. The pronouncements of "psychological egoism" or "fatalistic metaphysics" have an air of being profound, but they destroy sound thinking by obliterating the distinctions that we must have if we are to think straight and see things clearly and distinctly. Label it as you will; there is, after all, a difference between caring and uncaring behavior, between callous, selfish disregard for others and considerateness and concern. There is a difference between events that happen accidentally and those that are planned.

So, too, is there a difference between education and propaganda. The economist Thomas Sowell notes that the statement "All teaching is political" is trivially true in just the way the statement "Abraham Lincoln and Adolf Hitler were both imperfect human beings" is true.[21]

The blurring of vital distinctions is a mark of ideology or immaturity. We could be more tolerant of the pronouncement that *in some sense* all courses are political if campus feminists were prepared to acknowledge the vital difference between courses taught in a disinterested manner and those taught to promote an ideology. But that is precisely what so many deny.

This denial is so *perverse* that we are led to wonder what possible advantage the feminist ideologues could be getting from erasing the obvious and reasonable distinctions that most of us recognize and respect. On reflection, it is clear that their denial serves them very well indeed, by leaving them free to do what they please in their classrooms. Having denied the very possibility of objective learning, they are no longer bound by the need to adhere to traditional standards of a curriculum that seeks to convey an objective body of information. Putting "objectivity" in scare quotes, the feminists simply deny it as a possible pedagogical ideal. "Man is the measure of all things," said old Protagoras—and the gender feminists agree that in the past Man was the measure. Now it is Woman's turn.

This pedagogical philosophy licenses the feminist teacher to lay down "conclusions" or "rules" without feeling the need to argue for them. Consider the "ground rules" developed by the Center for Research on Women at Memphis State University and used at Rutgers University, the University of Minnesota, Penn State, and other schools around the country. The students are asked to accept them as a condition for taking the course:

> For the purposes of this course we agree to these rules:
> 1. Acknowledge that oppression (i.e., racism, sexism, classism) exists.
> 2. Acknowledge that one of the mechanisms of oppression (i.e., racism, sexism, classism, heterosexism) is that we are all systematically taught misinformation about our own groups and about members of both dominant and subordinate groups.
> 3. Assume that people (both the groups we study and the members of the class) always do the best they can.
> 4. If members of the class wish to make comments that they do not want repeated outside the classroom, they can preface their remarks with a request and the class will agree not to repeat the remarks.[22]

First, it should be pointed out that these "rules" are very unusual for a college class. Teachers frequently have rules about absences or late papers, but here the rules demand that the students adopt particular *beliefs,* none of which is self-evident. Consider rule no. 1, which asserts that "oppression exists." Stated in this unqualified way, it cannot be denied. But since the student is meant to understand that oppression exists in the United States in the form of classism and sexism, the matter is not nearly so simple. Is it not at least arguable that one of the good features of American life is that here, in contrast to most other countries, an individual can rise in the socioeconomic scale despite his or her background? Is this not one reason why many outsiders are so eager to come here? Why then speak of class oppression?

The coupling of sexism and racism is also problematic. Are they really that similar? Is sexism a national problem on a par with racism? The rule requires the student to accept that it is. Indeed, it is typical of the structure of many women's studies courses in putting a lot of loaded and controversial questions beyond the pale of discussion. And that is exactly what a college course should not be doing.

Rule no. 2 says: "One of the mechanisms of oppression is that we are all systematically taught misinformation." No doubt on occasion everyone is taught something that is not true. But are we "systematically" being given "misinformation"? When people were of the opinion that the world was flat, one might say they were "systematically" being taught that. But since everyone thought that was true, we shouldn't speak of "misinformation," which connotes more than unintentional error. As the women's studies scholars here use it, "systematically" connotes "deliberately" and with political purposes in mind. This alludes to the insidious workings of patriarchy, the "Hidden Unity" that keeps women in thrall to men. But it is certainly *false* that all of us are being deliberately (systematically) taught untruths.

Rule no. 3 asks students to assume that groups always do the best they can. But why should they be required to make such a plainly false assumption? People, especially in groups, often could do a lot better than they do. Why assume the opposite? This rule, too, is characteristic of the "feel good" spirit of many women's studies courses. Since every group is "doing its best," it is churlish to criticize any given group. (Does this assumption extend to fraternities? And to the football team?) Rule no. 3 serves another, unstated purpose: to preempt criticism that might disrupt the teacher's agenda.

Rule no. 4, which requires absolute confidentiality, is similarly objectionable. Classes should be free and open: anything said in the classroom should be repeatable outside. That an instructor invites or even allows her students to "speak out" about personal affairs is an unfailing sign that the course is unsubstantial and unscholarly. Moreover, the students who are encouraged to speak of painful incidents in their lives not only are being shortchanged scholastically, they are also at risk of being harmed by their disclosures. Even mental health professionals in clinical settings exercise great caution in eliciting traumatic disclosures. Any good school provides professional help to distressed students who need it. The amateur interventions of a teacher are intrusive and potentially harmful.

But getting students to make painful personal disclosures is a special feature of feminist pedagogy. Kali Tal, a cultural studies instructor, recently shared the "Rules of Conduct" she used at George Mason University with all the members of the women's studies electronic bulletin board: [23]

Rape and incest are touchy subjects. Some class participants will be survivors of sexual abuse. Everyone will likely have moments in this class when they are angry or sad or perhaps frightened. It is important . . . to make this classroom a safe place for students to share experiences, feelings, and intellectual ideas. I have therefore composed the following list of ground rules:

1. There will be no interruption of any speaker.
2. There will be no personal criticism of any kind directed by any member of the class to any other member of the class.
3. Because some of the material discussed and viewed in this course contains extremely graphic and violent material, some students

may find it necessary to take an occasional "breather." Students should feel free to stand up and walk out of class if they find themselves in need of a short break. It is permissible (and even encouraged) to ask a classmate to accompany you during such a break.

As a final ground rule, Professor Tal tells students "this class is not a therapy session."

Inevitably, some students who come to class to get information, to learn useful skills, and to analyze issues more deeply feel cheated by such approaches. They may feel that the teacher is wasting their time. What does the feminist teacher, intent on "creating agents of social change," think of her students when they react in this way?

Elizabeth Fay, a feminist writing instructor at the University of Massachusetts, tells about a student she calls Minnie, a young working-class woman from Puerto Rico who lived with her divorced mother. Minnie sat sullenly through her classes, occasionally asking angry questions and being "confrontational" in conference sessions.[24] When the course was over, Minnie filed a complaint that she had not learned any writing skills in the course. As Professor Fay describes it:

> Minnie's complaints rested on three main points: she was given no model essays to emulate; she was not given directive commentary that would have shown her how to rewrite; she was given no formulae to follow for each particular essay genre. In other words, she was denied constraint, she was asked to think on her own, and she was given the opportunity to give and receive peer feedback without an intruding master voice.[25]

Professor Fay's analysis of Minnie's grievance is complacently self-serving. It "silences" Minnie by treating her as someone who prefers "constraint" and a "master voice" to liberation. Professor Fay, who is not listening to Minnie, accuses Minnie of refusing to listen: "She made it clear that notions of multiple voices and visions, notions of gender politics, notions of student empowerment did not touch her need for the proper style, the proper accent, the Doolittle makeover she had signed up for."[26]

But Minnie hadn't signed up for voices, visions, and gender politics; she had signed up for a course in English composition. She wanted her essays corrected because she wanted to learn to write better English. That is not an unreasonable expectation for a writing course. But to Professor

Fay, Minnie had missed the real point of what the course in freshman composition was about:

> In freshman composition, what we try to give students is a con-
> sciousness about the social register and the range of voices they can
> and do adopt in order to get on with business. But it is their com-
> bination of demand and distrust (are you sure this is what I need?
> are you wasting my time and money?) that propels certain students
> into resistant postures. Minnie's out-of-class hostility and in-class
> silent propriety bespeak a surface socialization that itself resists the
> induction process; she desires an academically gilded armor but not
> a change of self, not a becoming.[27]

Professor Fay, who is disappointed that Minnie has failed to avail herself of the chance to "become," quite sincerely believes that Minnie's recalcitrant attitude comes from having been "socialized" in ways that "propel" her into a resistant posture. It simply never occurs to Professor Fay that her own attitude toward Minnie is disrespectful and that it is *she* who has been taught by her feminist mentors to adopt a patronizing posture toward women like her.[28]

Michael Olenick, a journalism major at the University of Minnesota, reported his experiences with Women's Studies 101 in an editorial in the school newspaper: "When I signed up for a women's studies class I expected to learn about feminism, famous women, women's history, and women's culture. . . . Instead of finding new insights into the world of women, I found . . . bizarre theories about world conspiracies dedicated to repressing and exploiting women."[29]

Heather Keena, a senior at the University of Minnesota, wrote a letter supporting Olenick's complaint about the atmosphere in the classroom. "I was made to feel as though I was dependent and weak for preferring men to women as sexual partners, and to feel that my opinions were not only insignificant, but somehow twisted."[30] Another class member, Kathleen Bittinger, thought the professor guilty of stereotyping the male gender as chauvinistic: "I was also told that my religious beliefs and sexual orientation are not the correct ones."[31]

I wondered what Professor Albrecht, who taught the course, thought of the controversy and phoned her. She was warm and personable, and her concern was undeniable. In response to the charges that her course was one-sided, she pointed out that students get their fill of standard viewpoints from "the mainstream media." It was her job to give them a deeper truth: "If scholarship isn't about improving people's lives, then what is it about?" Ms. Albrecht was clearly committed to her self-imposed task of telling students how they were being exploited within a patriarchal, classist, racist society. It was equally clear that she felt fully justified in not giving the other side a hearing. I have come across many devoted teachers who, like Professor Albrecht, refuse to listen to "voices" that could in any way affect their determination to produce students who are "agents of social change." Ms. Albrecht sent me her syllabus, which was unabashedly ideological: it even included a copy of the Rutgers "ground rules."

Students who complain about feminist pedagogy get little sympathy from the administration. Lynne Munson, a recent graduate of Northwestern, found the "feminist perspective" everywhere on her campus: "I took a classics course, and we were encouraged to take part in a feminist demonstration, 'Take Back the Night,' out of solidarity with the women of Sparta. In an art history class the professor attacked Manet's Olympia for its similarities to pornographic centerfolds."

Ms. Munson was especially critical of a freshman seminar called "The Menstrual Cycle: Fact or Fiction," in which students discussed their "raging hormonal imbalances." In the op-ed column of her school newspaper, Munson wrote that a course of this kind did not contribute much to a liberal arts education. She found the class silly and complained to the dean that the curriculum was becoming faddish and losing academic legitimacy.

The dean, Stephen Fisher, replied that the course was "a legitimate area of inquiry." He told me that Ms. Munson seemed to be distressed by women's studies and to be seeking ways to undermine it. I asked him whether he didn't think the menstrual cycle seemed an odd subject for a freshman seminar; wouldn't such a course be more appropriate in a medical school? Did he not share some of the current concerns that today's undergraduates have serious gaps in their knowledge of history, science, and literature and need a firm grounding in the "basics"? The dean replied that, unlike the University of Chicago, Northwestern had rejected the core curriculum in favor of general studies and that courses like the seminar on the menstrual cycle were appropriate to Northwestern's more pluralistic curriculum. When I pointed out that no one was giving seminars on prostate function or nocturnal emissions and other intimate male topics about which there is an equal amount of ignorance, he seemed amused, and we left it at that.

Menstruation is a favorite theme in women's studies courses. The Uni-

versity of Minnesota offers a course on "Blood Symbolism in Cross-Cul-
tural Perspective." Topics to be covered include "blood and sexual fluids"
and "menstruation and blood letting." At Vassar College they had a
"bleed-in." The flier announcing this event said: "Are you down on menstruation? The Women's Center warmly welcomes you to the first all-
campus BLEED IN October 16, 1993, 8:00 P.M. in the Women's Center."[32]

In a widely used textbook called *Feminism and Values,* the student will
read Carol P. Christ on the importance of menstrual fluids in the new
feminist goddess rituals. Ms. Christ, a former visiting lecturer at the Harvard Divinity School and Pomona College, tells students of "the joyful
affirmation of the female body and its cycles" in "Goddess-centered rituals" at the summer solstice: "From hidden dirty secret to symbol of the
life power of the Goddess, women's blood has come full circle."[33]

If women's blood has come full circle, the public at large has yet to
hear of it. From Finland comes this e-mail request by a feminist scholar
who is mentoring a student's research in this area:

> I have a student working on an MA thesis in sociology on different
> conceptions of menstruation in Finland. She has been going through
> medical literature. . . . All this material has shown her a dominant
> discourse based on traditional medical conceptions. . . . In order to
> have different voices, she has been interviewing women. . . . Her
> problem is that a) most women don't very much like to talk about
> menstruation, b) most have negative feelings about it . . . Does any-
> body have any suggestions on how to have also positive feelings
> expressed?[34]

Objective researchers do not usually ask for help in getting data more
in keeping with results they would view as "positive." On the other hand,
gender feminists are convinced that prevailing attitudes toward menstruation are fixed by a dominant (male) discourse. So the researcher tends to
discount the opinions of women (unfortunately a majority) whom they
regard as giving expression to negative male attitudes, and they look for
the countervailing "authentic" women's voices.

One such voice was sounded by feminist theorist Joan Straumanis
(later dean of Faculty at Rollins College). She concluded an address at a
women's study conference entitled "The Structure of Knowledge: A Feminist Perspective": "It is very consciousness-raising to have your period
during a conference like this one. . . . I don't know of any other conference where the speaker got up and said that she had her period. . . . For
that and other reasons, women's studies will never die"![35]

. . .

Lee Edelman is a popular professor of English literature at Tufts University. His course "Hitchcock: Cinema, Gender, Ideology" (English 91) caught my attention, so I called and asked if I might sit in on one of his classes.

I attended Professor Edelman's class on the day he discussed gender roles in Hitchcock's *The Thirty-Nine Steps*. Edelman, a thirtysomething associate professor, was analyzing the romance between Robert Donat and Madeleine Carroll. As he lectured he showed clips from the film, commenting all the while about the film's unstated sexual politics. The lecture was thematically one-dimensional, but interesting and engaging.

At the beginning of the film, Robert Donat, fleeing the authorities, enters a railway compartment and forcibly kisses Madeleine Carroll to avoid being spotted. Edelman asked, "What does it mean to think about romance always in terms of crime and violence?" He told the class that love is a social construct, first and foremost a political weapon: "How do masters of cinema get people to find war attractive? By suggesting Nazis want to hurt Mrs. Miniver. You show women as objects that men must protect. We bomb Hiroshima for Rita Hayworth."

Professor Edelman asked the class about a minor character: "How does Mr. Memory represent patriarchal knowledge?" No one volunteered an answer. One young man hesitantly pointed out that Carroll seems to enjoy Donat's kiss, since, after all, she closes her eyes and drops her glasses. From the back of the classroom a young woman condemned the male student along with Hitchcock. Both, she said, promote the idea that women enjoy assaults. The discussion became more animated. Edelman observed that the happy ending depends on "buying into the ideology of romantic love." Warming to this theme, another young woman said, "The moment the heroine falls in love, she ceases to have a distinct identity." Edelman agreed: "She wears a beatific smile, the smile of the fulfilled heterosexual relationship." The topic to be explored the following week: love and marriage in the conventional union. Assignment: *Rebecca*.

Later I spoke at length with Professor Edelman. His background is in literary deconstruction, a style of criticism he deploys to read every "text" (be it a novel, film, song, or TV commercial) as an expression, if not a weapon, of the oppressor culture. He believes the purpose of teaching is to challenge the culture by debunking ("deconstructing") its "texts." He believes good teaching is adversarial.

When I asked him if he felt he had an obligation to give arguments for the other side, Edelman made Professor Albrecht's point: he has the students for only a precious few hours a week; the dominant culture has them the rest of the time. It may be the only time in their lives they are exposed to iconoclastic thinking about their culture.

I had enjoyed the class and would not have minded hearing him on *Rebecca*. Edelman was fun to listen to, even when he kept insisting the students must learn to see how sex bias is inscribed in every cultural artifact, every work of art, every novel, every movie. The students were learning a lot about how Hitchcock exploited sexual themes, but from where I sat there was a lot they were not learning, including why Hitchcock is considered a great filmmaker. They were not learning about his mastery in building suspense. They were not told, nor could they explain, why *The Thirty-Nine Steps* had set a new style for cinematic dialogue. The Tufts students were being taught to "see through" Hitchcock's films before they had learned to look *at* them and before they knew much about why they should be studying them in the first place. Nothing the students said indicated they had learned much about Hitchcock or his work. By the time Edelman got through "unmasking" the sexism of *The Thirty-Nine Steps*, the students' disdain for it would have left them with little incentive to regard Hitchcock as a great filmmaker. They were learning what Hitchcock was "really" up to, and that, apparently, was what mattered.

These omissions are characteristic of much teaching that goes on in the contemporary classroom. Today's students are culturally undernourished. The college English class is the one opportunity for students to be exposed to great poetry, short stories, novels, and theater. If they do not learn to respect and enjoy good literature in college, they probably never will.

The feminist classroom strongly affects many an impressionable student. The effect on the teacher may also be dramatic, especially if she is a neophyte. Professor Dixie King tells how a course she was teaching transformed her: "In teaching my first women's studies course many years ago, I found myself changing as I talked; I discovered the extent to which I had been in complicity with the system, male-trained into the system; I deconstructed myself and reconstructed myself through dialogue in that class." [36]

In the course of inquiries into academic feminism I kept coming across students who marveled at how much they had been changed by their new perspective on the social reality. Students who see the workings of the sex/gender system "everywhere" are turning up in nonfeminist classrooms ready to challenge the "phallocentric reasoning" of their instructors. Some faculty consider such students virtually unteachable. One Midwestern English professor told me: "It is very difficult to teach students who have been trained to take the 'feminist perspective.' They have this steely look in their eyes. They distrust everything you say. For them *reason* itself is patriarchal, linear, and oppressive. You cannot argue with them. Everything is grist for their mill."

Kim Paffenroth, a former divinity student at Harvard, is one of several students who is disturbed at the extent to which the radical feminist perspective dominates his classes. One of his professors was sharply interrupted, midsentence, by an angry T.A. who "corrected" him because he had referred to God as "he." "I was quite shocked at the rudeness of her interruption, but even more aghast as I saw how much power she could wield with such petty rudeness when the professor meekly corrected himself and apologized."

College campuses used to be thought of as enclaves of high spirits and irreverence. Academic feminism has had a great deal to do with drastically changing that image. The political scientist Abigail Thernstrom describes American colleges as islands of intolerance in a sea of freedom. I visited one such island in the fall of 1989.

The College of Wooster in Ohio has a strong feminist presence. Opposition to feminist ideology is mainly surreptitious. One assistant professor, who requests anonymity, told me that it is "suicidal" to criticize campus feminists in any way. "They want people to be scared. Then you keep quiet and they don't have to deal with you." He described the atmosphere as "McCarthyist." Another silent critic excused his timidity on social grounds. Being perceived as confrontational in a small town is costly. "We have to live with these people." Yet another professor admitted his despair over the radical feminist encroachment at Wooster but said that to create a stir might be harmful to enrollments.

Four Wooster seniors agreed to talk to me about their experience in the feminist classroom. Peter Stratton, who took Women's Studies 110, was surprised on the first day of class to hear the professor declare the class a "liberated zone" where "suppressed" women would be free to speak out on any subject." Mr. Stratton says that at first he was very profeminist:

> But over and over again we heard how awful men are. That there is no point in caring for males, that romantic involvement is futile. Of course, there are some bad men in society, but you also have to look

at the good ones. When I first arrived at the College of Wooster, I accepted everything I was told. Now some of my friends and I will use words like "freshman" among ourselves as a sign of resistance.

Another senior, Michael Millican, believes the College of Wooster has "officially suspended the Bill of Rights." John Cassais says that few students dare to question the teacher's viewpoint. "The risks are too great." He believes students are being indoctrinated: "In the first-year seminar (not freshman seminar) they now concentrate exclusively on race and gender issues. That program resembles a university program a lot less than it does a reeducation camp."

The students read *Racism and Sexism,* a strongly ideological text edited by Paula Rothenberg (mentioned previously as head of the New Jersey Project and moderator at the Parsippany conference). Defenders of this book misdescribe it as a collection of "anti-discrimination court cases."[37] In fact, less than 20 percent of it deals with cases. The bulk of the book is a miscellany of mostly bad poetry and tendentious, tedious articles, full of graceless jargon, all written from a gender feminist perspective. It seems that Rothenberg saw no need to provide a hearing for other views. Nor, since relatively few selections have literary or stylistic merit, did she apparently feel responsible for offering the students a text that would teach them how to write well. At Wooster, however, *Racism and Sexism* was well suited to the purposes of the feminist activists and their administrative allies.

In 1990, the college invited a roster of speakers to campus to reinforce the message in Ms. Rothenberg's text: the speakers included Ms. Rothenberg, Angela Davis, Ronald Takaki, Derrick Bell, and a lone "conservative," former New York mayor Ed Koch. Koch was duly hissed and booed by the "well-trained" students.

The intolerance at Wooster for those who are critical of the gender feminist faith makes the faculty very circumspect about voicing criticism, and this has rendered them virtually unable to oppose any feminist program they think unworthy of support. "I am getting old and tired, and I do not want to get fired," said one professor:

What you have here are a lot of students and faculty who are very skeptical, but they are afraid to voice their reservations. On the other hand, women's studies faculty are well organized and they have very effective strategies. First they co-ordinate with other departments and offer a large group of courses, they bloc vote and get a number of themselves on educational policy committees. It's not hard these days to get a powerful administrator behind you. For them it is a way to make a name for themselves in college administration. They can say they initiated a new women's program.

Many students resent women's studies. They want less ideology and more objective content in their courses. One would think that the college administrations would be sympathetic to their complaints. But administrations have changed a lot in the last two decades. We now find deans and college presidents admonishing students not to be taken in by claims of objectivity and the allegedly disinterested scholarship of pedagogues who are fixed in the earlier phases of an untransformed curriculum. The more enlightened administrators preach the virtues of a new pedagogy that impugns all objectivity, even that of science. In a convocation address, Donald Harward, then vice president of academic affairs at the College of Wooster, said, "A major intellectual revolution has occurred. Within the last two decades the . . . effort 'to objectify' fields of inquiry has been called into question by a challenge to the objectivity of science —the preeminent prototype." [38]

Invoking the authority of the feminist epistemologist Sandra Harding, among others, Dr. Harward informed the students that "there is no objectivity, even in science." He then confided that "the new view of science, and thereby the new view of any field of intellectual inquiry, is only a whisker from irrationality and total skepticism. But fine lines are important." By the end of his address, the students were ready for the uplifting message that "learning and teaching have less to do with truth, reality, and objectivity than we had assumed."

Transformationists cannot always rely on a sympathetic faculty, but they can generally count on administrative support in furthering their projects. Schuster and Van Dyne, the Smith College transformation team, report that "informed administrators" are more likely than professors to acknowledge the need for curricular transformation. [39] At Wooster College it was Harward who initiated the policy of having students evaluate their teachers on their sensitivity to gender issues. He has since gone on to become president of Bates College in Maine.

Students who have been successfully trained in the feminist classroom to "become agents of change" may embarrass their mentors by practicing what they have learned right on the campus. At Simon's Rock of Bard College in Barrington, Massachusetts, twenty students who were not satisfied that the formal procedures of the university adequately protected students from sexual harassment formed "defense guard" groups to take matters into their own hands. "Defense guarding" consists of surrounding a targeted professor in an out-of-the-way place, charging him with sexual harassment, and then chanting, in unison, over and over again: "This will not be tolerated. This has got to stop."[40]

One of the participating students told me that if her group hears of behavior that sounds sexist or harassing, they will directly and repeatedly confront the perpetrator. "Defense guarding is a very effective means of convincing someone that what they are doing is wrong." I asked whether defense guarding was not unfairly intimidating to the accused and was told, "Why would they be intimidated unless they are guilty? If they have done nothing, they would not be intimidated."

One foreign professor subjected to this treatment became physically ill. The administration finally acted by putting sixteen "defense guards" under temporary suspension. Women's studies professor Patricia Sharp disclaimed all responsibility for the behavior of the defense guards; she insisted their attitude has nothing to do with feminism. Yet she expressed concern that nearly half of the eighteen students in her feminist theory class were members of the defense guard.

That the students' behavior should disconcert even the feminist teachers is understandable. It is equally understandable that the students feel betrayed. One member of the defense guard who was in Professor Sharp's class told me that in women's studies courses women are encouraged to empower themselves, but "when we put it into practice in a direct and effective way we are suspended."

Simon's Rock is part of Bard College. When asked about the tactics of the defense guards, Bard president Leon Botstein said, "The best face to put on it is that these kids do not possess a sufficient historical memory to understand that such behavior is extremely reminiscent of fascism, of brown shirts; it is a classic group intimidation and public humiliation which is associated with the thirties, and then finally with the Red Guards."[41]

Pennsylvania State College has an alternative newspaper called the *Lionhearted* that routinely pokes fun at campus political correctness. In its April 12, 1993, issue, it satirized an op-ed piece by a radical feminist student, Amanda Martin, that appeared in the college newspaper. Ms. Martin had recently attended the Penn State antirape march, which she called a march of "250 female warriors." She compared patriarchy to a bloodthirsty "monster" that is devouring all women. To those who would criticize her, she issued a warning: "I'll kick your ass."[42]

Ms. Martin's article invited parody, and the *Lionhearted* obliged by criticizing her harangue and irreverently printing a cartoon image of her in a blue bikini. The campus feminist activists reacted by seizing and destroying all six thousand copies of the *Lionhearted*. Several hundred were burned in a bonfire, late at night, outside the office of Ben Novak, a member of the Penn State board of trustees who serves as an advisor to the paper.

Mike Abrams, the editor of the Penn State school newspaper, the *Daily Collegian*, justified the burning of newspapers: "The individual(s) who burned copies of the *Lionhearted* were demonstrating the same freedom of expression that allowed the newspaper to print its views."[43] Donna Hughes, a Penn State women's studies professor, also saw nothing wrong with burning newspapers, given the circumstances. After all, the cartoon parody was a form of harassment. "I think it was an act of protest; considering the very personal, defaming attack on [Amanda Martin] in a full-page cartoon."[44]

It is difficult to estimate the proportion of students who become committed gender feminists. It is surely a minority. Even when the conversion seems to go deep it may be short-lived. But those who remain steadfast are tough and formidable. On the other hand, some of the "defectors" are just as formidable.

Heather Hart, a recent graduate of Brandeis University, tells of her disenchantment with academic feminism:

> At Brandeis I discovered feminism. And I instantly became a convert. And I did well, writing brilliant papers in my Myths of Patriarchy humanities class, in which I likened my fate as a woman to other victims throughout the ages. I joined the women's coalition, preached to anyone who would listen, and even came close to cutting men out of my life entirely.

Ms. Hart, however, came from Montreal, where lipstick is in fashion, and she refused to give it up: "They condemned me from the get-go. They talked about feeling excluded from the male-dominated, patriarchal society, and yet they were quick to dismiss me as a boy-toy just because I like the concept of decoration. . . . I was different and, therefore, a threat to the neat, closed, secret, homogeneous community."

Ms. Hart says that the near-ostracism she suffered kept her from enjoying the "strengths" that solidarity could have offered her; nevertheless, she accepted being disapproved of because she "did not wish to alienate" herself from those she felt allied to. The inevitable break came when Eddie

Murphy came to Brandeis to give a concert: "I was intent on going . . . yet at a meeting with my fellow feminists I was informed that we were boycotting the show as Murphy was a homophobic, misogynistic racist."

Ms. Hart crossed the picket line and had the revelation that in many ways her sisters in women's studies and the women's center were "frighteningly reminiscent" of the forces "they claimed to be fighting all those years."

Some who later defected look back with resentment on the feminists who held them in thrall. Annie Ballad, a 1988 graduate of Harvard, felt her private life to be intolerably incorrect, being in conflict with what she was learning in the feminist classroom. She had been persuaded that heterosexual lovemaking was basically a violation: "While taking women's studies (at Harvard) with a separatist teaching fellow there, I nearly had a nervous breakdown because I thought my boyfriend of five years was raping me every time he penetrated me." She set out to "deprogram" herself, using a technique of linguistic reversal that is known to be effective. Ms. Ballad had been trained to certain locutions, avoiding those that gender feminists deem condescending to women. She began to force herself to be "incorrect"; "I insisted on calling women 'girls,' 'chicks,' and 'babes.'" After a short while she felt free to enjoy her sexually incorrect life.

Irreverence is both an antidote and an immunizer. At strongly feminist Vassar College, two juniors, Regina Peters and Jennifer Lewis, founded the "Future Housewives of America." At first the group took themselves in a tongue-in-cheek spirit. One of their earliest projects (foiled at the last minute) was to sneak into the messy women's center late at night and clean it up, leaving a note signed "Compliments of the Future Housewives of America." Student groups are routinely given modest funds for running expenses: as a women's group, Future Housewives was entitled to apply for funds through the Feminist Alliance. Peters and Lewis showed up at an Alliance meeting and announced the formation of their group. They told about their first two planned activities: to publish their own cookbook and to host a Tupperware party. "I have never seen anything like it," said Peters later. "Fifty stunned women gaping in disbelief." They were not funded and have since disbanded.

Campus feminists have made the American campus a less happy place, having successfully browbeaten a once outspoken and free faculty. One of the saddest things about their influence is their effect on pedagogy outside their own classrooms. They have raised a generation of student watchdogs ever on the lookout for sexist bias in all its insidious manifestations. Students are careful rather than carefree. Humor is guarded. Many teachers now practice a kind of defensive pedagogy.

In December 1989 I received a phone call from a man who told me he was a graduate student at the University of Minnesota. He asked me to look into some "frightening" things campus feminists were up to. He mentioned the Scandinavian studies department. He told me he did not want to give me his name because he felt he would be hurt: "They are powerful, they are organized, and they are vindictive."

The University of Minnesota is heavily "colonized." In addition to its Women's Studies department, it has a Center for Advanced Feminist Studies, the Center for Women in International Development, a Women's Center, a Young Women's Association, the Center for Continuing Education for Women, and the Humphrey Center on Women and Public Policy. The feminist journal *Signs* is housed there, and the radical feminist review *Hurricane Alice* is associated with the English department. There is a Sexual Violence Program, as well as a Commission on Women.

After a few phone calls I found some faculty members who would speak up about the "campus feminists," provided anonymity was promised. One professor of social science told me:

> We have a hardened and embittered core of radical feminists. These women have been victorious in court: they have the ear of several powerful regents and administrators. They call the shots. Everywhere you look there are feminist faculty members concerned to divest departments of the white male viewpoint. If you question this, you are labeled a sexist. It is a nightmare. At faculty meetings we have learned to speak in code: you say things that alert other faculty members that you do not agree with the radical feminists, but you say nothing that could bring a charge of gender insensitivity. People are out for control and power. I did not fully understand what was happening until I read Nien Cheng's *Life and Death in Shanghai.*

Professor Norman Fruman, a distinguished scholar in the English department, was outspoken:

> If you resist feminists you are liable to the charge of sexism. You then may be socially or professionally isolated. With the rise of poststructuralism, Derrida, Foucault, Althusser, you have the basis

for a Stalinist position. Many faculty are now teaching students that there is no objectivity. All is subjective. This is their rallying cry. All of the literary masterpieces, including the very notion of aesthetic quality, are said to be a means of patriarchal control.

I then called Professor Lois Erickson, a feminist activist. She explained why the two men I had spoken to would of course be "hostile and defensive":

> It is a new era at the University of Minnesota. Our shared reality has been through a masculine lens. I spent a sabbatical at Harvard working with Carol Gilligan where I learned to honor the inner feminine voice. Until we can balance the feminine and the masculine, peace is not possible. For this we need a strong feminist studies department. . . . We have at least three hundred women on campus empowered by a favorable court ruling. This gives us a strong collective voice. Some men and women are threatened because they fear their feminine side.

Having heard "both sides" of the feminist question at Minnesota, I felt ready to tackle the mystery of the Scandinavian studies department. It turned out not to be a mystery at all—only a disturbing example of extreme feminist vigilance.

On April 12, 1989, four female graduate students filed sexual harassment charges against all six tenured members of the Scandinavian studies department (five men and one woman). The professors were called to Dean Fred Lukerman's office, notified of the charges and, according to the accused, told they'd better get themselves lawyers.

In a letter sent to Professor William Mishler of Scandinavian studies, Ms. Patricia Mullen, the university officer for sexual harassment, informed Mishler that he had been accused of sexual harassment and would be reported to the provost unless he responded within ten days. Similar letters were sent to the other five professors. Mishler's letters contained no specific facts that could be remotely considered to describe sexual harassment. When Mishler made further inquiries, he discovered he had been accused of giving a narrow and "patriarchal" interpretation of Isaak Dinesen's work, of not having read a novel a student deemed important, and of having greeted a student in a less than friendly manner. Two of Mishler's colleagues were accused of harassing the plaintiffs by not having given them higher grades.

The plaintiffs had drawn up a list of punitive demands, among them:

1. the denial of merit pay for a period of not less than five years;
2. monthly sexual harassment workshops for all Scandinavian core faculty for at least twelve months; and
3. annual sexual harassment workshops for all Scandinavian core faculty, adjunct faculty, visiting faculty, graduate assistants, reader-graders, and graduate students.

Lacking any support from the administration whatsoever, the professors were forced to seek legal counsel. On October 13, six months later, all charges against four of the accused were dropped. No explanation was offered. A few months later, the charges against the remaining two were dropped, again without explanation. All of them are still shaken from what they describe as a Kafkaesque ordeal. "When I saw the charges," says Professor Allen Simpson, "I panicked. It's the most terrifying thing . . . they want me fired. It cost me two thousand dollars to have my response drafted. I can't afford justice."

Professor Mishler requested that the contents of the complaints be made public to the Minnesota community. But, according to the *Minnesota Daily,* Patricia Mullen opposed disclosure on the grounds that "it would dampen people from coming forward."[45]

My efforts to reach someone who could give me the administration's side of the story were not successful. Ms. Mullen declined to speak with me. Fred Lukerman, who was dean of the College of Liberal Arts at the time, also proved to be inaccessible. I finally did talk to a dean who assured me he was very supportive of feminist causes on campus, but that he believed the Scandinavian studies affair was indeed a "witch hunt." "But please do not use my name," he implored.

More recently, at the University of New Hampshire, Professor Donald Silva was trying to dramatize the need for focus in writing essays. Unfortunately for him, he used sexual images to make his point: "Focus [in writing] is like sex. You seek a target. You zero in on your subject. You move from side to side. You close in on the subject. You bracket the subject and center on it. Focus connects experience and language. You and the subject become one."[46]

During another lecture he graphically illustrated the way some similes work, saying, "Belly dancing is like Jell-O on a plate, with a vibrator underneath."

The vast majority of his large lecture class found these remarks innocuous. Six female students filed formal harassment charges—claiming his words had demeaned women and created a hostile and intimidating environment. SHARPP—the Sexual Harassment and Rape Prevention Program on the New Hampshire campus—took up their cause. Professor Silva was found guilty of having used "two sexually explicit examples" that "a reasonable female student would find . . . offensive, intimidating, and contributing to a hostile environment." He was ordered to apologize in writing for having created a "hostile and offensive academic environment." He was fined two thousand dollars and formally reprimanded. He is now required to attend counseling sessions by a therapist approved by the university, and to report on his progress in therapy to his program director at the university. Silva has courageously refused to comply—and has been suspended from teaching without pay. The American Association of University Professors wrote a letter warning the university that any sanctions taken against Silva were a threat to academic freedom. At a meeting of more than sixty retired University of New Hampshire professors, they reviewed the case and voted unanimously to condemn the university's actions. But so far SHARPP and the University of New Hampshire have prevailed. Silva's attempt to get his side of the story heard is costing him thousands in legal fees, and it may cost him his career.

One expects faculty to protest encroachments on their traditional freedoms and prerogatives. One would expect them to be outraged at the "witch hunts" (and to express their outrage *before* they retire). But what sense of outrage there is comes, instead, from the gender feminists who, true to their self-image as "victims," urge gender feminists in the universities to be permanently alert for any signs of masculinist attempts to restore the status quo. Schuster and Van Dyne have charts and graphs outlining strategies for preparedness.[47] The Ford-funded National Council for Research on Women is now raising money for what it calls a "rapid response fund." As it explains in a fundraising letter dated December 8, 1993, the fund will enable it to act quickly to combat adverse publicity for such things as "feminist curriculum reforms."

Fears of resistance and backlash motivate preemptive strikes at critics and potential critics. The Modern Language Association Committee on the Status of Women has recently proposed "antifeminist harassment" and "intellectual harassment" as new and official categories of victimization. Examples of intellectual harassment include:

- easy dismissal of feminist writers, journals, and presses
- automatic deprecation of feminist work as "narrow," "partisan," and "lacking in rigor"
- malicious humor directed against feminists[48]

Toni McNaron, professor of English at the University of Minnesota, expresses the confidence of many when she predicts in the *Women's Review of Books* that gender feminist academics will transform the "academic establishment" in the nineties.[49] She makes the customary comparison between recent feminist theory and the scientific breakthrough made by Copernicus. But her exultant mood is laced with gloom. She reminds us that "proponents of Copernican theory were drummed out of their universities or, in extreme cases, excommunicated, jailed, and even killed." Acknowledging that contemporary feminists are not likely to suffer the more extreme retributions, she nevertheless warns of impending attacks. She exhorts feminist academics to "stand and resist wherever possible the onslaughts" of those who find fault with the feminist agenda. Professor McNaron's remarks were brought to my attention because she mentions me as one of the persecutors of the new Copernicans.

By now, feminists have a well-deserved reputation for being good at dishing it out but completely unable to take it. Many are known to deal with opponents by ad hominem or ad feminam counterattacks: accusations of misogyny, racism, homophobia, or opposition to diversity or inclusiveness. Some would-be critics fear for their very jobs. In these circumstances a critic may find himself suddenly alone. Others, watching, learn to keep a low profile. It is now quite clear that a self-protecting American faculty has been seriously derelict in its duty to defend the liberal traditions of the American academy.

Students are quick to learn that open criticism of the feminist classroom will not win them support from teachers who privately agree with them. The lesson they learn from the cravenness of their teachers is never lost on them: keep clear of controversy. Conformity is safest: practice it. That is a terrible lesson to convey to one's students and the antithesis of what the college experience should be.

In the story "The Emperor's New Clothes," the boy at the parade who dared to declare that the emperor had nothing on was immediately joined by his elders, who were grateful that someone had given voice to that innocent and obvious truth. Sadly, the story is not true to life. In real life the boy is more likely to be shunted aside by parading functionaries for failing to perceive the emperor's finery. In real life, the spectators do not take the boy's side. At Minnesota, Northwestern, Michigan, Wooster, New Hampshire, Harvard, and on campuses across the country, the gender feminists are unchallenged because the faculties have so far found it politic to look the other way.

Chapter 6

A Bureaucracy of One's Own

If there is one word that sums up everything that has gone wrong since the war, it's "workshop."
—ATTRIBUTED TO KINGSLEY AMIS

That the gender feminist perspective is comparable to a Copernican revolution is open to question. A revolution has undoubtedly taken place, but it is more a bureaucratic than an intellectual one.

In 1982 Peggy McIntosh, the associate director of the Wellesley College Center for Research on Women, gave a prescient and influential keynote address to an audience of feminist scholars in Geneva, Indiana:

> I think it is not so important for us to get women's bodies in high places, because that doesn't necessarily help at all in social change. But to promote women who carry a new consciousness of how the mountain strongholds of white men need valley values—this will change society. . . . Such persons placed high up in existing power structures can really make a difference.[1]

Ms. McIntosh's beguiling metaphors are matched by her unerring understanding of how to gain control of bureaucracies, a talent that has helped to make her one of the most influential and effective leaders among academic transformationists. The gender feminists that Dr. Mc-

Intosh addressed took her advice to heart. So did many others. Feminist academics have worked hard and successfully to get people "who carry a new consciousness" into administrative positions at every academic level. These now do their best to ensure that new appointments are not out of line. To criticize feminist ideology is now hazardous in the extreme, and even to have a "clean" record is no longer sufficient. Aspirants to university presidencies, deanships, program directorships, and other key posts are aware that they will probably have to show a record of demonstrated sympathy with gender feminist doctrines and policies. The same is rapidly becoming true for faculty appointments.

The Association of American Colleges (AAC), itself one of the "power structures" that have been colonized by women of the right consciousness, disseminates a widely used questionnaire entitled "It's All in What You Ask: Questions for Search Committees to Use." Prospective candidates for faculty or administrative positions are asked such questions as these:

- How have you demonstrated your commitment to women's issues in your current position? [Lead question]
- What is your relationship to the women's center?
- How do you incorporate new scholarship on women into undergraduate coursework? Into your research? Into graduate coursework? With your graduate students? How do you help your colleagues do so?
- How do you deal with backlash and denial?

The type of screening promoted by the AAC proved effective at the University of Maryland in its last presidential search. Speaking at the (self-styled) "historic" forum entitled "Transforming the Knowledge Base," Betty Schmitz, another major figure on the transformation circuit, described how the search committee had questioned all the candidates about their commitment to feminist transformation projects. Ms. Schmitz was pleased to report: "Every single candidate was prepared for the question. Two had funded programs on their own campuses, and the third had actually been involved in a project."[2]

Ms. Schmitz's confidence in the screening procedure was not misplaced. President William Kirwan has come through with more than $500,000 of the university's funds for a curriculum transformation project, without going through the faculty senate to do so.

Curricular matters are traditionally the province of the faculty or one of its representative bodies, such as the faculty senate. Changes in the curriculum normally involve intensive scrutiny and extensive debate followed by a vote. Kirwan's action seems most unusual. Ms. Schmitz, who had become Kirwan's assistant, reported how the president had to face a lot of "backlash" from the faculty and how she helped the president by giving him arguments to cope with the problem. She advised her sister transformationists to expect similar situations: "You will also have to prepare your administrators about what is going to happen. . . . It is wonderful to be able to supply appropriate words to the head of an institution, and it is important that people knowledgeable about the issues and well-versed in the language be in key positions to do so."[3] Faculty resistance does not faze Ms. Schmitz: "Speaking the unspeakable is a component of disrupting the patriarchy. The anger or disbelief that surfaces when faculty are forced to confront bias as a systemic, pervasive problem is the necessary first stage in the change process."[4]

Ms. Schmitz, who is better known as an activist than as a contributor to education theory or epistemology, is a confident apparatchik who goes about applying the insights of feminist theorists like Peggy McIntosh and Elizabeth Minnich to the urgent project of "breaking the disciplines" and transforming the curriculum. In these practical tasks she reports gratifying progress: A "heartening trend is the degree to which state monies and internal funds are being placed into curriculum transformation," she says, boasting of her success in establishing "a new position for a permanent director of the curriculum transformation project" at the University of Maryland.[5]

I dwell on Ms. Schmitz not because she is so unusual (though she is very good at what she does) but precisely because she is representative of the new breed of bureaucratic feminist. Skilled workshoppers, networkers, and fundraisers, they move within the corridors of academic power with ease and effectiveness, occasionally supplying "appropriate words" to those in power as needed to further the goals of the new pedagogy and to counter criticism. Schmitz is a great admirer of Dr. McIntosh, both for her insights into feminist pedagogical theory and for her prescient political analysis of how to get and hold power in the academy and, once attained, how to use it to further an agenda of transformation.

Since Maryland, Ms. Schmitz has moved to the state of Washington, where again she is working to install the apparatus of transformation. Here is more of her astute advice to her sisters in the transformation movement: "We . . . have to build our message into the mission of the institution, and we have to help those in the institution think about the future. . . . We have to see what the organization is aspiring to be and make sure that as the sentences articulating those goals are being formed, we provide language that informs them."[6]

Ms. Schmitz has written a handbook for transformationists. In it she uses Peggy McIntosh's five-phase theory to grade teachers and their classes. Phase one, you will remember, is the lowest stage of curricular consciousness. Phase five cannot be attained in today's culture, but phase four, in which "classes are wondrous and healing," is attainable. Even so, says Ms. Schmitz, "the amount of time it will take a given individual to reach Phase 4 is not predictable."[7] Schmitz refers to the five phases as if they were as scientifically established as the phases of the moon. Her handbook contains pointers on how to deal with "hostile" faculty "with an unwavering belief in traditional standards of excellence." These are the "respected scholars," an "unreachable" group of "Phase 1 thinkers."[8] According to Schmitz:

> These faculty may also be respected scholars in their field and popular teachers. They have no reason to change. If faced with pressure from administrators or project leaders, they will raise issues of academic freedom, the place of ideology in the curriculum, and their right to determine what is to be taught in their classes.[9]

Ms. Schmitz seems cynically aware that, despite their protests over the erosion of academic freedoms, the respected scholars no longer have the power they once had, and she reports that most project directors do not consider it "worth the effort to target this group specifically."[10]

Few on the faculty offer resistance to curricular change, nor do many raise issues of academic freedom. To get them to cooperate actively in their own "reeducation," Ms. Schmitz and her colleagues candidly recommend financial incentives: "How much faculty reeducation is possible without benefit of money for stipends? Our recent experience with regional consortia for curriculum integration suggests that even small amounts of seed money for initiating projects can result in concrete change."[11]

Large amounts of money work even better. At Maryland, for the past several summer vacations, the administration has offered faculty members a percentage of their annual salary to attend seminars on curriculum transformation. In 1991, for example, the classes met twice a week during July and August and faculty received 20 percent of their salary. Assuming an average $40,000 annual salary, this would mean that workshoppers earned about $500 for each class they attended.

Professor Herman Belz, a distinguished political scientist, noted with alarm that curriculum transformation was being implemented at Maryland, although it had never been voted on or endorsed by the faculty. Not having access to the administration's channels of distribution, he published his misgivings in the faculty newspaper:

> Faculty who are concerned to preserve and maintain intellectual integrity and freedom of academic inquiry in the University should examine carefully the recommendations of the [curriculum transformation committee] report. They should be aware of the potential threat to disciplinary autonomy that it contains. And they should take steps to bring the subject of curriculum transformation into the fresh air and open forums of public debate, where through the forms and procedures of critical deliberation we govern ourselves as an academic community.[12]

At the "historic" panel discussion, Ms. Schmitz would refer to protests in the school paper as "hysterical and extreme" backlash.[13] She assured her sister panelists that transformation at Maryland would be unaffected. "But we . . . have to keep educating the leadership."

Ms. Schmitz became known to the Middle Tennessee State University faculty when, under the sponsorship of the Tennessee Board of Regents, she conducted a curriculum transformation workshop in February 1990. In March 1990, the Advisory Committee for Curricular Transformation became prominent. This committee, which had been given no charge by the faculty senate, asserted that its authority to transform the curriculum stemmed from the regents: "This committee was formed in response to a mandate from the Board of Regents based on the findings published in the 1989 statewide report on the Status of Women in Academe."[14]

Pursuing what it took to be its mandate, the Advisory Committee for Curricular Transformation sent a lengthy (eighty-seven-item) questionnaire to the Middle Tennessee State faculty querying them in detail about how they ran their classes and asking questions designed to test their level of feminist consciousness. The advisory committee asked the professors to analyze their assigned readings, their lectures, and their audiovisual material and to reply to questions like "How often were the pronouns 'she' or 'her' used? How often did examples relate only to typical male experience or use only males in examples? How often are women shown in positions of power or action? How often are men shown in familial or domestic roles?" One section asks whether the instructors agree, agree strongly, disagree, or disagree strongly with such statements as "My students learned about how women feel about their lives. My students learned about changing gender roles."

One section entitled "Overall Course Evaluation" could be used to show where the professor ranks on Peggy McIntosh's five-phase scale. The pertinent question is:

Having looked at various components of your course, now look at your course as a whole. How would you classify this course?
1. neither men nor women were included in this course
2. womanless—no mention of women at all [a yes to No. 1 or No. 2 would signal to the interrogator that the respondent is in the first phase]
3. the only women depicted were treated as exceptional women or as anomalies [a second or third phaser]
4. women and men were described both separately and comparatively, stressing inter-relationships [a phase four lateral thinker]

Needless to say, most Tennessee professors were probably unaware that their answers in this section could be indicative of their place on that critical scale.

Actually, the faculty "scored" quite well on the feminist consciousness scale. Feminine pronouns were used just as much or *more* than male pronouns in the readings. Instructors reported they "rarely" used examples that related only to males. Females were more often the main focus of films and videos shown in class and appeared in two-thirds of the textbook illustrations. Professors reported that men and women spoke up in class at the same rate but that men were slightly more likely to be interrupted by other students than were the women. More than half the respondents reached "phase four" on Ms. McIntosh's scale.[15]

Nevertheless, many faculty felt the interrogations were fatuous and irritating, and they began to show some fight. The senate introduced a resolution against any language that "mandates revision, transformation, integration, or restructuring of the curriculum." Though that passed unanimously, the advisory committee ignored it. A new and equally intrusive questionnaire was soon on the way, and the regents and the Middle Tennessee State University administrators were spending more university funds on workshops and other transformation activities.

I called Middle Tennessee State's vice president of academic affairs, James Hindman, the administrator in charge of the transformation project. At first he expressed enthusiasm for it, but when he sensed I did not share his enthusiasm, he became defensive and claimed never to have seen the questionnaire. "It came from some outside organization. I had nothing to do with it," he said. He said he knew very little about the details of the transformation project and advised me to speak to the women's studies staff.

When I asked him about the workshops, conferences, and other trans-formationist activities, he got angry. "Who are you? You have no right to interview me or quote me." He slammed the phone down. I have since sent in a freedom-of-information form asking about the funding for the transformation activities at Middle Tennessee State University, with cop-ies to the attorney general's office and the Tennessee Board of Regents. The citizens of Tennessee have the right to know just how much of their money is being spent to have their college curriculum transformed to the liking of Ms. Stimpson, Ms. Schmitz, Ms. McIntosh, Ms. Schuster, Ms. Van Dyne, and Ms. Minnich.

Vice President Hindman was right about one thing. The questionnaire came from elsewhere: it was in fact designed by the Association of Amer-ican Colleges (AAC), an organization funded by dues from most of Amer-ica's colleges. The AAC used to be a nonpolitical professional organization devoted to monitoring the scholarly standards of American colleges. These days, though, it produces an impressive number of surveys, pack-ets, tracts, and brochures that promote gender feminist causes in the American academy. Among their many feminist publications are "Success and Survival Strategies for Women Faculty Members," "Students at the Center: Feminist Assessment," "Evaluating Courses for Inclusion of New Scholarship on Women," and "The Campus Climate Revisited: Chilly for Women Faculty, Administrators, and Graduate Students."

The Association of American Colleges was founded in 1915 to "im-prove undergraduate liberal education," a task to which it was conven-tionally faithful until fairly recently. As late as 1985, an AAC report defended the college major and spoke of "the joy of mastery, the thrill of moving forward in a formal body of knowledge and gaining some effective control over it, integrating it, perhaps even making some small contribu-tion to it."

Several women's studies luminaries—Johnnella Butler, Sandra Coyner, Marlene Longenecker, and Caryn McTighe Musil—found this remark offensive. In a scathing report to the AAC, made possible by "generous funding" from the cooperative Ford Foundation and the Fund for the

Improvement of Post-Secondary Education (FIPSE), they "deconstructed" the offending passage:

> A feminist analysis of this rhetoric reveals . . . an analogy between knowledge and sexual subjugation . . . , an idea of learning as mastery or control. Clearly embedded . . . are unconscious androcentric assumptions of dominance and subordination between the knower and the known, assumptions that too readily bring to mind the traditional relationship of men to women; of the colonizers to the colonized; indeed, of the masters to the slaves. Such phallocentric metaphors . . . [are not] the accidental usage of one report; they replicate the dominant discourses of Western empiricism that women's studies . . . critiques.[16]

The AAC is not likely to offend again. Even as it was being so sharply rebuked, the AAC was targeted for a gender feminist makeover. These days, it is an important resource for transformationists, and Caryn Mc-Tighe Musil is one of its senior fellows. She and Johnnella Butler, the feminist scholar from Washington University, are playing a principal role in the newly inaugurated $4.5 million AAC transformationist project.[17]

As for Ms. Schmitz, she is now a senior associate for the Cultural Pluralism Project at the Washington Center at Evergreen State College, where, amply funded by the Ford Foundation and the state government, she oversees the transformation project in several universities and colleges in the state. She, too, has recently served as a senior fellow at the AAC.

The AAC is not the only such organization to have caught the transformationist fever. Groups like the American Association of University Women and the prestigious American Council on Education now take it for granted that American education must be radically transformed. Consider, for example, this programmatic statement in a report sponsored by the American Council on Education entitled "The New Agenda of Women for Higher Education":

> What has yet to happen on all of our campuses is the transformation of knowledge and, therefore, of the curriculum demanded by this explosion of new information, and by challenges to conventional ways of thinking and knowing. Women's studies, the new scholarship on women, or transformation of the curriculum projects—the names vary according to campus and culture—should be goals of the faculty and academic administration on every campus.[18]

The transformation of the philosophy major at Mount Holyoke College is an example of change as it may affect an individual scholarly department. In the late eighties Mount Holyoke College was given funds by the Donner Foundation to conduct transformation seminars. Next it acquired a provost of the right consciousness, Peter Berek, who had been at Williams College. In the spring of 1992, this little item appeared in the college newspaper, under the headline "Philosophy Transforms Major":

> In an unusual move, the Philosophy Department has broken away from traditional requirements for philosophy majors and minors. . . . [As a result] students will be able to pursue in depth an area of special interest, including contemporary topics of philosophical thought—such as feminist philosophy, the philosophy of racism, and the philosophy of film.

The article noted the support the administration had given to the transformation of the philosophy major. Here is how the philosophy major was described before the transformation: "The major in philosophy is designed to provide the student with a broad understanding of the historical background of contemporary philosophical thought. . . . It shall consist of at least eight courses, including one each in the history of ancient philosophy, the history of modern philosophy, and logic." Here is the new description: "A major in philosophy should provide the student with a broad understanding of the background of contemporary philosophy. . . . Because philosophy admits of a diversity of sometimes competing conceptions of what philosophy is, the Department encourages each major to articulate her own major program."

The catalog does say that "most students" will be "encouraged to include . . . courses that provide an historical background for her area of special interest." But the old requirements are gone, and philosophy as a traditional major at Mount Holyoke no longer exists. Having broken away from the historic "phase one" demands that required the student to become thoroughly conversant with such "geniuses" as Plato, Descartes, and Kant, the rules now allow a philosophy student to get her degree by taking such courses as "Developments in Feminist Philosophy: Rethinking the World" (which explains how feminists reconstruct their "own . . . version of philosophy"), "Philosophy and Film" (including a special study of films that feature an "unlikely couple"), "Film Comedy" (which includes "feminist approaches to screwball comedy"), and "Feminist Science Fiction as Feminist Theory."[19]

Some colleges have instituted policies to screen out phase one "unreachables" early in the faculty hiring process. Cornell College in Iowa was one of the first to make such policies official. All applicants for teaching positions at Cornell College must show that they are conversant with and sympathetic to the new feminist scholarship. According to a 1988 issue of the *Chronicle of Higher Education,*

> Dennis Damon Moore, dean of the College, says that prospective faculty members are asked at interviews what impact feminist scholarship has had on their work and teaching. In addition, he says, when faculty members are reviewed, they are specifically asked to examine the relationship of the feminist perspective to their work.[20]

Six years later these sorts of developments are no longer "news," and the *Chronicle* does not report on them. The transformationists have come a long way in a very short time. How much farther they will go depends on the university faculties and the independent learned societies, which have so far shown little inclination to make a stand in defense of the traditional standards of liberal learning. Moreover, the transformationists are increasingly seeing to it that the faculties themselves are changing to include more and more people of the "right consciousness." As the number of doctrinally correct personnel grows, they, too, will see to it that only candidates of like qualifications are hired in the future. Ironically, the ongoing self-selection of faculty of the right feminist persuasion is being carried out in the name of "diversity" and "inclusiveness."

There are hundreds of well-funded transformationist projects throughout the country. Peggy McIntosh's Center for Research on Women at Wellesley College has a multimillion-dollar budget. The project at the University of Maryland has half a million to work with. The doyenne of transformationists, Caryn McTighe Musil, and her associates at the Association of American Colleges will have $4.5 million. Almost all transformationist projects are financially helped by being housed in the universities, where rent, postage, and other overhead is minimal. Many use the secretarial staffs and services of their host colleges.

Much of their funding comes from foundation grants, but the bulk of it comes from public funds, via state support for universities. In addition to the many individual projects supported within the universities, there are the umbrella organizations such as the AAC, which are now committed to the educational philosophy and agenda of the transformationists. And there, again, the university bureaucracies are paying.

It is a dismaying fact that only one organization—the National Association of Scholars—has been openly expressing concern at what the transformationists are doing in and to the American academy. The NAS has an office in Princeton, New Jersey, with a staff of six (two part-timers), a budget of $900,000, and a national membership of fewer than three thousand. In contrast to the transformationists, the NAS operates entirely on its own; no university supports it or offers it facilities.

Needless to say, the "politically correct" forces led by the gender feminists are continually blasting the NAS as a backlashing, sexist, racist, right-wing organization populated by "phase one" unreachables. In fact, like most professional educational or academic associations, the NAS has liberal as well as conservative members, including James David Barber, a Duke University political science professor, antiwar leader, and former president of Amnesty International; Richard Lamm, former Democratic governor of Colorado; Seymour Martin Lipset, current president of the American Sociological Association; and Eugene and Elizabeth Fox-Genovese, a Marxist historian and a socialist feminist, respectively. My husband, Fred Sommers, and I—both registered Democrats—are members of the Boston chapter, which has no distinctive political coloration. The common denominator is alarm at the loss of academic freedoms and a strong conviction that traditional academic standards must be protected.

The NAS, a tiny minority in the American academy, has a principled respect for open discussion. This requires it to give hearings to the opposition wherever it can. Steven Balch, its national director, and his staff make it a practice to invite major spokespersons with opposing points of view to NAS meetings and conventions. These gatherings are often the scenes of real debate on the very controversial issues that divide the NAS from its adversaries.

One reason the NAS has remained so small is that anyone who joins the organization faces opprobrium and labeling as a "reactionary." Untenured members place themselves in special jeopardy. Nevertheless, as more and more faculty are becoming fed up with the doctrinaire forces that are steadily reducing the degrees of freedom of both teachers and students on America's campuses, the membership keeps rising.

Professor Jim Hawkins teaches philosophy at Santa Monica City College. What happened at his college induced him to join with several of his colleagues to form an NAS chapter on his campus. During the 1989–90 academic year, a "Curriculum Transformation Task Force" was formed at Santa Monica by the administration without the usual faculty senate participation. The Curriculum Transformation Task Force issued a report whose central thesis seemed to be that the college's traditional curriculum had a "Eurocentric, white male orientation." It "prescribed a wholesale rethinking of 'all the categories on which we have come, consciously or not, to depend,' including our very definitions of courses, paradigms, disciplines, and departments."[21] Professor Hawkins and his colleagues also became aware that the administration was making substantial changes in the hiring processes, again without benefit of faculty input. For example, "a larger administrative contingent began to serve on previously faculty-dominated hiring committees, along with . . . people specifically trained to promote the cause of 'diversity.' " The hiring of new faculty at Santa Monica was soon being carefully monitored by the transformationists to ensure ideological rectitude. It is now a matter of routine at Santa Monica City College that applicants are asked multiple questions on transformationism. Hawkins cites one enthusiastic monitor as saying, "If you *have* to hire a white male, at least be sure his head is in the right place." Professor Hawkins concludes his report on transformationist activities at Santa Monica City College with the advice to "challenge your local transformationists to defend their proposals and premises. For many of them this will be, sadly, an unaccustomed experience."[22]

At many colleges and universities, administrators ask students to evaluate their professors on their sensitivity to gender issues. Some departments at American University, for example, now asks the student whether "the course examined the contributions of both women and men." One political science professor explained to me that at American your salary is directly linked to how well you do on these forms. He once made the mistake of saying "congressmen" instead of "congresspersons" and was rudely rebuked by two female students. He was convinced they would dock him several points for that lapse. The University of Minnesota has established a core of graduate students called "Classroom Climate Advisors" to help students offended by the remarks of professors or fellow students "develop a strategy for dealing with the problem."[23]

But more important changes have occurred at the level of staffing. Candidates for faculty positions are likely to be subject to careful screening to keep out persons of the wrong consciousness. To make this possible, the deciding committees must themselves be of the right consciousness. At the University of Arizona, faculty members who are not "keeping up with current trends" in postmodern and feminist thought may be disqualified from sitting on tenure and promotion committees. This new policy proposed by the (then) dean of the faculty of humanities, Annette Kolodny, would significantly curtail the traditional prerogatives of senior faculty to pass on appointments and promotions.[24] The impulse to doctrinal control by removing dissident opinion from positions of power sometimes takes a less subtle form. Incensed that an NAS chapter was being formed at Duke University, Professor Stanley Fish asked the dean to institute a policy that would exclude NAS members from serving on committees dealing with tenure and promotion decisions. In that case the dean did not comply.

In addition to tightening the bureaucratic screws, the forces of doctrinal rectitude work persistently and effectively to modify perspectives and group behavior. One example: In 1990, Virginia Polytechnic issued to the faculty copies of *Removing Bias,* a sixty-page guide presenting "tactics for attitudinal change." The guide advises professors on how they can avoid offensive humor: professors are encouraged to consult *Free to Be You and Me* by Marlo Thomas for help on how to be funny while "eliminating gender stereotyping."[25]

The tacit cooperation of government personnel is indispensable to the transformationists. I recently phoned the State Board of Education in Washington to inquire about a Transformation Conference being organized by Betty Schmitz for twelve community colleges. All four speakers —who included Johnnella Butler and Betty Schmitz—represented essentially the same point of view. I asked Alberta May, an assistant director for student services on the Washington State Board for Community and Technical Colleges who helps Ms. Schmitz to organize events, why they were not inviting speakers who had different ideas about curriculum reform. After all, I said, the educational philosophy advocated by Ms. Schmitz and her associates is quite controversial. "What do you mean?" asked a genuinely baffled Ms. May. "In what way could it be called controversial?"

Ms. May is a state employee. My question evidently rattled her, and she sent me a follow-up letter that gives some indication of the blind loyalty that transformationists command within some government bureaucracies: "Visionary leaders at a large percentage of institutions of higher education perceive the infusion of cultural pluralism as adding strength to the general educational curricula. . . . The State Board for Community and Technical Colleges . . . values the leadership and expertise of both Dr. Betty Schmitz and Dr. Johnnella Butler in this area."

News of my conversation with Ms. May must have reached Ms. Schmitz, for she wrote to me accusing me of "having attempted to persuade one of my clients to terminate my employment" and warning me that her "attorneys consider [my] conduct unlawful interference with a business relationship." She concluded: "If I learn that you have again attempted to interfere in any of my professional relationships, I shall take all available steps to assure that such conduct does not occur again and to redress any resulting damage."

Ms. Schmitz's readiness to use the masculinist courts to deal with "interference" does not surprise me. Nor is it surprising that her experience has given her the assurance that the government is on her side and that its largesse is rightfully hers.

Despite their overwhelming successes, the transformationists keep warning their supporters about an impending "right-wing backlash." Caryn McTighe Musil attacks the NAS in the 1992 anthology *The Courage to Question: Women's Studies and Student Learning* for purveying "misinformed and dangerous polemics."[26] No examples are given, although a footnote cites a 1988 NAS conference. Ms. Musil's reaction is instructive: criticism of any kind—even in a small scholarly conference four years ago—cannot be abided. It must be denounced, and those responsible must be impugned. Beverly Guy-Sheftall, director of the Women's Research Center at Spelman College, says it more soberly in a recent financial report she wrote for the Ford Foundation:

> We must not allow the current preoccupation with "political correctness" to obscure the reality of a modern-day, well-organized, right-wing movement (inside and outside the academy) whose old and popular racist, sexist, and homophobic schemes threaten to reverse the progressive reforms of the 1960's. . . . This makes it necessary to advocate loudly and clearly for the demise of the androcentric curriculum. . . . The support for Women's Studies should *intensify* during this paradoxical period of assault.[27]

It goes without saying that no one deserves to be called sexist or racist for defending the traditional curriculum. Nor should criticizing the educational philosophy of gender feminists be taken as any kind of sign that the critic belongs to a "right-wing movement." Although many conservatives oppose transformationism, many of the best-known critics who publicly express alarm about its effects on American education would be counted politically as left of center. These include Arthur Schlesinger, Jr., James David Barber, Nat Hentoff, James Atlas, Robert Hughes, C. Vann Woodward, Robert Alter, the late Irving Howe, Eugene Genovese, Alan Dershowitz, Paul Berman, and John Searle.

They are joined by a growing number of progressive women including such distinguished figures as Cynthia Ozick, Cynthia Wolff, Mary Lefkowitz, Iris Murdoch, Doris Lessing, Sylvia Hewlett, Elizabeth Fox-Genovese, Jean Bethke Elshtain, Rita Simon, Susan Haack, and Ruth Barcan Marcus.

The novelist Cynthia Ozick is a classical feminist who believes we are now witnessing the deterioration of feminism in the academy. She told me, "The whole point of feminism was to give women access to the great world. The new feminism on the campuses is regressive."

Mary Lefkowitz, a Wellesley classicist, is a pioneer in the study of women in the ancient world, but she does not read the lives of women of antiquity in terms of any rigid feminist system of interpretation. As a result, Professor Lefkowitz is persona non grata among many feminist historians. As a veteran equity feminist, Lefkowitz fought long and hard against the old boy network that once discriminated against women scholars. She believes it is being replaced by a new network, an old girl network of feminist preferment. "Just like many revolutions," she points out, "it becomes as bad as what it replaced."

I spoke with another distinguished classical scholar, Rebecca Hague, professor of classics at Amherst College. She expressed grave doubts about the value of a "feminist perspective on the ancient world" that focuses on women's absence from the government, taking that as proof that women were silenced and oppressed. "I am not sure that women in the ancient world wanted a role in the government. For them the religious life had far more value, and there women had a central role." Like Lefkowitz, Hague condemns the feminist intolerance to criticism. "I have the feeling that if you question them, you will be targeted."

Iris Murdoch fears that the progress being made in the cause of liberation, which she defines as freedom "to enjoy equal education, equal opportunities, equal rights, and to be treated as men are—as ordinary people on their own merits and not as a special tribe," is being seriously threatened by feminists who lay claim to female ethics, female criticism, and female knowledge.

When one thinks of "role models" for female college students of a liberal, artistic bent, women like Iris Murdoch, Joan Didion, Doris Lessing, Susan Sontag, and Cynthia Ozick come to mind. These women have expressed deep reservations about gynocentric feminism. Joan Didion articulated her abhorrence of the idea of designating "women" as a special class in a 1979 essay.[28] Susan Sontag wrote in a 1975 essay published in the *New York Review of Books* that she deplores feminist "anti-intellectualism" and felt it necessary to "dissociate myself from that wing of feminism that promotes the rancid and dangerous antithesis between mind . . . and emotion."[29]

In a 1991 lecture at the 92nd Street Y in New York City, Doris Lessing criticized the "rampaging kind of feminist" and called the denigration of male writers sheer "nonsense" that will alienate sensible women from feminism. "Hearing this kind of thing, many women think, oh my God, I don't want to have anything to do with this."[30] But such opinions are ignored by the women's studies and transformation movements. "That is what has made you marginal in the universities," Cynthia Ozick was warned by a campus feminist when she expressed the "wrong" views in a *New Yorker* article some years ago.

Perhaps the most conspicuous target of feminist opprobrium is Camille Paglia, who has managed to confound her attackers by striking back publicly and to great effect. After her book *Sexual Personae* not only became an unexpected best-seller but also was hailed by a number of scholarly critics, she could reasonably have expected to be acknowledged as an outstanding woman scholar even by those who take strong exception to her unfashionable views.

But the *Women's Review of Books* branded *Sexual Personae* a work of "crackpot extremism," "an apologia for a new post–Cold War fascism," patriarchy's "counter-assault on feminism."[31] Feminist professors at Connecticut College, attempting to get it removed from a reading list, compared it to *Mein Kampf*. When Paglia appeared at a Brown University forum, outraged faculty feminists signed a petition censuring her and demanding an investigation into procedures for inviting speakers to the campus.

Yale professor Harold Bloom has pointed out that "someone as brilliant, as learned, as talented, and as ferociously burning an intellect as Camille Paglia" belongs in the Ivy League or at someplace like the University of California at Berkeley or the University of Chicago. But the "bureaucrats of resentment who are appointed by others in the network because they are politically correct" will continue to do their utmost to make sure that this does not happen. "They will blackball her everywhere."[32]

Despite Paglia's continued defiance, the lesson is clear: anyone who dares to criticize the "New Feminist scholarship" must be prepared for rough treatment. When the Shakespearean scholar Richard Levin took issue with some feminist interpretations of Shakespeare's tragedies, he was denounced in a rude letter boasting no fewer than twenty-four signatories. Signing in groups is a standard feature of feminist critical response. In the letter, published in *PMLA*, they tell us they are "puzzled and disturbed that Richard Levin has made a successful academic career" in view of his way of interpreting literary texts. They censure the journal for having published Levin's article. If they had their way, Levin would effectively be denied the opportunity to publish his views.[33]

Neither Levin nor Paglia is fazed by such feminist onslaughts, but it would be hard to underestimate the inhibiting effects on others. Intimidation has enforced a stultifying conformity. To criticize the New Feminist scholarship without having tenure is reckless in the extreme: it is now virtually impossible to find public fault with academic feminism without paying for it in drastically diminished prospects for jobs or advancement in the American academy. The pressure to *refrain* from criticism is matched by the pressure to toe the line by zealously promoting feminist doctrine.

The New Feminism has been rapidly colonizing and "transforming" the American university. The influx was not invited, nor was it greeted with much enthusiasm. Yet it has not met with significant resistance. Why not?

Part of the answer is that some academic gender feminists regard the academy as a patriarchal institution whose normal procedures serve to keep European white males in power. Being morally convinced that they are not bound to adhere to rules of "fair play" devised by the oppressor, these gender feminist ideologues have no scruples about bypassing normal channels in gaining their ends.

A more important part of the answer is that a confused and well-meaning academic community has failed to distinguish clearly between equity and gender feminism. A befuddled liberalism has proved to be fertile soil for the growth of an intolerant gender feminism. The cannier feminists were quick to seize their opportunities. "You might wonder," says Paula Goldsmid, a former dean at Oberlin College, "how we managed to generate a women's studies program that has a catalog supplement listing more than twenty courses, that offers an individual major in women's studies, that has been able to involve several committees in really working to transform the academy in various ways." She describes one successful tactic: "There is a great reluctance to say or do anything publicly that goes against the liberal and 'progressive' Oberlin stance. Oberlin's liberal values can be turned to *our* advantage" (her emphasis).[34]

Paula Rothenberg, head of the New Jersey Project, gives much the same explanation for how she and her sister feminists got their own college, William Paterson, to institute a women's studies requirement: "Our surprising success was due to . . . the presence on the curriculum committee of some allies and old-style liberals who found it difficult to disagree with the idea of such a requirement, at least in public."[35]

Those who have their reservations about the costs of the rapid feminist colonization of the academy remain in disarray. Many of the feminists who entered the academy in the seventies and eighties had been activists in the antiwar sixties and seventies. Established academics, who might have been expected to resist some of the ideological baggage these feminists had brought with them, proved to be no match for these dedicated veterans. In the first place, many were inexperienced in dealing with people who *simply ignored* the unspoken understanding that no group on an American campus should promote a political agenda in its classrooms. And male faculty quickly became aware that resistance to feminist proposals would *automatically be condemned* as sexist and reactionary. The charge that the university itself was a male club kept them permanently off balance.

Moreover, part of the legacy of the sixties was that a significant part of the liberal academy had long since shifted away from the classical individualist liberalism of John Locke and John Stuart Mill to "anti-establishment liberalism." They were not averse to the gender feminists' message that the university itself was part of a morally discredited establishment.

Recently, I was discussing the subject of the gender feminist "colonization" of the academy with a prominent scholar and equity feminist. I told her of my view that well-meaning administrators and professors—mostly males—were failing to distinguish between equity feminism and its unscrupulous twin, gender feminism, and what harm their confusion was causing. My friend's theory was less flattering than mine. In her view, the male scholars who have given so much latitude to poorly qualified feminist ideologues knew very well what they were doing. Most academic men, she says, are themselves average scholars and not overly comfortable with competition from capable women. The female scholars whom they have allowed to outflank them strategically are at least intellectually less threatening than "vertical" thinkers like Helen Vendler, Ruth Barcan Marcus, or Elizabeth Fox-Genovese. If my friend is right, the inordinate influence of gender feminism in the academy is due at least in part to old-fashioned sexism. Her theory is mischievous and attractive, and it has elements of truth. For when a man of indifferent talents is conscious of being inferior to a woman, the problem of his own inferiority tends to be compounded by the fact that he is being bested by a woman.

On the whole, however, most women scholars I have spoken to about this do not support my friend's theory. Most competent women academics find that they are treated no worse and no better than their male counterparts. The far less interesting explanation they offer for the failure of men—especially male deans—to stand up to feminist ideologues and their projects is that they wished to avoid unpleasantness.

I once asked a prominent philosopher of science—a politically progressive, fair-minded man—what he thought of a lecture by Sandra Harding critiquing "male science." He told me he found it to be incomprehensible.

"Did you raise any objection in the question-and-answer period?" I inquired.

"No," he said. "I am just hoping it will all go away."

The problem is that "it" is not just going to go away. "It"—the gender feminist establishment—is well entrenched, and its numbers are increasing. It is confident, and it has little respect for scholars like my friend. If anything, it is this Oxford-trained philosopher, a "phase one vertical thinker," who is in danger of becoming irrelevant in the transformed university of the future.

The presence of a frankly ideological and politically powerful core of academics in America's universities has consequences far beyond the academy. Activist organizations like the National Organization of Women, the Ms. Foundation, and the American Association of University Women strive constantly to persuade the wider public that women are urgently in need of the protections they will help to provide. These organizations rely on a pool of academic feminists to faithfully produce books, data, and studies that demonstrate alarming amounts of sexism, discrimination, and gender bias.

Most feminist activists are sincerely committed to their mission, but there are material rewards that should not go unnoticed. In our tight economy, many productive people in depressed industries have lost or are in danger of losing their jobs. There is no comparable threat to the thriving careers of the professional feminists—the workshoppers, facilitators, and transformationists. Large numbers of professionals with job titles like "sex equity expert," "gender bias officer," and "harassment facilitator" are remuneratively engaged in finding, monitoring, and eradicating endless manifestations of gender bias.

That the feminist bureaucracies already command significant patronage and power is due in great part to their ability to influence local legislatures and school boards. More recently, they have shown a capacity to influence policy and law at the federal level. Here again, much of their effectiveness is due to their talents for persuading legislatures of the truth of some alarming "facts" about the plight of women, based on "studies that show . . ." The near-term prospect that they will have at their disposal an ever-larger number of ill-defined but well-paying jobs is bright indeed.

Chapter 7

The Self-Esteem Study

In 1991, newspapers around the country carried alarming reports about the plummeting self-esteem of American teenage girls. "Little girls lose their self-esteem on way to adolescence, study finds," said the *New York Times*.[1] "Girls' confidence erodes over years, study says" (*Chicago Tribune*).[2] "Study points to stark gender differences" (*Boston Globe*).[3]

The study had been commissioned by the American Association of University Women (AAUW), a women's organization founded in 1881, dedicated to promoting excellence in women's education. Like the League of Women Voters, it is one of the more respected women's organizations, with a current membership of about 140,000. Any study bearing its imprimatur is assured of wide and serious attention.

As part of its "Initiative for Educational Equity," the AAUW commissioned the Washington, D.C., polling firm of Greenberg-Lake Associates to measure the self-esteem of girls and boys between the ages of nine and fifteen. Three thousand children were asked about their self-confidence, career goals, and scholarly interests. According to the AAUW, the poll showed that between the ages of eleven and sixteen, girls experience a dramatic drop in self-esteem, which in turn significantly affects their ability to learn and to achieve. The AAUW took a very serious view of its findings, publishing them under the title "Shortchanging Girls, Short-changing America."

Not only did the report make headlines around the country, it led to hundreds of conferences and community action projects. Politicians, educators, and business leaders have been recruited by the AAUW to help America's "shortchanged" girls. Fifty congresspersons responded to the alarm by sponsoring a $360 million bill, the Gender Equity in Education Act, to deal with the problems raised by the AAUW study. When Pat Schroeder introduced the Gender Equity in Education Act before Congress in April 1993, she cited the AAUW report as if it were gospel:

> For too long, the needs of girls have been ignored or overlooked in crafting education policy. . . . Today, we know that little girls as young as 11 years old suffer from low levels of self-esteem. Where 9-year-old girls were once confident that they could conquer the world, girls at age 11 suddenly begin doubting their worth. They no longer like themselves and they begin to question their own abilities. . . . The Gender Equity in Education Act will help make schools an environment where girls are nurtured and respected, where they can learn that their lives are valuable at the same time they learn their ABC's.[4]

Although the self-esteem report is having an enormous impact, a most casual glance at its contents suffices to raise grave doubts about its philosophy, methodology, and conclusions. One glaring example is this major piece of evidence for the difference in boys' and girls' aspirations for success: "Self-esteem is critically related to young people's dreams and successes. The higher self-esteem of young men translates into bigger career dreams. . . . The number of boys who aspire to glamorous occupations (rock star, sports star) is greater than that of young women at every stage of adolescence, creating a kind of 'glamour gap.' "[5]

I did a double take on reading this. A *glamour gap*? Most kids do not have the talent and drive to be rock stars. The sensible ones know it.[6] What these responses suggest, and what many experts on adolescent development will tell you, is that girls mature earlier than boys, who at this age, apparently, suffer from a "reality gap."

We'll soon get to other dubious aspects of the AAUW's report. But first, let's see how the AAUW promoted it. For it was a model of how gender feminist activists tend to use "research" to political advantage.

When it completed the study in 1991, the AAUW held a blitz of press conferences. It distributed thousands of "Call to Action" brochures to its membership, to journalists, and to politicians. It also produced a highly professional documentary dramatizing the results of the study. The documentary was shown around the country at community conferences organized by local AAUW chapters. In the documentary, Anne Bryant, executive director of the AAUW, explains why we cannot afford to ignore the poll findings: "It is tragic to think about all the potential talent we lose. . . . It's frightening not only for our girls, but for our country. When we shortchange girls, we shortchange America."[7] Dr. David Sadker, an education theorist from American University who was interviewed in the documentary, offered a grim estimation of what America was losing by allowing this situation to persist: "If the cure for cancer is in the mind of a girl, there is a chance we will never get it."

The AAUW's findings were no surprise to psychologist Carol Gilligan of the Harvard University Graduate School of Education. Dr. Gilligan, who was featured in the AAUW self-esteem video, speaks of how her own research had helped her to see that girls experience a "loss of voice" that sometimes leads to serious psychological problems such as "depression, eating disorders and various kinds of dislocation." At eight or nine years old, she'd found, girls are forthright and self-confident. But as they enter adolescence they begin to fade, to retreat. They begin to notice that women are undervalued and that the cultural message is "keep quiet." Gilligan and her associates have become convinced that something dreadful happens to girls at age thirteen or fourteen. As Gilligan reported to the *New York Times*, "By 15 or 16 that resistance has gone underground. They start saying, 'I don't know, I don't know, I don't know.' They start not knowing what they had known."[8]

In her foreword to the "Call to Action" brochure, AAUW president Sharon Schuster makes a direct appeal to the reader on behalf of all the "shortchanged girls": "When you read this report, we ask you, most of all, to think of some special girl in your life—a daughter or granddaughter, a sister or student, a niece or a neighbor. Ask yourself, 'What can I do to make sure that our schools aren't shortchanging *her* future?' "[9]

In January 1991 the AAUW organized an "Educational Equity Roundtable" for leaders in government, education, and business to begin to address the problem of girls' precipitous loss of confidence. Participants included Governor Roy Romer of Colorado and Martha Frick, president of the National School Boards Association. Journalists were also invited.

As Sharon Schuster explains, "There was an impressive—and overwhelming—commitment by these leaders to address the needs of girls and young women." [10]

The response from the media was gratifying. The AAUW has its aura of repute and integrity, so it is perhaps understandable that the news reports about its self-esteem study were taken at face value. No one suggested that the AAUW's alarming findings about the plight of the nation's girls might be the product of "advocacy research," research undertaken with an eye to "proving" conclusions that advocates are ideologically committed to and that they find politically useful. Reporters who might normally seek out alternative points of view did not do so in this case.

Despite the sensational and sweeping nature of the findings that girls' self-esteem plummets, as far as I could ascertain, none of the journalists who reported on the study interviewed any social scientists to see whether the poll that reported this was properly designed and its results properly interpreted. Except for Carol Gilligan and her followers, no other experts in adolescent psychology were cited by the press. Indeed, in none of these stories was a single critic cited, despite the existence of a large body of findings and contrary opinions that the AAUW had ignored. Because the media made no effort to look beyond the news releases given them by the AAUW, it was left to skeptics to come forward on their own. As we shall see, some did.

In the meantime, however, the AAUW's rhetoric had taken hold. When the AAUW initiated its study in 1990, self-esteem was the hot topic of the moment. Everyone wanted it; some states had task forces to help people get it. Concern about children's self-image was so high the Children's Museum in Denver installed a "self-esteem corner." Self-esteem was the cure for what ails the country and a ticket to the best-seller list. [11]

Books with titles like *Learning to Love Yourself, The Inner Child Workbook, Co-Dependent's Guide to the Twelve Steps,* and *Children of Trauma: Recovering Your Discarded Self* sold in the millions. A National Council on Self-Esteem was established. [12] The New York State Education Department published a self-esteem manual that identifies four "components" of self-esteem. "I am somebody," "I belong," "I am competent," and "I have possibilities," it proclaims, sounding very much like Stuart Smalley on "Saturday Night Live" ("I'm good enough, I'm smart enough, and doggonit, people *like* me"). [13]

The charge that the self-esteem of the nation's girls was being undermined was made to order for the times. But was it true? That the report was so widely and uncritically credited cannot be taken as a sign of its soundness. The journalists and their readers, the concerned politicians and their constituents, did not know that the AAUW is yet another para-academic organization that has become highly political and ideological in recent years. Its charter is broad enough to include gender feminists, equity feminists, and nonfeminist women. But its present leadership has changed the association into an activist arm of gender feminism. Its current group of officers—executive director Anne Bryant, president Sharon Schuster, and Alice McKee, president of the AAUW educational foundation—are committed gender feminists who had expectations of what they would find when they initiated the self-esteem study. So a cool and objective look at the reported findings and the evidence for them is badly needed.

Here is how the AAUW summarizes the results of the survey in its "Call to Action" brochure:

> In a crucial measure of self-esteem, 60 percent of elementary school girls and 69 percent of elementary school boys say they are "happy the way I am." But, by high school, girls' self-esteem falls 31 points to only 29 percent, while boys' self-esteem falls only 23 points to 46 percent.[14]

> Girls are less likely than boys to say they are "pretty good at a lot of things." Less than a third of girls express this confidence, compared to almost half the boys. A 10-point gender gap in confidence in their abilities increases to 19 points in high school.[15]

The study found boys to be more likely to stick up for themselves in a disagreement with a teacher (28 percent of boys, 15 percent of girls); and boys are more likely than girls to "believe their career dreams will come true."[16]

The AAUW is happy to accommodate anyone who wants to see the "Call to Action" brochure and the "Shortchanging Girls" video: they have an 800 number for those who wish to order these and other gender bias materials they have developed. These readily available materials summarize the "findings." Getting hold of the actual Goldberg-Lake self-esteem study—the hard data on which all the claims are based—turned out to be far more difficult. You cannot order it through the 800 number. It is not available in libraries. The only way to get a look at it is to buy it directly from the AAUW for $85. I was willing to do that, though it is very unusual that a study cited as authoritative by members of the United States Congress would be unavailable in any library. Even buying it turned out to be a problem, though.

"Why do you want it?" asked a curious woman in the AAUW office in Washington. I said, truthfully enough, that I was doing research for a book and would like to review the data. She told me to leave my number and someone would get back to me. No one did. I tried again. This time, there was a tentative understanding that they would send me the study. But first they would send me a letter outlining certain terms. A letter eventually came, signed by Anne Bryant. She wrote: "Please send a statement outlining how you plan to use the survey instrument and results, along with your payment for the full research report. If your review and analysis of the data results in a possible publication or presentation, that use of data must receive advance written approval from AAUW."

I sent the money and a bland "statement" about my plans. I also used the 800 number to order all the high-priced pamphlets, newsletters, and summaries and, of course, the video. When the full report finally arrived, after several weeks and three more phone calls, I saw immediately why AAUW was so cautious. For one thing, it contained nothing like a definition of self-esteem, or even an informal discussion of what they meant by it.

The concept of self-esteem is generally considered to be unstable and controversial, yet few psychologists doubt its central importance. The instability and fluidity of the concept makes it ill-suited for a pollster approach. Polling firms are good at tallying opinions, but self-esteem is a complex personal characteristic, and people's expressed opinions of themselves may have little to do with their sense of inner worth. Yet the AAUW/Greenberg-Lake procedures relied almost exclusively on self-reports.

Self-esteem and a host of related personal characteristics such as self-love, humility, pride, and vanity have been under study since Aristotle. The scientific study of self-esteem by developmental psychologists and sociologists is in its infancy. At the moment, there is little agreement about how to define it and far less agreement on how to measure it.

Oxford University psychiatrist Philip Robson says, "It has even been questioned whether self-esteem exists as an independent entity."[17] What is more, different tests produce different results. According to Dr. Robson, "The same people do not get high scores on all of them." Self-reports on feelings of inner worth are not consistent over time, nor are they easy to interpret. High scores on a self-esteem test, says Dr. Robson, may indicate "conformity, rigidity, or insensitivity."[18]

Jack Block, a research psychologist at the University of California, Berkeley, has also criticized self-esteem questionnaires for failing to determine *why* people like or dislike themselves. Dr. Block points out that someone with high marks on a self-esteem test may 1) be deceiving the researchers; 2) be a self-absorbed egoist; or 3) have a healthy sense of self.[19]

Professor Susan Harter, another expert on adolescent self-esteem, warns of the difficulties in defining and measuring self-esteem:

> Ambiguous definitions of the construct, inadequate measuring instruments, and lack of theory have plagued self-esteem research. There is now a growing consensus . . . that self-esteem is poorly captured by measures that combine evaluations across diverse domains—such as scholastic competence, social acceptance, behavioral conduct, and appearance—into a single summary score.[20]

Setting aside for the moment the very serious problems of definition and measurement, we may ask whether researchers in the area of adolescent psychology are in any kind of agreement that girls do experience a dramatic drop in self-esteem.

Bruce Bower, behavioral science editor at *Science News,* was surprised when he read the AAUW's announcement in the *New York Times.* He calls the AAUW findings controversial, noting that they "have refocused attention on long-standing questions about the meaning of such studies and their implications, if any, for educational reform and . . . psychological development."[21] Bower canvassed the opinion of other researchers, and he found that the AAUW's finding that girls' self-esteem plummets did not square with what most of the experts in adolescent psychology were saying. He summarized the discrepancies between the AAUW findings and what the experts say in the March 23, 1991, issue of *Science News.* After reading Bower's article, I talked with several of the experts he cited.

Barton J. Hirsch, a professor of psychology at Northwestern University, has found comparable levels of self-esteem in adolescent boys and girls. I asked Professor Hirsch what he thought of the AAUW report. "Its findings are inconsistent with the recent literature. For a while there was said to be a small drop in self-esteem of high and middle school girls—now new results show otherwise." He also cautioned, and most experts in self-esteem seem to agree, that no one has been able to establish a clear correlation between self-esteem and behavior.[22] Yet the AAUW authors categorically assert: "Much of the difference between the educational aspirations and career goals of girls and boys can be traced to a gender gap in self-esteem that widens during their school years."[23]

Some researchers such as Susan Harter, Jack Block, Joseph Adelson, and the late Roberta Simmons say that adolescent girls do experience some drop in self-esteem. But their conclusions are nuanced and tentative: nothing like the dramatic, simplistic, and alarming contentions of the AAUW. I asked Susan Harter what she thought of the AAUW study. She said, "It was poorly designed and psychometrically unsound."

Roberta Simmons in her seminal work on adolescent psychology, *Moving into Adolescence,* says that girls experience a temporary drop as they go through junior high school, only to rebound once they establish a circle of friends. In high school there is a second drop. She says, "We don't know if that last self-esteem drop . . . was temporary or permanent."[24]

Wendy Wood at Texas A&M University did a statistical comparison of ninety-three independent studies on women's feelings of well-being. Bruce Bower has summarized Wood's research: "In examining these studies, which focused on well-being and life satisfaction among adult men and women, Wood and her colleagues found that women reported both greater happiness *and* more dissatisfaction and depression than men."[25]

I spoke with Dr. Wood. She claims that what may look like a self-esteem gender gap may be merely due to a gap in expressiveness. Wood and her colleagues believe that girls and women are more aware of their feelings and more articulate in expressing them, and so they are more candid about their negative emotions in self-reports than males are. "If you do not control for this difference, it is very easy to get a very distorted picture."

Naomi Gerstel, a sociologist at the University of Massachusetts, faults self-esteem surveys—including the AAUW study—for neglecting to interview high school dropouts. More males drop out than females. The fact that these boys do not get included in these studies may be creating a false picture of boys' self-esteem.[26]

The Berkeley psychologist Diana Baumrind is skeptical about the reliability of self-reporting altogether. She and her colleagues first measure children's overall achievements and competence. They then rely on trained observers to evaluate children's social and emotional well-being. Using objective measures as much as possible, they have found no significant lasting differences between boys and girls in areas of self-esteem.[27]

Anne Petersen, a University of Minnesota adolescent psychologist, recently summarized the opinion shared by most clinicians and researchers working in adolescent psychology:

It is now known that the majority of adolescents of both genders successfully negotiate this developmental period without any major psychological or emotional disorder, develop a positive sense of personal identity, and manage to forge adaptive peer relationships at the same time they maintain close relationships with their families.[28]

Roberta Simmons had said very much the same thing: "Most kids come through the years from 10 to 20 without major problems and with an increasing sense of self-esteem."[29]

If Petersen and Simmons are right, the AAUW's contentions are an expensive false alarm. In any case, the AAUW is less than candid when it speaks of its efforts to review the growing body of research on how girls learn. It is doing no such thing.

William Damon, the Director for the Center for Study of Human Development at Brown University, took some time to look into the claim that teenage girls were suffering a loss of self-esteem. "So far I have been unable to find a single article in any refereed journal that actually tests this thesis." He concedes that he did not spend months searching the literature. But, he says, if there is such an article, it's not easy to find. As he sees it, the debate over girls' self-esteem has never taken place among researchers. Rather, "the whole thing is being carried on in the court of the media."

I asked Joseph Adelson, a University of Michigan psychologist and editor of the *Handbook on Adolescent Psychology*, what he thought of the AAUW Report on self-esteem. "When I saw the report I thought, 'This is awful. I could prove it is awful, but it's not worth my time.'"

Given the hazards facing any investigator doing research in the area of self-esteem, and given that few adolescent psychologists corroborate the AAUW findings, the burden of proof is on the AAUW to show that its study was well designed and its findings carefully interpreted. But this is precisely what it has not shown. That may explain why the actual data for the Greenberg-Lake survey on which the AAUW based its sensational conclusions are so hard to come by. In fact, showing that the AAUW results are wrong is not as time-consuming as Adelson imagined it to be. A careful look at the self-reports quickly reveals the artful ways that the questions were asked and the answers tabulated to get the alarming conclusions of a national crisis in the self-esteem of adolescent girls.

The AAUW/Greenberg-Lake's self-esteem survey asked three thousand children to respond to statements such as "I'm happy the way I am," "I like most things about myself," "I am good at a lot of things," "My teacher is proud of me," and "I'm an important person." In its "Call to Action" brochure, the AAUW says the responses to such questions offer a "crucial measure" of self-esteem. Let us grant that this may be so and consider more closely the reported findings on the happiness query:

> The nationwide survey commissioned by AAUW found that 60 percent of elementary school girls and 69 percent of elementary school boys say they're "happy the way I am"—a key indicator of self-esteem. By high school, girls' self-esteem falls 31 percent to 29 percent, while boys' self-esteem falls only 23 percent to 46 percent —an increase from 7 to 17 points in the gender gap on this measure of self-esteem.[30]

One can see why any fair-minded person would be thoroughly alarmed by such a result. However, even if we accept that self-reports are reliable indicators of self-esteem, the claims stated in the brochure are seriously misleading. We are only told about how many boys and girls responded "*always* true" to "happy the way I am." We are not told that this was only one of *five* possible responses, including "sort of true," "sometimes true/sometimes false," "sort of false," or "always false" and that most responses were in the middle ranges. Few child psychologists would consider any but *the last two responses*—or perhaps *only the very last one*—as a sign of dangerously low self-esteem. The data presented to the public by the AAUW in all its literature and in its documentary suggest that the majority of girls are abnormally lacking in self-esteem. But this is deceptive because, in addition to the 29 percent of girls who checked "always true," 34 percent checked "sort of true" and another 25 percent "sometimes true/sometimes false"—a total of 88 percent, compared to 92 percent of boys. The AAUW claimed a seventeen-point gender gap in adolescent self-esteem.

The media, of course, followed the line laid down by the AAUW, which carefully and exclusively based its "happy the way I am" report on the "always true" respondents, ignoring all other respondents. Relying on this, *NEA Today,* the newspaper of the National Education Association, said, "By the time girls are in high school, only 29 percent say they are happy with themselves."[31]

An article in the *Chicago Tribune* was typical of the response in the popular press: "While 60 percent of elementary school girls and 69 percent of boys proclaim themselves 'happy the way I am,' by high school only 29 percent of girls and 46 percent of boys express such feelings."[32]

These deceptive figures made their way into Gloria Steinem's *Revolution from Within.* In fact, she mistakenly reversed the figures for nine-year-old boys and girls, making the girls' drop in self-esteem appear even more drastic:

> Even though girls get good grades, learn how to read sooner and have an edge over boys in verbal skills, the question we really need to ask is: "*What are these girls learning* [her emphasis]? According to a study commissioned by the American Association of University Women and released in 1991, a large part of the lesson is to undervalue oneself. As nine-year-olds, for instance, 67 [sic] percent of girls and 60 percent of boys said they were "happy with the way I am." By the time students were in high school, however, only 46 percent of boys said they felt that way—also a tragedy that needs every attention—and the girls had plummeted to 29 percent.[33]

The Women's Research and Education Institute in Washington, D.C., publishes an influential status report on American women called *The American Woman*.[34] "No book on the status of women is more important for government officials, members of Congress, and policy makers than *The American Woman*," says Governor Ann Richards.[35] "This book should be on the desk of every person and policy-maker interested in the status of women today," says Senator Barbara Mikulski. Here is how *The American Woman* reports on the AAUW findings: "Surveying youngsters ages 9 to 15 in 12 locations across the country, [AAUW] researchers found that by the time they are in high school, only 29 percent of girls say they are happy with themselves, compared to 46 percent of boys."[36] Apparently, neither Steinem, the journalists, nor the staff at the Women's Research and Education Institute looked at the data being used by the AAUW.[37] They must have relied instead on the AAUW's brochure.

Here is how the AAUW itself would soon be referring to its own findings:

> A nationwide survey commissioned by the American Association of University Women (AAUW) in 1990 found that on average 69 percent of elementary school boys and 60 percent of elementary school girls reported that they were "happy the way I am"; among high school students the percentages were 46 percent for boys and only 29 percent for girls.[38]

The brochure publicized another misleading conclusion: "Girls are less likely than boys to feel [they are] 'good at a lot of things.' Less than a third of girls express this confidence, compared to almost half the boys."

A 10-point gender gap in confidence in their abilities increases to 19 points in high school."[39] But again the reader is not informed that almost half of the high school girls (44 percent) chose the second possible response, "sort of true," which would have given a total of 67 percent girls and 79 percent boys who essentially feel they are "good at a lot of things." If the "sometimes true/sometimes false" response is included, the results for girls and boys are 95 percent and 98 percent, respectively, an altogether negligible difference.[40] The usual sequence of responses in such surveys, by the way, is "always true," "usually true," "sometimes true," "rarely true," and "never true." Can it be that the researchers suspected such answers might not yield useful results?[41]

Why, for that matter, should someone who answers "sometimes true/sometimes false" to "I'm good at a lot of things" be counted as lacking in self-confidence? In fact, aren't the "always true" answers suspect? The 42 percent of boys who say "always true" to "good at a lot of things" may be showing a lack of maturity or reflectiveness, or a want of humility. Similarly, a boy who thinks of himself as "always" "happy the way I am" may be suffering from a "maturity gap." Conversely, it is not necessarily a mark of insecurity or low self-esteem to admit to feeling blue or not prodigiously proficient some of the time.

The AAUW/Greenberg-Lake analysts may have been unaware that their "survey instrument" was seriously inadequate, and that their pollsters might have been measuring something different from self-esteem or self-confidence (e.g., maturity). Had the AAUW been less concerned to show that girls are being "shortchanged," it would have supplemented its poll by consulting with other experts to arrive at more responsible conclusions.

The AAUW study did find areas where boys and girls show nearly the same levels of self-confidence, but they do not emphasize these findings in the brochure, summary report, or documentary. On the "teacher is proud of me" statement, girls scored higher than boys (41 percent said "always true" or "sort of true," compared to 36 percent of boys). From an unhighlighted section called "classroom experience" we also learn that 80 percent of high school girls and 71 percent of the boys say the teachers think girls are smarter!

These results are available to anyone who cares to send in the $85 and sign the "Statement of Intent" form. Had the journalists who helped advertise the AAUW's message been less credulous—had they taken the time to review how the questionnaire was designed and the results interpreted—they would have seen that the study on which it was based was a lot of smoke and mirrors.

When gender feminists like Sharon Schuster, Anne Bryant, and Gloria Steinem discuss self-esteem, they assume as a matter of course that women are treated in ways that diminish their self-confidence, thereby keeping them subordinate to men. It remains only to persuade the public that this undermining of women is constantly taking place and that the nation's girls are suffering. The AAUW's "crucial measure of self-esteem" (self-reporting "always true" for "I am happy the way I am") is offered as evidence to confirm that high school girls are being undermined. But if we accept this as a "crucial measure," we find it yields a curious result. For it turns out that African-American girls scored *much higher* on self-esteem in the AAUW study than even white boys.

To the "happy the way I am" statement, 58 percent of the African-American high school girls say "always true"; 36 percent of white high school boys say "always true." For white high school girls, the figure is 22 percent. The white boys are fourteen points ahead of the white girls— a "gap" the AAUW finds shocking and unacceptable. But on their test, the African-American girls lead the white boys by twenty-two points, and the white girls by thirty-six points!

Clearly this finding does not square with the other basic assumption that the AAUW made: it claims there is a direct positive correlation between self-esteem and academic achievement. In many categories, African-American girls are at greater risk (for low grades and dropping out) than white girls or boys.

African-American boys are never mentioned in the brochures and the videos. But, if you look carefully enough in the full five-hundred-page data report from Greenberg-Lake, you find them. You also see why the AAUW researchers must have been discomfited by the data on these children. The Greenberg-Lake data report informs us that African-American boys score *highest* of all on the indices of self-esteem, "lead[ing] black girls by margins of 10 to 18 percent on measures of general happiness."[42] If their data are correct, about three of every four African-American boys are "always" "happy the way I am," versus one in five white girls. As for the "glamour gap," the African-American boys turn out to be the most confident and ambitious of all. Far more of them plan to become doctors, scientists, governors, or senators than their white counterparts. Sixty-seven percent said yes when asked, "Do you *really* think you will ever end up being a sports star?"[43]

These results must have startled the designers of the survey. They claim that self-esteem, as they measured it by the self-reports, is directly and positively correlated with future achievement. *Isn't future achievement what all the fuss is about?* So how is it that those who score highest on the

AAUW's self-esteem measure are educationally at risk, while *the group with the lowest confidence does so well?* White girls are getting the better grades and going to college in far greater numbers than any other group.[44]

In the report itself, the authors scramble to make sense of these inconvenient responses. African-American students, they speculate, "have a greater tendency to provide [pollsters] the 'right' answers to survey questions on self-esteem. They have learned that others depict their culture as self-hating or self-deprecating and strive to put a 'best foot forward.' "[45] But putting one's best foot forward is not known to be a racial trait.

The AAUW explains that they did not report their findings on the African-American boys because the sample was too small to be statistically reliable. But surely it was not too small to have alerted them that something might have been seriously amiss in their methodology. Given the fact that the AAUW researchers had found unusually high levels of self-esteem in a statistically significant sample of African-American girls, they had to consider the strong possibility that the high scores of the black boys were not a fluke. They were now bound to investigate the hypothesis, so devastating to their entire project, that "self-esteem" as they were measuring it was not correlated with academic achievement.

One researcher did try to explain why African-American girls have higher self-esteem scores than white girls and boys. Dr. Janie Ward speculates that the self-esteem of African-American girls is unaffected by their academic performance. "Black girls seem to be maintaining high levels of self-esteem by disassociating themselves from school," she says.[46] But why would only African-American girls be so little affected? How do we know that the white boys' high scores are not due to *their* relative indifference to academic worth?

If one takes the AAUW's way of measuring self-esteem seriously, then one should now begin to take seriously the suggestion that there is an *inverse* relation between self-esteem reports and success in school, for *that* is what the study actually suggests. Of course, that is exactly the opposite of what the AAUW claims. Yet, it is not altogether out of the question: Asian children test very much higher than American students in math and science, yet American students express far more confidence in their math and science abilities than do their Asian counterparts. In other words, our children rank near the bottom, but they're "happy the way they are."

This brings us to perhaps the most serious failing of the AAUW "call to action." The report begins by telling us that our children cannot thrive in the next century unless "they become the best educated people on on Earth." But the education reform movement has missed the point, it continues, because "most of this debate has ignored more than half the people whose futures are shaped by the schools: girls."[47] After that, we hear no more about the learning gap between American and foreign children, but the implication is clear: the learning gap will be bridged when we bridge the gender gap. Although that assumption sounds superficially plausible, such facts as we have point to its unlikelihood.

Professor Harold Stevenson of the University of Michigan is one of several researchers who has been studying the differences between American and Asian students in both skills and self-esteem. His influential article in *Education Digest* (December 1992), "Children Deserve Better than Phony Self-Esteem," reported on scholarly research done over many years. It did not rely on polls, and it had no preconceived notions on what the outcome would be. The AAUW researchers do not cite his work, nor was he invited to their roundtable. He has found that though there is a serious learning gap between American and foreign children, the American children are unaware of their shortcomings:

Our University of Michigan research group spent the last decade studying the academic performance of American students, and one of our most consistent findings is that the academic achievement of our students is inferior to that of students in many other societies. . . . The low scores of the American students are distressing, but of equal concern is the discrepancy between their low levels of performance and the positive evaluations they gave of their ability in math.[48]

In math, at least, it appears that the vaunted correlation between self-esteem and achievement does not hold. Instead of a bill called "Gender Equity in Education," we need a bill called "Common Sense in Education," which would oversee the way the government spends money on phony education issues. The measure would not need a very big budget, but it could save millions by cutting out unneeded projects like the ones proposed for raising self-esteem and force us instead to address directly the very real problems we must solve if we are to give our students the academic competence they need and to which they are entitled.

Meantime, the feminist alarms over the self-esteem of female adolescents keep sounding. The AAUW ignored the views of many reputable experts on adolescent psychology, but it had its own scholar and philosopher in Carol Gilligan. Gilligan has written voluminously on adolescent girls and their self-esteem. The AAUW's "Call to Action" brochure invoked her authority in promoting its findings. She is in the video. According to the *New York Times,* she was also "an advisor on the development of questions asked in the survey."[49]

In her influential book *In a Different Voice,* Gilligan claims that women have special ways of dealing with moral dilemmas; she maintains that, being more caring, less competitive, less abstract, and more sensitive than men in making moral decisions, women speak "in a different voice." She argues that their culture of nurturing and caring and their habits of peaceful accommodation could be the salvation of a world governed by hypercompetitive males and their habits of abstract moral reasoning. She has since argued that our society silences, denigrates, and squelches women's voices and that this often causes serious pathologies. Her recent work has placed her at the center of the self-esteem movement.

Gilligan's standing is generally higher among gender feminist intellectuals than among scholars at large. As her general popularity has skyrocketed, her reputation as a researcher has been attacked. Professionally, Gilligan is a social psychologist concentrating on moral development. But, for want of empirical evidence, she has failed to convince many of her peers of the validity of her theories. Wendy Wood, the specialist in women's psychology at Texas A&M, voices a considered judgment shared by many professionals in the field of women's psychology: "Independent research in moral psychology has not confirmed [Gilligan's] findings."

On the contrary, independent research tends to *disconfirm* Gilligan's thesis that there is a substantive difference in the moral psychology of men and women. Lawrence Walker of the University of British Columbia has reviewed 108 studies on gender difference in solving moral dilemmas. He concludes, "Sex differences in moral reasoning in late adolescence and youth are rare."[50] William Damon (Brown University) and Anne Colby (Radcliffe College) point out that though males are viewed as more analytical and independent, and women more empathetic and tactful, there is little evidence to support these stereotypes: "There is very little support in the psychological literature for the notion that girls are more aware of others' feelings or are more altruistic than boys. Sex differences in empathy are inconsistently found and are generally very small when they are reported."[51]

In *The Mismeasure of Woman,* the psychologist Carol Tavris reviews the literature on sex differences and moral development. Her assessment echoes Walker's, Wood's, Damon's, and Colby's. Tavris says, "In study after study, researchers report no average differences in the kind of moral reasoning that men and women apply."[52] Tavris rejects the "woman is better" school of feminism for lack of convincing evidence that women are more "planet-saving . . . pacifistic, empathic or earth-loving."[53]

Even other feminist research psychologists have taken to criticizing Gilligan's findings. Faye Crosby, a psychologist at Smith College, questions Gilligan's methodological approach:

> Gilligan referred throughout her book to the information obtained in her studies, but did not present any tabulations. Indeed she never quantified anything. The reader never learns anything about 136 of the 144 people from [one of her three studies], as only 8 are quoted in the book. One probably does not have to be a trained researcher to worry about this tactic.[54]

Martha Mednick, a Howard University psychologist, refers to a "spate of articles" that have challenged the validity of Gilligan's data. But she acknowledges, "The belief in a 'different voice' persists; it appears to be a symbol for a cluster of widely held social beliefs that argue for women's difference, for reasons that are quite independent of scientific merit."[55]

Gilligan herself seems untouched by the criticism and shows little sign of tempering her theories or her methods of research and reporting. Her recent work on the "silenced voice" continues to use the same anecdotal method that Crosby and others have criticized. As Gilligan sees them, young girls are spontaneous, forthright, and truthful, only to be betrayed in adolescence by an acculturation, an acquired "patina of niceness and piety" that diminishes their spirit, inducing in them a kind of "self-silencing."[56]

Christopher Lasch, one of Gilligan's sharper critics, argues that Gilligan's idealized view of female children as noble, spontaneous, and naturally virtuous beings who are progressively spoiled by a corrupting socialization has its roots in Jean-Jacques Rousseau's theory of education. Rousseau, however, sentimentalized boys as well as girls. Lasch insists that both Rousseau and Gilligan are wrong. In particular, real girls do not change from a Rousseauian ideal of natural virtue to something more muted, pious, conformist, and "nice." On the contrary, when researchers look at junior high school girls without preconceptions they are often struck by a glaring absence of niceness and piety, including the privileged private schools Gilligan studied. Of Gilligan and her associates, Lasch says:

> They would have done better to remind themselves, on the strength of their own evidence, that women are just as likely as men to

misuse power, to relish cruelty, and to indulge the taste for cruelty in enforcing conformity. Study of a girls' school would seem to provide the ideal corrective to sentimental views of women's natural gift for nurture and compassion.[57]

Whatever Gilligan's shortcomings as an empirical psychologist may be, they seem not to matter. Her most recent book on the "silenced voice," *Meeting at the Crossroads,* received an adulatory review from Carolyn Heilbrun. Heilbrun concedes that Gilligan's research has been challenged but insists that her contribution remains a "landmark in psychology."[58]

Indeed, Gilligan remains a feminist icon who "valorized" women by arguing for their special gifts and describing their special fragilities. It was only natural that the AAUW would turn to her and like feminists for "expert" support. Gilligan herself is not an author of the AAUW report. It is not easy to determine who the authors are, but in one document we find a note thanking Nancy Goldberger and Janie Victoria Ward, "who gave us hundreds of hours of expertise and guidance in developing the questionnaire and interpreting the poll data."[59] Gilligan was Ward's teacher and dissertation advisor at the Harvard School of Education. Dr. Goldberger, a psychologist at the Fielding Institute in Santa Barbara, is a coauthor of *Women's Way of Knowing,* the bible of gynocentric epistemology. Ward and Goldberger were probably "sympathetic." Had the AAUW consulted some of the well-known experts in the field cited in Bruce Bower's article in *Science News,* it is not at all certain that the AAUW would have had the clear finding of gender bias it presented to the public.

The Ms. Foundation declared April 28, 1993, "Take Our Daughters to Work Day." The event was a great success; more than 500,000 girls went to work with their mothers or fathers, and the Ms. Foundation expects to make it an annual event. It has created a special "Take Our Daughters to Work" teacher's guide, which addresses the question "Why such extra effort on behalf of girls?" The teacher's guide recites the AAUW/Gilligan formula: "Recent studies point to adolescence as a time of crisis and loss for girls. While most girls are outspoken and self-confident at the age of nine, levels of self-esteem plummet ... by the time they reach high school."[60]

The Ms. Foundation had originally planned to confine "Take Our Daughters to Work Day" to the New York City area. But then Gloria Steinem mentioned the event in an interview in *Parade* magazine in which she spoke of girls' dramatic loss of self-esteem. According to Judy Mann of the *Washington Post,* the event "took off like Mother's Day."[61] What was Steinem's galvanizing comment? "At age 11, girls are sure of what they know. . . . But at 12 or 13, when they take on the feminine role, they become uncertain. They begin to say, 'I don't know.' Their true selves go underground."[62] Steinem added that this makes girls vulnerable to depression, teenage pregnancy, and even eating disorders. From the day her comments appeared in *Parade,* the Ms. Foundation says it was inundated with calls—more than five hundred per day. The event quickly developed into a national happening. The foundation prepared information kits, a teacher's guide, leaflets, fliers, and pamphlets, even a "minimagazine" and T-shirts. The advisory committee established to help organize the day included some of the New Feminism's brightest stars: Marlo Thomas, Gloria Steinem, Carol Gilligan, Naomi Wolf, and Callie Khouri (the scriptwriter of *Thelma and Louise*).[63]

The theme of the event was that for one day, at least, girls would be "visible, valued, and heard." As for the boys left behind at school, the Ms. Foundation suggested they spend the day doing exercises to help them understand how our society shortchanges women.[64] The teacher's guide suggests that boys ponder the question "In the classroom, who speaks more, boys or girls?" Using "guided imagery," the teacher is supposed to ask them to imagine themselves living inside a box:

Describe the box to them: its size, airholes and light (if any). Ask them to reach out and touch the roof and the sides with their hands. Now make the box even smaller. While their eyes are still closed ask them: "What if you want to get out of the box and you can't? . . . What do people say to girls to keep them in a box? What happens to girls who step outside of the box?"

The object is to get boys "to experience the limitations defined by gender."[65]

So the girls are off for a fun day with their parents, being "visible, valued, and heard," and the boys are left behind to learn their lesson. I am not opposed to the idea of taking a child to work (though I think it should be done in the summer, to avoid missing a school day). I am sure many parents and daughters had a good experience. But if having children join parents for a day at work is a good idea, then boys must not be excluded. Of course, boys must learn to be thoughtful and respectful of girls, but they are not culprits; they are not silencing girls or lowering their self-esteem, and no one should be sending the boys the message that they are doing any of these things. A day that singles out the girls inevitably conveys that kind of message.

The gender feminist self-esteem alarm should not be allowed to become thematic in our public schools. The Ms. Foundation is now making an all-out effort to make April 28 an annual girls' holiday. That should not be allowed. Parents and school officials must step in to insist that a day with parents must be gender-neutral and nondivisive; it must include the sons as well as the daughters.

Chapter 8

The Wellesley Report:
A Gender at Risk

&

The American Association of University Women had every reason to be gratified and exhilarated by the public success of the self-esteem report. It had "proved" that American girls "do not believe in themselves." The association moved quickly to commission a second study. This new study would show *how* schoolgirls are being undermined and point to remedies. Its advent was announced by Sharon Schuster: "The survey and the roundtable are just the first steps in AAUW's effort to stimulate a national discussion on how our schools—and our entire society—can encourage girls to believe in themselves. . . . We have awarded a grant to the Wellesley College Center for Research on Women to review the growing body of research on how girls learn."[1]

The Wellesley Report was completed in 1992, a year after the self-esteem report was released. Not surprisingly, it appeared to dramatically reinforce the tragic tidings of the earlier report. The AAUW had called the self-esteem study "Shortchanging Girls, Shortchanging America"; they called the Wellesley Report "How Schools Shortchange Girls."

The AAUW distributed the findings in attractive little booklets and pamphlets, providing all interested parties, especially journalists, with convenient summaries and highlights that could serve as the basis for their stories. Writing the foreword for the new report, Alice McKee, president of the AAUW Educational Foundation, repeated and reinforced the theme of the AAUW's first study: "The wealth of statistical evidence must convince even the most skeptical that gender bias in our schools is shortchanging girls—and compromising our country. . . . The evidence is in, and the picture is clear: shortchanging girls—the women of tomorrow—shortchanges America."[2]

The Wellesley revelations turned out to be even more newsworthy than the Greenberg-Lake poll on self-esteem, generating more than fourteen hundred stories by journalists and newscasters. The San Francisco Chronicle reported the "Dreadful Waste of Female Talent."[3] "Powerful Impact of Bias Against Girls," cried the Los Angeles Times.[4] Time magazine informed its readers that "the latest research finds that the gender gap goes well beyond boys' persistent edge in math and science."[5] The Boston Globe emphasized the distress of girls: "From the very first days in school American girls face a drum-fire of gender bias, ranging from sexual harassment to discrimination in the curriculum to lack of attention from teachers, according to a survey released today in Washington."[6] The New York Times weighed in with "Bias Against Girls Is Found Rife in Schools, with Lasting Damage."[7]

The AAUW was quick to seize on the largesse provided by a cooperative and trusting press. Most of the press stories cited above were reprinted in brochures showing how "AAUW is making headlines." The whole of Time magazine's adulatory article became part of the AAUW's promotional packet.

Once again, the release of a sensational AAUW study was the occasion for a gathering of notables who would be influential in the association's "call for action." In April 1992, the Council on Foundations, an umbrella organization of leaders of the most powerful philanthropic organizations in America, met at the Fountainbleau Hilton Resort in Miami. One of the most popular events, entitled "How Schools Shortchange Girls," included a wine and cheese party and a talk by Susan Bailey, principal author of the AAUW-Wellesley report. Guests received handsomely produced information kits presenting the AAUW findings and hailing their significance. The day before Susan Faludi had delivered a keynote address on "the undeclared war against American women."

The next step was already in the works. The $360 million "Gender

Equity in Education" bill was introduced in Congress in April of 1993 by the bipartisan Congressional Caucus for Women's Issues.[8] Among the bill's sponsors were Patricia Schroeder, Olympia Snowe, Susan Molinari, Patsy Mink, Connie Morella, Nita Lowey, Dale Kildee, Lynn Woolsey, Cardiss Collins, Jolene Unsoeld, and Louise Slaughter. The Gender Equity in Education Act (H.R. 1793) would establish a permanent and well-funded gender equity bureaucracy. It calls for an Office of Women's Equity within the Department of Education, charged with "promoting and coordinating women's equity policies, programs, activities and initiatives in all federal education programs and offices."

Politically, a bill calling for gender equity would seem to have clear sailing apart from any merits it might or might not have. On the one hand, it offered some members of Congress a welcome opportunity to show they were sensitive to women's issues. On the other hand, the dangers of challenging the AAUW or the Wellesley College Center for Research on Women were obvious.

Congresswoman Patricia Schroeder cited the Wellesley Report in introducing the bill. For her, the report was an unquestioned source of truth: our nation's girls are being systematically undermined, and Congress must act. In September of 1993, Senators Edward Kennedy, Tom Harkin, Carol Moseley-Braun, Paul Simon, and Barbara Mikulski introduced a Senate version of the Gender Equity in Education Act. Referring to the Wellesley Report, Senator Kennedy said: [It] "refutes the common assumption that boys and girls are treated equally in our educational system. Clearly they are not."[9]

Walteen Grady Truely, President and CEO, Women and Foundations/ Corporate Philanthropy, which had sponsored Susan Bailey and Susan Faludi in Miami, appeared before the congressional subcommittee to argue for the Gender Equity in Education Act. She pointed out that "girls' self-esteem plummets between pre-adolescence and the 10th grade."[10] Like Pat Schroeder, Senator Kennedy, and others, Ms. Truely appears to have relied in part on the AAUW brochures.

Everyone expects the bill to pass. The National Council for Research on Women reported the AAUW's success as an inspiring example of how women's research can lead directly to congressional action:

Last year a report by the American Association of University Women (AAUW) documented serious inequities in education for girls and women. As a result of that work, an omnibus package of legislation, the Gender Equity in Education Act (H.R. 1793), was recently introduced in the House of Representatives. . . . The introduction of H.R.

1793 is a milestone for demonstrating valuable linkages between feminist research and policy in investigating gender discrimination in education.[11]

That the linkages are of value to those doing the research is unquestionable. What is highly questionable is the value and integrity of the research and the way the advocates have deployed the "findings" to activate the United States Congress.

Are girls really being insidiously damaged by our school systems? That question actually remains to be investigated. Everyone knows we need to improve our schools, but are the girls worse off than the boys? If one does insist on focusing on who is worse off, then it doesn't take long to see that, educationally speaking, boys are the weaker gender. Consider that today 55 percent of college students are female. In 1971, women received 43 percent of the bachelor's degrees, 40 percent of the master's degrees, and 14 percent of the doctorates. By 1989 the figures grew to 52 percent for B.A.'s, 52 percent for M.A.'s, and 36 percent for doctoral degrees. Women are still behind men in earning doctorates, but according to the U.S. Department of Education, the number of doctorates awarded to women has increased by 185 percent since 1971.[12]

The Wellesley study gives a lot of attention to how girls are behind in math and science, though the math and science test differentials are small compared to large differentials favoring girls in reading and writing. On the National Assessment of Education Progress Tests (NAEP), administered to seventeen-year-olds in 1990, males outperformed females by three points in math and eleven points in science. The girls outperformed boys by thirteen points in reading and twenty-four points in writing.[13]

Girls outnumber boys in all extracurricular activities except sports and hobby clubs. Almost twice as many girls as boys participate in student government, band and orchestra, and drama or service clubs. More girls work on the school newspapers and yearbooks. More are members of honor and service societies.[14] Boys far outnumber girls in sports, but that gap is narrowing each year. In 1972, only 4 percent of girls were in high school athletic programs. By 1987 the figure was up to 26 percent, more than a sixfold increase.[15]

On the purely academic front, progress continues apace. The UCLA Higher Education Research Institute's annual survey of college freshmen shows more women (66 percent) than men (63 percent) planning to pursue advanced degrees.[16] The UCLA data show a tripling in the percentage of women aiming for higher degrees in less than twenty-five years. As the institute's director, Alexander Astin, notes, "To close such a wide gap in the relatively short span of two decades is truly remarkable." David Merkowitz of the American Council on Education agrees: "If you want a long-term indicator of major social change, this is one." But indicators that girls are doing well are not the stuff of the Wellesley Report.

The report illegitimately bolsters its "shortchanged girls" thesis by omitting all comparisons of boys and girls in areas where boys are clearly in trouble. In a study of self-reports by high school seniors, the U.S. Department of Education found that more boys than girls cut classes, fail to do homework assignments, had disciplinary problems, had been suspended, and had been in trouble with the police.[17] Studying transcripts of 1982 high school graduates, the Department of Education found girls outperforming boys in *all* subjects, from math to English to science.[18] It also learned that in all racial and ethnic groups, "females were generally more likely than males to report their parents wanted them to attend college."[19]

The Wellesley researchers looked at girls' better grades in math and science classes and concluded that the standardized tests must be biased. Girls get better grades, but boys are doing better on the tests. But their conclusion would have had more credibility had they also considered the possibility that there could be a grading bias against boys.

According to the 1992 *Digest of Educational Statistics*, more boys drop out. Between 1980 and 1982, 19 percent of males and 15 percent of females between the tenth and twelfth grade dropped out of school. Boys are more likely to be robbed, threatened, and attacked in and out of school. Just about every pathology—including alcoholism and drug abuse—hits boys harder.[20] According to the Wellesley Report, "adolescent girls are four to five times more likely than boys to attempt suicide."[21] It mentions parenthetically that more boys actually die. It does not say that *five* times as many boys as girls actually succeed in killing themselves. For boys fifteen to twenty-four the figure is 21.9 per 100,000; for girls it is 4.2 per 100,000. The adult suicide rate is not very different. In the United States in 1990, 24,724 men and 6,182 women committed suicide.[22] What would the Wellesley investigators and other advocates have made of these statistics were the numbers reversed?

The tribulations of schoolboys are not an urgent concern of the leadership of the AAUW; its interest is in studies that uncover bias against girls and women. For details on how American girls are suffering from inequitable treatment in the nation's classrooms, the Wellesley investigators relied heavily on the expertise of Myra and David Sadker of the

American University School of Education, who had already found just the kind of thing the AAUW was concerned about: "In a study conducted by Myra and David Sadker, boys in elementary and middle school called out answers eight times more often than girls. When boys called out, teachers listened. But when girls called out, they were told to 'raise your hand if you want to speak.'"[23] The telling difference in "call-outs" has become a favorite with those who seek to show how girls are being cheated. Pat Schroeder faithfully echoed the claim in introducing the Gender Equity in Education Act: "Teachers are more likely to call on boys and to give them constructive feedback. When boys call out answers, teachers tend to listen to their comments. But girls who call out their answers are reprimanded and told to raise their hands."[24]

The Sadkers have been observing teachers in the classroom for more than two decades, gathering their data on gender bias. Convinced that "America's schools cheat girls," as the subtitle of their new book, *Failing at Fairness,* claims, they have devised strategies for ridding teachers (a majority of whom happen to be women) of their unconscious gender bias that the Sadkers feel is at the root of the problem. The Sadkers' latest book describes their work as the "backbone" of the Wellesley Report, and they are among the report's chief authors. Certainly their work provided key support for the report's claim that "whether one looks at preschool classrooms or university lecture halls, at female teachers or male teachers, research spanning the past twenty years consistently reveals that males receive more teacher attention than do females."[25]

Teachers tend not to be surprised to hear that boys in their classes may be getting more attention—boys tend to be rowdier in the classrooms and to require more supervision. But is that a sign or form of discrimination? Despite their decades of attention to the problem, the Sadkers supply us with no plausible evidence that girls are losing out because teachers are less attentive to them. Instead, they argue that it stands to reason: "The most valuable resource in a classroom is the teacher's attention. If the teacher is giving more of that valuable resource to one group, it should come as no surprise that group shows greater educational gains."[26]

As we have seen, however, the evidence suggests that it is boys who are suffering an overall academic deficit. Boys do perform slightly better on standardized math tests, but even that gap is small, and closing. In the 1991 International Assessment of Educational Progress (IAEP), the Educational Testing Service found that on a scale of 100, thirteen-year-old American girls average 1 point below boys. And this slight gap is altogether negligible in comparison with the gap that separates American students from their foreign counterparts. Taiwanese and Korean girls are more than 16 points ahead of American boys on this same test.[27]

In addition to measuring abilities, the Educational Testing Service asked students around the world whether or not they thought math was "for boys and girls equally." In most countries, including the United States, almost all students agreed it was. The exceptions were Korea, Taiwan, and Jordan. In Korea, 27 percent said that math was more for boys; for Taiwan and Jordan, the figure was 15 percent. "Interestingly," the report notes, "the three countries that were more likely to view mathematics as gender linked . . . did not exhibit significant differences in performance by gender."[28] And girls in two of those countries—Korea and Taiwan—outperformed American boys.

From the IAEP at least, it appears that gender-linked attitudes about math are not strongly correlated to performance. The Educational Testing Service did find one key variable positively related with achievement throughout the world: the amount of time students spent on their math homework—irrespective of gender.

Despite this, the Wellesley Report sticks to its guns. Tackling the gender problem is the first priority in making America educationally strong for the global economy of the future.

In any case, gender inequity in the form of teacher inattention to girls is what the Sadkers' research is all about, and many of the Wellesley conclusions stand or fall with their expertise and probity. The Sadkers, who collected data from more than one hundred fourth-, sixth-, and eighth-grade classes, reportedly found that boys did not merely get more reprimands but received more feedback of all kinds: "Classrooms were characterized by a more general environment of inequity: there were the 'haves' and the 'have nots' of teacher attention. . . . Male students received significantly more remediation, criticism, and praise than female students."[29]

How much is that? I wondered. And how well, if at all, is the disparity in attention correlated with a disparity in student achievement? I was curious to read the Sadkers' research papers. The Wellesley Report leads readers to the *Phi Delta Kappan* for technical details on the Sadkers' findings. But the *Phi Delta Kappan* is not a research journal, and the Sadkers' publications in it are very short—less than four pages each, including illustrations and cartoons—and merely restate the Sadkers' claims without giving details concerning the research that backs them up.

In two exhaustive searches in the education data base (ERIC), I was unable to find any peer-reviewed, scholarly articles by the Sadkers in which their data and their claims on classroom interactions are laid out. The Sadkers themselves make no reference to such articles in the Wellesley Report, nor in their 1991 review of the literature on gender bias in the *Review of Research in Education,* nor in *Failing at Fairness.* The Wellesley Report does refer readers to the final reports on the Sadkers' unpublished studies on classroom inequities. The Sadkers did two of these, in 1984 and 1985, both supported by government grants. The first is called *Year Three: Final Report, Promoting Effectiveness in Classroom Instruction* (funded by the National Institute of Education, 1984); the other is called *Final Report: Faculty Development for Effectiveness and Equity in College Teaching* (sponsored by the Fund for the Improvement of Post-Secondary Education—FIPSE—1985). Since the conclusions of the Wellesley Report rely on studies like these, I was determined to get hold of them. But I found it even harder to get my hands on them than on the AAUW's research on self-esteem.

The 1985 FIPSE study seems to have vanished altogether. After exhaustive library and computer searches, I called the Department of Education, which informed me it no longer had a copy. The librarian at the Widener Library at Harvard University did a computer search as thorough and high-tech as any I have ever seen. Finally, she requested it from the Library of Congress. "If they do not have it, no one does," she said—and they did not.

In the meantime, one of my undergraduate assistants called David Sadker himself to ask how to find it. He told her that *he* did not have a copy and urged her to have a look at the article in the *Phi Delta Kappan.* We had come full circle.

I did find the other study: *Year Three: Final Report, Promoting Effectiveness in Classroom Instruction.* It was available in the Education Library at Harvard University on microfilm, for twenty-five cents per page. Holding the 189 pages photocopied from the microfilm, I wondered if I might be the only person in the world—besides the Sadkers and some of their graduate students—to have looked at its contents. Yet it contains the data behind the contention, now on the tip of many politicians' tongues, that girls are suffering an attention gap that seriously compromises their education.

What had the Sadkers found? They and their assistants visited hundreds of elementary classrooms and observed the teachers' interactions with students. They identified four types of teacher comments: praise ("Good answer"), acceptance ("Okay"), remediation ("Give it another try; think a littler harder this time"), and criticism ("Wrong"). They determined that fewer than 5 percent of teachers' interactions constituted criticism. Praise accounted for about 11 percent of interaction; 33 percent was remediation. The remainder (approximately 51–56 percent) was bland acceptance.[30] Although boys and girls got close to the same amount of bland acceptance ("Okay"), boys got a larger share of the other categories. The exact number is difficult to determine from the data. In their many published articles, the Sadkers generally do not specify the actual size of the difference, but instead make claims about discrepancies without specifying them: "Girls received less than their share in all categories."[31]

In the kind of observations the Sadkers and their researchers made, the chances of observer bias in selecting the data are extraordinarily high. It is all too easy to "find" just what one believes is there. As I have noted, the Wellesley Report relies strongly on research by the Sadkers that purportedly found boys calling out eight times more often than girls, with boys being respectfully attended to, while the relatively few girls who called out were told to "please raise your hands if you want to speak." Professor Jere Brophy of Michigan State, who is perhaps the most prominent scholar working in the area of classroom interaction, is suspicious of the Sadkers' findings on call-outs. "It is too extreme," he says. "It all depends on the neighborhood, the level of the class, and the teacher. Many teachers simply do not allow call-outs." I asked him about the Sadkers' claim that boys get more careful and thoughtful teacher comments. According to Brophy, any differences that are showing up are negligibly slight. Did he see a link between the ways teachers interact with boys and girls and their overall achievement? "No, and that is why I have never tried to make that much of the sex difference findings."

For details of the Sadkers' findings, the Wellesley Report refers to research reported in a 1981 volume of a journal called *The Pointer*.[32] *The Pointer* is now defunct, but when I finally got to read the article I was surprised to see that what it said about classroom discipline in particular was not, in my view, at all indicative of bias against girls. This portion of the *Pointer* article focuses not on "call-outs," but on how teachers reprimand boys and girls differently, emphasizing that boys are disciplined more than girls. Here is what the Sadkers and their coauthor, Dawn Thomas, found:

Boys, particularly low-achieving boys, receive eight to ten times as many reprimands as do their female classmates. . . . When both girls and boys are misbehaving equally, boys still receive more frequent discipline. Research shows that when teachers are faced with disruptive behavior from both boys and girls, they are over three times as likely to reprimand the boys than the girls. Also, boys are more likely to get reprimanded in a harsh and public manner and to receive heavy penalties; girls are more likely to get reprimanded in a softer, private manner and to receive lighter penalties.[33]

The article says nothing at all about "call-outs," and nothing about girls being told to raise their hands if they want to speak. Yet it is cited as the source for the Report's oft-repeated claims about this matter. Thinking that I must be in error, I looked at a 1991 article in the *Review of Research in Education* by the Sadkers themselves, in which they, too, cite the research reported in the *Pointer* article:

D. Sadker, Sadker, and Thomas (1981) reported that boys were eight times more likely than girls to call out in elementary- and middle-school classrooms. When boys called out, the teacher's most frequent response was to accept the call-out and continue with the class. When girls called out, a much rarer phenomenon, the teacher's most typical response was to remediate or correct the inappropriate behavior with comments such as "in this class, we raise our hands."[34]

But the Sadkers are misquoting themselves; *The Pointer* contains no such findings. Support for the Sadkers' claim about "call-outs" may well exist. But putting aside both the Wellesley Report and the Sadkers' apparent error in citing the *Pointer* article for support, one can note that the claim about "call-outs" keeps the drums of outrage beating and gives fuel to the notion that American girls "spend years learning the lessons of silence in elementary, secondary, and college classrooms," after which they find it difficult or impossible to "regain their voices."[35]

Suppose, indeed, that teachers do call on boys more often. There is no clear evidence that girls lose because of that. Girls are getting the better grades, they like school better, they drop out less, and more of them go to college. If teacher attention were crudely to be correlated with student achievement, we would be led to the perverse conclusion that more attention causes poorer performance.

In any case, I could find no study showing a direct relation between teacher and student interaction and student output. Looking back at the Sadkers' *Year Three: Final Report,* I notice that they, too, acknowledge that "at this point it is not possible to draw direct cause and effect links between teacher behavior and student outcomes."[36]

The Wellesley Report cites other studies supposedly corroborative of the claim that teachers' inattention inequitably shortchanges America's schoolgirls. But again, the sources cited do not make the case. For example, a government study entitled *Final Report: A Study of Sex Equity in Classroom Education* by Marlaine Lockheed, an education specialist in the Education and Social Policy Department at the World Bank, does say that boys get more teacher reaction; however, in summing up her findings, Lockheed *denies* that this is to be interpreted in terms of gender inequity: "Data from the study do not support the notion that classroom teachers play a major role in creating and maintaining inequities. Despite findings that boys are more disruptive (and thus receive more teacher attention), data suggest that teachers respond to the nature of the student behavior rather than to student gender."[37]

Another study cited in the report warns that "at this point, all comments on the potential effects of various patterns of teacher-child behavior on social and cognitive development are highly speculative."[38] The report also includes a reference to a 1989 survey by M. Gail Jones.[39] The article does not itself contain any original data, but rather gives a brief summary of twenty articles on bias in classroom interaction. From Jones's survey, the studies—some better designed than others—appear to be inconclusive. Many researchers find more teacher interaction with the rowdier boys—but none have shown that it harms the girls. A 1987 study by K. Tobin and P. Garnett had found that a few "target" students in the science classroom tended to dominate classroom interactions, and these targets tended to be males.[40] But a further study of target students by Jones herself found that "although there were more male than female target students, the female target students averaged more interactions per class session than male target students."[41] That kind of result is typical of the status of research in this area. It makes one wonder whether the study of student-teacher interaction, using gender as a key category and "unconscious bias" as a possible parameter, is worth all the trouble.

Oddly enough, the authors of the Wellesley Report do mention, almost as an aside, that "new evidence indicates that it is too soon to state a definitive connection between a specific teacher behavior and a particular student outcome."[42] The report does not say what this new evidence is and never mentions it again. Nor are we told why the existence of such evidence does not vitiate the report's sensational conclusion that gender bias favoring boys is rife and its correction a matter of national urgency. To put it mildly, the literature on the subject of classroom bias seems confusing and not a little confused.

•   •   •

The advocacy research on classroom bias would not matter much were it not for the lack of skepticism on the part of legislators who now see gender equity in the classroom as a critical national issue. The testimony of Anne Bryant, the executive director of the AAUW, before Congress in April 1993 in favor of the Gender Equity in Education Act is typical of what it has heard:

> Myra and David Sadker of the American University and other re-
> searchers have extensively documented gender bias in teacher-
> student interactions. . . . Teachers tend to give girls less attention,
> with some studies showing teachers directing 80 percent of all their
> questions to boys.[43]

In her presentation, Ms. Bryant indicated that the AAUW had worked with the Congressional Caucus on Women's Issues to develop the bill and vowed that "we will continue to work with you as the omnibus educational equity package moves through Congress."[44]

It was a close relationship. The wording of the bill echoed that of the AAUW brochure:

> Research reveals that, at all classroom levels, girls receive different
> treatment from teachers than do boys. . . . To address this problem,
> this legislation would create programs to provide teacher training in
> identifying and eliminating inequitable practices in the classroom.[45]

Members of Congress have competent and intelligent staffs who are accustomed to checking up on all kinds of claims made by special interest groups. One hopes they will look into the data behind the AAUW and Wellesley brochures before voting millions of dollars for the Gender Equity Act and reaping us the bitter fruits of the AAUW's irresponsible and divisive initiative.

Because of the key role the Sadkers were playing in the AAUW and Wellesley initiatives, I was curious to find out more about them. The opportunity came when I was invited to participate in a discussion of gender bias in the schools on the PBS radio show "Talk of the Nation."[46] The producer explained that there would be four of us: the Sadkers, Sharon Steindam, a school administrator from Arlington, Virginia, and me. I knew nothing about Ms. Steindam, but the PBS producer told me she had some familiarity with the Sadkers' gender bias workshops and was prepared to discuss the difficulties of applying their recommendations in the classroom. For my part, I was grateful to have the opinion of an experienced educator.

Once on the air, the Sadkers held forth on their ideas. I raised questions about their research methods and conclusions. After a while, the mediator, Ira Glass, introduced Dr. Steindam as someone who was prepared to talk about "some of the *problems* of being attuned to gender bias in the classroom" (his emphasis).

But Dr. Steindam had no problem to report. She had only the highest praise for the Sadkers' program and she told us how "aghast" teachers were to discover how sexist they had been. Ira Glass clearly had not expected this response. He said: "Now were there *problems* implementing it (his emphasis)?" Again she raved on about how enlightening the workshops had been. She was pleased that the state of Virginia had given a "$5,000 or $10,000 grant to fund the Sadkers' workshop" and assured us the money was "absolutely minimal."

After the program aired, my phone rang: it was a colleague of the Sadkers from American University. He told me that Ms. Steindam was not the objective outsider she appeared to be on the PBS show. She had been a student of the Sadkers and had written her doctoral thesis with them. She had even coauthored an article with them called "Gender Equity and Educational Reform."[47]

I could not believe that PBS knew about this relationship without telling me before the show, so I called Ira Glass. He knew that Ms. Steindam was acquainted with the Sadkers' training methods but had no idea she was their colleague and coauthor.

The professor from American University was skeptical of the Sadkers' data-gathering techniques in general. "They, or their graduate students, sit in classrooms and tally up how many times teachers praise, criticize, etc., boys versus girls. The possibilities for subjective interpretation are endless."

He also told me about his encounter with one of the Sadkers' students, who was doing research for her own thesis:

A doctoral student of theirs used one of my classes in her research. At the end of her first visit, she said, "You are screwing up my data." When I showed surprise, she said, "Yes, you're one of the control classes and you're supposed to show bias but you don't." She came to that class two more times, and each time she discovered more bias. In fact, the last time she observed, the numbers looked so lopsided and not at all reflective of the way the class went, I asked my graduate assistant to take a sample poll of students to see how their recollections jibed with the numbers she wrote down. In every case, the male students recalled being called on far fewer times, and the female students several more times than her numbers indicated. I am distrustful of such research.

Something else happened during the PBS show that increased my own doubt about such research methods. Halfway into the program, a woman named Lisa called in. She identified herself as a feminist and proceeded to admonish Ira Glass, the very polite and respectful PBS moderator, for interrupting Myra and me "seven times" and David Sadker, the lone male, "not at all." Glass was clearly shaken by this attack. David Sadker was happy to have this neat confirmation of his thesis. "Lisa is right," he said, and proceeded to give a brief lecture on how many more times women are interrupted than men.

I went back to the PBS tape with a stopwatch. Up to the point Lisa called, David Sadker had spoken for a total of two minutes, and Ms. Sadker and I had spoken for six minutes each. True, we were interrupted more—but we had talked three times as much! Glass interrupted Mr. Sadker approximately once every fifty-two seconds. He interrupted Ms. Sadker and me once every ninety-three seconds. In effect, Mr. Glass had interrupted his male guest nearly twice as often as he had interrupted his female guests. Furthermore, whereas an interrupted Mr. Sadker lapsed into silence, Ms. Sadker and I both insisted on finishing what we were saying.

On April 7, 1992, NBC News' "Dateline" with Jane Pauley and Stone Phillips had Myra and David Sadker on as guests. Ms. Pauley began:

> The [Wellesley] report cites data compiled over the last decade by a husband-and-wife research team. Drs. David and Myra Sadker of American University are the nation's leading experts on gender bias. We hired them as consultants to observe Miss Lowe [a teacher] and analyze our videotape for evidence of bias against girls.[48]

A "Dateline" crew had filmed Ms. Lowe's elementary school class for several hours. A few minutes of this were shown. In one scene children were working quietly at their desks, and Ms. Lowe was moving from one boy to the next making brief, thoughtful comments. She then went on to a girl but said nothing of consequence to her. In a voice-over, Ms. Pauley excitedly pointed out, "Remember, she knows our cameras are there, and she knows we are looking for gender bias." Pauley was visibly stunned by what she regarded as Ms. Lowe's sexist behavior: "So boys are getting the message that what they have to say is important, and girls begin to conclude just the opposite, with serious consequences."

I called Ms. Lowe. She agrees with the *goals* of the Sadkers' research and believes teachers may exhibit unconscious bias. She herself took part in a teachers' presentation in support of the Gender Equity in Education Act. Nevertheless, she felt that the "Dateline" program was a sham. "That class was boy-heavy," she said. "Of course I called on more boys. A good documentary should tell you the proportion of boys to girls in the class. There were four or five more boys than girls." Moreover, she pointed out, the "Dateline" crew had filmed her for eight to ten hours, but only a few minutes were shown. Of course it was possible to find in all that footage some small sequence that appeared to show bias. "By that method," Ms. Lowe observed derisively, "they could document most anything." (The segment, by the way, aired just after NBC had weathered the embarrassment of airing a "documentary" on the dangers of GM trucks whose gas tanks were located on the side. It turned out that an NBC crew had fitted a truck with an explosive and then graphically "showed" how impact caused the fuel tank to explode without explaining how the footage had been rigged.)

Ms. Lowe told me that her fifth-graders were incensed by what "Dateline" had made of the long hours of filming. The kids knew there were more boys than girls in the class. Why wasn't that made clear, they wondered. Their general feeling was that "Dateline" was stretching to drive home a message. I asked Ms. Lowe how the "Dateline" staff and Ms. Pauley had happened to choose her school to film. Ms. Lowe informed me that the contact was made through Dr. Sharon Steindam, one of her school administrators who had worked with the Sadkers.

"Dateline" did interview one skeptic. Ms. Pauley asked Diane Ravitch, then assistant secretary of education under Lamar Alexander, what she thought of the Wellesley Report. Ms. Ravitch told Pauley all about the overwhelming data that show *boys* to be in serious trouble. She spoke about dropout rates, the grading gap that favors girls, the far greater number of boys with learning disabilities. According to Ravitch, Pauley showed no interest in the boys' plight but kept after her to concede that girls were suffering from gender bias. When it became clear that Ravitch was not going to capitulate, Pauley asked her, "Well, what if people *believe* there is bias?" Ms. Ravitch, by then nettled, retorted, "If people believe this is a serious problem, they should send their daughters to single-sex schools." All that aired of her comments was that isolated exasperated remark.[49]

No fewer than fifty members of Congress sent a letter to Lamar Alexander, professing themselves outraged by Ravitch's comment, and they cited the AAUW/Wellesley report "How Schools Shortchange Girls" to contradict her. They demanded that the secretary take serious steps with regard to Ms. Ravitch. The letter also put the secretary on notice: if he opposed the Gender Equity in Education Act, there would be fireworks.

Stone Phillips may well have been right when he said on a recent "Dateline" update on the Gender Equity in Education Act, "With women playing a bigger role than ever in Washington . . . this may be one bill immune from congressional gridlock."[50] But the women who are playing a bigger role are not necessarily members of Congress; they are more likely to be the determined women of organizations like the AAUW and the Wellesley College Center for Research on Women.

Jane Pauley was clearly moved by the Wellesley Report. Her husband, Garry Trudeau, was too; he used his "Doonesbury" column to popularize its findings. It is understandable that Ms. Pauley and Mr. Trudeau should assume that the Wellesley scholars and the AAUW had been fair and competent in their research. To Pauley and Trudeau, as to most other intelligent and informed Americans, Wellesley and the AAUW are synonymous with professional integrity and scholarly authority.

On the other hand, the American public relies on Ms. Pauley's reputation as an investigative reporter to be accurate—even on issues that passionately concern her. Ironically, the title of her gender bias documentary was "Failing at Fairness."

I have had yet another brush with the Sadkers. On the afternoon of Monday, January 10, 1994, I received a call from a producer of the Oprah Winfrey show. The Sadkers would be appearing on the show on Thursday morning to discuss their findings on how girls are being shortchanged in the nation's schools. I was invited to join them on the show to provide a contrasting point of view. Despite the short notice, I was delighted. It is so rare that the gender-bias experts are confronted with any kind of criticism. I accepted and we planned that I would leave for Chicago Wednesday morning to avoid transportation problems from a predicted storm. But on late Tuesday afternoon, the producer called to tell me that there had been an extraordinary development. The Sadkers were refusing to appear with me. The producer was apologetic, but he was in a bind. The show would go on without my criticism—which is just what the Sadkers wanted. I told the producer that this was a pattern with gender-bias advocates; they meet only in like-minded groups and speak only in uncontested venues. They do not feel obligated to deal with objections to their views and doctrines. What is extraordinary is that, so far, they have been able to get their way.

The Sadkers are just two of several authors of the Wellesley Report. Peggy McIntosh is another. She is listed as a "core team member" who helped to do the research and to write the report and who "discussed, reviewed, and debated every aspect of the project for its entire twelve-month life."[51] In addition to the charge that schools undermine girls' self-esteem by "silencing" them in our nation's classrooms, the report claims that girls "do not see themselves" reflected in the curriculum. That is Ms. McIntosh's pet charge.

Blandly accepting Ms. McIntosh's quirky distinction between (feminine) "lateral" and (masculine) "vertical" thinking, the report urges that girls' special ways of thinking and knowing be recognized and emphasized in the nation's elementary schools. Likewise, the report refers to McIntosh's five interactive phases of curricular development as if these were recognized scientific findings:

Phases I, II, and III have a vertical axis of "either/or thinking" that views winning and losing as the only alternatives. An important conceptual and emotional shift occurs in Phase IV. . . . In Phase IV we see, for the first time, the cyclical nature of daily life, the making and mending of the social fabric. . . . Phase IV features lateral and plural thinking, sees "vertical" thinking as simply one version of thinking, and encourages all students to "make textbooks of their lives."[52]

The report does not explain the meaning of "vertical" and "lateral" thinking or what it might mean to "make textbooks of [one's life]," but it repeats as gospel McIntosh's assessment of the traditional curriculum as insidious: "Many school subjects, as presently taught, fall within the general descriptions of Phases I and II. In the upper grades especially, the curriculum narrows and definitions of knowing take on gender-specific and culture-specific qualities associated with Anglo-European male values."[53] Such passages provide insight into what the gender feminists mean by gender inequity—a definition far from what most people understand it to mean. As an example of a phase one Anglo-European male activity, the report cites civics classes that focus on controversy. It suggests that girls would be more comfortable in classes that are more personal and less contentious—that address what the report calls "the daily texture of life."

To get at the philosophy underlying the Wellesley Report, it is instructive to return to McIntosh's fall 1990 workshop for grade school teachers in Brookline, Massachusetts, when she condemned "young white males" as a group, calling them "dangerous to themselves and to the rest of us." [54] To give her audience an idea of the harm inflicted by the vertical approach, she told of a young girl who had trouble adding a column of numbers: $1 + 3 + 5$. The problem, as McIntosh saw it, was that the worksheet required her to think vertically, thereby undermining her self-esteem and causing her to become discouraged. She urged the Brookline teachers to find ways to "put . . . [students] off the right-wrong axis, the win-lose axis."

What that might mean for learning sums, McIntosh never explicitly said. One exasperated parent who saw the video, Robert Costrell, a professor of economics at the University of Massachusetts at Amherst wrote a piece in the local newspaper critical of Ms. McIntosh's educational philosophy:

> Since the child could not add $1 + 3 + 5$, we need to know if she could add $1 + 3$. If not, then she would only be further demoralized by more three-term exercises, no matter how non-hierarchical. If she *can* add $1 + 3$, then the child is ready for a breakthrough, since she could then add $4 + 5$ and finish the problem. The child would not only have found the answer, but would have the basis for later study of the associative law in algebra, not to mention the self-esteem that goes along with it. But of course, this is "vertical thinking." [55]

Professor Costrell here touches on a fundamental inconsistency within the Wellesley Report. On the one hand, it tells us that girls are left behind in math, science, and engineering and that we must take steps to help them catch up. Though the report exaggerates the significance of the disparity between the math skills of boys and those of girls, we may all acknowledge the need to address any deficiency girls may have in math and science. But the report goes on to denigrate vertical approaches to subjects like math and science, despite the fact that they depend on exact thinking and calculation. It's not that the authors of the report could not make up their minds; in fact, they seem to have little use for exact thinking and real science. But the reporters and politicians needed some evidence that girls are being shortchanged. The discrepancy in science and math, though small, was useful for that purpose. So the report cites the boys' advantage in these areas, ignoring for the moment its own prejudice against those subjects.

Debating clubs, which take for granted an "adversarial, win/lose orientation," are cited in the report as another example of a male approach to knowledge. Yet most analytical disciplines, from philosophy to history to law, require skill in argument. As an equity feminist who wants girls to excel, I see debating clubs as an important tool for teaching students to be articulate, cogent, persuasive, and forceful. True, adversarial competitiveness is a part of every debate, and so favoring skill in debate may be made to seem like favoring aggression. So what? Adversarial rhetoric is a tradition of the greatest schools, from the dialectical practices of the Greek academies and the ancient yeshivas of Babylonia to the great debating clubs of Oxford and Cambridge. What would our modern system of democratic parliaments be without debates? More than ever women are called upon to use debating skills in their professions and in politics. To talk about "kill or be killed" practices and to suggest that women are "above" that sort of thing is to relegate them to ineffectiveness.

McIntosh's theories are depressingly reminiscent of the canard that women are innately irrational and too delicate for the rough-and-tumble world we associate with effective intellectual exchange and clear thinking. How far, after all, is McIntosh from the eighteenth-century German philosopher Johann Gottlieb Fichte, who had his own views about male and female "ways of knowing." "Man reduces all that is in and for him to clear conceptions, and discovers it only through reasoning. . . . Woman, on the other hand, has a natural sentiment of what is good, true, and proper." Not surprisingly, Fichte offers this left-handed compliment to women and their wondrous "sentiments" in the course of arguing against granting them the right to vote.[56]

The women at the AAUW and the Wellesley College Center for Research on Women cannot have it both ways: if you want girls to succeed in math, science, and engineering, then you have to teach them, along with boys, to be analytical thinkers, to value the very things Ms. McIntosh was warning the Brookline teachers against—"exact thinking, decisiveness, mastery of something—right and wrong answers, win lest you lose." As John Leo of *U.S. News & World Report*—one of the few journalists who took the trouble to read past the first few pages of the report—put it, "McIntosh wants to promote 'lateral thinking' in the curriculum, the aim of which is not to win or excel but 'to be in a decent relationship to the invisible elements of the universe.' Consider that an alarm bell. This report needs a full vertical analysis."[57]

Colleges use both the Scholastic Aptitude Test and the high school records in selecting students for admission. On average, girls have better grades but do slightly worse on the SAT. The mean math scores in 1992 were 499 for boys, and 456 for girls; in English, 428 for boys, and 419 for girls.[58] The SAT is supposed to predict how well a student will do in college; however, once they get to college, it is the girls who get the better grades.

Ever on the alert for how schools are "shortchanging" girls, the Wellesley Report takes these facts as clear evidence that the SAT is biased in favor of boys. It is possible that the test score differentials are indicative of bias and that the test should be altered to minimize or eliminate such bias. But we cannot accept that conclusion without better (and more impartial) research. Scores by themselves do not necessarily show bias. There are many other factors to consider.

More girls than boys take the SAT (girls, 52 percent; boys, 48 percent); moreover, according to the 1992 College Board *Profile of the SAT Test Takers,* more females from "at risk" categories take the test than males. Specifically, more girls from lower-income homes or with parents who never attended college are likely to attempt the SAT exam than are boys from the same background. "These characteristics are associated with lower than average SAT scores," says the College Board.[59]

Men and women take different kinds of courses in college; more males enroll in math and science, more females in the humanities. The advent of radical grade inflation in the humanities, and comparatively little in the sciences, might explain why, despite lower SAT scores, women students net higher grade point averages. The Wellesley researchers were aware of this possibility, but they insist that even when course difficulty is taken into account, the SAT test still turns out to be biased against girls:

> The underprediction of women's college grades does not result from women taking easier courses. In math courses at all levels, grades of females and males are very similar, but male SAT-Math scores are higher than female scores. Even when grades are weighted to allow for differences in the difficulty of first-year courses taken by women and men, the underprediction of women's grades is reduced but not eliminated.[60]

If that were right, we would certainly be inclined to say that the test is skewed in favor of the boys. On this point the report claims support from an article entitled "Gender Bias in the Prediction of College Course Performance" in a 1988 issue of the *Journal of Educational Measurement*. But, as journalist Daniel Seligman reported in a March 1992 issue of *Fortune*, that article is a weak reed indeed.[61] Its authors, Robert McCormack and Mary McLeod of San Diego State University, take pains to say that once the difficulty of the courses is considered, there is *no* evidence of gender bias. In fact, McCormack and McLeod found, "Curiously, in those few courses in which a gender bias was found, it most often involved over-predicting for women in a course in which men earned a higher average grade."[62]

Seligman's observations provoked a letter to *Fortune* from Susan Bailey and Patricia Campbell—two of the report's authors. They did not defend, explain, or apologize for their reliance on the McCormack/McLeod article; instead they claimed that other studies do support the finding of bias. Furthermore, they asserted, "It is hard to take seriously [Seligman's] critique . . . when girls are referred to as 'dolls.' . . . The Report was written to document gender bias and to suggest positive steps to combat it. Reference to guys [and] dolls . . . does little to help our schools or our students."[63] Mr. Seligman's choice of words may have been frivolous, but his point was not. And what are we to think when those who claim to be helping our schools refuse to answer a criticism that presents a simple finding of error?

Criticism by the education writer Rita Kramer in *Commentary* provoked another angry letter from Sharon Schuster, the president of the AAUW. Ms. Schuster argued that girls' weaker performance was caused by the biased content of the tests:

> Research studies reviewed in the report also found substantial gender bias in standardized tests. One analysis of tests found twice as many references to men as to women, and more pictures of and references to boys than girls. A later study of the Scholastic Aptitude Test (SAT) found references to 42 men and only three women in the reading-comprehension passages used in the four 1984–85 exams. Of the 42 men, 34 were famous and their work was cited; one of the three women was famous (Margaret Mead) and her work was criticized.[64]

Ms. Schuster seems to imply that if the SAT and other standardized tests had more word problems that girls could relate to—say, about famous women or perhaps about cooking, sewing, quilting, or relationships—then girls' scores would go up.

But surely Ms. Schuster read the report which rejects this argument, noting that "references to male or female names, pronouns, possessions, or occupations in the place of neutral language *had no demonstrable effect at all* on the examinee performance on mathematics word problems [my emphasis]." Boys still averaged better than girls on SAT problem solving, "even when the problem related to food and cooking." The content of examples had no effect on performance one way or the other.

The report did find that girls are better than boys in computation, a rather small consolation in an era of hand-held calculators. Not to be discouraged, the AAUW-Wellesley team seized the opportunity to recommend that boys' and girls' test results be equalized by testing more on computation and less on problem solving. Of course, this sets precisely the wrong emphasis, since it is the higher-order skills—problem solving —that are most important, and in which our children are weakest. International exams document that our schoolchildren come closer to our competitors in arithmetic (though even here they still lag behind) than they do in more challenging areas.

So, once again we find that the gender feminists' ideological and partisan treatment of a problem—which is in principle amenable to an objective and nonpartisan solution—ends up confusing the issues, creating acrimony, and helping nobody. The question of test fairness is important, too important to be left to the mercies of advocacy research. Who is shortchanging whom?

The Wellesley Report is correct when it points out that American girls are trailing boys in math and science. The gap is small but real, and the report is right to suggest that schools must make every effort to "dispel myths about math and science as 'inappropriate' fields for women."[65] Unfortunately, that sound suggestion is accompanied by more than twenty questionable and distressing recommendations that would, if acted upon, create a nightmarish "gender equity" bureaucracy with plenty of time and money on its hands—just the sort of recommendation anyone who cares about the well-being of American schools should fear and loathe: "The U.S Department of Education's Office of Educational Research and Improvement (OERI) should establish an advisory panel of gender equity experts to work with OERI to develop a research and dissemination agenda to foster gender-equitable education in the nation's classrooms."[66]

Who would be training the gender experts? Who would monitor the nation's schools on how well they conform to the ideals of a correct sexual politics? More generally, who would benefit most from the millions being requested for the Gender Equity in Education Act? Would it not be those who insist that gender equity is our foremost educational problem? Our system cannot handle much more pressure from these muddled but determined women with their multistage theories and their metaphors about windows, mirrors, and voices, their workshops, and above all their constant alarms about the state of male-female relations in American society.

Which leads us back to what is most wrongheaded about the Wellesley Report: its exploitation of America's very real problem as a nation educationally at risk. Despite its suggestion that solving the "problem of gender equity" will somehow help us to bridge the gap between American children and the educationally superior children of other countries—what the education researcher Harold Stevenson aptly calls the "learning gap" —the report never says how. The reason for the omission is obvious: the authors have no plausible solution to offer.

In 1992, the Mathematical Association of America published a translation of the math section of Japan's 1990 college entrance exam. American mathematicians were startled by what they saw. Professor Richard Askey, a mathematician at the University of Wisconsin, spoke for many American scientists and mathematicians when he said, "The level at which [Japanese] students perform on these [exams] is just incredible."[67]

Science magazine recently printed a sample question from the entrance examination to Tokyo University. To solve it would require a lot of "vertical thinking": "Given a regular pyramid, there is a ball with its center on the bottom of the pyramid and tangent to all edges. (A regular pyramid has four isosceles triangles adjoined to a square base.) If each edge of the pyramid base is of length a, find the height of the pyramid and the volume of the portion it has in common with the ball."[68]

The *Science* editors point out that this question is being asked not of future math and science majors but of Japanese high school students who were planning to major in the humanities. They noted: "When U.S. math majors might trail even lit students in Japan, there's a lot of catching up to do."[69]

American educators sometimes explain away the discrepancies by pointing out that only the best students in Japan take the test. In 1987, for example, 31 percent of American college-age students took the SAT; in Japan the figure was 14 percent for the Japanese equivalent of the SAT. But even our very *best* students had a hard time matching the *average* score of the Japanese students.[70] Studies by Professor Jerry Becker, of Southern Illinois University, and by Floyd Mattheis, of East Carolina University, tell the same story. Becker reports that the problem is not simply that Japanese students as a whole outperform our students but that "*average* students in Japan show greater achievement than the top five percent of U.S. students" (his emphasis).[71] Mattheis compared junior high students in Japan and North Carolina. Reporting on his study, *Science* magazine says, "It shows Japanese students out front at every age group in a test that measures six logical thinking operations."[72]

Professor Stevenson has done some of the most thorough comparative studies. He found a big difference between the *average* American score and the *average* for Japanese and Taiwanese students. (Only 14.5 percent of Taiwanese and 8 percent of Japanese eleventh-graders had scores *below* the American average.) Among fifth-graders only 4.1 percent of Taiwanese children and 10.3 percent of Japanese children score as low or lower than the American average.[73] Stevenson points out that we cannot attribute the disparity to "differential sampling." He studied first-, fifth-, and eleventh-graders in Japan, Taiwan, and the United States, in all three of which enrollment in first and fifth grades is close to 100 percent. If vocational schools are included in the figures for high school, the representation of adolescents is also the same.

What of the gender gap between American boys and girls in math? As noted earlier, the Educational Testing Service (in its International Assessment of Mathematics and Science) found that although thirteen-year-old American girls lag a point behind the boys, that gap is insignificant compared to the one between American children and foreign children. Recall that the disparity between our boys and Taiwanese and Korean *girls* was 16 points.[74]

Some theorists speculate that Asian children do better at math because their languages are so complex and abstract, providing better preparation in the cognitive skills required for math and science. That does not help to explain why American children lag behind European and Canadian students too. Girls in French-speaking Quebec outperform our boys by 12 points on the IAEP math test. In fact, American boys lag behind girls in such countries as Ireland, Italy, and Hungary.[75] In science the results, although not quite so dismaying, continue the pattern: American boys trail significantly behind the foreign girls.

The president of the Educational Testing Service, Gregory Anrig, has cited three factors that contribute to Asians' and Europeans' higher performance: rigorous content in the curriculum, high expectations from parents and teachers, and positive cultural attitudes toward learning.[76] Absurdly, cynically, or foolishly, the AAUW and the Wellesley experts are focusing on the one area in which American students surpass students in other countries, and where they need the least amount of help—self-esteem!

Reacting to the alarms of the AAUW and the Wellesley College Center for Research on Women, Congress is now likely to pass the Gender Equity in Education Act. Unfortunately, a legislative emphasis on gender gaps is an unhelpful diversion. Dr. Stevenson's findings, backed by serious studies from many other quarters, highlight the real problems of a nation that is educationally at risk. The recommendations that Stevenson and other experts on the "learning gap" problem are making are straightforward, constructive, commonsensical, and practicable. Must we wait for Congress to exhaust its need to show that its feminist credentials are in order before we see a serious effort to get our educational act together?

The AAUW and the Wellesley researchers had every right to be gratified at their success. It had all been so easy. The media had been cooperative and uncritical. The strategy of "do a study, declare a crisis, get politicians worked up" was proving to be astonishingly effective.

The Wellesley Center took the lead for the next study, focusing on the sexual harassment of girls by boys in the grade schools. Nan Stein was the obvious choice to carry out such a study. A "project director" at the Wellesley College Center for Research on Women, she had been prominent on the workshop circuit for many years. Working closely with the National Organization for Women, Dr. Stein designed a questionnaire and placed it in the September 1992 issue of *Seventeen*. The editors at *Seventeen* preceded the questionnaire by an article that told a disturbing story about a Minnesota girl named Katy Lyle who was tormented and humiliated on a daily basis by her peers and eventually took legal action. Certain passages from the story were highlighted in large boldface letters: "It's probably happened to you" and "You don't have to put up with it—in fact it's illegal. And your school is responsible for stopping it." The article ended with a word from Dr. Stein about the importance of creating more caring and just schools—"girls included." Then came the half-page tear-off questionnaire entitled "What's Happening to You?" Among the thirteen questions asked of the *Seventeen* readers were these:

- Did anyone do any of the following to you *when you didn't want them to* in the last school year?
  (a) touch, pinch, or grab you
  (b) lean over you or corner you

  (c) give you sexual notes or pictures
  (d) make suggestive or sexual gestures, looks, comments, or jokes
  (e) pressure you to do something sexual
  (f)   force you to do something sexual
  • If you've been sexually harassed at school, how did it make you feel?

Forty-two hundred of the magazine's 1.9 million subscribers returned the questionnaire, a 0.2 percent response.[77] Nearly all the respondents reported they had been harassed as defined by the questionnaire. Specifically, the data showed that 89 percent of the respondents had received suggestive gestures, looks, comments, or jokes; 83 percent had been touched, pinched, or grabbed; 47 percent were leaned over or cornered; 28 percent received sexual notes or pictures; 27 percent were pressured to do something sexual; and 10 percent were forced to do something sexual.

Ms. Stein, who was much moved by the responses, began to write about them even before she completed the study. In the November 1992 issue of *Education Week,* she wrote:

> Their letters arrive by the hundreds daily, screaming to be read: "OPEN," "URGENT," "PLEASE READ" are scribbled on the envelopes. Sometimes the writers give their names and addresses, sometimes they don't. . . . Inside the envelopes are chilling stories, handwritten on lined notebook paper. . . . All beg for attention, for answers, and above all, for some type of justice.[78]

"To thousands of adolescent girls," she concludes, "school may be teaching more about oppression than freedom; more about silence than autonomy. We need to heed their warnings and listen to their stories."

When Ms. Stein's final report came out on March 24, 1993, the results were carried in newspapers around the country. The reporters cited Ms. Stein's figures in just the way she and the Wellesley researchers must have hoped: Instead of pointing out that the "9 out of 10" of those who reported being sexually harassed were girls who had taken the trouble to answer a magazine survey—and who constituted no more than two-tenths of 1 percent of the magazine's readership—the reporters simply spoke of an epidemic of harassment. The story headline from the *Boston Globe* was typical: "A U.S. survey shows wide harassment of girls in school."[79]

What Ms. Stein and the National Organization of Women had devised is known as a self-selecting poll. Responsible pollsters call them SLOPs—self-selected listener opinion polls—and they avoid doing them, or crediting them when other pollsters do them.[80] A famous example used in introductory statistics classes shows their failings—the 1936 SLOP published by the *Literary Digest* that showed Alf Landon beating FDR by a landslide. SLOPs continue to be popular with some mass-market publications as a form of entertainment, but no serious researcher relies on them.

I asked Tom W. Smith, a director at the National Opinion Research Center at the University of Chicago, whether we learn *anything* from a poll of this kind: "No, because there is a crucial fallacy in self-selected research: you get a biased response." He pointed out that the Wellesley harassment survey was in fact the result of not one but two stages of self-selection. The study was confined to readers of *Seventeen*, whose readers are not necessarily representative of the population of adolescent girls; and readers who respond to such a survey tend to be those who feel most strongly about the problem. "Even if they had forty thousand responses it would still prove very little," said Smith. "You still have to wonder about the other million and a half–plus who did not respond."

It is not hard to see how SLOPs could be used to generate alarm in almost any area of social interaction. Using Nan Stein's methodology, we could easily get people worked up about the problem of neighborly harassment. We begin by writing a story describing a case of horrifying neighbor behavior. Assume that we print this in a publication like the *Reader's Digest.* Certain passages would be highlighted—"It's probably happened to you" and "You don't have to put up with it—in fact it's illegal. And your city government is responsible for stopping it." We would then enclose a convenient one-page survey called "What's Happening to You?" asking whether your neighbor did any of a list of things to you in the past year—"generally annoy you by asking for burdensome favors," "scream at your children," "play loud music or have loud parties," "damage your lawn, your car, your garden, your pet, or any other property," "frighten you by reckless, threatening behavior—involving alcohol, drugs, or guns," "steal from you or physically attack you or any member of your family." And we would end by asking, "If you have been tormented by your neighbor, how did it make you feel?"

It would be expected that the *Digest* would receive responses from some small percentage of its readers and that *the vast majority of this small percentage* would give details of being victimized by a neighbor. The "researcher" could then tally up the results in a scientific-looking brochure full of tables, charts, and percentages (86 percent were accosted by their neighbor, 62 percent threatened with physical attack, 45 percent physically beaten, 91 percent subjected to loud music, etc.). Interspersed throughout the report would be disturbing passages from letters by the sufferers.

Though its findings would surely be depressing, a SLOP survey on neighborly harassment would tell us very little that we did not know. Everyone knows that some neighbors are intolerable. What we want to know is how *prevalent* neighbor harassment is, and for that we need to know about the experience of those who did not return the questionnaire.

An SLOP survey is of little value to most social scientists. In using one as her survey instrument, Nan Stein was virtually assured of the alarming results. A serious study of juvenile harassment needs another kind of approach. We need to know whether the cases cited were part of a more general problem of a breakdown of civility and discipline among American adolescents, for example. Sexual harassment may indeed be more prevalent today than it has been in the past. On the other hand, its greater prevalence may be due to the overall rise of antisocial behavior in American life rather than to a rise in gender bias. We'd also want to get a sense of how adolescent *girls* harass other girls.

The point is that the Wellesley harassment study is less concerned with girls' unhappiness than with how *boys* make them unhappy. The study tells us once again how our society "shortchanges" and "silences" its females, giving the gender feminists a fresh supply of stories of female victimization and male malfeasance. The survey may have been unscientific, but it was perfectly designed for its real purpose.

Susan McGee Bailey, a director at the Wellesley College Center for Research on Women, called the *Seventeen* survey a "wake-up call" and urged everyone to "listen to the girls' voices."[81] She acknowledged, however, that the survey was unscientific. The AAUW soon took up the implicit challenge. In a survey conducted by the Louis Harris polling firm, a *random sample* of fifteen hundred boys and girls (grades eight through eleven) were queried about harassment. The findings surprised everyone including the AAUW. Four of five students, male as well as female, reported being harassed. The study does suggest that our schools are the setting for a lot of incivility and even outright violence. It suggests that many kids are erotically overstimulated. More than half the girls and nearly half the boys had been touched, grabbed, or pinched "in a sexual way." Some of the students had been rubbed up against (57 percent of girls, 36 percent of boys), some had had clothing pulled at, and some had received sexual notes.[82]

The high incidence of sexually harassed males did not jibe with the shortchanging theme. How do you put a gender bias spin on that kind of finding? Once again, the AAUW was up to the challenge. Speaking to the *Boston Globe,* Alice McKee argued that the *effects* of the harassment differ: "The bottom line is that girls suffer adverse emotional, behavioral and educational impacts three times more often than boys as a result of sexual harassment." The *Globe* writer, Alison Bass, explained and amplified the point:

> Even though boys reported being harassed almost as often as did girls, the survey . . . found that girls were far more likely than boys to want to cut class and stay home from school as a result of the harassment. Girls were also more hesitant to speak up in class and less confident about themselves after being sexually harassed, the survey found.[83]

So once again we are given to understand that "research suggests" the girls are being shortchanged. The effects on them (in wanting to cut classes and stay home) were markedly worse. But *wanting* to cut classes and actually cutting classes are not the same, and the latter effect is just the sort of thing we can check.[84] If McKee is right, girls should be showing high rates of absenteeism, cutting class, and getting lower grades. In fact, girls have better attendance and earn better grades than boys, and more of them graduate. This is not to say that girls and boys react to harassment in the same way. The response of girls to insults or slights may indeed be more dramatic, leading them to *express* the desire to cut classes more than boys do—a finding that would be in keeping with those of Wendy Wood and her colleagues at Texas A&M, that "girls are more aware of their feelings and more accurate in reporting on negative emotions."

This time the AAUW's pollsters had come up with findings that did not readily lend themselves to the "shortchanging" theme. And for the first time some skeptical voices began to speak up in the popular press. In a *New York Times* story, Felicity Barringer cited students who criticized the survey for "characterizing too many behaviors as sexual harassment." After the *Boston Globe* ran a story giving the exact spin the AAUW dictated, reporter Thomas Palmer had doubts about the validity of the harassment survey. He and Alison Bass wrote a story questioning the AAUW findings and incorporating outside opinions. Billie Dziech, an expert on sexual harassment and the author of one of the most respected books on the subject, *The Lecherous Professor,* pointed out that the inexact terminology vitiated the AAUW report.[85] "There is a difference between something I would call 'sexual hassle' and 'sexual harassment.' "

Jerry Weiner, president-elect of the American Psychiatry Association, told the *Globe,* "I have many reservations and concerns about the reliability of the data and using that kind of data to draw the broad sweeping conclusions that were drawn in the report." Tom W. Smith, the director of the National Opinion Research Center at the University of Chicago, also criticized the vagueness of the questions and the wide range of possible interpretation.

For the first time the *merits* of an AAUW study alleging gender inequity were not simply reported but actually debated on national television. Ted Koppel chose the AAUW's report on sexual harassment in grade schools as a subject for "Nightline." He arranged a confrontation between Nan Stein and me to debate its significance. Ms. Stein is an excellent protagonist, but she faltered when I reminded her that she had spoken of the little boys who flipped up the skirts of little girls in the schoolyard as "gender terrorists." A skeptical Mr. Koppel asked whether she would call a schoolyard bully picking on another boy a "terrorist" too. Ms. Stein must not have enjoyed the experience—after our "Nightline" encounter, she backed out of another debate between us scheduled for a Boston television program the following week. The producer was too diplomatic to tell me what Ms. Stein had said about me. "Let us just say she does not like you very much."

In December 1993 I took part in another debate about harassment in the workplace with Anne Bryant, executive director of the AAUW, on ABC's "Lifetime Magazine." I said that the AAUW surveys were "tendentious and biased." I brought up the fact that their harassment study had failed to distinguish between "casual banter, teasing, and serious harassment." Shaking her finger at me, Bryant admonished me, "Christina, stop it! Do you want to know something? This is the last time you'll criticize the incredibly prestigious and well-run organization—the American Association of University Women."[86] It would seem she feels that any criticism of the AAUW is simply out of order and should not be given a public airing. In any case, the producer told me that the AAUW's public relations director later tried to persuade ABC not to run the debate.

Feminism is not well served by biased studies or by media that tolerate and help to promote them. Had journalists, politicians, and education leaders been doing a proper job of checking sources, looking at the original data, and seeking dissenting opinions from scholars, had they not put their faith in glossy brochures and press releases, the alarming findings on self-esteem, gender bias in the classroom, and harassment in the hallways would not be automatically credited. In a soundly critical climate, the federal government would not be on the verge of pouring tens of millions of dollars into projects that will enrich the gender-bias industry and further weaken our schools. And Ms. Bryant and the other current leaders of the AAUW would have learned some time ago that the reputation of the AAUW must inevitably be compromised by anyone who uses its "incredible prestige" to promote research whose probity and objectivity cannot be defended.

Chapter 9

Noble Lies

Pity, wrath, heroism filled them, but the power of putting two and two together was annihilated.
—E. M. FORSTER, *A Passage to India*

Statistics and studies on such provocative subjects as eating disorders, rape, battery, and wage differentials are used to underscore the plight of women in the oppressive gender system and to help recruit adherents to the gender feminist cause. But if the figures are not true, they almost never serve the interests of the victimized women they concern. Anorexia is a disease; blaming men does nothing to help cure it. Battery and rape are crimes that shatter lives; those who suffer must be cared for, and those who cause their suffering must be kept from doing further harm. But in all we do to help, the most loyal ally is truth. Truth brought to public light recruits the best of us to work for change. On the other hand, even the best-intentioned "noble lie" ultimately discredits the finest cause.

Gender feminist ideology holds that physical menace toward women is the norm. The cause of battered women has been a handy bandwagon for this creed. Gloria Steinem's portrait of male-female intimacy under patriarchy is typical: "Patriarchy *requires* violence or the subliminal threat of violence in order to maintain itself. . . . The most dangerous situation for a woman is not an unknown man in the street, or even the enemy in wartime, but a husband or lover in the isolation of their own home."[1]

Steinem's description of the dangers women face in their own home is reminiscent of the Super Bowl hoax of January 1993.[2]

Some days before that Super Bowl, American women were alerted that a sharp increase in battering was to be expected on the day of the game. The implications were sensational, but purportedly there were reliable studies. In the current climate, the story had a certain ring of plausibility, and it quickly spread. Here is the chronology.

Thursday, January 28

A news conference was called in Pasadena, California, the site of the forthcoming Super Bowl game, by a coalition of women's groups. At the news conference reporters were informed that significant anecdotal evidence suggested that Super Bowl Sunday is "the biggest day of the year for violence against women."[3] Prior to the conference, there had been reports of increases as high as 40 percent in calls for help from victims that day. At the conference, Sheila Kuehl of the California Women's Law Center cited a study done at Virginia's Old Dominion University three years before, saying that it found that police reports of beatings and hospital admissions in northern Virginia rose 40 percent after games won by the Redskins during the 1988–89 season. The presence of Linda Mitchell at the conference, a representative of a media "watchdog" group called Fairness and Accuracy in Reporting (FAIR), lent credibility to the cause.

At about this time a very large media mailing was sent by Dobisky Associates, warning at-risk women, "Don't remain at home with him during the game." The idea that sports fans are prone to attack wives or girlfriends on that climactic day persuaded many men as well: Robert Lipsyte of the *New York Times* would soon be referring to the "Abuse Bowl."[4]

Friday, January 29

Lenore Walker, a Denver psychologist and author of *The Battered Woman,* appeared on "Good Morning America" claiming to have compiled a ten-year record showing a sharp increase in violent incidents against women on Super Bowl Sundays. Here, again, a representative from FAIR, Laura Flanders, was present to lend credibility to the cause.

Saturday, January 30

A story in the *Boston Globe* written by Lynda Gorov reported that women's shelters and hotlines are "flooded with more calls from victims [on Super Bowl Sunday] than on any other day of the year." Gorov cited "one study of women's shelters out West" that "showed a 40 percent climb in calls, a pattern advocates said is repeated nationwide, including in Massachusetts."[5]

Ms. Gorov asked specialists in domestic violence to explain the phenomenon. Many felt that everything about the Super Bowl is calculated to give men the idea that women are there for their use and abuse. "More than one advocate mentioned provocatively dressed cheerleaders at the game may reinforce abusers' perceptions that women are intended to serve men," she wrote. According to Nancy Isaac, an expert on domestic violence at the Harvard School of Public Health, men see the violence as their right: "It's: 'I'm supposed to be king of my castle, it's supposed to be my day, and if you don't have dinner ready on time, you're going to get it.' "

Other newspapers joined in. Robert Lipsyte described the connection between the tension generated by the big game and the violence it causes: "Someone shut up that kid or someone's going to get pounded."[6] Michael Collier of the *Oakland Tribune* wrote that the Super Bowl causes "boyfriends, husbands and fathers" to "explode like mad linemen, leaving girlfriends, wives and children beaten."[7] Journalists and television commentators all over the country sounded the alarm. CBS and the Associated Press called Super Bowl Sunday a "day of dread," and just before the game, NBC broadcast a public service spot reminding men that domestic violence is a crime.

In this roiling sea of media credulity was a lone island of professional integrity. Ken Ringle, a *Washington Post* staff writer, took the time to call around to check on the sources of the story.[8] When Ringle asked Janet Katz, professor of sociology and criminal justice at Old Dominion and one of the principal authors of the study cited by Ms. Kuehl at the Thursday press conference, about the connection between violence and football games, she said: "That's not what we found at all." Instead, she told Ringle, they had found that an increase in emergency room admissions "was not associated with the occurrence of football games in general."[9]

Ringle then called Charles Patrick Ewing, a professor at the University of Buffalo, whom Dobisky Associates had quoted as saying, "Super Bowl Sunday is one day in the year when hot lines, shelters and other agencies that work with battered women get the most reports and complaints of domestic violence." "I never said that," Ewing told Ringle. When told about Ewing's denial, Frank Dobisky corrected himself, saying that the quote should have read *"one of the days* of the year." But that explanation either makes the claim incoherent, since only one day can have "the most" battery complaints, or trivializes it, since *any* day (including April Fool's Day) could now be said to be the day of heightened brutality.

Ringle checked with Lynda Gorov, the *Boston Globe* reporter. Gorov told him she had never seen the study she cited but had been told of it by FAIR. Ms. Mitchell of FAIR told Ringle that the authority for the 40 percent figure was Lenore Walker. Walker's office, in turn, referred calls on the subject to Michael Lindsey, a Denver psychologist and an authority on battered women.

Pressed by Ringle, Lindsey admitted he could find no basis for the report. "I haven't been any more successful than you in tracking down any of this," he said. "You think maybe we have one of these myth things here?" Later, other reporters got to Ms. Walker, pressing her to detail her findings. "We don't use them for public consumption," she explained, "we used them to guide us in advocacy projects."[10]

It would have been more honest for the feminists who initiated the campaign to admit that there was no scientific basis for saying that foot-ball fans are more brutal to women than are chess players or Democrats; nor was there any hard data for the claim that there was a significant rise in domestic violence on Super Bowl Sunday.

Ringle's unraveling of the "myth thing" was published on the front page of the *Washington Post* on January 31. On February 2, *Boston Globe* staff writer Bob Hohler published what amounted to a retraction of Ms. Gorov's story. Hohler had done some more digging and had gotten FAIR's Steven Rendall to back off from the organization's earlier support of the claim. "It should not have gone out in FAIR materials," said Rendall.

Hohler got another set of interviews, this time with psychologists who told him that they had their doubts about the story from the very begin-ning. One expert, Joan Stiles, public education coordinator for the Mas-sachusetts Coalition of Battered Women's Service Groups, told the *Globe* that the Super Bowl story "sensationalized and trivialized" the battering problem, and damaged the cause's credibility. Lundy Bancroft, a training director for a Cambridge-based counseling program for men who batter, said, "I disbelieved the 40 percent thing from the moment I heard it." Bancroft also suggested that the campaign to pressure NBC to air the domestic-violence spot "unfairly stigmatized" football fans. "There is no stereotypical batterer," he said. As Michael Lindsey commented to Ken Ringle, "When people make crazy statements like this, the credibility of the whole cause can go right out the window."

According to Ringle, Linda Mitchell from FAIR would later acknowl-edge that she was aware during the original news conference that Ms.

Kuehl was misrepresenting the Old Dominion study. Ringle asked her whether she did not feel obligated to challenge her colleague. "I wouldn't do that in front of the media," Mitchell said. "She has a right to report it as she wants." (FAIR would later take issue with Ringle's interpretation of Mitchell's remarks.)

Hohler's investigations fully supported the conclusions Ringle had reached. Ringle wrote: "Despite their dramatic claims, none of the activists appears to have any evidence that a link actually exists between football and wife-beating. Yet the concept has gained such credence that their campaign has rolled on anyway, unabated." [11]

Of the shelters and hot lines monitored on the Sunday of the twenty-seventh Super Bowl, some reported variations in the number of calls for help that day, and others did not. In Buffalo, whose team (and fans) had suffered a crushing defeat, there were no unusual increases.

Not surprisingly, Ringle's story generated a flurry of media activity. FAIR sent a letter to the *Washington Post* attacking the piece, claiming that it contained errors and quotes taken out of context. A subsequent column in the *Washington Post* mentioned that FAIR was unhappy with Ringle's reporting, but the paper otherwise supported the gist of his piece. And then there was more. The *American Journalism Review* did its own investigation of Ringle's reporting. Its conclusion was both that Ringle was correct in reporting that there was no solid data to support the 40 percent figure but that Ringle had twisted and used quotes selectively to support his thesis. Ringle's response? He stands by his story. [12]

Despite Ringle's exposé and the ensuing media attention, the Super Bowl Sunday "statistic" will be with us for a while, doing its divisive work. In the book *How to Make the World a Better Place for Women in Five Minutes a Day*, a comment under the heading "Did You Know?" informs readers that "Super Bowl Sunday is the most violent day of the year, with the highest reported number of domestic battering cases." [13] How a belief in that misandrist canard can make the world a better place for women is not explained.

How many women in the United States are brutalized by the men in their lives? Here is a cross section of the various answers:

During the 9-year period, intimates committed 5.6 million violent victimizations against women, an annual average of 626,000. (U.S. Department of Justice, 1991) [14]

Approximately 1.8 million women a year are physically assaulted by their husbands or boyfriends. (*Behind Closed Doors: Violence in the American Family*) [15]

In the past year, 3 million women have been battered. (Senator Joseph Biden, 1991) [16]

Total domestic violence, reported and unreported, affects a many as 4 million women a year. (Senator Biden's staff report, 1992) [17]

An estimated three to four million women are brutally beaten each year in the U.S. (*Feminist Dictionary*) [18]

Nearly 6 million wives will be abused by their husbands in any one year. (*Time* magazine, September 5, 1983)

More than 50 percent of all women will experience some form of violence from their spouses during marriage. More than one-third are battered repeatedly every year. (National Coalition Against Domestic Violence) [19]

The estimates of the number of women beaten per second vary:

A woman is beaten every eighteen seconds. (Gail Dines, 1992) [20]

An American woman is beaten by her husband or boyfriend every 15 seconds. (*New York Times*, April 23, 1993)

Every twelve seconds, a woman in the United States is beaten by her husband or lover. (*Mirabella*, November 1993) [21]

A gong [will be] sounded every ten seconds for a woman being battered in the United States. ("The Clothesline Project," Johns Hopkins University) [22]

In the United States, every 7.4 seconds a woman is beaten by her husband. (*Annals of Emergency Medicine*, June 1989)

6.5 million women annually are assaulted by their partners . . . one every five seconds. (BrotherPeace, 1993) [23]

Sometimes the same source will give the figure both in millions of women and in seconds—without acknowledging that the two are inconsistent. Since there are 31,536,000 seconds in a year, the fifteen-second rate would amount to 2.1 million assaults. Three to four million would mean one every 7.9 or 10.5 seconds. This mistake is common:

According to the National Coalition Against Domestic Violence, 3 million to 4 million women are battered every year in the U.S., one every 15 seconds. (Mary McGrory, *Washington Post,* October 20, 1987)

Domestic violence affects an estimated 4 to 5 million women a year. Every 15 seconds, an American woman is abused by her partner. (*Christian Science Monitor,* October 12, 1990)

There are 3 million to 4 million women beaten by husbands or lovers every year; that's one every 15 seconds. (*Chicago Tribune,* February 10, 1992)

Richard J. Gelles and Murray A. Straus are academic social scientists (from the University of Rhode Island and the University of New Hampshire, respectively) who have been studying domestic violence for more than twenty-five years. Their research is among the most respected and frequently cited by other social scientists, by police, by the FBI, and by the personnel in domestic violence agencies.

For a long time, Gelles and Straus were highly regarded by feminist activists for the pioneer work they had done in this once-neglected area. But they fell out of favor in the late 1970s because their findings were not informed by the "battery is caused by patriarchy" thesis. The fact that they were men was also held against them.

Gelles and Straus do find high levels of violence in many American families; but in both of their national surveys they found that women were just as likely to engage in it as men. They also found that siblings are the most violent of all.[24] They distinguish between minor violence, such as throwing objects, pushing, shoving, and slapping (no injuries, no serious intimidation), and severe violence, such as kicking, hitting or trying to hit with an object, hitting with fist, beating up, and threatening with gun or knife—actions that have a high probability of leading to injury or are accompanied by the serious threat of injury. The vast majority of family disputes involve minor violence rather than severe violence. In their 1985 Second National Family Violence Survey, sponsored by the National Institute of Mental Health, they found that 16 percent of couples were violent—the "Saturday Night Brawlers" (with the wife just as likely as the husband to slap, grab, shove, or throw things). In 3 to 4 percent of couples, there was at least one act of severe violence by the husband against the wife. But in their surveys they also found that "women assault their partners at about the same rate as men assault their partners. This applies to both minor and severe assaults."[25]

Gelles and Straus are careful to say that women are *far more likely* to be injured and to need medical care. But overall, the percentage of women who are injured seriously enough to need medical care is still relatively small compared to the inflated claims of the gender feminists and the politicians—fewer than 1 percent.[26] Murray Straus estimates that approximately 100,000 women per year are victims of the severe kinds of violence shown in the TV film *The Burning Bed*. That is a shockingly high number of victims, but it is far short of Senator Biden's claim, derived from feminist advocacy studies, that more that three or four million women are victims of "horrifying" violence.

Straus and Gelles have made other discoveries not appreciated by gender feminists. Among them is the finding that because of changing demographics and improved public awareness, there was a significant *decrease* in wife battery between 1975 and 1985.[27] Moreover, though they once reported that battery increased during pregnancy, they now say they were mistaken: "Data from the 1985 Second National Family Violence Survey indicate that the previously reported association between pregnancy and husband-to-wife violence is spurious, and is an artifact of the effect of another variable, age."[28]

Gelles and Straus consider domestic violence to be a serious national problem. They have for years been advocates for social, medical, and legal intervention to help battered women. All the same, according to their studies, more than 84 percent of families are not violent, and among the 16 percent who are, nearly half the violence (though not half the injuries) is perpetrated by women.

Journalists, activists, and even gender feminists make extensive use of Gelles and Straus's research. Some researchers manipulate their data to get shocking figures on abuse. If you overlook the researchers' distinction between minor and severe violence, if you never mention that women do just as much of the shoving, grabbing, pushing, and slapping, you arrive at very high figures for battery: three million, four million, six million, depending on how slack you are in what you count as battery.

The National Coalition Against Domestic Violence gives shocking figures on abuse in their fundraising brochure: "More than 50 percent of all women will experience some form of violence from their spouses during marriage. More than one-third are battered repeatedly every year." We get the impression that one-third of all married women (18 million) are repeatedly being battered. Where did the coalition get these figures? Either they relied on their own special gender feminist sources or they creatively interpreted the FBI's, Department of Justice's, or Gelles and

Straus's studies to suit their purposes. The latter is what the Common-wealth Fund, a New York State philanthropy concerned with public health, did in their Women's Health Survey.

In July 1993, the Commonwealth Fund released the results of a tele-phone survey of 2,500 women, designed and carried out by Louis Harris and Associates. The Commonwealth and Harris investigators took their questions directly from the Gelles and Straus survey and got the following results:

I would like you to tell me whether, in the past twelve months, your spouse or partner ever:

		YES	NO
1.	Insulted you or swore at you	34%	66%
2.	Stomped out of the room or house or yard	34	66
3.	Threatened to hit you or throw something at you	5	95
4.	Threw or smashed or hit or kicked something	11	89
5.	Threw something at you	3	97
6.	Pushed, grabbed, shoved, or slapped you	5	95
7.	Kicked, bit, or hit you with a fist or some other object	2	98
8.	Beat you up	0	100
9.	Choked you	0	99
10.	Threatened you with a knife or gun	0	100
11.	Used a knife or gun	0	100

Using these findings, and based on the assumption that there are approximately 55 million women married or living with someone as a couple, the Harris/Commonwealth survey concluded that as many as four million women a year were victims of physical assaults, and 20.7 million were verbally or emotionally abused by their partners.[29]

Newspapers around the country, including the *Wall Street Journal*, the *Washington Post*, the *Detroit News*, and the *San Francisco Chronicle*,[30] carried the bleak tidings that 37 percent of married women are emotionally abused and 3.9 million are physically assaulted every year.

No one mentioned that all the survey questions were taken from the questionnaire that Gelles and Straus had used in their 1975 and 1985 Family Violence Surveys with very different results. Interpreted as Gelles and Straus interpret the data, the survey actually showed that domestic violence was still *decreasing*. The survey had found that 2–3 percent of the respondents had suffered what Gelles and Straus classify as "severe violence."

But the most interesting finding of all, and one entirely overlooked by the press, for it did not harmonize with the notes of alarm in the Harris/ Commonwealth press releases, was the response the poll received to questions 8 through 11, about the most severe forms of violence. Gelles and Straus had estimated that these things happen to fewer than 1 percent of women. According to the survey sample, the percentage of women who had these experiences was virtually *zero*: all respondents answered "no" to all the questions on severe violence.[31] This finding does not, of course, mean that no one was brutally attacked. But it does suggest that severe violence is relatively rare.[32]

So where did the four million figure for physical assault come from? And the twenty million for psychological abuse? Clearly the interpreters of the Harris/Commonwealth poll data were operating with a much wider conception of "abuse" than Gelles and Straus. Looking at the "survey instrument," we find that they had indeed opened the door wide to the alarmist conclusions they disseminated. For some of the answers that Gelles and Straus counted as minor and not indicative of abuse, the Harris/Commonwealth people took seriously. For example, the questionnaire asked "whether in the past 12 months your partner ever: 1) insulted you or swore at you; or 2) stomped out of the room or house or yard." Thirty-four percent of women answered "yes" to these questions, and all were classified as victims of "emotional and verbal abuse." Had men been included, one wonders whether they would not have proved to be equally "abused."

To arrive at the figure of four million for *physical* abuse, the survey used the simple expedient of ignoring the distinction between minor and severe violent acts, counting all acts of violence as acts of abuse. Five percent of the women they spoke to said they had been "pushed, grabbed, shoved, or slapped"; they were all classified as victims of domestic violence and added in to get a projection of four million victims nationwide. No effort was made to find out if the aggression was mutual or whether it was physically harmful or seriously intimidating. If a couple has a fight, and she stomps out of the room (or yard), and he grabs her arm, this would count as a violent physical assault on her.[33]

If the survey's *data* can be trusted and we interpret them in the careful and reasonable way that Gelles and Straus recommend, then we may learn that the worst kinds of abuse may be abating. That is still nothing to celebrate. If up to 3 percent of American women who are married or living with partners are at risk of serious abuse, that would amount to 1.6 million women. If the higher figures Gelles and Straus found are right (3–4 percent), then the number of women at risk is 2.2 million. Both numbers are tragically large and speak of an urgent need for prevention and for shelters and other help for the victims.

But how does this help the gender feminist in her misandrist campaign? She needs to find that a large proportion of men are batterers; a meager 3 or 4 percent will not serve her purpose. As for journalists and the newscasters, their interests too often lie in giving a sensational rather than an accurate picture of gender violence, and they tend to credit the advocacy sources. Better four million or five than one or two. Evidently, *Time* magazine felt six was even better. And all the better, too, if the media's readers and viewers get the impression that the inflated figures refer not to slaps, shoves, or pushes but to brutal, terrifying, life-threatening assaults.

Gender feminists are committed to the doctrine that the vast majority of batterers or rapists are not fringe characters but men whom society regards as normal—sports fans, former fraternity brothers, pillars of the community. For these "normal" men, women are not so much persons as "objects." In the gender feminist view, once a woman is "objectified" and therefore no longer human, battering her is simply the next logical step.

Just how "normal" are men who batter? Are they ordinary husbands? These are legitimate questions, but the road to reasonable answers is all too often blocked by feminist dogmas. By setting aside the feminist roadblocks, we can discern some important truths.

Are the batterers really just your average Joe? If the state of Massachusetts is typical—*the large majority of batterers are criminals.* Andrew Klein, chief probation officer in Quincy Court, Quincy, Massachusetts, studied repeat batterers for the Ford Foundation. In his final report he said, "When Massachusetts computerized its civil restraining order files in 1992, linking them with the state's criminal offender record data base, it found that almost 80 percent of the first 8,500 male subjects of restraining orders had prior criminal records in the state." [34]

Many of the batterers' records were for offenses like drunk driving and drugs, but almost half had prior histories of violence against male and female victims. Klein continues: "In other words, these men were generally violent, *assaulting other males as well as female intimates*. The average number of prior crimes against persons complaints was 4.5" (my emphasis). [35]

The gender feminist believes that the average man is a potential batterer because that is how men are "socialized" in the patriarchy. But ideology aside, there are indications that those who batter are *not* average. Talk of a generalized misogyny may be preventing us from seeing and facing the particular effect on women and men of the large criminal element in our society.

Massachusetts may not be typical. Still, the Massachusetts batterers' profile suggests it is not helpful to think of battery exclusively in terms of misogyny, patriarchy, or gender bias. We need to understand why the number of sociopaths in our society, especially violent male sociopaths, is so high.

My prediction is that Mr. Klein's important findings will be ignored. What use is it to gender warriors like Marilyn French and Gloria Steinem to show that violent *criminals* tend to abuse their wives and girlfriends and other males as well? Their primary concern is to persuade the public that the so-called normal man is a morally defective human being who gets off on hurting women.

There are other important studies that could help shed light on battering and could ultimately help many victims who are ignored because their batterers do not fit the gender feminist stereotype. [36] It turns out that lesbians may be battering each other at the same rate as heterosexuals. Several books and articles document the problem of violence among lesbians. [37] Professor Claire Renzetti, a professor of sociology at St. Joseph's University in Philadelphia, has studied the problem of lesbian violence and summarized the findings in *Violent Betrayal: Partner Abuse in Lesbian Relationships*:

It appears that violence in lesbian relationships occurs at about the same frequency as violence in heterosexual relationships. The abuse may. . . . [range] from verbal threats and insults to stabbings and shootings. Indeed, batterers display a terrifying ingenuity in their selection of abusive tactics, frequently tailoring the abuse to the specific vulnerabilities of their partners.[38]

Once again, it appears that battery may have very little to do with patriarchy or gender bias. Where noncriminals are involved, battery seems to be a pathology of intimacy, as frequent among gays as among straight people.

Battery and rape research is the very stuff of gender feminist advocacy. Researchers who try to pursue their investigations in a nonpolitical way are often subject to attack by the advocates. Murray Straus reports that he and some of his co-workers "became the object of bitter scholarly and personal attacks, including threats and attempts at intimidation."[39] In the late seventies and early eighties his scholarly presentations were sometimes obstructed by booing, shouting, or picketing. When he was being considered for offices in scientific societies, he was labeled an antifeminist.

In the November 1993 issue of *Mirabella,* Richard Gelles and Murray Straus were accused of using "sexist 'reasoning' " and of producing works of "pop 'scholarship.' " The article offers no evidence for these judgments.[40] In 1992 a rumor was circulated that Murray Straus had beaten his wife and sexually harassed his students. Straus fought back as best he could and in one instance was able to elicit a written apology from a domestic violence activist.

Richard Gelles claims that whenever male researchers question exaggerated findings on domestic battery, it is never long before rumors begin circulating that he is himself a batterer. For female skeptics, however, the situation appears to be equally intimidating. When Suzanne K. Steinmetz, a co-investigator in the First National Family Violence Survey, was being considered for promotion, the feminists launched a letter-writing campaign urging that it be denied. She also received calls threatening her and her family, and there was a bomb threat at a conference where she spoke. As long as researchers are thus intimidated, we will probably remain in the dark about the true dimension of a problem that affects the lives of millions of American women.

Another factor limiting the prospects for sound research in this area is the absence of a rigorous system of review. In most fields, when a well-known study is flawed, critics can make a name for themselves by showing up its defects. This process keeps researchers honest. However, in today's environment for feminist research, the higher your figures for abuse, the more likely you'll reap rewards, regardless of your methodology. You'll be mentioned in feminist encyclopedias, dictionaries, "fact sheets," and textbooks. Your research will be widely publicized; Ellen Goodman, Anna Quindlen, and Judy Mann will put you in their columns. Fashion magazines will reproduce your charts and graphs. You may be quoted by Pat Schroeder, Joseph Biden, and surgeon generals from both parties. Senator Kennedy's office will call. You should expect to be invited to give expert testimony before Congress. As for would-be critics, they're in for grief.

The same *Time* magazine story that reported on the nonexistent March of Dimes study also informed readers that "between 22 percent and 35 percent of all visits by females to emergency rooms are for injuries from domestic assaults." This bit of data is one of the most frequently cited statistics in the literature on violence against women. It regularly turns up in news stories on wife abuse. It is in the brochures from domestic violence agencies, and it is on the tip of many politicians' tongues. Where does it come from? The primary source is a 1984 article entitled "Domestic Violence Victims in the Emergency Department," in the *Journal of the American Medical Association*.[41] Going to the study, we find that it was conducted at the Henry Ford Hospital in downtown Detroit. The authors candidly inform us that their sample group was not representative of the American population at large. Of the 492 patients who responded to a questionnaire about domestic violence, they report that 90 percent were from inner-city Detroit and 60 percent were unemployed.[42] We also learn that the 22 percent figure covers *both* women and men. Thirty-eight percent of those complaining of abuse were men.[43]

The authors of the Detroit study took care to point out its limited scope, but the editors at the *Journal of the American Medical Association* who reported their results were not as careful. In a 1990 column called "News Update" we read that "22 percent to 35 percent of women presenting with any complaints are there because of symptoms relating to ongoing abuse." In the footnotes they cite the 1984 Detroit study, a paper by Evan Stark and Anne Flitcraft,[44] and a 1989 study published in the *Annals of Emergency Medicine*.

Stark and Flitcraft are perhaps the two best-known researchers on domestic battery and emergency room admissions. Their figures for emergency room visits caused by domestic battering go as high as 50 percent.[45] But they, too, base their numbers on studies at large urban hospitals. Their figures are higher than those of the Detroit study because their method is to review old medical records and *estimate* how many women were battered—not relying simply on what the woman or the attending clinician may have said. They have developed what they call an "index of suspicion." If a woman was assaulted but the records do not say who hit her, Stark and Flitcraft classify this as a case of "probable" domestic abuse; if she has injuries to her face and torso that are inadequately explained ("I ran into a door"), they classify it as "suggestive" of abuse. They say: "Overall, the nonabusive injuries tend to be to the extremities, whereas the abuse injuries tend to be central (face or torso)." This method, coupled with their exclusive reliance on records from large urban hospitals, leads them to very high numbers on abuse.

Stark and Flitcraft's methodology is innovative and imaginative, and may indeed help practitioners identify more women who are victimized by abuse. Still, the methodology is highly subjective. Stark and Flitcraft's tendency to lapse into gender feminist jargon raises questions about their objectivity. In an article called "Medicine and Patriarchal Violence," they speculate on why women marry: "Economic discrimination against women in capitalist societies—job segregation by sex, marginal employment and lower wages—drives women to marry, apply their undervalued labor time to household drudgery, and to remain dependent on men generally, if not on a specific husband, boyfriend or father."[46]

They worry that women's shelters may be co-opted by a "bourgeois ideology" that diverts women from the need for a "fundamental social revolution."[47] They cite Karl Marx, Franz Fanon, Herbert Marcuse, and Michel Foucault as if they are unquestioned authorities on gender politics and on capitalism. They criticize Friedrich Engels—but only because they say he sounds too much like a "bourgeois moralist."[48] Flitcraft and Stark appear to regard the abuse they claim to have found as the sort of thing one should expect to find in a bourgeois capitalist patriarchy. But it often works the other way, too: you choose a research methodology that will give you the findings you expect.

The *Journal of the American Medical Association* cites a third source for the 22–35 percent statistic, an article called "Education Is Not Enough: A Systems Failure in Protecting Battered Women," from the *Annals of Emergency Medicine*. That article reports on a small study done of the "emergency department records of a medical school serving the inner-city population" of Philadelphia. Like Flitcraft and Stark, by using "guess-timates" and focusing on the segment of the population with highest overall rates of violence, the researchers were able to get very high figures —up to 30 percent.

In examining research on battery, one sees that respected medical

periodicals uncritically indulge the feminists in their inflationary tenden-
cies. It is hard to avoid the impression that the medical journals have
dropped their usual standards when reporting the findings of the battery
studies. It is pretty clear that studies of this poor caliber on some other
subject of medical interest and importance would either not be reported
or be reported with many caveats. To my mind, giving research on "wom-
en's topics" abnormal latitude is patronizingly sexist.

In November of 1992 the Family Violence Prevention Fund did a
survey of all 397 emergency departments in California hospitals. Nurse
managers were asked, "During a typical month, approximately how many
patients have been diagnosed with an injury caused by domestic violence?" The nurses' estimates ranged from two per month for small hospitals to eight per month for the large hospitals. This finding corresponds
to Gelles and Straus's low figure for violence that could require hospital-
ization.

Those who did the fund survey did not accept its results; they concluded instead that the nurses are simply not equipped to deal with the
problem and are vastly understating it. "The low identity rates reported
in this survey might be explained by the marked lack of domestic violence–specific training." One may agree that nurses and doctors do need
that kind of training. On the other hand, the low rates of battery they
found sound plausible; for unlike all the other studies on emergency
rooms and violence, this one actually polled a fair cross section of hospitals.

Because many feminist activists and researchers have so great a stake
in exaggerating the problem and so little compunction in doing so, objective information on battery is very hard to come by. The Super Bowl story
was a bald untruth from the start. The "rule of thumb" story is an example
of revisionist history that feminists happily fell into believing. It reinforces
their perspective on society, and they tell it as a way of winning converts
to their angry creed.

As it is told in the opening essay in one of the most popular textbooks
in women's studies, *Women: A Feminist Perspective,* "The popular expression 'rule of thumb' originated from English common law, which allowed
a husband to beat his wife with a whip or stick no bigger in diameter
than his thumb. The husband's prerogative was incorporated into American law. Several states had statutes that essentially allowed a man to beat
his wife without interference from the courts."[49]

The story is supposed to bring home to students the realization that
they have been born into a system that tolerates violence against women.
Sheila Kuehl, the feminist legal activist who had played a central role in

launching the "Abuse Bowl" hoax, appeared on CNN's "Sonya Live" four months after the incident, holding forth on the supposed history of the rule and acclaiming the New Feminists for finally striking back: "I think we're undoing thousands and thousands of years of human history. You know the phrase 'rule of thumb' that everybody thinks is the standard measure of everything? It was a law in England that said you could beat your wife with a stick as long as it was no thicker . . . than your thumb."[50]

Columnists and journalists writing about domestic violence were quick to pick up on the anecdote.

> The colloquial phrase "rule of thumb" is supposedly derived from the ancient right of a husband to discipline his wife with a rod "no thicker than his thumb." (*Time* magazine, September 5, 1983)

> A husband's right to beat his wife is included in Blackstone's 1768 codification of the common law. Husbands had the right to "physically chastise" an errant wife so long as the stick was no bigger than their thumb—the so-called "rule of thumb." (*Washington Post,* January 3, 1989)

> Violence against women does not have to be the rule of thumb—an idiom from an old English law that said a man could beat his wife if the stick was no thicker than his thumb. (*Atlanta Constitution,* April 22, 1993)

The "rule of thumb," however, turns out to be an excellent example of what may be called a feminist fiction.[51] It is not to be found in William Blackstone's treatise on English common law. On the contrary, British law since the 1700s and our American laws predating the Revolution prohibit wife beating, though there have been periods and places in which the prohibition was only indifferently enforced.

That the phrase did not even originate in legal practice could have been ascertained by any fact-checker who took the trouble to look it up in the Oxford English Dictionary, which notes that the term has been used metaphorically for at least three hundred years to refer to any method of measurement or technique of estimation derived from experience rather than science.

According to Canadian folklorist Philip Hiscock, "The real explanation of 'rule of thumb' is that it derives from wood workers . . . who knew their trade so well they rarely or never fell back on the use of such things as rulers. Instead, they would measure things by, for example, the length of their thumbs." Hiscock adds that the phrase came into metaphorical use by the late seventeenth century.[52] Hiscock could not track the source of the idea that the term derives from a principle governing wife beating, but he believes it is an example of "modern folklore" and compares it to other "back-formed explanations," such as the claim that asparagus comes from "sparrow-grass" or that "ring around the rosy" is about the plague.

We shall see that Hiscock's hunch was correct, but we must begin by exonerating William Blackstone (1723–80), the Englishman who codified centuries of legal customs and practices into the elegant and clearly organized tome known as *Commentaries on the Laws of England*. The *Commentaries*, a classic of legal literature, became the basis for the development of American law. The so-called rule of thumb as a guideline for wife beating does not occur in Blackstone's compendium, although he does refer to an ancient law that permitted physical chastisement and contrasts it with the more enlightened standards of his own day:

> The husband also, by the old law, might give his wife moderate correction. For, as he is to answer for her misbehaviour, the law thought it reasonable to intrust him with this power of restraining her, by domestic chastisement, in the same moderation that a man is allowed to correct his apprentices or children. . . . But this power of correction was confined within reasonable bounds and the husband was prohibited from using any violence to his wife *aliter quam ad virum, ex causa regiminis et castigationis uxoris suae, licite et rationabiliter pertinet* [other than what lawfully and reasonably belongs to the husband for the due government and correction of his wife]. . . . *But with us, in the politer reign of Charles the Second, this power of correction began to be doubted; and a wife may now have security of the peace against her husband.* . . . Yet [among] the lower rank of people . . . the courts of law will still permit a husband to restrain a wife of her liberty in case of any gross misbehaviour [emphasis added].[53]

In America, there have been laws against wife beating since before the Revolution. By 1870, it was illegal in almost every state; but even before then, wife-beaters were arrested and punished for assault and battery.[54] The historian and feminist Elizabeth Pleck observes in a scholarly article entitled "Wife-Battering in Nineteenth-Century America":

> It has often been claimed that wife-beating in nineteenth-century America was legal. . . . Actually, though, several states passed stat-

utes legally prohibiting wife-beating; and at least one statute even predates the American Revolution. The Massachusetts Bay Colony prohibited wife-beating as early as 1655. The edict states: "No man shall strike his wife nor any woman her husband on penalty of such fine not exceeding ten pounds for one offense, or such corporal punishment as the County shall determine."[55]

She points out that punishments for wife-beaters could be severe: according to an 1882 Maryland statute, the culprit could receive forty lashes at the whipping post; in Delaware, the number was thirty. In New Mexico, fines ranging from $255 to $1,000 were levied, or sentences of one to five years in prison imposed.[56] For most of our history, in fact, wife beating has been considered a sin comparable to thievery or adultery. Religious groups—especially Protestant groups such as Quakers, Methodists, and Baptists—punished, shunned, and excommunicated wife-beaters. Husbands, brothers, and neighbors often took vengeance against the batterer. Vigilante parties sometimes abducted wife-beaters and whipped them.[57]

Just how did the false account originate, and how did it achieve authority and currency? As with many myths, there is a small core of fact surrounded by an accretion of error. In the course of rendering rulings on cases before them, two Southern judges had alluded to an "ancient law" according to which a man could beat his wife as long as the implement was not wider than his thumb. The judges, one from North Carolina and one from Mississippi, did not accept the authority of the "ancient law." The North Carolina judge referred to it as "barbarism," and both judges found the husband in the case in question guilty of wife abuse.[58] Nevertheless, their rulings seemed to tolerate the notion that men had a measure of latitude in physically chastising their wives. Fortunately, as Pleck takes pains to remind us, they were not representative of judicial opinion in the rest of the country.[59]

In 1976, Del Martin, a coordinator of the NOW Task Force on Battered Women, came across a reference to the two judges and their remarks.[60] Neither judge had used the phrase "rule of thumb," but a thumb had been mentioned, and Ms. Martin took note of it:

Our law, based upon the old English common-law doctrines, explicitly permitted wife-beating for correctional purposes. However, certain restrictions did exist. . . . For instance, the common-law doctrine had been modified to allow the husband "the right to whip his wife, provided that he used a switch no bigger than his thumb"—a rule of thumb, so to speak.[61]

Ms. Martin had not claimed that the term "rule of thumb" originated from common law. Before long, however, the "ancient law" alluded to by two obscure Southern judges was being treated as an unchallenged principle of both British and American law, and journalists and academics alike were bandying the notion about. Feminist Terry Davidson, in an article entitled "Wife Beating: A Recurring Phenomenon Throughout History," claims that "one of the reasons nineteenth century British wives were dealt with so harshly by their husbands and by their legal system was the 'rule of thumb' "[62] and castigates Blackstone himself. "Blackstone saw nothing unreasonable about the wife-beating law. In fact, he believed it to be quite moderate."[63]

These interpretive errors were given added authority by a group of scholars and lawyers who, in 1982, prepared a report on wife abuse for the United States Commission on Civil Rights, *Under the Rule of Thumb: Battered Women and the Administration of Justice—A Report of the United States Commission on Civil Rights.* On the second page, they note: "American law is built upon the British common law that condoned wife beating and even prescribed the weapon to be used. This 'rule of thumb' stipulated that a man could only beat his wife with a 'rod not thicker than his thumb.' "[64] It went on to speak of Blackstone as the jurist who "greatly influenced the making of the law in the American colonies [and who] commented on the 'rule of thumb,' " justifying the rule by noting that "the law thought it reasonable to intrust [the husband] with this power of . . . chastisement, in the same moderation that a man is allowed to correct his apprentices or children."[65]

The publication of the report established the feminist fable about the origins of the term in popular lore, and the misogyny of Blackstone and "our law" as "fact." Misstatements about the "rule of thumb" still appear in the popular press.

The same 1993 *Time* magazine article that popularized the nonexistent March of Dimes study on domestic violence and birth defects and reported that "between 22 percent and 35 percent of all visits by females to emergency rooms are for injuries from domestic assaults" also cited New York University law professor Holly Maguigan: "We talk about the notion of the rule of thumb, forgetting that it had to do with the restriction on a man's right to use a weapon against his wife: he couldn't use a rod that was larger than his thumb."[66] Professor Maguigan's law students would do well to check their Blackstone.

• • •

We react to batterers with revulsion—first, because of what they do, which is ugly and cruel; and second, because of what they are, which is cowardly and often sadistic. As those working in the social services and the shelters well know, helping battered women is as difficult as it is exigent. Resources are limited, and strategies for help are often controversial. On a wider canvas, we need good legislation and good public policy as well as funds earmarked toward the problem. But sound public policy on battery cannot be made without credible and trustworthy information. In promulgating sensational untruths, the gender feminists systematically diminish public trust. Experts concerned about battery and devoted to alleviating it are worried. As Michael Lindsey said to Ken Ringle, "When people make crazy statements like this, the credibility of the whole cause can go right out the window."

Chapter 10

Rape Research

એ

I apologize to the reader for the clinical tone of this chapter. As a crime against the person, rape is uniquely horrible in its long-term effects. The anguish it brings is often followed by an abiding sense of fear and shame. Discussions of the data on rape inevitably seem callous. How can one quantify the sense of deep violation behind the statistics? Terms like *incidence* and *prevalence* are statistical jargon; once we use them, we necessarily abstract ourselves from the misery. Yet, it remains clear that to arrive at intelligent policies and strategies to decrease the occurrence of rape, we have no alternative but to gather and analyze data, and to do so does not make us callous. Truth is no enemy to compassion, and falsehood is no friend.

Some feminists routinely refer to American society as a "rape culture." Yet estimates on the prevalence of rape vary wildly. According to the FBI *Uniform Crime Report,* there were 102,560 reported rapes or attempted rapes in 1990.[1] The Bureau of Justice Statistics estimates that 130,000 women were victims of rape in 1990.[2] A Harris poll sets the figure at

380,000 rapes or sexual assaults for 1993.[3] According to a study by the National Victims Center, there were 683,000 completed forcible rapes in 1990.[4] The Justice Department says that 8 percent of all American women will be victims of rape or attempted rape in their lifetime. The radical feminist legal scholar Catharine MacKinnon, however, claims that "by conservative definition [rape] happens to almost half of all women at least once in their lives."[5]

Who is right? Feminist activists and others have plausibly argued that the relatively low figures of the FBI and the Bureau of Justice Statistics are not trustworthy. The FBI survey is based on the number of cases reported to the police, but rape is among the most underreported of crimes. The Bureau of Justice Statistics National Crime Survey is based on interviews with 100,000 randomly selected women. It, too, is said to be flawed because the women were never directly questioned about rape. Rape was discussed only if the woman happened to bring it up in the course of answering more general questions about criminal victimization. The Justice Department has changed its method of questioning to meet this criticism, so we will know in a year or two whether this has a significant effect on its numbers. Clearly, independent studies on the incidence and prevalence of rape are badly needed. Unfortunately, research groups investigating in this area have no common definition of rape, and the results so far have led to confusion and acrimony.

Of the rape studies by nongovernment groups, the two most frequently cited are the 1985 Ms. magazine report by Mary Koss and the 1992 National Women's Study by Dr. Dean Kilpatrick of the Crime Victims Research and Treatment Center at the Medical School of South Carolina. In 1982, Mary Koss, then a professor of psychology at Kent State University in Ohio, published an article on rape in which she expressed the orthodox gender feminist view that "rape represents an extreme behavior but *one that is on a continuum with normal male behavior within the culture*" (my emphasis).[6] Some well-placed feminist activists were impressed by her. As Koss tells it, she received a phone call out of the blue inviting her to lunch with Gloria Steinem.[7] For Koss, the lunch was a turning point. Ms. magazine had decided to do a national rape survey on college campuses, and Koss was chosen to direct it. Koss's findings would become the most frequently cited research on women's victimization, not so much by established scholars in the field of rape research as by journalists, politicians, and activists.

Koss and her associates interviewed slightly more than three thousand college women, randomly selected nationwide.[8] The young women were asked ten questions about sexual violation. These were followed by several questions about the precise nature of the violation. Had they been drinking? What were their emotions during and after the event? What forms of resistance did they use? How would they label the event? Koss counted anyone who answered affirmatively to any of the last three questions as having been raped:

8. Have you had sexual intercourse when you didn't want to because a man gave you alcohol or drugs?
9. Have you had sexual intercourse when you didn't want to because a man threatened or used some degree of physical force (twisting your arm, holding you down, etc.) to make you?
10. Have you had sexual acts (anal or oral intercourse or penetration by objects other than the penis) when you didn't want to because a man threatened or used some degree of physical force (twisting your arm, holding you down, etc.) to make you?

Koss and her colleagues concluded that 15.4 percent of respondents had been raped, and that 12.1 percent had been victims of attempted rape.[9] Thus, a total of 27.5 percent of the respondents were determined to have been victims of rape or attempted rape because they gave answers that fit Koss's criteria for rape (penetration by penis, finger, or other object under coercive influence such as physical force, alcohol, or threats). However, that is not how the so-called rape victims saw it. Only about a quarter of the women Koss calls rape victims labeled what happened to them as rape. According to Koss, the answers to the follow-up questions revealed that "only 27 percent" of the women she counted as having been raped labeled themselves as rape victims.[10] Of the remainder, 49 percent said it was "miscommunication," 14 percent said it was a "crime but not rape," and 11 percent said they "don't feel victimized."[11]

In line with her view of rape as existing on a continuum of male sexual aggression, Koss also asked: "Have you given in to sex play (fondling, kissing, or petting, but not intercourse) when you didn't want to because you were overwhelmed by a man's continual arguments and pressure?" To this question, 53.7 percent responded affirmatively, and they were counted as having been sexually victimized.

The Koss study, released in 1988, became known as the Ms. Report. Here is how the Ms. Foundation characterizes the results: "The Ms. project—the largest scientific investigation ever undertaken on the subject—revealed some disquieting statistics, including this astonishing fact: one in four female respondents had an experience that met the legal definition of rape or attempted rape."[12]

"One in four" has since become the official figure on women's rape victimization cited in women's studies departments, rape crisis centers, women's magazines, and on protest buttons and posters. Susan Faludi defended it in a *Newsweek* story on sexual correctness.[13] Naomi Wolf refers to it in *The Beauty Myth,* calculating that acquaintance rape is "more common than lefthandedness, alcoholism, and heart attacks."[14] "One in four" is chanted in "Take Back the Night" processions, and it is the number given in the date rape brochures handed out at freshman orientation at colleges and universities around the country.[15] Politicians, from Senator Joseph Biden of Delaware, a Democrat, to Republican Congressman Jim Ramstad of Minnesota, cite it regularly, and it is the primary reason for the Title IV, "Safe Campuses for Women" provision of the Violence Against Women Act of 1993, which provides twenty million dollars to combat rape on college campuses.[16]

When Neil Gilbert, a professor at Berkeley's School of Social Welfare, first read the "one in four" figure in the school newspaper, he was convinced it could not be accurate. The results did not tally with the findings of almost all previous research on rape. When he read the study he was able to see where the high figures came from and why Koss's approach was unsound.

He noticed, for example, that Koss and her colleagues counted as victims of rape any respondent who answered "yes" to the question "Have you had sexual intercourse when you didn't want to because a man gave you alcohol or drugs?" That opened the door wide to regarding as a rape victim anyone who regretted her liaison of the previous night. If your date mixes a pitcher of margaritas and encourages you to drink with him and you accept a drink, have you been "administered" an intoxicant, and has your judgment been impaired? Certainly, if you pass out and are molested, one would call it rape. But if you drink and, while intoxicated, engage in sex that you later come to regret, have you been raped? Koss does not address these questions specifically, she merely counts your date as a rapist and you as a rape statistic if you drank with your date and regret having had sex with him. As Gilbert points out, the question, as Koss posed it, is far too ambiguous:

> What does having sex "because" a man gives you drugs or alcohol signify? A positive response does not indicate whether duress, intoxication, force, or the threat of force were present; whether the woman's judgment or control were substantially impaired; or whether the man purposefully got the woman drunk in order to prevent her resistance to sexual advances. . . . While the item could have been

clearly worded to denote "intentional incapacitation of the victim," as the question stands it would require a mind reader to detect whether any affirmative response corresponds to this legal definition of rape.[17]

Koss, however, insisted that her criteria conformed with the legal definitions of rape used in some states, and she cited in particular the statute on rape of her own state, Ohio: "No person shall engage in sexual conduct with another person . . . when . . . for the purpose of preventing resistance the offender substantially impairs the other person's judgment or control by administering any drug or intoxicant to the other person" (Ohio revised code 1980, 2907.01A, 2907.02).[18]

Two reporters from the *Blade*—a small, progressive Toledo, Ohio, newspaper that has won awards for the excellence of its investigative articles—were also not convinced that the "one in four" figure was accurate. They took a close look at Koss's study and at several others that were being cited to support the alarming tidings of widespread sexual abuse on college campuses. In a special three-part series on rape called "The Making of an Epidemic," published in October 1992, the reporters, Nara Shoenberg and Sam Roe, revealed that Koss was quoting the Ohio statute in a very misleading way: she had stopped short of mentioning the qualifying clause of the statute, which specifically *excludes* "the situation where a person plies his intended partner with drink or drugs in hopes that lowered inhibition might lead to a liaison."[19] Koss now concedes that question eight was badly worded. Indeed, she told the *Blade* reporters, "At the time I viewed the question as legal; I now concede that it's ambiguous."[20] As Koss herself told the *Blade,* once you remove the positive responses to the alcohol question, the finding that one in seven college women is a victim of rape drops to one in nine.[21] But, as we shall see, this figure too is unacceptably high.

For Gilbert, the most serious indication that something was basically awry in the *Ms.*/Koss study was that the majority of women she classified as having been raped *did not believe they had been raped*. Of those Koss counts as having been raped, only 27 percent thought they had been; 73 percent did not say that what happened to them was rape. In effect, Koss and her followers present us with a picture of confused young women overwhelmed by threatening males who force their attentions on them during the course of a date but are unable or unwilling to classify their experience as rape. Does that picture fit the average female undergraduate? For that matter, does it plausibly apply to the larger community? As

the journalist Cathy Young observes, "Women have sex after initial reluctance for a number of reasons . . . fear of being beaten up by their dates
is rarely reported as one of them."[22]

Katie Roiphe, a graduate student in English at Princeton and author of
The Morning After: Sex, Fear, and Feminism on Campus, argues along similar lines when she claims that Koss had no right to reject the judgment of
the college women who didn't think they were raped. But Katha Pollitt of
The Nation defends Koss, pointing out that in many cases people are
wronged without knowing it. Thus we do not say that "victims of other
injustices—fraud, malpractice, job discrimination—have suffered no
wrong as long as they are unaware of the law."[23]

Pollitt's analogy is faulty, however. If Jane has ugly financial dealings
with Tom and an expert explains to Jane that Tom has defrauded her,
then Jane usually thanks the expert for having enlightened her about the
legal facts. To make her case, Pollitt would have to show that the rape
victims who were unaware that they were raped would accept Koss's
judgment that they really were. But that has not been shown; Koss did
not enlighten the women she counts as rape victims, and they did not say
"now that you explain it, we can see we were."

Koss and Pollitt make a technical (and in fact dubious) legal point:
women are ignorant about what counts as rape. Roiphe makes a straightforward human point: the women were there, and they know best how
to judge what happened to them. Since when do feminists consider "law"
to override women's experience?

Koss also found that 42 percent of those she counted as rape victims
went on to have sex with their attackers on a later occasion. For victims
of attempted rape, the figure for subsequent sex with reported assailants
was 35 percent. Koss is quick to point out that "it is not known if [the
subsequent sex] was forced or voluntary" and that most of the relationships "did eventually break up subsequent to the victimization."[24] But of
course, *most* college relationships break up eventually for one reason or
another. Yet, instead of taking these young women at their word, Koss
casts about for explanations of why so many "raped" women would return
to their assailants, implying that they may have been coerced. She ends
by treating her subjects' rejection of her findings as evidence that they
were confused and sexually naive. There is a more respectful explanation.
Since most of those Koss counts as rape victims did not regard themselves
as having been raped, why not take this fact and the fact that so many
went back to their partners as reasonable indications that they had not
been raped to begin with?

The Toledo reporters calculated that if you eliminate the affirmative responses to the alcohol or drugs question, and also subtract from Koss's results the women who did not think they were raped, her one in four figure for rape and attempted rape "drops to between one in twenty-two and one in thirty-three." [25]

The other frequently cited nongovernment rape study, the National Women's Study, was conducted by Dean Kilpatrick. From an interview sample of 4,008 women, the study projected that there were 683,000 rapes in 1990. As to prevalence, it concluded that "in America, one out of every eight adult women, or at least 12.1 million American women, has been the victim of forcible rape sometime in her lifetime." [26]

Unlike the Koss report, which tallied rape attempts as well as rapes, the Kilpatrick study focused exclusively on rape. Interviews were conducted by phone, by female interviewers. A woman who agreed to become part of the study heard the following from the interviewer: "Women do not always report such experiences to police or discuss them with family or friends. The person making the advances isn't always a stranger, but can be a friend, boyfriend, or even a family member. Such experiences can occur anytime in a woman's life—even as a child." [27] Pointing out that she wants to hear about any such experiences "regardless of how long ago it happened or who made the advances," the interviewer proceeds to ask four questions:

1. Has a man or boy ever made you have sex by using force or threatening to harm you or someone close to you? Just so there is no mistake, by sex we mean putting a penis in your vagina.
2. Has anyone ever made you have oral sex by force or threat of harm? Just so there is no mistake, by oral sex we mean that a man or boy put his penis in your mouth or somebody penetrated your vagina or anus with his mouth or tongue.
3. Has anyone ever made you have anal sex by force or threat of harm?
4. Has anyone ever put fingers or objects in your vagina or anus against your will by using force or threat?

Any woman who answered yes to any one of the four questions was classified as a victim of rape.

This seems to be a fairly straightforward and well-designed survey that provides a window into the private horror that many women, especially very young women, experience. One of the more disturbing findings of the survey was that 61 percent of the victims said they were seventeen or younger when the rape occurred.

There is, however, one flaw that affects the significance of Kilpatrick's findings. An affirmative answer to any one of the first three questions does reasonably put one in the category of rape victim. The fourth is problematic, for it includes cases in which a boy penetrated a girl with his finger, against her will, in a heavy petting situation. Certainly the boy behaved badly. But is he a rapist? Probably neither he nor his date would say so. Yet, the survey classifies him as a rapist and her as a rape victim.

I called Dr. Kilpatrick and asked him about the fourth question. "Well," he said, "if a woman is forcibly penetrated by an object such as a broomstick, we would call that rape."

"So would I," I said. "But isn't there a big difference between being violated by a broomstick and being violated by a finger?" Dr. Kilpatrick acknowledged this: "We should have split out fingers versus objects," he said. Still, he assured me that the question did not significantly affect the outcome. But I wondered. The study had found an epidemic of rape among teenagers—just the age group most likely to get into situations like the one I have described.

The more serious worry is that Kilpatrick's findings, and many other findings on rape, vary wildly unless the respondents are explicitly asked whether they have been raped. In 1993, Louis Harris and Associates did a telephone survey and came up with quite different results. Harris was commissioned by the Commonwealth Fund to do a study of women's health. As we shall see, their high figures on women's depression and psychological abuse by men caused a stir.[28] But their finding on rape went altogether unnoticed. Among the questions asked of its random sample population of 2,500 women was, "In the last five years, have you been a victim of a rape or sexual assault?" Two percent of the respondents said yes; 98 percent said no. Since attempted rape counts as sexual assault, the combined figures for rape and attempted rape would be 1.9 million over five years or 380,000 for a single year. Since there are approximately twice as many attempted rapes as completed rapes, the Commonwealth/Harris figure for completed rapes would come to approximately 190,000. That is dramatically lower than Kilpatrick's finding of 683,000 *completed forcible rapes*.

The Harris interviewer also asked a question about acquaintance and marital rape that is worded very much like Kilpatrick's and Koss's: "In the past year, did your partner ever try to, or force you to, have sexual relations by using physical force, such as holding you down, or hitting you, or threatening to hit you, or not?"[29] Not a single respondent of the Harris poll's sample answered yes.

How to explain the discrepancy? True, women are often extremely reluctant to talk about sexual violence that they have experienced. But the Harris pollsters had asked a lot of other awkward personal questions to which the women responded with candor: 6 percent said they had considered suicide, 5 percent admitted to using hard drugs, 10 percent said they had been sexually abused when they were growing up. I don't have the answer, though it seems obvious to me that such wide variances should make us appreciate the difficulty of getting reliable figures on the risk of rape from the research. That the real risk should be known is obvious. The *Blade* reporters interviewed students on their fears and found them anxious and bewildered. "It makes a big difference if it's one in three or one in fifty," said April Groff of the University of Michigan, who says she is "very scared." "I'd have to say, honestly, I'd think about rape a lot less if I knew the number was one in fifty." [30]

When the *Blade* reporters asked Kilpatrick why he had not asked women whether they had been raped, he told them there had been no time in the thirty-five-minute interview. "That was probably something that ended up on the cutting-room floor." [31] But Kilpatrick's exclusion of such a question resulted in very much higher figures. When pressed about why he omitted it from a study for which he had received a million-dollar federal grant, he replied, "If people think that is a key question, let them get their own grant and do their own study." [32]

Kilpatrick had done an earlier study in which respondents were explicitly asked whether they had been raped. That study showed a relatively low prevalence of 5 percent—one in twenty—and it got very little publicity. [33] Kilpatrick subsequently abandoned his former methodology in favor of the *Ms.*/Koss method, which allows the surveyor to decide whether a rape occurred. Like Koss, he used an expanded definition of rape (both include penetration by a finger). Kilpatrick's new approach yielded him high numbers (one in eight), and citations in major newspapers around the country. His graphs were reproduced in *Time* magazine under the heading, "Unsettling Report on an Epidemic of Rape." [34] Now he shares with Koss the honor of being a principal expert cited by media, politicians, and activists.

There are many researchers who study rape victimization, but their relatively low figures generate no headlines. The reporters from the *Blade* interviewed several scholars whose findings on rape were not sensational but whose research methods were sound and were not based on controversial definitions. Eugene Kanin, a retired professor of sociology from Purdue University and a pioneer in the field of acquaintance rape, is upset by the intrusion of politics into the field of inquiry: "This is highly convoluted activism rather than social science research." [35] Professor Margaret Gordon of the University of Washington did a study in 1981 that came up with relatively low figures for rape (one in fifty). She tells of the negative reaction to her findings: "There was some pressure—at least I felt pressure—to have rape be as prevalent as possible. . . . I'm a pretty strong feminist, but one of the things I was fighting was that the really avid feminists were trying to get me to say that things were worse than they really are."[36] Dr. Linda George of Duke University also found relatively low rates of rape (one in seventeen), even though she asked questions very close to Kilpatrick's. She told the *Blade* she is concerned that many of her colleagues treat the high numbers as if they are "cast in stone."[37] Dr. Naomi Breslau, director of research in the psychiatry department at the Henry Ford Health Science Center in Detroit, who also found low numbers, feels that it is important to challenge the popular view that higher numbers are necessarily more accurate. Dr. Breslau sees the need for a new and more objective program of research: "It's really an open question. . . . We really don't know a whole lot about it."[38]

An intrepid few in the academy have publicly criticized those who have proclaimed a "rape crisis" for irresponsibly exaggerating the problem and causing needless anxiety. Camille Paglia claims that they have been especially hysterical about date rape: "Date rape has swelled into a catastrophic cosmic event, like an asteroid threatening the earth in a fifties science-fiction film."[39] She bluntly rejects the contention that " 'No' always means no. . . .'No' has always been, and always will be, part of the dangerous, alluring courtship ritual of sex and seduction, observable even in the animal kingdom."[40]

Paglia's dismissal of date rape hype infuriates campus feminists, for whom the rape crisis is very real. On most campuses, date-rape groups hold meetings, marches, rallies. Victims are "survivors," and their friends are "co-survivors" who also suffer and need counseling.[41] At some rape awareness meetings, women who have not yet been date raped are referred to as "potential survivors." Their male classmates are "potential rapists."[42]

Has date rape in fact reached critical proportions on the college campus? Having heard about an outbreak of rape at Columbia University, Peter Hellman of *New York* magazine decided to do a story about it.[43] To his surprise, he found that campus police logs showed no evidence of it whatsoever. Only two rapes were reported to the Columbia campus police in 1990, and in both cases, charges were dropped for lack of evidence. Hellman checked the figures at other campuses and found that in 1990 fewer than one thousand rapes were reported to campus security on college campuses *in the entire country*.[44] That works out to fewer than one-half of one rape per campus. Yet despite the existence of a rape crisis center at St. Luke's–Roosevelt Hospital two blocks from Columbia University, campus feminists pressured the administration into installing an expensive rape crisis center inside the university. Peter Hellman describes a typical night at the center in February 1992: "On a recent Saturday night, a shift of three peer counselors sat in the Rape Crisis Center—one a backup to the other two. . . . Nobody called; nobody came. As if in a firehouse, the three women sat alertly and waited for disaster to strike. It was easy to forget these were the fading hours of the eve of Valentine's Day."[45]

In *The Morning After,* Katie Roiphe describes the elaborate measures taken to prevent sexual assaults at Princeton. Blue lights have been installed around the campus, freshman women are issued whistles at orientation. There are marches, rape counseling sessions, emergency telephones. But as Roiphe tells it, Princeton is a very safe town, and whenever she walked across a deserted golf course to get to classes, she was more afraid of the wild geese than of a rapist. Roiphe reports that between 1982 and 1993 only two rapes were reported to the campus police. And, when it comes to violent attacks in general, male students are actually more likely to be the victims. Roiphe sees the campus rape crisis movement as a phenomenon of privilege: these young women have had it all, and when they find out that the world can be dangerous and unpredictable, they are outraged:

> Many of these girls [in rape marches] came to Princeton from Milton and Exeter. Many of their lives have been full of summers in Nantucket and horseback-riding lessons. These are women who have grown up expecting fairness, consideration, and politeness.[46]

The *Blade* story on rape is unique in contemporary journalism because the authors dared to question the popular feminist statistics on this terribly sensitive problem. But to my mind, the important and intriguing story they tell about unreliable advocacy statistics is overshadowed by the even more important discoveries they made about the morally indefensible way that public funds for combatting rape are being allocated. Schoenberg and Roe studied Toledo neighborhoods and calculated that women in the poorer areas were nearly thirty times more likely to be raped than those in the wealthy areas. They also found that campus rape rates were thirty times lower than the rape rates for the general population of eighteen- to twenty-four-year-olds in Toledo. The attention and the money are disproportionately going to those least at risk. According to the *Blade* reporters:

Across the nation, public universities are spending millions of dollars a year on rapidly growing programs to combat rape. Videos,
self-defense classes, and full-time rape educators are commonplace.
. . . But the new spending comes at a time when community rape
programs—also dependent on tax dollars—are desperately scram-
bling for money to help populations at much higher risk than college students.[47]

One obvious reason for this inequity is that feminist advocates come
largely from the middle class and so exert great pressure to protect their
own. To render their claims plausible, they dramatize themselves as victims—survivors or "potential survivors." Another device is to expand the
definition of rape (as Koss and Kilpatrick do). Dr. Andrea Parrot, chair of
the Cornell University Coalition Advocating Rape Education and author
of *Sexual Assault on Campus,* begins her date rape prevention manual with
the words, "Any sexual intercourse without mutual desire is a form of
rape. Anyone who is psychologically or physically pressured into sexual
contact on any occasion is *as much a victim* as the person who is attacked
in the streets" (my emphasis).[48] By such a definition, privileged young
women in our nation's colleges gain moral parity with the real victims in
the community at large. Parrot's novel conception of rape also justifies
the salaries being paid to all the new personnel in the burgeoning college
date rape industry. After all, it is much more pleasant to deal with rape
from an office in Princeton than on the streets of downtown Trenton.
    Another reason that college women are getting a lion's share of public
resources for combatting rape is that collegiate money, though originally
public, is allocated by college officials. As the *Blade* points out:

Public universities have multi-million dollar budgets heavily subsi-
dized by state dollars. School officials decide how the money is
spent, and are eager to address the high-profile issues like rape on
campus. In contrast, rape crisis centers—nonprofit agencies that
provide free services in the community—must appeal directly to
federal and state governments for money.[49]

Schoenberg and Roe describe typical cases of women in communities
around the country—in Madison, Wisconsin, in Columbus, Ohio, in
Austin, Texas, and in Newport, Kentucky—who have been raped and
have to wait months for rape counseling services. There were three rapes
reported to police at the University of Minnesota in 1992; in New York
City there were close to three thousand. Minnesota students have a

twenty-four-hour rape crisis hot line of their own. In New York City, the "hot line" leads to detectives in the sex crimes unit. The *Blade* reports that the sponsors of the Violence Against Women Act of 1993 reflect the same bizarre priorities: "If Senator Biden has his way, campuses will get at least twenty million more dollars for rape education and prevention." In the meantime, Gail Rawlings of the Pennsylvania Coalition Against Rape complains that the bill guarantees nothing for basic services, counseling, and support groups for women in the larger community: "It's ridiculous. This bill is supposed to encourage prosecution of violence against women, [and] one of the main keys is to have support for the victim. . . . I just don't understand why [the money] isn't there."[50]

Because rape is the most underreported of crimes, the campus activists tell us we cannot learn the true dimensions of campus rape from police logs or hospital reports. But as an explanation of why there are so few known and proven incidents of rape on campus, that won't do. Underreporting of sexual crimes is not confined to the campus, and wherever there is a high level of *reported* rape—say in poor urban communities where the funds for combatting rape are almost nonexistent—the level of underreported rape will be greater still. No matter how you look at it, women on campus do not face anywhere near the same risk of rape as women elsewhere. The fact that college women continue to get a disproportionate and ever-growing share of the very scarce public resources allocated for rape prevention and for aid to rape victims underscores how disproportionately powerful and *self-preoccupied* the campus feminists are despite all their vaunted concern for "women" writ large.

Once again we see what a long way the New Feminism has come from Seneca Falls. The privileged and protected women who launched the women's movement, as Elizabeth Cady Stanton and Susan B. Anthony took pains to point out, did not regard *themselves* as the primary victims of gender inequity: "They had souls large enough to feel the wrongs of others without being scarified in their own flesh." They did not act as if they had "in their own experience endured the coarser forms of tyranny resulting from unjust laws, or association with immoral and unscrupulous men."[51] Ms. Stanton and Ms. Anthony concentrated their efforts on the Hester Vaughns and the other defenseless women whose need for gender equity was urgent and unquestionable.

Much of the unattractive self-preoccupation and victimology that we find on today's campuses have been irresponsibly engendered by the inflated and scarifying "one in four" statistic on campus rape. In some cases the campaign of alarmism arouses exasperation of another kind. In an article in the *New York Times Magazine,* Katie Roiphe questioned Koss's figures: "If 25 percent of my women friends were really being raped, wouldn't I know it?"[52] She also questioned the feminist perspective on male/female relations: "These feminists are endorsing their own utopian vision of sexual relations: sex without struggle, sex without power, sex without persuasion, sex without pursuit. If verbal coercion constitutes rape, then the word rape itself expands to include any kind of sex a woman experiences as negative."[53]

The publication of Ms. Roiphe's piece incensed the campus feminists. "The *New York Times* should be shot," railed Laurie Fink, a professor at Kenyon College.[54] "Don't invite [Katie Roiphe] to your school if you can prevent it," counseled Pauline Bart of the University of Illinois.[55] Gail Dines, a women's studies professor and date rape activist from Wheelock College, called Roiphe a traitor who has sold out to the "white male patriarchy."[56]

Other critics, such as Camille Paglia and Berkeley professor of social welfare Neil Gilbert, have been targeted for demonstrations, boycotts, and denunciations. Gilbert began to publish his critical analyses of the *Ms./ Koss* study in 1990.[57] Many feminist activists did not look kindly on Gilbert's challenge to their "one in four" figure. A date rape clearinghouse in San Francisco devotes itself to "refuting" Gilbert; it sends out masses of literature attacking him. It advertises at feminist conferences with green and orange fliers bearing the headline STOP IT, BITCH! The words are not Gilbert's, but the tactic is an effective way of drawing attention to his work. At one demonstration against Gilbert on the Berkeley campus, students chanted, "Cut it out or cut it off," and carried signs that read, KILL NEIL GILBERT![58] Sheila Kuehl, the director of the California Women's Law Center, confided to readers of the *Los Angeles Daily Journal,* "I found myself wishing that Gilbert, himself, might be raped and . . . be told, to his face, it had never happened."[59]

The findings being cited in support of an "epidemic" of campus rape are the products of advocacy research. Those promoting the research are bitterly opposed to seeing it exposed as inaccurate. On the other hand, rape is indeed the most underreported of crimes. We need the truth for policy to be fair and effective. If the feminist advocates would stop muddying the waters we could probably get at it.

High rape numbers serve the gender feminists by promoting the belief that American culture is sexist and misogynist. But the common assumption that rape is a manifestation of misogyny is open to question. Assume for the sake of argument that Koss and Kilpatrick are right and that the lower numbers of the FBI, the Justice Department, the Harris poll, of Kilpatrick's earlier study, and the many other studies mentioned earlier are wrong. Would it then follow that we are a "patriarchal rape culture"? Not necessarily. American society is exceptionally violent, and the violence is not specifically patriarchal or misogynist. According to *International Crime Rates,* a report from the United States Department of Justice, "Crimes of violence (homicide, rape, and robbery) are four to nine times more frequent in the United States than they are in Europe. The U.S. crime rate for rape was . . . roughly seven times higher than the average for Europe."[60] The incidence of rape is many times lower in such countries as Greece, Portugal, or Japan—countries far more overtly patriarchal than ours.

It might be said that places like Greece, Portugal, and Japan do not keep good records on rape. But the fact is that Greece, Portugal, and Japan are significantly less violent than we are. I have walked through the equivalent of Central Park in Kyoto at night. I felt safe, and I was safe, not because Japan is a feminist society (it is the opposite), but because crime is relatively rare. The international studies on violence suggest that patriarchy is not the primary cause of rape but that rape, along with other crimes against the person, is caused by whatever it is that makes our society among the most violent of the so-called advanced nations.

But the suggestion that criminal violence, not patriarchal misogyny, is the primary reason for our relatively high rate of rape is unwelcome to gender feminists like Susan Faludi, who insist, in the face of all evidence to the contrary, that "the highest rate of rapes appears in cultures that have the highest degree of gender inequality, where sexes are segregated at work, that have patriarchal religions, that celebrate all-male sporting and hunting rituals, i.e., a society such as us."[61]

In the spring of 1992, Peter Jennings hosted an ABC special on the subject of rape. Catharine MacKinnon, Susan Faludi, Naomi Wolf, and Mary Koss were among the panelists, along with John Leo of *U.S. News & World Report.* When MacKinnon trotted out the claim that 25 percent of women are victims of rape, Mr. Leo replied, "I don't believe those statistics. . . . That's totally false."[62] MacKinnon countered, "That means you don't believe women. It's not cooked, it's interviews with women by people who believed them when they said it. That's the methodology."[63] The accusation that Leo did not believe "women" silenced him, as it was meant to. But as we have seen, believing what women actually say is precisely *not* the methodology by which some feminist advocates get their incendiary statistics.

MacKinnon's next volley was certainly on target. She pointed out that the statistics she had cited "are starting to become nationally accepted by the government." *That* claim could not be gainsaid, and MacKinnon may be pardoned for crowing about it. The government, like the media, is accepting the gender feminist claims and is introducing legislation whose "whole purpose . . . is to raise the consciousness of the American public."[64] The words are Joseph Biden's, and the bill to which he referred— the Violence Against Women Act—introduces the principle that violence against women is much like racial violence, calling for civil as well as criminal remedies. Like a lynching or a cross burning, an act of violence by a man against a woman would be prosecuted as a crime of gender bias, under title 3 of the bill: "State and Federal criminal laws do not adequately protect against the bias element of gender-motivated crimes, which separates these crimes from acts of random violence, nor do those laws adequately provide victims of gender-motivated crimes the opportunity to vindicate their interests."[65] Whereas ordinary violence is "random," "violence against women" may be discriminatory in the literal sense in which we speak of a bigot as discriminating against someone because of race or religion.

Mary Koss and Sarah Buel were invited to give testimony on the subject of violence against women before the House Judiciary Committee. Dean Kilpatrick's findings were cited. Neil Gilbert was not there; nor were any of the other scholars interviewed by the Toledo *Blade*.

The litigation that the bill invites gladdens the hearts of gender feminists. If we consider that a boy getting fresh in the backseat of a car may be prosecuted both as an attempted rapist and as a gender bigot who has violated his date's civil rights, we can see why the title 3 provision is being hailed by radical feminists like Catharine MacKinnon and Andrea Dworkin. Dworkin, who was surprised and delighted at the support the bill was getting, candidly observed that the senators "don't understand the meaning of the legislation they pass."[66]

Senator Biden invites us to see the bill's potential as an instrument of moral education on a national scale. "I have become convinced . . . that violence against women reflects as much a failure of our nation's collective moral imagination as it does the failure of our nation's laws and regulations."[67] Fair enough, but then why not include crimes against the elderly or children? What constitutional or moral ground is there for singling out female crime victims for special treatment under civil rights laws? Can it be that Biden and the others are buying into the gender feminist ontology of a society divided against itself along the fault line of gender?

Equity feminists are as upset as anyone else about the prevalence of violence against women, but they are not possessed of the worldview that licenses their overzealous sisters to present inflammatory but inaccurate data on male abuse. They want social scientists to tell them the objective truth about the prevalence of rape. And because they are not committed to the view that men are arrayed against women, they are able to see violence against women in the context of what, in our country, appears to be a general crisis of violence against persons. By distinguishing between acts of random violence and acts of violence against women, the sponsors of the Violence Against Women Act believe that they are showing sensitivity to feminist concerns. In fact, they may be doing social harm by accepting a divisive, gender-specific approach to a problem that is not caused by gender bias, misogyny, or "patriarchy"—an approach that can obscure real and urgent problems such as lesbian battering or male-on-male sexual violence.[68]

According to Stephen Donaldson, president of Stop Prison Rape, more than 290,000 male prisoners are assaulted each year. Prison rape, says Donaldson in a *New York Times* opinion piece, "is an entrenched tradition." Donaldson, who was himself a victim of prison rape twenty years ago when he was incarcerated for antiwar activities, has calculated that there may be as many as 45,000 rapes *every day* in our prison population of 1.2 million men. The number of rapes is vastly higher than the number of victims because the same men are often attacked repeatedly. Many of the rapes are "gang bangs" repeated day after day. To report such a rape is a terribly dangerous thing to do, so these rapes may be the most underreported of all. No one knows how accurate Donaldson's figures are. They seem incredible to me. But the tragic and neglected atrocities he is concerned about are not the kind whose study attracts grants from the Ford or Ms. foundations. If he is anywhere near right, the incidence of male rape would be as high or higher than that of female rape.

Equity feminists find it reasonable to approach the problem of violence against women by addressing the root causes of the general rise in violence and the decline in civility. To view rape as a crime of gender bias (encouraged by a patriarchy that looks with tolerance on the victimization of women) is perversely to miss its true nature. Rape is perpetrated by criminals, which is to say, it is perpetrated by people who are wont to gratify themselves in criminal ways and who care very little about the suffering they inflict on others.

That most violence is male isn't news. But very little of it appears to be misogynist. This country has more than its share of violent males; statistically we must expect them to gratify themselves at the expense of people weaker than themselves, male or female; and so they do. Gender feminist ideologues bemuse and alarm the public with inflated statistics. And they have made no case for the claim that violence against women is symptomatic of a deeply misogynist culture.

Rape is just one variety of crime against the person, and rape of women is just one subvariety. The real challenge we face in our society is how to reverse the tide of violence. How to achieve this is a true challenge to our moral imagination. It is clear that we must learn more about why so many of our male children are so violent. And it is clear we must find ways to educate all of our children to regard violence with abhorrence and contempt. We must once again teach decency and considerateness. And this, too, must become clear: in any constructive agenda for the future, the gender feminist's divisive social philosophy has no place.

Chapter 11

The Backlash Myth

When regard for truth has been broken down or even
slightly weakened, all things will remain doubtful.
                                        —ST. AUGUSTINE

A couple of years ago, American publishing was enlivened by the release of Susan Faludi's *Backlash* and Naomi Wolf's *The Beauty Myth,* two impassioned feminist screeds uncovering and denouncing the schemes that have prevented women from enjoying the fruits of the women's movement.[1] For our purposes, what these books have in common is more interesting and important than what distinguishes them. Both reported a widespread conspiracy against women. In both, the putative conspiracy has the same goal: to prevent today's women from making use of their hard-won freedoms—to punish them, in other words, for liberating themselves. As Ms. Wolf informs us: "After the success of the women's movement's second wave, the beauty myth was perfected to checkmate power at every level in individual women's lives."[2]

Conspiracy theories are always popular, but in this case the authors, writing primarily for middle-class readers, faced a tricky problem. No reasonable person in this day and age could be expected to believe that somewhere in America a group of male "elders" has sat down to plot ways to perpetuate the subjugation of women. How, then, could they persuade anyone of the existence of a widespread effort to control women for the good of men?

The solution that they hit upon made it possible for them to have their conspiracy while disavowing it. Faludi and Wolf argued that the conspiracy against women is being carried out by malevolent but invisible backlash forces or beauty-myth forces that act in purposeful ways. The forces in question are subtle, powerful, and insidiously efficient, and women are largely unconscious of them. What is more, the primary enforcers of the conspiracy are not a group of sequestered males plotting and planning their next backlash maneuvers: it is women themselves who "internalize" the aims of the backlash, who, unwittingly, do its bidding. In other words, the backlash is Us. Or, as Wolf puts it, "many women internalize Big Brother's eye."[3]

Faludi's scope is wider than Wolf's; she argues that the media and the political system have been co-opted by the backlash, as well:

> The backlash is not a conspiracy, with a council dispatching agents from some central control room, nor are the people who serve its ends often aware of their role; some even consider themselves feminists. For the most part, its workings are encoded and internalized, diffuse and chameleonic . . . generated by a culture machine that is always scrounging for a "fresh" angle. Taken as a whole, however, these codes and cajolings, these whispers and threats and myths, move overwhelmingly in one direction: they try to push women back into their "acceptable" roles.[4]

Wolf focuses more narrowly on the "beauty backlash," which pressures women to diet, dress up, make up, and work out in ways that are "destroying women physically and depleting us psychologically":[5] "The beauty backlash against feminism is no conspiracy, but a million separate individual reflexes . . . that coalesce into a national mood weighing women down; the backlash is all the more oppressive because the source of the suffocation is so diffuse as to be almost invisible."[6]

Having thus skirted a claim of outright conspiracy, Faludi and Wolf nevertheless freely use the *language* of subterfuge to arouse anger and bitterness. In their systems, the backlash and the beauty myth become malevolent personified forces behind plot after plot against women.

They incite unscrupulous stooges in the media to write articles that make "single and childless women feel like circus freaks." Cosmetics saleswomen are backlash agents, "trained," Wolf says, "with techniques akin to those used by professional cult converters and hypnotists." She calls Weight Watchers a "cult" and compares its disciplines to those of the Unification Church, Scientology, est, and Lifespring. In aerobics classes, "robotic" women do the "same bouncing dance . . . practiced by the Hare Krishnas for the same effect." [7]

What the backlash "wants" is clear to both Faludi and Wolf. By the seventies, women had been granted a great deal of equality. The primary aim of the backlash is to retake lost ground, to put women to rout. [8] The subtitle of Faludi's book is *The Undeclared War Against American Women*. *Backlash* itself may be regarded as a feminist counterattack in this supposed war. As Patricia Schroeder noted in a review of the book, women are not "riled up enough," and Faludi "may be able to do what political activists have tried to do for years." [9] Indeed, she and Wolf together succeeded in moving countless women to anger and dismay.

Where did Faludi and Wolf get the idea that masses of seemingly free women were being mysteriously manipulated from within? A look at their source of inspiration illustrates the workings of a law of intellectual fashion that the journalist Paul Berman calls "Parisian determinism"—that is, whatever is the rage in Paris will be fashionable in America fifteen years later. [10]

Michel Foucault, a professor of philosophy at the distinguished Collège de France and an irreverent social thinker who felt deeply alienated from the society in which he lived, introduced his theory of interior disciplines in 1975. His book *Discipline and Punish,* with its novel explanation of how large groups of people could be controlled without the need of exterior controllers, took intellectual Paris by storm. Foucault had little love for the modern democratic state. Like Marx, he was interested in the forces that keep citizens of democracies law-abiding and obedient.

According to Foucault, the individual subjects of contemporary democracies are not free at all. Instead, democratic societies turn out to be even more rigidly authoritarian than the tyrannies they replaced. Modern citizens find themselves subject to the rules (he calls them "disciplines") of modern bureaucratic institutions: schools, factories, hospitals, the military, the prisons. In premodern societies, where power was overtly authoritarian, enforcement was inconsistent, haphazard, and inefficient: the king's minions could not be everywhere all the time. In contemporary societies, control is pervasive and unceasing: the modern citizen, having internalized the disciplines of the institutions, polices himself. This results in a "disciplinary society" of "docile" subjects who keep themselves in line with what is expected. According to the philosopher Richard Rorty, Foucault believed he was exposing "a vast organization of repression and injustice." [11] He regarded the multitude of self-disciplined individuals as constituting a "microfascism" that is even more efficiently constraining than the macrofascism of totalitarian states.

How seriously can one take Foucault's theory? Not very, says Princeton political philosopher Michael Walzer, who characterizes Foucault's politics as "infantile leftism."[12] Foucault was aware that he was equating modern democracies with repressively brutal systems like the Soviet prison camps in the Gulag. In a 1977 interview, he showed some concern about how his ideas might be interpreted: "I am indeed worried by a certain use . . . which consists in saying, 'Everyone has their own Gulag, the Gulag is here at our door, in our cities, our hospitals, our prisons, it's here in our heads.' "[13] But, as Walzer points out, so long as Foucault rejected the possibility of individual freedom, which is the moral basis for liberal democracy, it was unclear how he could sustain the distinction between the real Gulag and the one inside the heads of bourgeois citizens.

Foucault's theory has few adherents among social philosophers, but it is nonetheless highly popular among gender feminist theorists, who find his critique of liberal democracy useful for their purposes. Foucault has given them an all-purpose weapon to be used against traditional-minded feminists.

Equity feminists believe that American women have made great progress and that our system of government allows them to expect more. They do not believe that women are "socially subordinate." By contrast, the gender feminists believe that modern women are still in thrall to patriarchy, and Foucault helps them to make their case. When equity feminists point to the gains made by women in recent decades, gender feminists consider them naive. Applying Foucault, they insist that male power *remains* all-pervasive, only now it has become "interiorized" and therefore even more efficient; force is no longer necessary. In effect, they have adopted Foucault's "discourses" to argue that "femininity" itself is really a discipline that continues to degrade and oppress women, even those in the so-called free democracies. As Sandra Lee Bartky puts it:

> No one is marched off for electrolysis at the end of a rifle. . . . Nevertheless . . . the disciplinary practices of femininity . . . must be understood as aspects of a far larger discipline, an oppressive and inegalitarian system of sexual subordination. This system aims at turning women into the docile and compliant companions of men just as surely as the army aims to turn its raw recruits into soldiers.[14]

For Bartky, contemporary American women live in a kind of sexual prison, subject to disciplines that ordain much of their daily lives:

The woman who checks her make-up half a dozen times a day to see if her foundation has caked or her mascara run, who worries that the wind or rain may spoil her hairdo, who looks frequently to see if her stockings have bagged at the ankle, or who, feeling fat, monitors everything she eats, has become, just as surely as the inmate [under constant surveillance], a self-policing subject, a self committed to a relentless self-surveillance. *This self-surveillance is a form of obedience to patriarchy* [my emphasis].[15]

Catharine MacKinnon presents her own, sexier version of how contemporary women have "interiorized" a self-destructive, self-sustaining, despairing, craven identity that serves men very well and continues to humiliate women:

Sexual desire in women, at least in this culture, is socially constructed as that by which we come to want our own self-annihilation; that is, our subordination is eroticized; . . . we get off on it, to a degree. This is our stake in this system that is not in our interest, our stake in this system that is killing us. I'm saying that femininity as we know it is how we come to want male dominance, which most emphatically is not in our interest.[16]

MacKinnon rejects "femininity as we know it" because it has come to mean accepting and even desiring male domination. Her militant, gynocentric feminism would teach women to see how deeply, craftily, and deceptively the male culture has socialized them to compliance: "Male dominance is perhaps the most pervasive and tenacious system of power in history. . . . Its force is exercised as consent, its authority as participation."[17]

It would be a mistake to think that the idea of a tenacious internalized power that is keeping women subjugated is on the fringe of the New Feminism and not at its center. To most feminist leaders, the backlash is very real. It was the theme of a 1992 conference I attended at Radcliffe College called "In the Eye of the Storm: Feminist Research and Action in the 90s." One of the purposes of the conference was to "explore the backlash—against the women's movement, against women's research, women's studies . . . and against public policy equity agendas." The conference was sponsored by the prestigious National Council for Research on Women—an umbrella organization that represents more than seventy women's groups, including the Wellesley College Center for Research on Women and the American Association of University Women. Expenses were covered by the Ford Foundation. Though the conference featured extremists like Charlotte Bunch (who referred to Dan Quayle as a Klansman), it also had Nannerl Keohane, now president of Duke University, who seemed not to be disturbed by all the backlash rhetoric.

The assumption that women must defend themselves against an enemy who is waging an undeclared war against them has by now achieved the status of conventional feminist wisdom. In large part, this has happened because seemingly reasonable and highly placed feminists like Ms. Keohane have not seen fit to challenge it. Whether they have been silent because they agree or because they have found it politic to refrain from criticism, I do not know.

Foucault promulgated his doctrine of self-surveillance in the midseventies. By the mideighties, it had turned up in the books of feminist theorists; by the nineties, it had become thematic in feminist best-sellers. Wolf mentions Foucault in her bibliography. Faludi offers him no acknowledgment, but her characterization of the backlash bespeaks his influence:

> The lack of orchestration, the absence of a single string-puller, only makes it harder to see—and perhaps more effective. A backlash against women's rights succeeds to the degree that it appears *not* to be political, that it appears not to be a struggle at all. It is most powerful when it goes private, when it lodges inside a woman's mind and turns her vision inward, until she imagines the pressure is all in her head, until she begins to enforce the backlash too—on herself.[18]

Wolf and Faludi tend to portray the "disciplined" and docile women in the grip of the backlash as Stepford wives—helpless, possessed, and robotic. Wolf sometimes speaks of women as victims of "mass hypnosis." "This is not a conspiracy theory," she reminds us. "It doesn't have to be."[19] Faludi explains how the backlash managed to "infiltrate the thoughts of women, broadcasting on these private channels its soundwaves of shame and reproach."[20]

In addition to Foucauldian theory, Faludi and Wolf have appropriated masses of statistics and studies that "consistently show" the workings of the backlash and the beauty myth and their effects on American women. But although their books are massively footnoted, reliable statistical evidence for the backlash hypothesis is in terribly short supply. According to Wolf, "Recent research consistently shows that inside the majority of the West's controlled, attractive, successful working women, there is a secret 'underlife' poisoning our freedom; infused with notions of beauty, it is a dark vein of self-hatred, physical obsessions, terror of aging, and dread of lost control."[21] The research she cites was done in 1983 at Old Dominion University. She claims that the researchers found that attractive women "compare themselves only to models, not to other women," and feel unattractive. This kind of claim is central to Wolf's contention that images of beautiful, willowy women in fashion magazines demoralize real women. In fact, the study she cited suggested the opposite. The Old Dominion researchers compared the self-reports of three groups of college-age women: one group evaluated themselves after looking at photos of fashion models, another group after looking at pictures of unattractive peers, and a third group after looking at pictures of very attractive peers. The researchers were careful not to exaggerate the significance of this small experiment, but they (tentatively) concluded that although reactions to attractive *peers* negatively influenced women's self-evaluation, exposure to the models had no such effect:

> Perhaps in the eyes of most of our subjects, peer beauty qualified as a more appropriate standard for social comparison than professional beauty. . . . Viewed in a practical sense, our results further suggest that thumbing through popular magazines filled with beautiful models may have little immediate effect on the self-images of most women.[22]

I called the principal author of the study, Thomas Cash, a psychologist at Old Dominion, and asked him what he thought about Ms. Wolf's use of his research. "It had nothing to do with what we found. It made no sense. What I reported was just the opposite of what Wolf claimed. . . . She grabbed it, ran with it, and got it backward."[23] We have already discussed her sensational disclosure that the beauty backlash is wreaking havoc with young women by leading them into a lethal epidemic of anorexia with annual fatalities of 150,000. The actual fatalities may be as low as 100 per year.

Much of the support Wolf brings for her beauty-myth theory consists of merely labeling an activity insidious rather than showing it to be so—exercising, dieting, and buying Lancôme products at the cosmetics counter in Bloomingdale's all come under attack. Characterizing Weight Watchers as a cult does not constitute evidence that it is one. In her zeal to construe every effort of American women to lose weight as a symptom of a male-induced anxiety, she overlooks the fact that many people—men as well as women—suffer from obesity and are threatened by diseases that do not affect people who are fit. Stressing the importance of diet and fitness can hardly be considered as an insidious attempt by the male establishment to disempower women. The desire to achieve greater fitness is perhaps the main motive inspiring both men and women to exercise and to monitor their diets.

Wolf recycled results from every alarmist-advocacy study she could get her hands on. Mary Koss's results on date rape are duly reported: "One in four women respondents had an experience that met the American legal definition of rape or attempted rape."[24] She does not mention that Koss's definition of rape was controversial. She does not tell us that almost half the women Koss classified as victims dated their "rapists" again. Wolf does sometimes point to real problems, such as the overwhelming fear of being "unfeminine," the excessive rate of cosmetic surgery, and the high incidence of domestic violence. But she errs in systematically ascribing them to the same misogynist cause. Good social theorists are painfully aware of the complexity of the phenomena they seek to explain, and honest researchers tend to be suspicious of single-factor explanations, no matter how beguiling.

Faludi's approach is that of the muckraking reporter bent on saving women by exposing the lies, half-truths, and deceits that the male-oriented media have created to demoralize women and keep them out of the workplace. Her readers might naturally assume that she herself has taken care to be truthful. However, not a few astonished reviewers discovered that *Backlash* relies for its impact on many untruths—some far more serious than any it exposes. In her *New York Times* review, the journalist and feminist Ellen Goodman gently chastised Faludi for overlooking evidence that did not fit her puzzle. But Goodman's tone was so enthusiastic—she praised the book for its "sharp style" and thoroughness—that few heeded her criticisms.[25] Within weeks *Backlash* jumped to the top of the best-seller lists, becoming the hottest feminist book in decades. Faludi was in demand—on the lecture circuit, on talk shows, in book stores, and in print. The more serious criticism came a few months later.

In a letter to the *New York Times Book Review*, Barbara Lovenheim, author of *Beating the Marriage Odds*, reported that she had looked into some of Faludi's major claims and found them to be erroneous. Her letter presented some egregious examples and concluded that Faludi "skews data, misquotes primary sources, and makes serious errors of omission."[26]

Although Lovenheim is a respected and responsible journalist, the review editors of the *Times* have a policy of fact-checking controversial material, and they asked Lovenheim to provide detailed proof that her criticisms of Faludi were well-grounded. She complied, and the *Times* devoted half a page to the publication of Lovenheim's letter. Here is a portion of Lovenheim's argument and findings.

Faludi had written: "Women under thirty-five now give birth to children with Down syndrome at a higher rate than women over thirty-five."[27] That claim fits well with Faludi's central thesis that the backlash is particularly aimed at professionally successful single women. By propagating false reports that women over thirty-five are at a higher risk of bearing a child with birth defects, the backlash seeks to discourage women and to harm their careers by causing them to worry about their decision to delay childbirth.

But, says Ms. Lovenheim, the deplorable truth is that age *sharply* increases a woman's chance of having a baby with Down syndrome. The chances are one in 1,000 under age twenty-five, one in 400 at thirty-five, one in 100 at forty, and one in 35 at forty-four.[28] Lovenheim points out that, in making her false claim, Faludi misrepresents her own source, *Working Woman* (August 1990). For *Working Woman* had warned its readers that a variety of abnormalities are associated with maternal age, among them that older women "are more likely to conceive fetuses with chromosomal defects such as Down syndrome."[29]

One of Faludi's more sensational claims—it opens her book—is that there is a concerted effort under way to demoralize successful women by spooking them about a man shortage. Faludi denies that there is a shortage, but Lovenheim shows that the facts do not support her. Though there is no man shortage for women in their twenties and early thirties, things change by the time women reach their midthirties. The census data indicate that between the ages of thirty-five and forty-four, there are 84 single men for every 100 women.[30] There are as many as one million more single women than single men between ages thirty-five and fifty-four. Lovenheim points out that Faludi made it look otherwise by leaving out all divorced and widowed singles.

Faludi responded to Lovenheim's letter two weeks later. She said she "welcomed" attempts to correct "minor inaccuracies." But she could not "help wondering at the possible motives of the letter writer, who is the author of a book called *Beating the Marriage Odds*." She made an attempt to explain her bizarre claim that older women have a lower incidence of Down's births. The claim was poorly worded, she conceded: she really meant to say that since women over thirty-five tend to be screened for birth defects, many abort their defective fetuses, lowering their rate of live births to babies with this abnormality. She neglected to add that this concession undercuts her larger argument.

After Lovenheim's letter was published, reviewers in several journals began to turn up other serious errors in Faludi's arguments. She had cited, for example, a 1986 article in *Fortune* magazine reporting that many successful women were finding demanding careers unsatisfying and were "bailing out" to accommodate marriage and children. According to Faludi, "The *Fortune* story left an especially deep and troubled impression on young women aspiring to business and management careers. . . . The year after *Fortune* launched the 'bailing out' trend, the proportion of women applying to business schools suddenly began to shrink—for the first time in a decade."

In a review, Gretchen Morgenson of *Forbes* magazine called this thesis "interesting but wrong." She wrote, "There was no shrinkage following the *Fortune* story. According to the American Assembly of Collegiate Schools of Business, which reports on business school graduates, the proportion of women graduates increased every year from 1967 through 1989, the most recent figures available." [31]

Morgenson also deflated Faludi's claim that in the eighties, "women were pouring into many low-paid female work ghettos." United States Bureau of Labor statistics, she pointed out, show that "the percentage of women executives, administrators, and managers among all managers in the American work force has risen from 32.4 percent in 1983 to 41 percent in 1991." Morgenson judged Faludi's book "a labyrinth of nonsense followed by eighty pages of footnotes." [32]

Time magazine, which was preparing an article on Faludi, found other glaring inconsistencies, primarily in Faludi's economic reckonings, which apparently led them to modify the ebullient tone of their story with the admonition that Faludi "rightly slams journalists who distort data in order to promote what they view as a larger truth; but in a number of instances, she can be accused of the same tactics." [33] *Time* reporter Nancy Gibbs looked into some of Faludi's complaints about the way the media have dealt with the economic effects of divorce on women:

> Faludi demonstrates that the studies on the impact of divorce greatly exaggerate the fall in the average woman's living standard in the year after she leaves her husband. But she adds that five years after divorce, most women's standard of living has actually improved. She relegates to a footnote the fact that this is because most have remarried. [34]

Faludi is especially critical of anyone in the media who finds fault with current day-care arrangements. She treats a 1984 *Newsweek* story as a diatribe against day care that glorifies women who give up careers to raise their kids. But Cathy Young, the reviewer from *Reason* magazine, points out that Faludi carefully refrained from mentioning that the author of the article called for quality day care and considered it to be "a basic family need."[35] To make her general case for a media backlash, Faludi assiduously collected media stories that question the joys of single life or the wisdom of a mother with small children choosing to work. Young observed that Faludi nowhere mentions the numerous articles that *encourage* women in these choices, nor those that celebrate "the new fatherhood, the benefits for girls of having working mothers, women in business and nontraditional jobs." Throughout her long book, Faludi gives the clear impression that the slant of coverage in major newspapers and magazines is distinctly antifeminist. According to Ms. Young, the opposite is true.

In a review for *Working Woman* magazine, Carol Pogash finds that Faludi "misconstrues statistics to suit her view that American women are no longer very anxious to wed."[36] Faludi interprets a 1990 Virginia Slims poll as finding that women placed the quest for a husband way at the bottom of their list of concerns. "Perhaps," says Ms. Pogash, "that's because 62 percent of the women in the sample were already married, a fact [Faludi] doesn't mention."[37] Ms. Pogash notes that Faludi also misstated the results of another Virginia Slims poll as showing that "70 percent of women believed they could have a 'happy and complete life' without a wedding ring." In fact the question was, "Do you think it is possible for a woman to have a complete and happy life if she is single?"—not whether the respondent herself could be happy as a single woman.

Faludi talks about "the wages of the backlash," and her most insistent theme is that women are being severely punished economically for the social and civic progress they had made prior to the eighties. How a feminist reacts to data about gender gaps in salaries and economic opportunities is an excellent indication of the kind of feminist she is. In general, the equity feminist points with pride to the many gains women have made toward achieving parity in the workplace. By contrast, the gender feminist makes it a point to disparage these gains and to speak of backlash. It disturbs her that the public may be lulled into thinking that women are doing well and that men are allowing it. The gender feminist insists that any so-called progress is illusory.

I felt the force of this insistence two years ago when my stepson, Tamler, was a junior at the University of Pennsylvania. He had written a term paper on *Jane Eyre* in which he made the "insensitive" observation that vocational opportunities for women are wider today than they were for Jane Eyre. "No!" wrote his instructor in the margin. "Even today women only make 59 percent of what men make!" (I was later to see this professor on one of the panels at the Heilbrun conference.) The next semester, in another course and for another English professor, Tamler "erred" again by saying of one female character that she had a more satisfying job than her husband did. Again, his teacher expressed her irritation in the margin: "How would you rationalize women earning 49 percent of men's salaries in *all* fields?" As monitored by Pennsylvania's English department, the condition of women seemed to have grown appreciably worse in less than a year!

We have all seen these angry figures. But there is not much truth in them. By most measures, the eighties were a time of rather spectacular gains by American women—in education, in wages, and in such traditionally male professions as business, law, and medicine. The gender feminist will have none of this. According to Susan Faludi, the eighties were the backlash decade, in which men successfully retracted many of the gains wrested from them in preceding decades. This view, inconveniently, does not square with the facts.

Since any criticism of Faludi's claim of a wages backlash is apt to be construed as just more backlashing, one must be grateful to the editors of the *New York Times* business section for braving the wrath of feminist ideologues by presenting an objective account of the economic picture as it affects women. Surveying several reports by women economists on women's gains in the 1980s, *New York Times* business writer Sylvia Nasar rejected Faludi's thesis. She pointed to masses of empirical data showing that "Far from losing ground, women gained more in the 1980s than in the entire postwar era before that. And almost as much as between 1890 and 1980."[38]

Today more than ever, economic position is a function of education. In 1970, 41 percent of college students were women; in 1979, 50 percent were women; and in 1992, 55 percent were women. In 1970, 5 percent of law degrees were granted to women. In 1989, the figure was 41 percent; by 1991 it was 43 percent, and it has since gone up. In 1970, women earned 8 percent of medical degrees. This rose to 33 percent in 1989; by 1991 it was 36 percent. The giant strides in education are reflected in accelerated progress in the professions and business. Diane Ravitch, a fellow at the Brookings Institution, reports that women have made great advancements toward full equality in every professional field, and "in some, such as pharmacy and veterinary medicine, women have become the majority in what was previously a male-dominated profession."[39]

The *New York Times* article summarized the research as follows:

A fresh body of research—mostly by a new generation of female economists who've mined a mountain of unexplored data—shows compellingly that women were big economic winners in the 1980s expansion and that their gains are likely to keep coming in the 1990s regardless of who is in the White House. . . . Conventional wisdom—enshrined in the best-selling book *Backlash: The Undeclared War Against American Women,* among other places—has it that women made no progress in the past decade. In fact, women were stuck earning around 60 cents to the men's dollar from 1960 through 1980, but started catching up fast as the economy expanded during the 1980s.[40]

The *Times* reports that the proportion women earn of each dollar of men's wages rose to a record 72 cents by 1990. But the *Times* points out that even this figure is misleadingly pessimistic, because it includes older women who are only marginally in the work force, such as "the mother who graduated from high school, left the work force at twenty and returned to a minimum wage at a local store." Younger women, says the *Times,* "now earn 80 cents for every dollar earned by men of the same age, up from 69 cents in 1980."

It might be supposed that it was not so much that women did well but that men did poorly in the recent recession. However, Baruch College economics professor June O'Neill, director of the Center for Study of Business and Government, showed that even in areas where men did well, women did better: "At the upper end, where men did very well, women went through the roof." According to Francine Blau, a University of Illinois economist cited in the *Times* story, the eighties were years in which "everything started to come together for women."

None of these facts has made the slightest impression on the backlash mongerers. For years, feminist activists have been wearing buttons claiming women earn "59 cents to a man's dollar." Some journalists have questioned this figure: Faludi calls them "spokesmen" for the backlash.[41] According to Faludi, "By 1988, women with a college diploma could still wear the famous 59-cent buttons. They were still making 59 cents to their male counterpart's dollar. In fact, the pay gap for them was now a bit worse than five years earlier."[42]

The sources Faludi cites do not sustain her figure. The actual figure for 1988 is 68 cents, both for all women and for women with a college diploma. This is substantially higher, not lower, than it was five years earlier. The most recent figures, for 1992, are considerably higher yet, the highest they have ever been: 71 cents for all women and 73 cents for women with a college diploma.[43]

The figure of 59 cents may be a useful rallying cry for gender feminist activists, but like many such slogans it is highly misleading and now egregiously out of date. The following diagram shows the dramatic rise of the female-to-male, year-round, full-time earnings ratio, from about 59 cents throughout the 1970s to 71 cents in 1992.[44]

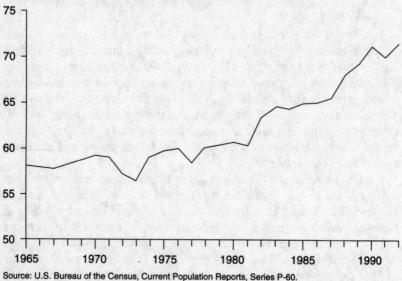

Female-to-Male YRFT Earnings Ratio

Source: U.S. Bureau of the Census, Current Population Reports, Series P-60.

Evidently the 59 cent figure is chosen for its propaganda value rather than for true insights into any remaining discrimination.

What of the remaining gap between male and female earnings? For the gender feminists, the answer is simple: the wage gap is the result of discrimination against women. But in fact, serious economics scholars who are trained to interpret these data (including many eminent female economists) point out that most of the differences in earnings reflect such prosaic matters as shorter work weeks and lesser workplace experience. For example, the average work week for full-time, year-round females is shorter than for males. When economists compare men's and women's *hourly* earnings instead of their *yearly* earnings, the wage gap narrows even more.[45]

Economists differ on exactly how much, if any, of the remaining gap is discrimination. Most economists agree that much of it simply represents the fact that, on average, women have accrued less workplace experience than men of the same age. One recent scholarly estimate shows that as of 1987, females who were currently working full-time and year-round had, on average, one-quarter fewer years of work experience than comparable males.[46] Moreover, a year of average female work experience generally represents fewer hours than a year of average male work experience, because of women's shorter average work week.

The experience gap is particularly important in explaining the earnings gap between older women and men, which is considerably wider than that for younger workers (67 cents for ages fifty-five through sixty-four vs. 82 cents for ages twenty-five through thirty-four). For older women, the experience gap is wider than one-quarter, and adds up over time to a sizable gap in years of experience and an even wider gap in hours of experience.

These data are important in understanding the oft-cited claim of a "glass ceiling" for women. Promotion in high-powered professional jobs often goes to those who have put in long hours in evenings and on weekends. Husbands may be more likely to do so than wives, for a variety of reasons, including unequal division of responsibilities at home, in which case the source of the difficulty is at home, not in the marketplace.[47]

Obviously, the experience gap also reflects the fact that many women choose to move into and out of the work force during childbearing and child-rearing years. This reduces the amount of experience they acquire in the workplace and naturally results in lower earnings, quite apart from any possible discrimination. Some evidence of this is provided by data on childless workers, for whom the experience gap should be much narrower, resulting in a narrower earnings gap. This, in fact, is the case: the female-to-male ratio of hourly earnings for childless white workers aged twenty to forty-four was 86–91 percent, as of 1987.[48]

The bottom line is that although economists still differ on how much discrimination remains, virtually all of them would agree that the 59 cent figure is highly misleading. For example, June O'Neill finds that "differences in earnings attributable solely to gender are likely to be much smaller than is commonly believed, probably less than 10 percent."[49] This contrasts rather starkly with the 41 percent figure claimed by Faludi.

This is not to say that there is no room for improvement. An obvious case in point is the modern university's failure to adjust its tenure system to the growing number of females entering academic careers. Since all new professors are required to "publish or perish" in the first six years of their career, the tenure clock ticks away at exactly the same rate as young women's biological clocks.[50] Adjustments are called for since this state of affairs seriously affects equality of opportunity. It is important to note, however, that the slow adjustment of the universities to changed circumstances is at least in part *because* they are public or nonprofit institutions that are somewhat insulated from the market. The private sector, arguably, has been more creative with respect to flextime, on-site day care, and home office options, and is likely to evolve further, out of economic imperative, rather than through the kind of government intrusion favored by many of the gender warriors.[51]

The generally sober economics profession has a few of its own gender feminists, too. One of its more prominent exponents is American University's professor of economics Barbara Bergmann, who claims "widespread, severe, ongoing discrimination by employers and fellow workers."[52] Professor Bergmann recently surprised some of her fellow feminist (and nonfeminist) economists by opposing a long-standing proposal to include the value of nonmarket activity, such as housework and child care, in the official gross domestic product figures. Her reason was revealing: "Part of the motive [of the proposal] is to lend some dignity to the position of housewives. What I think feminism is about is getting women off of the housewife track."[53] Professor Bergmann has proposed that all candidates for office in the American Economic Association be questioned regarding "their memberships in feminist and antifeminist organizations."[54] She did not specify which "antifeminist" memberships she was targeting, but the tone of her proposal is particularly disturbing because she had recently served as president of the American Association of University Professors.

As Ms. Nasar reminds us, women have not yet achieved parity. Nevertheless, the glass is at least three-quarters full and getting fuller. Someone ought to inform the University of Pennsylvania English department about this—and, more crucially, the many *Backlash* readers who may have been discouraged by misleading statistics.

According to Faludi and Wolf, there are three kinds of women to consider. The majority are naifs who are in one way or another pawns of the patriarchy that shapes their minds and desires. The sophisticated minority of aware women can be divided into two classes: those who have not sold out to the patriarchy and those who have. Not surprisingly, Faludi places herself in the first group, while those who disagree with them are consigned to the second. Faludi includes in their number such dedicated feminists as Betty Friedan, Germaine Greer, Sylvia Hewlett, Erica Jong, and Susan Brownmiller.

Friedan, who has criticized radical feminists for "wallowing" in victimhood and who even dared to suggest that feminists were wrong to slight Girl Scout leaders and Junior League members, is accused of using New Right rhetoric and of being part and parcel of its "profamily" agenda. But the question is not why Betty Friedan may be wrong but why she is, in Faludi's words, "stomping on a movement that she did so much to create and lead." Faludi's "explanation" is that Friedan is having "the tantrums of a fallen leader who is clearly distressed and angry that she wasn't allowed to be the Alpha wolf as long as she would have liked."[55] According to Faludi, Friedan's pettiness rendered her susceptible to treason.

Sylvia Ann Hewlett is a former Barnard professor of economics who is known for her work on family-policy issues. She had worked hard in the seventies canvassing for the Equal Rights Amendment. Her shock and dismay at its defeat moved her to ask, in her book *A Lesser Life: The Myth of Women's Liberation in America,* "Why did *women* fail to give the ERA the support necessary for victory?"

The conclusions she reached put her high on Faludi's backlash blacklist. "In a profound way," Hewlett writes, "feminists have failed to connect with the needs and aspirations of ordinary American women."[56] According to Hewlett, the ERA did not pass because of a widespread defection of women who no longer felt well represented by the feminist leaders who advocated its passage. "It is sobering to realize that the ERA was defeated not by Barry Goldwater, Jerry Falwell, or any combination of male chauvinist pigs, but by women who were alienated from a feminist movement the values of which seemed elitist and disconnected from the lives of ordinary people."[57]

Faludi is, of course, committed to the view that women as well as men are participating in and abetting the backlash. So Hewlett's contentions are in that sense not unwelcome to Faludi: both agree that women no less than men are responsible for the defeat of the ERA. But whereas Hewlett ascribes women's opposition to the ERA to their alienation from the women's movement due to its lack of sympathy for "ordinary women," Faludi insists on seeing it as a direct effect of the backlash that isolated and discredited the leaders of the women's movement. For Faludi, there is no way to explain the phenomenon but to pity the masses of women who did not support the ERA as craven, frightened victims of the backlash. And since Hewlett cannot conceivably be so cavalierly dismissed, she must be an agent of the backlash itself. Faludi avails herself of a classic technique for dealing with sophisticated opponents: accuse them of having sold out to the enemy. She slyly informs the reader that Hewlett lives at a "fashionable Manhattan address" and is a member of an establishment think tank. She mentions that publishers vied for Hewlett's book when they found it was critical of feminism and insinuates that she makes lots of money as an authority on family policy, citing a black-tie dinner Hewlett sponsored on Capitol Hill. In short, she implies, Hewlett is an opportunist with a substantial pecuniary interest in holding and promoting the opinions she expresses.[58]

Faludi deals with Germaine Greer, Susan Brownmiller, and Erica Jong in much the same way. Just as Friedan is described as having a "tantrum," Greer and Brownmiller are said to be "revisionists" and "recanters."[59] As for Ms. Jong, Faludi informs us that her support for feminism "had actually always been rather equivocal."[60] But the plain truth is that Faludi has painted herself into a position that allows no room for criticism.

Wolf does not have Faludi's brassy temperament. She prefers to say that her critics are misguided and to forgive them, for they know not what they do. After seeing Wolf interviewed on "20/20," Barbara Walters called her theory of the beauty myth "a crock." Wolf took this as additional evidence of how deeply the myth is embedded in the minds of seemingly free women: even Ms. Walters has been bodysnatched. Wolf admits she finds it troubling when women deny their own oppression. But, she explains, "Those initial impulses of denial are understandable: People most need the mechanism of denial when an intolerable situation has been pointed out to them."[61]

However, the fact that most women *reject* the divisive radical feminism she has been promoting appears finally to have impressed Ms. Wolf, whose new book, *Fire with Fire*,[62] trumpets a shift from what she calls "victim feminism" to a new "power feminism." Wolf's power feminism turns out to be a version of the classically liberal mainstream feminism with the addition of some contemporary "feel good" themes. To the dismay of many who admired the heated claims of her first book, Wolf now seems to regard American women as individuals who must be encouraged to take charge of their lives rather than whine about mass hypnosis and male conspiracies. The victim feminism whose able spokesperson she had hitherto been she now regards as "obsolete": "It no longer matches up with what women see happening in their lives. And, if feminism, locked for years in the siege mentality that once was necessary, fails to see this change, it may fail to embrace this new era's opportunities."[63]

The new Wolf calls for a feminism that "is tolerant about other women's choices about equality and appearance," a feminism that "does not attack men on the basis of gender," one that "knows that making social change does not contradict the principle that girls just want to have fun."[64]

When I read this, I felt like calling Ms. Wolf to tell her, "All is forgiven!" But I probably would have been unable to refrain from adding, "Well, almost all: was the siege mentality to which you so cleverly contributed in *The Beauty Myth* really necessary?" In the end I'm inclined to chalk up her earlier extremism to the effective indoctrination she got in women's studies at Yale.

Her former allies are not so forgiving. After all, it was only just yesterday that they had been cheering Wolf's descriptions of how women are in mass hypnosis and in thrall to the men who exploit them. On the academic feminist e-mail network, one now sees Wolf reviled and attacked. A typical reaction comes from e-mailer Suzanna Walters, a sociology professor at Georgetown University: "Wolf's book is trash and backlash and everything nasty (including homophobic and racist)."[65]

Get used to this, Ms. Wolf. You'll soon be finding out how it feels to be called antifeminist simply because you refuse to regard men as the enemy and women as their hapless victims. You speak of "the principle that girls just want to have fun." That will doubly offend your erstwhile sisters in arms. First, they prefer all female Americans above the age of fourteen to be referred to as "women." Second, they find the idea that women want to have fun, frivolous and retrograde. You'll be monitored for more such breaches of doctrine. And, in particular, Susan Faludi will now classify you as just another backlasher.

Barbara Walters had found Naomi Wolf's beauty-myth thesis about the secret misery of professional women offensive and absurd. Kathleen Gilles Seidel, a best-selling writer and avid reader of romance novels, was offended by American University feminist scholar Kay Mussell's analysis of women who enjoy reading romance novels. Ms. Mussell describes romance readers as unhappy women seeking to escape from their own "powerlessness, *from* meaninglessness, and *from* lack of self-esteem and identity."[66] Seidel finds that arrogantly wrong:

I am a romance reader, and I strongly object to anyone describing my life in those terms. I have my moments of dissatisfaction, of course, but I have power and meaning, I do not lack self-esteem or identity. Granted not all women have living room window treatments that they like as much as I like mine, or a mother such as mine or work that they feel about as I feel about mine, but I do think it is possible for women to find contentment, fulfillment, peace, and happiness within our culture, and I believe that a great many of them are doing a good job of it.[67]

It isn't hard to imagine how the feminist Foucauldians would go about explaining Ms. Seidel's enthusiasm for her window treatments—or her sanguine view about the lives of other American women. For them it is a tenet of faith that the life of women under patriarchy is one of quiet desperation. But when asked, the majority of women seem to agree with Ms. Seidel.

Occasionally a study designed to document the woes of American women inadvertently turns up data that suggest most American women are enjoying life. An interesting case in point is the already-mentioned study on women's ills commissioned by the Commonwealth Fund in 1992 and carried out by Louis Harris and Associates.

The Harris pollsters asked a series of questions of a random sample of 2,500 women and 1,000 men about their physical and mental well-being.[68] When asked how they had felt in the past week, the respondents answered as follows:

		NEVER	RARELY	SOME OF THE TIME	MOST OF THE TIME
1. I felt	Men:	48	25	22	5
depressed.	Women:	36	29	29	5
2. My sleep	Men:	40	21	28	11
was restless.	Women:	29	22	36	12
3. I enjoyed	Men:	1	2	13	83
life.	Women:	1	2	15	82
4. I had crying	Men:	88	6	5	—
spells.	Women:	63	19	16	2
5. I felt sad.	Men:	41	29	28	2
	Women:	33	27	35	4
6. I felt that	Men:	61	22	14	2
people	Women:	61	22	14	2
disliked me.					

A large majority of women (82 percent) claimed they "enjoyed life most of the time." The same small proportion (5 percent of men and women) said they had been depressed most of that week. That a lot of American women are enjoying life may not be newsworthy. But here is the astonishing way the Commonwealth Fund and Harris and Associates summarized the results of the questionnaire in their press release: "Survey results indicate that depression and low self-esteem are pervasive problems for American women. Forty percent of the women surveyed report being severely depressed in the past week, compared with 26 percent of men."[69]

This conclusion was somehow arrived at by the way the Harris poll interpreted the responses to the six questions. The survey's report represented this result graphically:[70]

Women and Depression
Younger Women Are More Depressed than Older Women

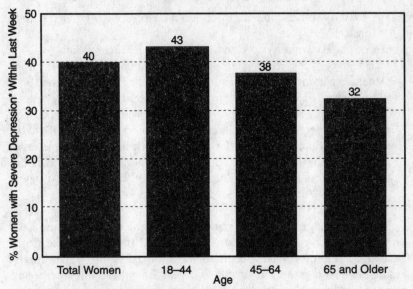

* Derived from ranking responses to six statements regarding symptoms of depression.

Humphrey Taylor, president of Louis Harris and Associates, announced at the news conference that the results on women's depression surprised him the most.[71] He said that the survey can "accurately be projected to the American female population [of 94.6 million]. This is far and away the most comprehensive survey ever done on women's health."[72]

Following the press conference and the news release on July 14, 1993, the bleak news about the mental condition of American women went out over the Reuters news wire under the headline SURVEY SHOWS 4 OF 10 WOMEN DEPRESSED:

> • A survey called the most comprehensive ever done on women's health has found a large number—4 out of 10—suffered "severe depression." . . . The study was called "important" by U.S. Health and Human Services Secretary Donna Shalala who attended the [press] conference. "For too long health care [and] health research has been addressed from one point of view, the white male point of view."[73]

The next day these stories appeared in news stories around the country:

> • 4 in ten women polled suffer severe depression. (*Orange County Register*)
> • 4 out of 10 women depressed, survey finds. (*Baltimore Sun*)
> • In a given week, 40 percent of women, compared to 26 percent of men, experienced "severe depression." (*Seattle Post-Intelligencer*)
> • 40 percent of women compared to 26 percent of men experienced "severe depression" in the previous week. (*Newark Star-Ledger*)
> • Study: 40 percent of women feel severe depression. (*Boston Herald*)
> • The Harris poll conducted for the New York-based charitable organization [the Commonwealth Fund] . . . found 40 percent of the women had suffered severe depression recently. (WCBS-AM news-radio, New York)[74]

These newspapers and radio station were relying on Reuters, and Reuters had relied on a special "Survey Highlights" prepared by the Commonwealth Fund. No one seems to have looked at the actual survey results. But I did, and I was unable to fathom how those who interpreted them could possibly have come up with the finding about women's depression.

I called the Commonwealth Fund and was put through to Mary Johnson, the same polite program assistant I had spoken to when I questioned the inclusion of heated exchanges and insults between couples as instances of "psychological abuse" of women. This time I asked her how they had arrived at the statistic that 40 percent of women were severely depressed. What about the 82 percent of women who said they enjoyed life most of the time? "We pulled out certain findings that seemed sur-prising," Ms. Johnson responded. "We are not saying they are clinically depressed."

I told her that "severe depression" certainly sounded like the real thing —after all, this was a women's health survey. I asked her again why the report paid no attention to the strong positive responses suggesting that most women were, overall, fairly happy. Ms. Johnson assured me again that the 40 percent figure was reliable, the product of a diagnostic method that had been developed by the Center for Epidemiologic Studies (CES) and adapted by a team of "consultants" who had reduced the CES ques-tionnaire from twenty questions to six. I asked her for more details. She told me she had not been around when the survey was developed and put me on to her supervisor, Evelyn Walz, a program coordinator, who suggested that I address any further questions to the Harris poll.

I called Harris and Associates and reached Liz Cooner, a vice president, who told me that a Lois Hoeffler had been in charge of the women's health survey but had since left to attend graduate school in sociology. Ms. Cooner offered to answer my questions in her stead.

I asked her how the Harris people had come up with 40 percent of women severely depressed and told her that the responses suggested the opposite. She immediately rebuked me for using the term "severe depres-sion." She said that was strong language and inappropriate for the find-ings. When I told her that I was only quoting the report, she said, "I have not seen it reported as 'severe depression.' " I referred her to page 3 of the report, and to the "Highlights" and the graph. She agreed that if the report had indeed used the term "severe depression," it was inappropriate. She said she did not know what I needed the information for, but since I had so many questions about the validity of the conclusions, I should proba-bly "just not reference it" in whatever I was writing.

I reminded her of all the journalists who had already "referenced it," not to mention Donna Shalala. Since she herself agreed that the an-nounced finding was incorrect, I asked her whether she might now wish to disassociate the Harris poll from this claim. She said she was in no position to do that, but I was free to write to Humphrey Taylor and ask him to reconsider. It seemed to me, however, that having been apprised of their error, Harris and Associates should now be taking the initiative in correcting it and making the correction public, not me.

There was, moreover, another section of the Harris questionnaire, which never made it into the charts or newspaper stories. The 2,500 women and 1,000 men were asked: "All things considered, how satisfied are you with your life these days?" Here are the percentage results:

MEN		WOMEN
55	very satisfied	54
38	somewhat satisfied	40
4	not very satisfied	4
2	not satisfied at all	2
1	not sure	1

If we project from these responses, we should conclude that 94 percent of women (and 93 percent of men) are at least somewhat content with their lives, a finding that hardly squares with the headline-grabbing figure of 40 percent severely depressed. Indeed, other polls, surveys, and studies suggest high levels of satisfaction among American women and men. The Gallup poll organization periodically takes a "Satisfaction with U.S. Personal Life" survey in which it asks, "In general, are you satisfied or dissatisfied with the way things are going in your own personal life?" In March of 1992, 78 percent of women and 80 percent of men responded that they were satisfied.[75] In 1993, the *San Francisco Chronicle* did a survey on the life satisfaction of "baby boomers" (ages thirty through forty-seven) living in the Bay area and found that "baby boomer women are happier and more sexually satisfied than boomer men."[76]

It is probably impossible to get accurate figures on something as ambiguous as life satisfaction. Depression, on the other hand, is a fairly well-defined disorder. If the guidelines and definitions laid down by the American Psychiatric Association are followed, there are several questions pollsters could ask that would give them a fairly good idea of the prevalence of depression. Here are two used by the American Psychiatric Association (in conjunction with several others):

- Have you been in a depressed mood most of the day, nearly every day?
- Do you have a markedly diminished interest or pleasure in all, or almost all, activities most of the day, nearly every day?[77]

Psychiatrists ask such questions to arrive at a diagnosis of depression, and epidemiologists use them to get an idea of its prevalence in the population. According to the National Institute of Mental Health's *Psychiatric Disorders in America,* the yearly prevalence of depression is 2.2 percent for men and 5.0 percent for women; the lifetime rate is 3.6 percent for men and 8.7 percent for women.[78] I decided to check out the CES survey that Mary Johnson had told me the Harris researchers had adapted. I called the NIMH and was put in touch with Karen Bourdon, the psychologist in charge of researching symptoms of community distress. What did they think of the way the Harris poll had used their scale? She said immediately, "We wish they would not do this. They should know better."

She explained that the survey instrument was never intended as a measure of depression: if all twenty questions are asked and carefully interpreted, it can be helpful in measuring symptoms of distress in a community but not in diagnosing a medical illness. She added that in some of her other studies she had found a similar percentage of men and women showing signs of affective distress: women have more symptoms of depression; men, of antisocial behavior and alcoholism.[79]

In informal conversations with several psychiatrists, I quickly learned that they considered a 40 percent depression finding (not to speak of "severe depression") preposterous, because the responses to the six questions the Harris pollsters had selected from the CES's twenty did not show depression. They showed only that some women (and men) had felt "blue" during the week in question. They were at a loss to understand how Harris and Associates had come up with such a bizarre result.

Faludi's *Backlash* appeared before Harris and Associates published their figures on women's depression, but she, too, found significantly higher rates of depression among women—married women, that is:[80] "Married women have more nervous breakdowns, nervousness, heart palpitations, and inertia . . . insomnia, trembling hands, dizzy spells, nightmares, hypochondria, passivity, agoraphobia . . . wives have the lowest self-esteem, felt the least attractive, reported the most loneliness."[81] Her finding echoed feminist sociologist Jessie Bernard's 1972 warning that "marriage may be hazardous to women's health." Yet in *Psychiatric Disorders in America,* we read, "The strong protective effect of marriage against affective disorders is confirmed in much of the epidemiologic literature."[82] Here are the findings of a major National Institute of Mental Health Study:[83]

	MAJOR DEPRESSION ANNUAL RATE PER 100
married (no divorce)	1.5
never married	2.4
divorced once	4.1
divorced twice	5.8
cohabiting	5.1

In a 1989 review of the literature on marital happiness in *Psychological Bulletin,* the authors conclude, "For both sexes the married state (vs.

unmarried) was associated with favorable well-being, but the favorable outcomes proved stronger for women than men."[84]

The day after I talked to Mary Johnson and Liz Cooner, I received a call from Lois Hoeffler, the principal investigator who had left Harris and Associates to pursue a graduate degree in sociology. She was contacting me at the behest of Harris and Associates to explain the 40 percent finding.

Ms. Hoeffler was charming, candid, and very sure of herself. When I asked her how she had selected the six questions from the NIMH/CES diagnostic questionnaire, she said, "We picked them out arbitrarily." She told me that a footnote on page 185 of the Harris poll's full report "explains that the findings were not meant as an indication of clinical depression."

I told her that the footnote she alluded to was nowhere in the Commonwealth Fund report. Nowhere was there any public mention that "severe depression" was not meant literally. She agreed that the actual responses were not helpful for determining the prevalence of clinical depression, but they did show that more women are depressed than men. "If you are interested in gender differences, you can use these findings."

I asked her about the ideas that guided her in designing and interpreting the questionnaire. She told me she was very concerned that the Harris poll study not be just another study reflecting "white male norms" of research. She wanted to avoid the usual "phallocentric" bias. She said: "I am not really into phallocentric theory. So much of psychology is based on the fact that men are repressing women. I can't handle it. Most of the mainstream theories are based on white male norms."

She had written her master's thesis in Hunter College's Social Research Program. Her topic was "feminist social theories of the self," and her research analyzed the ideas of Carol Gilligan. She finds Gilligan inadequate because "Gilligan is still grounded in male psychological theory." Ms. Hoeffler told me that the radical feminist theologian Mary Daly was a more direct influence on her work. Another influence was *Women's Ways of Knowing,* the book that introduced the dubious epistemological distinction between "connected knowers" (women) and "separate knowers" (men).

Ms. Hoeffler told me that her work as a primary investigator for Harris and Associates provided her with a unique opportunity to implement her ideas. "It's not everyone who can apply what they wrote in their master's thesis. I was lucky." I asked her whether her input had been an important factor in the final product, to which she replied, "I got in some stuff, but less than I might have." "How open was Harris and Associates president Humphrey Taylor to her ideas?" I asked.

Humphrey was attuned to feminist things when I was there. In the course of this project he became more aware. . . . But I do not try to reeducate men. I speak in their language. You have to speak in male language. You say: we should do this survey because it's a hot topic and will make money, not we should do this because it's the right thing to do.

I asked her if there are other polling organizations in which feminist activists are influential. She said: "Oh yes. Greenberg-Lake." The reader will remember that the AAUW used Greenberg-Lake as its polling agency in studying the self-esteem of adolescents. It came up with the dramatic and inaccurate figure that schoolgirls experience a "31 point drop in self-esteem."

Hoeffler went on to say that with the increase in the number of feminists who are doing research, she expects more polls and surveys to reflect the new consciousness. "We are hitting the peak moment. A researcher's politics are always in the research. We [feminist pollsters] balance it out." Since she considers most research politically biased against women, she saw little reason to apologize for her feminist bias.

Then she brought up Foucault. She had found most male researchers to be extremely unenlightened. Foucault had helped her to see why "those who are subjugated and marginal are positioned to see the situation more clearly." "Foucault is great," she concluded, and affirmed that his theories had "influenced my participation at Harris while I was there."

I had looked into two areas of the women's health survey—those on psychological abuse and depression. Both revealed severe flaws and a pronounced ideological slant. There may well be problems with other parts of the survey. Did the Commonwealth Fund—one of the oldest foundations in America, with an endowment of $340 million—know that a study commissioned from a distinguished, long-established pollster would use a gynocentric researcher who sought to avoid "phallocentric" methods?

But perhaps the Commonwealth Fund is not merely sinned against. Ellen Futter, president of Barnard College, is chair of the Commonwealth Fund's Commission on Women's Health, which sponsored the Harris survey. She is among the many academic administrators who take pains to deny the existence of political correctness on America's campuses. On the contrary, as she sees it, those who claim there is a problem are doing harm. In a recent interview with Anna Quindlen for *Mirabella,* Futter said that the "PC" debate had given the public a "skewed" picture of the academy.[85] "Because of these characterizations, some very . . . thoughtful efforts to broaden the presentation of intellectual ideas . . . have been miscast." President Futter should take a close look at the "thoughtful efforts" that went into the women's health survey, commissioned under her watch.[86]

Hoeffler had successfully seen to it that the Harris report was not just another study applying "white male norms" of research. Donna Shalala spotted this feature of the report and commended it as a distinguishing virtue. One must hope that her comment that "white male" research has prevailed "for too long" does not represent a considered judgment. For unlike Ms. Hoeffler, an ideological Ms. Shalala would be no bit player in the misandrist game that the gender feminist zealots are playing. The professionalism of American research is an enormous and precious national resource. And Ms. Shalala heads a department whose outlays are almost double that of the Department of Defense.

Robert Reich, the U.S secretary of labor, wrote a blurb for *Backlash* describing it as "spellbinding and frightening . . . a wake-up call to the men as well as the women who are struggling to build a gender-respectful society."[87] One can only hope, again, that Reich was too spellbound to have read *Backlash* with a discriminating mind. What is more alarming than anything Faludi has to say about an undeclared war against American women is the credulity it has met in high public officials on whose judgment we ought to be able to rely.

Chapter 12

The Gender Wardens

Censorship is the strongest drive in human nature; sex is a weak second.
        —PHIL KERBY, *Los Angeles Times*
                    editorial writer, on a postcard to
                    Nat Hentoff [1]

Question: How many feminists does it take to screw in a light bulb?
Feminist answer: That's not funny.

It is sometimes said that feminists don't have a sense of humor. Yet, there are some situations, not funny to most women, that gender feminists seem to find very amusing.

About a thousand feminists were present at Manhattan's 92nd Street Y on Mother's Day 1992 to hear a debate between Susan Faludi and *Playboy* columnist Asa Baber. Baber opened his talk by observing that on Mother's Day, the phone lines throughout the United States are jammed because everyone is trying to call home to talk to their mothers. On Father's Day, the lines are free. "We have to ask why there is so much less interest in fathers," said Baber. [2]

The assembled women, most of them fans of Ms. Faludi, found this uproarious. "It brought down the house," said Baber. "At first, I didn't get it. I thought my fly was open." But then he caught on and said, "If you think that is funny, you are going to think this is a laugh riot: I think the fact that our fathers are so much out of the loop is a major tragedy in our culture."

Baber had taken another misstep, but this time he didn't tickle anyone's funny bone. An outraged audience hissed and booed him. Later, when he was asked whether this was because his hecklers believed that men were useless, irrelevant, and potentially dangerous, Baber answered, "You got it."[3] To them he appeared to be just another patriarch exacting homage.

The jeering, hooting atmosphere in which Baber found himself was familiar to me. I had encountered it in the "safe spaces" where gender feminists gather to tell one another put-down stories describing how a sister had routed some male who didn't have a clue at how offensive he was (recall the "Shut up, you fucker" with which one partisan had squelched an unsuspecting male student critic in a feminist classroom). I'd heard it in the appreciative laughter of the audience when feminist academics reported to them on how they had played on the liberal guilt of the faculty to get their projects approved. Baber was in the camp of the enemy, and anything he had to say was regarded as offensive or, if he were lucky, laughable.

The derision of the women who were hooting at Baber was safely directed at "men." One must wonder what Baber's audience would make of the millions of women who still observe the amenities of Father's Day. So intent are gender feminists on condemning the "patriarchy" that they rarely let on how they feel about women who "go along." Nevertheless, it is not hard to see that in jeering at Baber, they were also jeering at most American women.

That is the corrosive paradox of gender feminism's misandrist stance: no group of women can wage war on men without at the same time denigrating the women who respect those men. It is just not possible to incriminate men without implying that large numbers of women are fools or worse. Other groups have had their official enemies—workers against capitalists, whites against blacks, Hindus against Muslims—and for a while such enmities may be stable. But when women set themselves against men, they simultaneously set themselves against other women in a group antagonism that is untenable from the outset. In the end, the gender feminist is always forced to show her disappointment and annoyance with the women who are to be found in the camp of the enemy. Misandry moves on to misogyny.

Betty Friedan once told Simone de Beauvoir that she believed women should have the choice to stay home to raise their children if that is what they wish to do. Beauvoir answered: "No, we don't believe that any woman should have this choice. No woman should be authorized to stay at home to raise her children. Society should be totally different. Women should not have that choice, precisely because if there is such a choice, too many women will make that one."[4]

De Beauvoir thought this drastic policy was needed to prevent women from leading blighted conventional lives. Though she does not spell it out, she must have been aware that her "totally different" society would require a legion of Big Sisters endowed by the state with the power to prohibit any woman who wants to marry and stay home with children from carrying out her plans. She betrays the patronizing attitude typical of many gender feminists toward "uninitiated" women.

An illiberal authoritarianism is implicit in the doctrine that women are socialized to want the things the gender feminist believes they *should not want*. For those who believe that what women want and hope for is "constrained" or "coerced" by their upbringing in the patriarchy are led to dismiss the values and aspirations of most women. The next step may not be inevitable, but it is almost irresistible: to regard women as badly brought-up children whose harmful desires and immature choices must be discounted.

Gender feminists, such as Sandra Lee Bartky, argue for a "feminist reconstruction of self and society [that] must go far beyond anything now contemplated in the theory or politics of the mainstream women's movement."[5] Bartky, who writes on "the phenomenology of feminist consciousness," is concerned with what a proper feminist consciousness should be like. In her book *Femininity and Domination,* she says, "A thorough overhaul of desire is clearly on the feminist agenda: the fantasy that we are overwhelmed by Rhett Butler should be traded in for one in which we seize state power and reeducate him."[6] Bartky, however, does not advocate any authoritarian measures to protect women from incorrect values and preferences shaped by "the masters of patriarchal society." She points out that at present we do not know how to "decolonize the imagination."[7] She cautions that "overhauling" desires and "trading in" popular fantasies may have to wait for the day when feminist theorists develop an "adequate theory of sexuality." In her apocalyptic feminist vision, women as well as men may one day be radically reconstructed. We will have learned to *prefer* the "right" way to live.

Although they may disagree politically about what measures to take with women who make the wrong choices, de Beauvoir and her latter-day descendants share a common posture: they condescend to, patronize, and pity the benighted females who, because they have been "socialized" in the sex/gender system, cannot help wanting the wrong things in life. Their disdain for the hapless victims of patriarchy is rarely acknowledged.

When feminists talk of a new society and of how people must be changed, they invariably have in mind men who exploit and abuse women. But it is not difficult to see that they regard most women as men's dupes.

Consider how Naomi Wolf (in the *Beauty Myth*) regards the eight million American women members of Weight Watchers—as cultists in need of deprogramming. Most gender feminists may not be ready to advocate coercion of women of low feminist consciousness, but they are very much in favor of a massive and concerted effort to give the desires, aspirations, and values of American women a thorough makeover. As the feminist philosopher Alison Jaggar puts it, "If individual desires and interests are socially constituted . . . , the ultimate authority of individual judgment comes into question. Perhaps people may be mistaken about truth, morality or even their own interests; perhaps they may be systematically self-deceived."[8] Note that Jaggar explicitly impugns the traditional liberal principle that the many individual judgments and preferences are the ultimate authority. I find that a chilling doctrine: when the people are systematically self-deceived, the ultimate authority is presumed to be vested in a vanguard that unmasks their self-deception. As Ms. Jaggar says, "Certain historical circumstances allow specific groups of women to transcend at least partially the perceptions and theoretical constructs of male dominance."[9] It is these women of high feminist consciousness who "inspire and guide women in a struggle for social change."

Respect for people's preferences is generally thought to be fundamental for democracy. But ideologues find ways of denying this principle. The gender feminist who claims to represent the true interests of women is convinced that she profoundly understands their situation and so is in an exceptional position to know their true interests. In practice, this means she is prepared to dismiss popular preferences in an illiberal way. To justify this, feminist philosopher Marilyn Friedman argues that popular preferences are often "inauthentic" and that even liberals are aware of this:

> Liberal feminists can easily join with other feminists in recognizing that political democracy by itself is insufficient to ensure that preferences are formed without coercion, constraint, undue restriction of options, and so forth. Social, cultural, and economic conditions are as important as political conditions, if not more so, in ensuring that preferences are, in some important sense, authentic.[10]

Friedman is quite wrong in her assumptions: anyone, liberal or conservative, who believes in democracy will sense danger in them. Who will "ensure" that preferences are "authentic"? What additions to political democracy does Friedman have in mind? A constitutional amendment to provide reeducation camps for men and women of false consciousness? Is she prepared to go the authoritarian route indicated by de Beauvoir?

The feminist who thinks that democracy is insufficient believes that seemingly free and enlightened American women have values and desires that, unbeknownst to them, are being manipulated by a system intent on keeping women subjugated to men. Romance, a major cause of defection from the gynocentric enclave, is ever a sticking point with gender feminists. Gloria Steinem, writing on the subject, engages in this kind of debunking "critique": "Romance itself serves a larger political purpose by offering at least a temporary reward for gender roles and threatening rebels with loneliness and rejection. . . . It privatizes our hopes and distracts us from making societal changes. The Roman 'bread and circuses' way of keeping the masses happy. . . . might now be updated." [11] Jaggar, too, sees in romance a distraction from sexual politics: "The ideology of romantic love has now become so pervasive that most women in contemporary capitalism probably believe that they marry for love rather than for economic support." [12]

For her authoritarian disdain, de Beauvoir deserves our liberal censure. But the less authoritarian feminists also deserve it. No intelligent and liberal person—no one who has read and appreciated the limpid political prose of George Orwell or who has learned from the savage history of twentieth-century totalitarianism—can accept the idea of a social agenda to "overhaul" the desires of large numbers of people to make them more "authentic."

In her defense, the gender feminist replies that effective teachers or political leaders must always try to help others overcome benightedness. When women are caught in a system designed to perpetuate male domination, they must be enlightened. There is nothing intrinsically illiberal about seeking to make them conscious of their subjugation. It is the very essence of a liberal education to open minds and enlighten consciousness. If that entails "reeducating" them and overhauling their desires, so be it.

This argument could easily be made in an earlier era when classically liberal principles were being applied to men but not to women. In the nineteenth century, the proposition that all men are created equal was taken to mean "all males." Women did not have the rights that men had, and, what is more, they were being taught that their subordinate status was fitting and natural. Feminist philosophers like John Stuart Mill and Harriet Taylor rightly feared that such teaching was helping to perpetuate inequities. Under the circumstances, political democracy applied only minimally to women. Because they did not vote, their preferences were not in play, and the question of how authentic their preferences were was of importance inasmuch as it affected their ability to agitate for the rights that were being withheld from them.

But women are no longer disenfranchised, and their preferences are being taken into account. Nor are they now taught that they are subordinate or that a subordinate role for them is fitting and proper. Have any women in history been better informed, more aware of their rights and options? Since women today can no longer be regarded as the victims of an undemocratic indoctrination, we must regard their preferences as "authentic." Any other attitude toward American women is unacceptably patronizing and profoundly illiberal.

Gender feminists are especially disapproving of the lives of traditionally religious women such as evangelical Christian women, Catholic women, or Orthodox Jewish women, whom they see as being conditioned for highly restricted roles. Surely, they say, it is evident that such women are subjugated, and the choices they make inauthentic. As Gloria Steinem explains it, the appeal of religious fundamentalism for women is that "the promise is safety in return for obedience, respectability in return for self-respect and freedom—a sad bargain."[13]

That is a harsh judgment to make about millions of American women. Ms. Steinem is of course free to disagree with conventionally religious women on any number of issues, but she is not morally free to cast aspersions on their autonomy and self-respect. The New Feminism is supposed to be about sisterhood. Why are its most prominent practitioners so condescending?

Steinem herself knows a thing or two about how to recruit adherents to a cause by promises of "safety" and "self-respect." The feminist orthodoxy she portrays promises safety in a sisterhood that will offer unhappy or insecure women a venue where they can build self-esteem and attain an authenticity enjoyed by no other group of women.[14]

The traditionally religious women of today, be they Protestant Christians, Orthodox Jews, or observant Catholics—emphatically do not think of themselves as subjugated, lacking in self-respect, or unfree. Indeed, they very properly resent being described that way. For they are perfectly aware that they have all the rights that men have. If they choose to lead the lives they do, that is their affair.

Of course there are feminists who disapprove of the way these women live, and some may even think of them as pitiable. These feminists are perfectly at liberty to try to persuade them to change their way of life. For their part, traditional women might try to persuade the feminists of the merits of the religious way of life. Mostly, however, gender feminists are content to dismiss and even jeer at the religious women without engaging or confronting them in a respectful dialogue, and it is not surprising that the latter have grown increasingly impatient with their feminist critics.

Several years ago, Liz Harris wrote an extraordinary and much-talked-about article for the New Yorker on the ultraorthodox Hasidic women of Brooklyn, New York.[15] She had expected to find oppressed women— "self-effacing drudges" worn down by a family system that exalted men and denigrated women. Instead, she was impressed by their strong marriages, their large, thriving families, and their "remarkably energetic, mutually supportive community of women, an almost Amazonian society." "Most of the [Hasidic] women sped around like intergalactic missiles, and the greater majority of those I was to encounter seemed . . . to be as occupied with worthy projects as Eleanor Roosevelt, as hospitable as Welcome Wagoneers."[16]

My relatives on my husband's side are Jewish, and most are Orthodox. Ms. Harris's description fits them to a T. At family gatherings, I sometimes tell my sister-in-law, my nieces, and their friends about the feminist theorists who pity them and would liberate them from their "gendered families." They are more amused than offended. It might surprise Gloria Steinem to hear they have a rather shrewd understanding of her kind of feminism. They simply want no part of it. They believe they have made an autonomous choice: they also believe their way of life offers them such basic advantages as community, grace, dignity, and spirituality. They see the patriarchal aspects of their tradition as generally benign. Some of them find aspects of Judaism insensitive to important concerns of women, but they are even more put off by the gender feminist's rejection of traditional religion.

But of course it is not only religious women who reject the gender feminist perspective. A clear majority of secular American women enjoy many aspects of "la différence." Many want things that gender feminists are trying to free them from, be it conventional marriages and families, or fashions and makeup that sometimes render them "sex objects." Such feminists are uncomfortably aware that they are not reaching these women; but instead of asking themselves where they may be going wrong, they fall back on the question-begging theory of false consciousness to explain the mass indifference of the women they want to save.

For the gender feminists do want to save women—from themselves. False consciousness is said to be endemic in the patriarchy. And every feminist has her theory. Feminists who specialize in the theory of feminist consciousness talk about mechanisms by which "patriarchy invades the intimate recesses of personality where it may maim and cripple the spirit forever."[17] However, a growing number of women are questioning whether gender feminism, with its insistence that personal relationships be construed in terms of political power, has taken much of the joy out of male/female intimacy, maiming and crippling the spirit of some of its devotees forever.

A few years ago, an op-ed piece I wrote for the *Chronicle of Higher Education* aroused a storm of protest because it defended the "many women [who] continue to swoon at the sight of Rhett Butler carrying Scarlett O'Hara up the stairs to a fate undreamt of in feminist philosophy."[18] The Society for Women in Philosophy (SWIP), an organization within the American Philosophical Association, arranged for a public debate between Marilyn Friedman, a philosopher from the University of Washington, and me. Ms. Friedman informed the overflow audience that she was stunned by my flippant reaction to Rhett's rape of Scarlett—for rape she considered it to be. "The name of Richard Speck, to take one example, can remind us that real rape is not the pleasurable fantasy intimated in *Gone with the Wind*. To put the point graphically: would 'many women' still swoon over Butler's rape of O'Hara if they knew that he urinated on her?"[19] Lest readers wonder how they could have missed that lurid scene in *Gone with the Wind,* I hasten to say that Ms. Friedman made up this detail presumably to bolster her point. In my rejoinder, I told the audience about a recent poll taken by Harriet Taylor, the feminist author of *Scarlett's Women: "Gone with the Wind" and Its Female Fans.*[20] Ms. Taylor did not pretend that her survey was scientific, but what she found has the ring of truth. She asked GWTW fans what they thought had happened when Scarlett was carried up the stairs. The overwhelming majority of the four hundred respondents indicated that they did not think Rhett raped Scarlett, though there was some "mutually pleasurable rough sex."[21] Almost all reported that they found the scene "erotically exciting." As one respondent put it:

> Scarlett's story is that of a woman who has had lousy sex from two
> incompetent husbands (a "boy" and an "old man," as Rhett reminds
> her) [who] knew nothing about women. At last she finds out what

good sex feels like, even if (or probably because) her first experience takes place in mutual inebriation and a spirit of vengeful anger.[22]

The idea of "mutually pleasurable rough sex" is not high on the gender feminist list of entertainments. All the same, if the New Feminist philosophers were honest about taking women seriously, they would be paying attention to what, in most women's minds, is a fundamental distinction: Scarlett was ravished, not raped. The next morning finds her relishing the memory. Ms. Friedman's insistence that Scarlett was raped was just another example of how gender feminists, estranged from the women they claim to represent, tend to view male/female relations as violent or humiliating to women.

Friedman, like Bartky, takes comfort in the idea that women's desires and aspirations will change in time. Younger women, she says, are already less inclined to be taken in by the Rhett Butler mystique, and his fascination should continue to diminish. That is, unless people like me give younger women the idea that there is nothing wrong with taking pleasure in Scarlett's enraptured submission.

"How sad it would be," she writes, "if Sommers's writings acted as an obstacle to change, bolstering those who interpret the sexual domination of women as pleasurable, and intimidating those who speak out against such domination."[23]

Ms. Friedman considers Sandra Bartky to be one of her mentors and Bartky is, indeed, of the opinion that active measures should be taken to prevent the spread of "harmful" writings. In 1990 I was commissioned by the *Atlantic* to do a piece on campus feminism. When Sandra Bartky somehow learned of this, she wrote to the editors, pleading with them not to publish it. She told them that I was a disreputable philosopher and "a right-wing ideologue." The *Chronicle of Higher Education* found out about the flap, and called Ms. Bartky to ask her why she had written the letter. At first she denied having asked them to suppress my piece, claiming that she had only requested that my article be accompanied by another giving a different point of view. But when the *Chronicle* reporter pointed out that he had a copy of the letter and that it contained no such request, she defiantly admitted having tried to stop the piece: "I wouldn't want a nut case who thinks there wasn't a Holocaust to write about the Holocaust. Editors exercise discretion. By not asking someone to write a piece, that's not censorship, that's discretion."[24]

Inadvertently, Bartky got her way. By the time the whole matter was sorted out, the *Atlantic* had gone on to other issues. Editor Michael Curtis told the *Chronicle* that he was embarrassed that the piece had not been

published. The *Chronicle* reporter asked what he thought of Bartky's letter. "It seemed to confirm some of the darker aspects of Ms. Sommers's
article, which pointed out the extraordinary lengths some of the women
were prepared to go to shape all discussion in which they had an interest,"
he replied.[25]

Rhett Butler continues to pique the gender feminists. Naomi Wolf, at
least in her earlier incarnation, was fond of explaining to the public how
women cooperate in their own degradation. When asked why women
enjoyed the "rape scene" in *Gone with the Wind,* Ms. Wolf answered that
they had been "trained" to accept that kind of treatment and so grew to
like it: "It's not surprising that, after decades of being exposed to a culture
that consistently eroticizes violence against women, women, too, would
often internalize their own training."[26]

I can't help being amused by how upset the New Feminists get over
the vicarious pleasure women take in Scarlett's transports. All that incorrect swooning! How are we ever going to get women to see how wrong it
is? Nevertheless, the gender feminists seem to believe that thirty years
from now, with the academy transformed and the feminist consciousness
of the population raised, there will be a new Zeitgeist. Women who
interpret sexual domination as pleasurable will then be few and far between, and Scarlett, alas, will be out of style.

Is this scenario out of the question? I think it is. Sexuality has always
been part of our natures, and there is no one right way. Men like Rhett
Butler will continue to fascinate many women. Nor will the doctrine that
this demeans them have much of an effect. How many women who like
Rhett Butler–types are in search of support groups to help them change?
Such women are not grateful to the gender feminists for going to war
against male lust. They may even be offended at the suggestion that they
themselves are being degraded and humiliated; for that treats their enjoy-
ment as pathological.

Defending women who enjoy the idea of ravishment is not the same as
holding a brief for any specific kind of fantasy or sexual preference.
Fantasies of female domination are also popular. Women are clearly capable of treating men as "sex objects" with an enthusiasm equal to, and
in some cases exceeding, that of men for treating women as such. Male
strip-shows seem to be as popular as Tupperware parties.

The dissident feminist Camille Paglia uses the term *pagan gazers* for
those who publicly watch males or females as sex objects. She has no
quarrel with the male gazers, but she positively applauds the female ones.
"Women are getting much more honest about looking at men, and about
leering. Finally we're getting somewhere."[27]

If Paglia is right, sexual liberation may not be going in the direction of eliminating the Other as a sex object; it may instead be going in the direction of encouraging women to objectify the male as Other, too. Such a development would certainly be a far cry from the gender feminist utopia described by University of Massachusetts philosopher Ann Ferguson:

> With the elimination of sex roles, and the disappearance, in an overpopulated world, of any biological need for sex to be associated with procreation, there would be no reason why such a society could not transcend sexual gender. It would no longer matter what biological sex individuals had. Love relationships, and the sexual relationships developing out of them, would be based on the individual meshing together of androgynous human beings.[28]

Ferguson's utopia conjures up visions of a world of gender-neutral characters like Pat on "Saturday Night Live." Although Pat-like people can be very nice (doubtless, never rough), their sexually correct meshings do not invite heated speculation. To put the matter bluntly: the androgynous society has always been a boring feminist fairy tale with no roots in psychological or social reality.

A group of gay women who call themselves "lipstick lesbians" are rebelling against the androgynous ideal that feminists like Ann Ferguson and Joyce Trebilcot celebrate. According to Lindsy Van Gelder, a writer for *Allure* magazine, the lipstick lesbians are tired of Birkenstock and L. L. Bean couture, "womyn's" music festivals, potluck dinners, and all the "rigid dos and don'ts of feminist ideology."[29] She reports on several lesbian go-go bars in different parts of the country where lipstick lesbians congregate and treat each other in ways that are very much frowned upon in most gender feminist circles.

I believe that the Bartkys, the Friedmans, and the Fergusons are doomed to disappointment but that in any case no feminist should ever have an agenda of managing women's desires and fantasies. For suppose we could succeed in "trading in the fantasy of being overwhelmed by Rhett Butler for one in which we seize state power and reeducate him." Suppose, indeed, that we succeeded in getting most people to feel and to behave in ways that are sexually correct by gender feminist lights. Once the methods and institutions for overhauling desires are in place, what would prevent their deployment by new groups who have different conceptions of what is sexually correct and incorrect? Having seized state power, some zealous faction would find ready to hand the apparatus needed for reeducating people to *its* idea of what is "authentic," not only sexually but politically and culturally.

So far, the efforts to get women to overhaul their fantasies and desires have been noncoercive, but they do not seem to have been particularly effective. To get the results they want, the gender feminists have turned their attention to art and literature, where fantasies are manufactured and reinforced. Ms. Friedman calls our attention to Angela Carter's feminist rewrite of the "morning after" scene in *Gone with the Wind:* "Scarlett lies in bed smiling the next morning because she broke Rhett's kneecaps the night before. And the reason that he disappeared before she awoke was to go off to Europe to visit a good kneecap specialist."[30]

This is meant to be amusing, but of course the point is serious. For the gender feminist believes that Margaret Mitchell got it wrong. If Mitchell had understood better how to make a true heroine of Scarlett, she would have made her different. Scarlett would then have been the kind of person who would plainly see that Rhett must be severely punished for what he had inflicted on her the night before. More generally, the gender feminist believes she must *rebut* and replace the fiction that glorifies dominant males and the women who find them attractive. This popular literature, which "eroticizes" male dominance, must be opposed and, if possible, eradicated. Furthermore, the feminist establishment must seek ways to foster the popularity of a new genre of romantic film and fiction that sends a more edifying message to the women and men of America. A widely used textbook gives us a fair idea of what that message *should* be:

> Plots for nonsexist films could include women in traditionally male jobs (e.g., long-distance truck driver). . . . For example, a high-ranking female Army officer, treated with respect by men and women alike, could be shown not only in various sexual encounters with other people but also carrying out her job in a humane manner. Or perhaps the main character could be a female urologist. She could interact with nurses and other medical personnel, diagnose illnesses brilliantly, and treat patients with great sympathy as well as have sex with them. When the Army officer or the urologist engage in sexual activities, they will treat their partners and be treated by them in some of the considerate ways described above.[31]

The truck driver and the urologist are meant to be serious role models for the free feminist woman, humane, forthrightly sexual, but not discriminating against either gender in her preferences for partners, so considerate that all will respect her. These models are projected in the hope that

someday films and novels with such themes and heroines will be preferred, replacing the currently popular "incorrect" romances with a more
acceptable ideal.

It seems a futile hope. Perhaps the best way to see what the gender
feminists are up against is to compare their version of romance with that
embodied in contemporary romance fiction that sells in the millions. Here
is a typical example:

> Townsfolk called him devil. For dark and enigmatic Julian, Earl of
> Ravenwood, was a man with a legendary temper and a first wife
> whose mysterious death would not be forgotten. . . . Now country-
> bred Sophy Dorring is about to become Ravenwood's new bride.
> Drawn to his masculine strength and the glitter of desire that burned
> in his emerald eyes, the tawny-haired lass had her own reasons for
> agreeing to a marriage of convenience. . . . Sophy Dorring intended
> to teach the devil to love.[32]

Romance novels amount to almost 40 percent of all mass-market paperback sales. Harlequin Enterprises alone has sales of close to 200 million books worldwide. They appear in many languages, including
Japanese, Swedish, and Greek, and they are now beginning to appear in
Eastern Europe. The readership is almost exclusively women.[33] The challenge this presents to gender feminist ideologues is most formidable since
almost every hero in this fictional genre is an "alpha male" like Rhett
Butler or the Earl of Ravenwood. It was therefore to be expected that the
New Feminists would make a concerted attempt to correct this literature
and to replace it by a new one.

Kathleen Gilles Seidel reports that "young, politically conscious editors" have been pressuring writers "to conform to at least the appearance
of a more feminist fantasy."[34] But these authors "felt that an alien sensibility was being forced on their work, that they weren't being allowed to
speak to their readers in their own voices. They didn't want to write about
heroines who repair helicopters."[35] Ms. Seidel notes that editorial pressure was especially strong on writers who were drawn to the macho,
domineering hero.

Seidel is echoed by Jayne Ann Krentz, the hugely successful writer of
romance fiction who created the intriguing earl and his Sophy:

> Much of this effort was exerted by a wave of young editors fresh out
> of East Coast colleges who arrived in New York to take up their first
> positions in publishing. . . . They set about trying to make romances

respectable. They looked for new authors who shared their views of what a respectable romance should be, and they tried to change the books being written by the established, successful authors they inherited. The first target of these reforming editors was what has come to be known in the trade as the alpha male.[36]

Ms. Krentz lists several more "targets," among them "the aggressive seduction of the heroine by the hero" and the convention that the heroine is a virgin. The young editors' failure was "resounding."[37] Their exhortations to change had little effect on the more established writers. Nor did they succeed in their aim of getting new writers to introduce a new and popular genre of "politically correct romances . . . featuring sensitive, unaggressive heroes and sexually experienced, right-thinking heroines in 'modern' stories dealing with trendy issues. . . . Across the board, from series romance to single title release, it is the writers who have steadfastly resisted the efforts to reform the genre whose books consistently outsell all others."[38]

Sales are the true gauge of public preference; in the last analysis, it was the *readers'* resistance to the "right-thinking" heroines and heros that caused the zealous editors to unbend and retreat.

The effort to impose feminist rectitude sometimes surfaces in less popular literary genres. The Israeli poet Gershom Gorenberg, who had submitted several poems to Marge Piercy, poetry editor of *Tikkun* magazine, received a letter from her that read: "I found your work witty and original, and I am taking parts of [it] for . . . *Tikkun.* I have to say I am not fond of the way you write about women, but I have left out those parts. When I blot out those parts, I like what you are doing."[39]

Gorenberg's first impulse was to search his poetry for the "criminal stanzas," although he could find nothing in his writing that struck him as sexist: "And then I realize that the inquisitor is succeeding admirably: The very vagueness of the charge has driven me to search for my sins, incriminate myself, confess."[40]

Gorenberg saw that the blotting had larger implications and described it in an op-ed column for the *New York Times.* It was published along with a rebuttal by Piercy. Piercy was indignant: "I try to pick the best work that comes through the mailbox—and the best has to consider the implications of the language used and the sensitivities of many groups, including women. Why would I publish work that degrades me?"[41]

Piercy defends a censorship that she herself has never been subjected to. We may imagine her outrage if an editor had tried to blot out any part of her novel *Women on the Edge of Time* for its treatment of traditional family values. She there described a gender feminist utopia in which both women and men are able to bear children and to nurse. It is unfortunate that Ms. Piercy's concern for liberating women from biological constraints is not matched by a passionate regard for free expression.

Established and successful writers have not found it too difficult to resist the gender feminist pressures. Younger writers are more vulnerable. In 1992, Pam Houston published a collection of critically esteemed short stories entitled *Cowboys Are My Weakness*. Some of her female characters "have a susceptibility to a certain kind of emotionally unavailable man," and Ms. Houston, who gives workshops to other young writers, often finds herself in the line of fire from feminists who are convinced she is doing great harm to the cause.[42] During one of her opening sessions, she was confronted by a woman who asked, "How can you take responsibility for putting stories like these out in the world?" Houston points out that her feminist critics "confuse fiction with self-help literature."

Because she writes as she does, Ms. Houston receives hate mail, harassing phone calls, and threats. She tells of other writers like herself, young and old, who feel compelled to "apologize for their female characters if they were anything short of amazonian . . . if their character was 'only a waitress,' sorry if she stayed at home and took care of the kids . . . sorry if she failed at the bar, or lost her keys, or loved a man." Houston warns that with "Big Sister" watching, women seem not to be "grant[ing] one another the right to tell the story of their own experience." She believes "the pressure women are putting on each other" to be "more insidious and far harder to resist than the pressure men have used to try to silence women for centuries." Indeed, she says, "in 1994, women are silencing each other and we are doing it so effectively that we are even silencing ourselves."[43]

In some ways, the art world offers even better prospects than literature for an ideologically correct censorious revisionism. A recent exhibit at New York's Whitney Museum Sixty-Seventh Biennial presented examples of art that is acceptably didactic in celebrating "women's rage." One work by Sue Williams explains itself: "The art world can suck my proverbial . . . ," which the catalog says "wrenches painting away from its white male domain." Two works express the artist's fury over women's vulnerability to eating disorders: one consists of a large amount of plastic vomit on the floor; the other, called "Gnaw," consists of two six-hundred-pound cubes of chocolate and lard with the artist's teeth marks in them. Another installation contains three casts of a larynx and tongue, which we are meant to take as the remains of a mutilated woman, and is accompanied by sounds of women's laughter and crying. The casts are made out of lipstick, to represent, as the catalog explains, "the silencing of women through the use of a specifically gendered material."[44]

Political art freely created can be exciting. But art wrought under the constraint of a political ideology is at best boring and at worst dreadful. That much is known from the history of "socialist realism," long a blight on Soviet literature and art. The more serious constraints, however, do not come in what is produced but in what is choked off.

Elizabeth Broun, director of the Smithsonian National Museum of American Art, invoked "two decades of feminist writing" as support for her decision to remove from an exhibit a work of Sol LeWitt that she deemed "degrading and offensive." The offending work was described by the New York Times:

It consists of a black box, about one foot tall, one foot deep and eight feet long, across the front of which 10 tiny holes have been drilled. The inside of the box is illuminated to reveal a series of photographs visible through the holes. The photographs depict a nude woman moving toward the viewer, beginning with a distant grainy image of her entire body and concluding with a closeup of her navel.[45]

Sol LeWitt had made the exhibit to honor the pioneer photographer Eadweard Muybridge. The little holes were references to the openings in Muybridge's multiple cameras, which gave the illusion of motion before the era of motion pictures. Ms. Broun saw it otherwise. "Peering through successive peepholes and focusing increasingly on the pubic region invokes unequivocal references to a degrading pornographic experience. I cannot in good conscience offer this experience to our visitors as a meaningful and important one."[46] After a protest, LeWitt's piece was reinstated.

Unfortunately, the great Spanish artist Francisco de Goya did not meet with such luck at Pennsylvania State University. Nancy Stumhofer, an instructor in the English department, took offense at a reproduction of the Goya painting The Naked Maja, which, along with reproductions of several other European paintings, had hung in her classroom longer than anyone could remember. Ms. Stumhofer turned to Bonnie Ortiz, a harassment officer at the college. Together they delivered a complaint to the campus chief executive officer, Dr. Wayne Lammie, claiming that the painting was creating "a chilly climate for women." Ms. Stumhofer refused to switch classrooms and rejected a compromise plan to take down the painting while she was teaching, saying, "Every female student in every class scheduled in that room would be subject to the chill."[47] Dr.

Lammie and the University Women's Commission agreed. Goya's paint-ing was removed.

It does not take much to chill an environment. Chris Robison, a grad-uate student at the University of Nebraska, had placed on his desk a small photograph of his wife at the beach wearing a bikini. Two of his office mates, both female graduate students in psychology, demanded he re-move it because "it created a hostile work environment."[48] I talked with Mr. and Mrs. Robison, who told me that at first they thought the women were kidding. But then the offended office mates made it clear to Mr. Robison that "the photo conveyed a message about [his] attitude toward women" that they did not approve of.

The department chair, Professor John Berman, took the women's side, warning that female students who came into the office could be offended. Mr. Robison removed his wife's picture from his desk, telling the local newspaper, "I cannot risk the very real consequences of putting the photo up again."

The charge of offending by creating a hostile or "intimidating" environ-ment is now being made with great frequency, and, almost always, those accused retreat, for they know they cannot depend on support from those in authority. Never mind that such a charge usually creates a hostile, intimidating, or "chilling" environment of its own or that they could have used less confrontational ways of dealing with an uncomfortable situation —such as calling the buildings and grounds department to have an un-wanted painting removed. Making a case of it puts everyone on notice that feminist sensibilities, no matter how precious or odd, are not to be trifled with.

The "hostile environment" created by those who are hypersensitive to every possible offense is no longer strictly an academic phenomenon. We are beginning to see it in the museums, in the press (witness the *Boston Globe* with its "Women on the Verge"), and in many a workplace, where the employers are practicing defensive suppression of innocent behavior in fear that it could be considered harassment by litigious feminists.

For the time being, however, the "chill" of rectitude is still most intense on the modern American campus, where cadres of well-trained zealots from the feminist classrooms are vengefully poised to find sexism in every cranny of their environment. One of the precious and fragile things that wither in the hostile and intolerant climate of feminist rectitude is artistic creativity.

The attack on art by self-righteous students has begun to cause alarm in quarters that are usually sympathetic to gender feminist concerns. Liza Mundy, writing in the Fall 1993 issue of *Lingua Franca,* reports on the shocking successes that students, affronted by the art on their campuses, have had in censoring it.

At the University of North Carolina, feminist students took offense at a sculpture called *The Student Body,* by Julia Balk. It consists of several students walking across campus—a male has his arm around a female, and he is reading a book; she is eating an apple. Students organized a Committee Against Offensive Statues and were able to persuade the chancellor, Paul Hardin, to move the work to an out-of-the-way place where no one would be forced to see it.[49] At Colgate University, a mix of students and faculty successfully challenged the exhibition of nude photographs by one of America's premier photographers, Lee Friedlander. At the University of Arizona, enough students denounced the nude self-photos of graduate student Laurie Blakeslee to cause their removal. The University of Pittsburgh banned a nude painting from last year's open exhibit of student art at the insistence of an all-female panel, who considered it obscene and sexually offensive. Anthropologist Carol Vance of Columbia University is unhappy about these acts of censorship. As she told Liza Mundy, "What may strike me as sexist might not strike you as sexist." She finds fault with the administrations for caving in: "Administrations that really show inertia when it comes to addressing the problem of sexism and so on, will snap to when someone says that a film or work of art is offensive. . . . It's a relatively inexpensive way for an administration to show its concern."[50]

At the University of Michigan, where Catharine MacKinnon inspires censorship, the students simply removed a videotape they regarded as offensive from an exhibit by the artist Carol Jacobsen. Jacobsen then demanded that they either censor the whole thing or replace the tape. After meeting with MacKinnon and her fellow anti-pornography crusader Andrea Dworkin, the students went into another room and then "independently" asked Jacobsen to take down the entire exhibit. MacKinnon is adamant about the need for feminist monitoring of art and makes no bones about her own insight and expertise into what cannot pass muster: "What you need is people who see through literature like Andrea Dworkin, who see through law like me, to see through art and create the uncompromised women's visual vocabulary."[51] Commenting on the "deafening silence" of the Michigan faculty, Carol Vance suggested that "no one wanted to cross Catharine MacKinnon."

With gender monitors in a position of influence, the more creative writers and artists are shunted aside. The effect on novices and the unrecognized is especially serious. How many works are unpublished (or unwritten) out of fear of offending the feminist sensibilities of funders, curators, editors, and other gender wardens inside and outside the academy? How many paintings are unexhibited (or unpainted), how many lyrics unrecorded (or unsung)? Artists need courage, but ideological intimidation deeply affects and inhibits creativity.

The government could help if it understood the problem. But far from discouraging the cultural apparatchiks, the government may soon be "empowering" them by offering federal support for monitors of "gender equity" in every school and every workplace. Such monitors are already strongly entrenched in our cultural institutions, and there they will continue to hold sway until their power is challenged.

But who will challenge them? The answer to that question transcends the politics of liberalism and conservatism. Too often, those who find fault with the intolerance of the feminist ideologues are tarred as right-wing reactionaries. It is true that "the right" has tended to be more alarmed about the censoriousness of the "liberal" left. But there are relatively few conservatives in our educational institutions and cultural temples, and it would be most unrealistic to count on them to be very effective in combatting gender feminism. Nor, if we judge by the sorry record of their faintheartedness in the academic world, should we count on intellectual men to engage the gender feminists in open battle. So the unpleasant but necessary task of confrontation falls to women who believe in free expression and who scorn those who would stifle it. Such women waged and won the battle for the suffrage and for all the basic rights American women now enjoy. Such women are still in the majority, but out of a lack of awareness of the extent of the problem or a reluctance to criticize their zealous sisters, they have remained silent. The price has been great—the ideologues have made off with the women's movement.

It would be difficult to exaggerate the extent of the difficulties we now face. The gender feminists have proved very adroit in getting financial support from governmental and private sources. They hold the keys to many bureaucratic fiefdoms, research centers, womens' studies programs, tenure committees, and para-academic organizations. It is now virtually impossible to be appointed to high administrative office in any university system without having passed muster with the gender feminists. If bills that are now before Congress pass, there will be paid gender monitors in every primary and secondary school in the country and harassment officers in every secondary school and college. Nor will this phenomenon be restricted to schools; experts on harassment will be needed to monitor the workplace. Needless to say, the only available "experts" are gender feminists whose very raison d'être is to find more and more abuse.

Moreover, the gender feminists will continue to do everything in their power to ensure that their patronage goes to women of the right consciousness. And, it must be acknowledged, they have certain inherent advantages over the mainstream. Now that it has overthrown most of the legal impediments to women's rights, equity feminism is no longer galvanizing: it does not produce fanatics. Moderates in general are not temperamentally suited to activism. They tend to be reflective and individualistic. They do not network. They do not rally. They do not recruit. They do not threaten their opponents with loss of jobs or loss of patronage. They are not especially litigious. In short, they have so far been no match politically for the gender warriors.

On the other hand, the mainstream feminists are only just becoming aware of the fact that the Faludis and the Steinems speak in the name of women *but do not represent them*. With the new awareness that the feminist leaders and theorists are patronizing them, there is a very real possibility that the mainstream is the tide of the not-too-distant future. I began the research for this book in 1989. Since then, the public has learned that academic feminism has been playing a leading role in promoting the illiberal movement known as "PC" in the nation's colleges. Now it is beginning to realize that the New Feminism is socially divisive and that it generally lacks a constituency in the population at large.

Classical equity feminism is very much alive in the hearts of American women. It is unfortunate that part of its energies must now be diverted to defend the women's movement from the grave threat posed to it by the gender feminist ideologues. Ironically a concerted effort to deal with the threat may well prove revitalizing to the languishing mainstream. Getting out from under the stifling, condescending ministrations of the ideologues is a bracing cause and an exhilarating necessary step for the truly liberated women to take. When enough women take it, the gender feminists' lack of a constituency among American women will be exposed, and their power structure will not survive.

Inside the academy, it would take only a courageous few to launch the long-overdue critique that will puncture the intellectual affectations of the gender feminists. Open criticism of an academic feminism that has subordinated scholarship to ideology would quickly halt the pretentious campaign to "transform the knowledge base" and eventually open the doors to more representative, less doctrinaire, and more capable women scholars in the women's studies programs. We should then see the end of "feminist classrooms" that recruit students for the more extreme wing of the women's movement.

Outside the academy individual voices have already begun to be heard in protest, from women as diverse as Camille Paglia, Betty Friedan, Katie

Roiphe, Midge Decter, Mary Lefkowitz, Cathy Young, Erica Jong, Diane Ravitch, Karen Lehrman, and Wendy Kaminer, women who are not fazed by being denounced as traitors and backlashers. We may expect that more and more women will be expressing their frustration and annoyance with feminists who speak in their name but do not share their values. When that happens, we may expect that the public will become alert to what the gender feminists stand for; their influence should then decline precipitously. For some time to come, the gender monitors will still be there—in the schools, in the feminist centers, in the workplace—but, increasingly, their intrusions will not be welcome.

The reader of this book may wonder whether there is *anything* I like about the gender feminists. I have sat among them in many a gathering and have occasionally found myself in relaxed agreement with them. For I do like the features they share with classical feminism: a concern for women and a determination to see them fairly treated. We very much need that concern and energy, but we decidedly do not need their militant gynocentrism and misandrism. It's too bad that in the case of the gender feminists we can't have the concern without the rest of the baggage. I believe, however, that once their ideology becomes unfashionable, many a gender feminist will quietly divest herself of the sex/gender lens through which she now views social reality and join the equity feminist mainstream. I do not think this will happen tomorrow, but I am convinced it will happen. Credos and intellectual fashions come and go but feminism itself—the pure and wholesome article first displayed at Seneca Falls in 1848—is as American as apple pie, and it will stay.

Notes

Preface

1. Gloria Steinem, *Revolution from Within: A Book of Self-Esteem* (Boston: Little, Brown, 1992), p. 222.
2. Naomi Wolf, *The Beauty Myth: How Images of Beauty Are Used Against Women* (New York: Doubleday, 1992), pp. 180–82.
3. Ibid., p. 207.
4. Joan Jacobs Brumberg, *Fasting Girls: The Emergence of Anorexia Nervosa as a Modern Disease* (Cambridge, Mass.: Harvard University Press, 1988), pp. 19–20.
5. Ibid., p. 33.
6. *FDA Consumer,* May 1986 and March 1992. The report is based on figures provided by the National Center of Health Statistics (NCHS).
7. Ann Landers, "Women and Distorted Body Images," *Boston Globe,* April 29, 1992.
8. Wolf sent me a copy of a letter that she had written to her editors, which said, "I have . . . learned that the statistic, taken from Brumberg's *Fasting Girls* and provided to her by the American Anorexia and Bulimia Association, is not accurate. Please let me know how to correct this error in future editions."
9. Wolf, *The Beauty Myth,* p. 208.
10. Cheris Kramarae and Dale Spender, eds., *The Knowledge Explosion: Generations of Feminist Scholarship* (New York: Teachers College Press, Columbia University, 1992), p. 15.

11. Women's Studies Network (Internet: LISTSERV@UMDD.UMD.EDU), November 4, 1992.
12. *Time,* December 6, 1993, p. 10.
13. Ms. Buel has taken a leave from the Suffolk County office to return to Harvard. She is now a fellow at the Bunting Institute, a feminist research center at Radcliffe College.
14. Tracing it further, I found that Esta Soler, the executive director of the Family Violence Prevention Foundation, repeated Buel's claim in a 1990 grant application. She had given that grant application to *Time* writer McDowell, who relied on it in making the claim about the March of Dimes. That was it: it had gone from White-head's introductory remark, to Sarah Buel's unpublished manuscript, to the domestic violence people, to the *Globe* and *Time,* then to all the rest of the newspapers.
15. *Boston Globe,* January 29, 1993, p. 16.
16. Ken Ringle, *Washington Post,* January 31, 1993, p. A1.
17. Louis Harris and Associates, "Commonwealth Fund Survey on Women's Health" (New York: Commonwealth Fund, 1993), p. 8.
18. Reported in *Time,* March 9, 1992, p. 54.
19. *Los Angeles Times Magazine,* February 2, 1992. See also *In View: Issues and Insights for College Women* 1, no. 3 (September–October 1989).

Chapter 1: Women Under Siege

1. Winifred Holtby, "Feminism Divided," in *Modern Feminisms,* ed. Maggie Humm (New York: Columbia University Press, 1992), p. 42.
2. Marilyn French, *The War Against Women* (New York: Simon & Schuster, 1992). Heilbrun is quoted on the jacket cover.
3. Anne Mathews, "Rage in a Tenured Position," *New York Times Magazine,* November 8, 1992, p. 47.
4. Ibid., p. 72.
5. *Chronicle of Higher Education,* November 11, 1992, p. A18.
6. Ibid., p. A17.
7. Pauline Bart's comments were made in the context of notifying women's studies teachers about the *New York Times* story on Carolyn Heilbrun and her trials at Columbia. The text appears on the Women's Studies Network (Internet: LISTSERV@UMDD.UMD.EDU), November 9, 1992.
8. The Heilbrun conference is on videotape. The tape is available through the women's studies program at the CUNY Graduate Center.
9. *The Elizabeth Cady Stanton–Susan B. Anthony Reader,* ed. Ellen Carol Dubois (Boston: Northeastern University Press, 1992), p. 51.
10. Sandra Lee Bartky, *Femininity and Domination: Studies in the Phenomenology of Oppression* (New York: Routledge, 1990), p. 50. Bartky is relying on the work of the feminist anthropologist Gayle Rubin, who was among the first to speak of the "sex/gender system." Here is Rubin's definition: "While particular socio-sexual systems vary, each one is specific and individuals within it will have to conform to a finite set of possibilities. Each new generation must learn and become its sexual destiny, each person must be encoded with its appropriate status within the system." From Gayle Rubin, "The Traffic in Women," in Rayna Reiter, ed., *Toward an Anthropology of Women* (New York: Monthly Review Press, 1975), p. 161.
11. Kate Millett, *Sexual Politics* (New York: Ballantine Books, 1970). The quoted passage is taken from the back cover.

12. Alison M. Jaggar, *Feminist Politics and Human Nature* (Totowa, N.J.: Rowman and Littlefield, 1988), p. 148.
13. Iris Marion Young, *"Throwing like a Girl" and Other Essays in Feminist Philosophy and Social Theory* (Bloomington: Indiana University Press, 1990), p. 93.
14. Iris Marion Young, "Humanism, Gynocentrism, and Feminist Politics," in ibid., p. 73.
15. Andrea Nye, *Feminist Theory and the Philosophies of Man* (New York: Routledge, 1988), p. 23.
16. Holtby, "Feminism Divided," p. 42.
17. Catharine A. MacKinnon, *New York Times,* December 15, 1991, p. 11.
18. *Harvard Crimson,* December 13, 1989.
19. Virginia Held, "Feminism and Epistemology: Recent Work on the Connection between Gender and Knowledge," *Philosophy and Public Affairs* 14, no. 3 (Summer 1985): 296.
20. Ibid., p. 297.
21. Kathryn Allen Rabuzzi, *Motherself: A Mythic Analysis of Motherhood* (Bloomington: Indiana University Press, 1988) p. 1.
22. Bartky, *Femininity and Domination,* p. 27.
23. Marilyn French, *The War Against Women* (New York: Simon & Schuster, 1992), p. 163.
24. Janet Radcliffe Richards, *The Skeptical Feminist: A Philosophical Enquiry* (Middlesex, England: Penguin Books, 1980), p. 323.
25. Susan McClary, "Getting Down off the Beanstalk: The Presence of Woman's Voice in Janika Vandervelde's *Genesis 11,*" *Minnesota Composers' Forum Newsletter* (January 1987).
26. Naomi Wolf, "A Woman's Place," *New York Times,* May 31, 1992. Ms. Wolf's piece was a shortened version of a commencement speech she had just delivered to the Scripps College class of 1992.
27. Ibid.
28. Letters to the editor, *New York Times,* June 12, 1992.
29. The 1992 NWSA conference in Austin was both audiotaped and videotaped. The tapes are available through the NWSA office at the University of Maryland in College Park, Maryland.
30. For an account of past NWSA conferences see Carol Sternhell's review of Gloria Steinem's *Revolution from Within,* in *Women's Review of Books* 9, no. 9 (June 1992): 5.
31. Alice Rossi, ed., *The Feminist Papers: From Adams to de Beauvoir* (New York: Columbia University Press, 1993), p. 413.
32. Ibid., p. 414.
33. Ibid.
34. Ibid., p. 415.
35. Ibid., p. 416.
36. Elisabeth Griffith, *In Her Own Right: The Life of Elizabeth Cady Stanton* (New York: Oxford University Press, 1984), p. 159.
37. Historian Elisabeth Griffith reports that some scholars believe that it was Richard Hunt who came up with the idea of a women's rights conference. See ibid., p. 52.
38. The conference, called "Taking the Lead: Balancing the Educational Equation," was cosponsored by Mills College and the American Association of University Women (AAUW). It took place October 23–25, 1992, at Mills College. The program is

available through the AAUW's Washington office. I attended the conference with my sister, Louise Hoff, and with journalist Barbara Rhoades Ellis. See also Ms. Ellis's entertaining and insightful "Pod People Infest AAUW," an account of the Mills conference, in *Heterodoxy*, December 1992. Ms. Ellis's article includes my description of its "Perils of Feminist Teaching" workshop.

39. David Gurevich, "Lost in Translation," *American Spectator*, August 1991, pp. 28–29.
40. Gurevich notes that he had no trouble translating these parts of Ms. Kauffman's speech: "Her clichés have perfect Russian equivalents, finessed over the past seventy years."

Chapter 2: Indignation, Resentment, and Collective Guilt

1. *Boston Globe*, April 30, 1992, p. 29.
2. Sandra Lee Bartky, *Femininity and Domination: Studies in the Phenomenology of Oppression* (New York: Routledge, 1990), p. 15.
3. *Daily Hampshire Gazette*, March 18, 1992.
4. Marilyn French, *The War Against Women* (New York: Simon & Schuster, 1992), p. 182.
5. Ibid.
6. Ibid., p. 199.
7. Diana Scully, on the Women's Studies Network (Internet: LISTSERV@UMDD.UMD.EDU), January 27, 1993. See also her book, *Understanding Sexual Violence* (New York: Routledge, 1990).
8. *Time*, June 3, 1991, p. 52.
9. Story reported in the *Washington Times*, May 7, 1993.
10. *Ms.* magazine, September/October 1993, p. 94. Cited in Daniel Wattenberg, "Sharia Feminists," in *American Spectator*, December 1993, p. 60.
11. *Vanity Fair*, November, 1993, p. 170; quoted in ibid., from Kim Masters, *Vanity Fair*, November 1993.
12. Wattenberg, "Sharia Feminists," p. 62.
13. Ruth Shalit, "Romper Room: Sexual Harassment—by Tots," *New Republic*, March 29, 1993, p. 14.
14. Nan Stein, "Secrets in Public: Sexual Harassment in Public (and Private) Schools," working paper no. 256 (Wellesley, Mass.: Wellesley College Center for Research on Women, 1993), p. 4.
15. Shalit, "Romper Room," p. 13.
16. Lionel Tiger, *Newsday*, October 15, 1991.
17. *Boston Phoenix*, October 11, 1991, p. 14.
18. Ibid.
19. Ibid., p. 21.
20. Ibid., April 16, 1993.
21. The full account of the Nyhan affair is to be found in ibid. See also Joe Queenan, "What's New Pussy-Whipped?" in *GQ*, August 1993, p. 144. See also "Fighting Words," *The New Yorker*, May 3, 1993, p. 34.

Chapter 3: Transforming the Academy

1. Joyce Trebilcot, ed., *Mothering: Essays in Feminist Theory* (Totowa, N.J.: Rowman and Allanheld, 1984), p. vii.

2. Copies of the Women's Studies Constitution are available through the National Women's Studies Association, University of Maryland, College Park.
3. Carolyn Heilbrun, "Feminist Criticism in Departments of Literature," *Academe*, September–October 1983, p. 14.

Elaine Marks, Nannerl Keohane, and Elizabeth Minnich have also given enthusiastic support to the comparison between the discoveries made in women's studies and those of Copernicus and Darwin. See Elaine Marks, "Deconstructing in Women's Studies to Reconstructing the Humanities," Marilyn R. Schuster and Susan R. Van Dyne, eds., in *Women's Place in the Academy: Transforming the Liberal Arts Curriculum* (Totowa, N.J.: Rowman and Allanheld, 1985), p. 174. Nannerl Keohane made the comparison in her address "Challenges for the Future" at the June 15, 1992, conference at Radcliffe College entitled "In the Eye of the Storm: Feminist Research and Action in the Nineties." Elizabeth Minnich makes it as well: "What we [feminists] are doing is comparable to Copernicus shattering our geo-centricity, Darwin shattering our species-centricity. We are shattering andro-centricity, and the change is as fundamental, as dangerous, as exciting." Keynote address, "The Feminist Academy," reprinted in *Proceedings of Great Lakes Women's Studies Association*, November 1979, p. 7.
4. Gerda Lerner, quoted in *Chronicle of Higher Education*, September 28, 1988, p. 7.
5. Jessie Bernard in the foreword to Angela Simeone, *Academic Women* (South Hadley, Mass.: Bergin and Garvey, 1987), pp. xii and xiii.
6. *Ms.* magazine, October 1985, p. 50.
7. Ann Ferguson, "Feminist Teaching: A Practice Developed in Undergraduate Courses," *Radical Teacher*, April 1982, p. 28.
8. "Access to Resources" (Towson, Md.: Towson State University, National Clearinghouse for Curriculum Transformation Resources, April 1993), p. 7.
9. Caryn McTighe Musil, *The Courage to Question: Women's Studies and Student Learning* (Washington, D.C.: Association of American Colleges, 1992), p. 3.
10. Louise Bernikow, introduction to *The World Split Open: Four Centuries of Women Poets in England and America, 1552–1950* (New York: Random House, 1974), p. 3.
11. Geraldine Ruthchild, "The Best Feminist Criticism Is a *New* Criticism," in *Feminist Pedagogy and the Learning Climate: Proceedings of the Ninth Annual Great Lakes Colleges Association Women's Studies Conference* (Ann Arbor, Mich.: Great Lakes Colleges Association, 1983), p. 34.
12. Gerda Lerner, *The Creation of Patriarchy* (New York: Oxford University Press, 1986), p. 224.
13. Ibid., p. 225.
14. "Evaluating Courses for Inclusion of New Scholarship on Women" (Washington D.C.: Association of American Colleges, May 1988), p. 1.
15. *The AAUW Report: How Schools Shortchange Girls* (Washington, D.C.: American Association of University Women Educational Foundation, 1992), p. 63.
16. Leonard C. Wood et al., *America: Its People and Values* (Dallas: Harcourt Brace Jovanovich, 1985), pp. 145, 170, 509, 701. See also Daniel Boorstin and Brooks Mather Kelley, *A History of the United States* (Lexington, Mass.: Ginn, 1986).
17. Elizabeth Kamarck Minnich, *Transforming Knowledge* (Philadelphia: Temple University Press, 1990), p. 133.
18. Boorstin and Kelley, *A History of the United States*. Example cited in Robert Lerner, Althea K. Nagai, and Stanley Rothman, "Filler Feminism in High School History,"

Academic Questions 5, no. 1 (Winter 1991–92): 34. For a frank but sympathetic biography of Anne Morrow Lindbergh, see Dorothy Herrmann, *Anne Morrow Lindbergh* (New York: Penguin, 1993).

19. Lerner, Nagai, and Rothman, "Filler Feminism in High School History," p. 29.
20. *American Voices,* ed. Carol Berkin, Alan Brinkly, et al. (Glenview, Ill.: Scott Freedman, 1992), p. 18.
21. Gilbert Sewall, *Social Studies Review* (New York: American Textbook Council, 1993), p. 7.
22. Paul C. Vitz, *Censorship: Evidence of Bias in Our Children's Textbooks* (Ann Arbor, Mich.: Servant Books, 1986).
23. Ibid., p. 73.
24. Diane Ravitch and Chester E. Finn, *What Do Our Seventeen-Year-Olds Know?* (New York: Harper & Row, 1987). The figures cited are taken from the appendix, pp. 262–77.
25. Reported in the *Boston Globe:* "Top Students Get Low Scores in Civics," April 6, 1993, p. 3.
26. "Standards for Evaluation of Instructional Materials with Respect to Social Content" (California State Department of Education, 1986), p. 2.
27. Peggy Means McIntosh, "Curricular Re-Vision: The New Knowledge for a New Age," in *Educating the Majority: Women Challenge Tradition in Higher Education,* ed. Carol Pearson, Donna Shavlik, and Judith Touchton (New York: Macmillan, 1989), p. 404. To make their point about the masculinist character of artistic and literary judgment, the transformationist revisionists almost always encase terms like *masterpiece, genius,* and *literary canon* in scare quotes.
28. Janis C. Bell, "Teaching Art History: A Strategy for the Survival of Women's Studies," in "Looking Forward: Women's Strategies for Survival," *Proceedings of the Eleventh Annual Great Lakes Colleges Association* (Ann Arbor, Mich.: Great Lakes Colleges Association, 1985), p. 28.
29. Ibid., p. 23.
30. Marks, "Deconstructing in Women's Studies," p. 178.
31. Quoted in Minnich, *Transforming Knowledge,* p. 27.
32. Peggy McIntosh, keynote address, "Seeing Our Way Clear: Feminist Re-Vision of the Academy," *Proceedings of the Eighth Annual Great Lakes Colleges Association Women's Studies Conference* (Ann Arbor, Mich.: Great Lakes Colleges Association, 1983), p. 8.
33. *Boston Globe,* June 30, 1991.
34. "Transforming the Knowledge Base: A Panel Discussion at the National Network of Women's Caucuses" (New York: National Council for Research on Women, 1990), p. 4. Minnich's attack on the ancient Greeks reminded me of my own more traditional introduction to "The Greeks." When I was in high school, my mother gave me Edith Hamilton's *The Greek Way*. It inspired in me a great interest in philosophy and classical art. Today, the many pedagogues who follow the Minnich line protect high school girls from such books.
35. Minnich, *Transforming Knowledge,* p. 113.
36. Joyce Trebilcot, "Dyke Methods," *Hypatia: A Journal of Feminist Philosophy* 3, no. 2 (Summer 1988): 3.
37. "Feminist Scholarship Guidelines," distributed by the New Jersey Project (Wayne, N.J.: William Paterson College, 1991).

38. Catharine MacKinnon, "Feminism, Marxism, Method, and the State," in *Signs* (Summer 1993): 636.
39. Sandra Harding, *The Science Question in Feminism* (Ithaca, N.Y.: Cornell University Press, 1986), p. 113.
40. Mary Field Belenky, Blythe McVicker Clinchy, Nancy Rule Goldberger, and Jill Mattuck Tarule, *Women's Ways of Knowing* (New York: Basic Books, 1986), p. 104.
41. Ibid.
42. Ibid., p. 113.
43. Peggy McIntosh, "Seeing Our Way Clear: Feminist Revision and the Academy," *Proceedings of the Eighth Annual GLCA Women's Studies Conference* (Ann Arbor, Mich.: Great Lakes Colleges Association, November 5–7, 1982), p. 13.
44. Dr. McIntosh outlined her five-phase theory in a 1990 workshop for the public school teachers and staff in Brookline, Massachusetts, which was videotaped by the Brookline School Department and is available through that office.
45. Peggy McIntosh, "Interactive Phases of Curricular and Personal Re-Vision with Regard to Race," working paper no. 219 (Wellesley, Mass.: Wellesley College Center for Research on Women, 1990), p. 6.
46. McIntosh, working paper no. 124, p. 11.
47. Workshop, Brookline, Massachusetts, 1990 (see note 44 above).
48. McIntosh, working paper no. 219, p. 5.
49. Ibid., no. 124, p. 7.
50. Ibid., p. 10.
51. Ibid., no. 219, p. 10.
52. Ibid.
53. Ibid., p. 11.
54. Ibid., p. 6.
55. Ibid., no. 124, p. 21.
56. Schuster and Van Dyne, *Women's Place in the Academy*, p. 26.
57. All the quotations concerning Dean Stimpson's "Dream Curriculum" are from Catharine R. Stimpson, "Is There a Core in Their Curriculum? And Is It Really Necessary?" *Change* (March–April 1988): 27–31.
58. Ibid., p. 30.
59. Linda Gardiner, "Can This Discipline Be Saved? Feminist Theory Challenges Mainstream Philosophy," working paper no. 118 (Wellesley, Mass.: Wellesley College Center for Research on Women, 1983), p. 4.
60. Ibid., p. 12.
61. Evelyn Fox Keller, *Reflections on Gender and Science* (New Haven, Conn.: Yale University Press, 1985), p. 174.
62. Ibid., p. 175.
63. Ibid., p. 173.
64. Interview with Meg Urry of the Space Telescope and Science Institute, "CNN Headline News," June 14, 1993, 9:55 P.M.
65. Sue Rosser, "Integrating the Feminist Perspective into Courses in Introductory Biology," in Schuster and Van Dyne, *Women's Place in the Academy*, p. 263.
66. Ibid., p. 267.
67. Harding, *The Science Question in Feminism*, p. 251.
68. Margarita Levin, "Caring New World: Feminism and Science," *American Scholar* (Winter 1988): 105.

Chapter 4: New Epistemologies

1. See, for example, Nancy Hartsock, "The Feminist Standpoint: Developing the Ground for a Specifically Feminist Historical Materialism," in Sandra Harding and Merrill B. Hintikka, eds., *Discovering Reality: Feminist Perspectives on Epistemology, Metaphysics, Methodology, and Philosophy of Science* (Dordrecht, Holland: D. Reidel, 1983), p. 284, cited in *Feminist Epistemologies,* ed. Linda Alcoff and Elizabeth Potter (New York: Routledge, 1993), p. 85; or Charlotte Bunch, "Not for Lesbians Only," in *Passionate Politics: Feminist Theory in Action* (New York: St. Martin's Press, 1987), pp. 279–309, cited in *Feminist Epistemologies.*
2. Cited in *Feminist Epistemologies,* p. 90.
3. Virginia Held, "Feminism and Epistemology: Recent Work on the Connection between Gender and Knowledge," *Philosophy and Public Affairs* 14, no. 3 (Summer 1985): 299.
4. Susan Haack, "Epistemological Reflections of an Old Feminist," presented at annual meetings of the Eastern division of the American Philosophical Association, Washington, D.C. (December 1992). Sponsored by the Social Philosophy and Policy Center, Bowling Green. Haack's paper was published in *Reason Papers* 18 (Fall 1993): 31–43.
5. Ibid., p. 33.
6. Yolanda T. Moses, "The Challenge of Diversity," in *Education and Urban Society* 22, no. 4 (August 1990): 404. Cited in an article by Jim Sleeper in *New Republic,* June 28, 1993, p. 11.
7. Ibid., *Education and Urban Society*: 409.
8. Elizabeth Cady Stanton, "Motherhood," in Alice Rossi, ed., *The Feminist Papers: From Adams to de Beauvoir* (New York: Bantam Books, 1973), pp. 399–400.
9. Ibid.
10. Iris Murdoch, in a private letter to me.
11. Robyn R. Warhol and Diane Price Herndl, eds., *Feminisms: An Anthology of Literary Theory and Criticism* (New Brunswick, N.J.: Rutgers University Press, 1991), p. ix.
12. By a familiar irony, though most Christians would object to Mary being considered a goddess, none of the women who organized the conference thought that Christian sensibilities needed to be considered.
13. Peter Steinfels, "Beliefs," *New York Times,* May 1, 1993, p. 10.
14. Barbara Smith and Beverly Smith, "Across the Kitchen Table: A Sister-to-Sister Dialogue," in Cherríe Moraga and Gloria Anzaldua, eds., *This Bridge Called My Back: Writings by Radical Women of Color* (Watertown, Mass.: Persephone Press, 1981), p. 114.
15. Johnnella Butler called in sick.
16. Beverly Guy-Sheftall, "Consultant's Report," Ford Foundation Program on Education and Culture, March 1993, p. 11.
17. "The Monday Group," June 14, 1993.
18. *Transformations* 4, no. 1 (Spring 1993): 2.
19. The "historic" pamphlet "Transforming the Knowledge Base" can be ordered through the National Council for Research on Women in New York.

Notes

Chapter 5: The Feminist Classroom

1. Margo Culley, Arlyn Diamond, Lee Edwards, Sara Lennox, and Catherine Portuges, "The Politics of Nurturance," in *Gendered Subjects: The Dynamics of Feminist Teaching* (Boston: Routledge and Kegan Paul, 1985), p. 19.

2. Carole Sheffield, "Sexual Terrorism," in *Women: A Feminist Perspective,* ed. Jo Freeman (Mountain View, Calif.: Mayfield, 1989, p. 4). Ms. Sheffield is professor of political science at William Paterson College, where she serves as co-chair of the campus violence project.

3. The "model syllabus" can be found in Johnnella Butler, Sandra Coynes, Margaret Homans, Marlene Longenecker, and Caryn McTighe Musil, *Liberal Learning and the Women's Studies Major: A Report to the Professions* (Washington, D.C.: Association of American Colleges, 1991), appendix B.

4. Ibid., pp. 14–15.

5. Susan S. Arpad, "The Personal Cost of the Feminist Knowledge Explosion," in Cheris Kramarae and Dale Spender, eds., *The Knowledge Explosion* (New York: Teachers College Press, 1992), pp. 333–34.

6. Karen Lehrman, "Off Course," *Mother Jones,* September–October 1993, pp. 46–47.

7. Ibid., p. 49.

8. Joyce Trebilcot, "Dyke Methods," *Hypatia: A Journal of Feminist Philosophy* 3, no. 2 (Summer 1988): 7.

9. Ann Ferguson, "Feminist Teaching: A Practice Developed in Undergraduate Courses," *Radical Teacher* (April 1982): 28.

10. Ibid., p. 29.

11. Marcia Bedard and Beth Hartung, " 'Blackboard Jungle' Revisited," *Thought and Action* 7, no. 1 (Spring 1991): 11.

12. Ibid., p. 9.

13. Shawn Brown's paper (October 8, 1992) for Political Science 111, University of Michigan, p. 4.

14. Letter to *Michigan Review,* November 5, 1992.

15. Dale M. Bauer, "The Other 'F' Word: The Feminist in the Classroom," *College English* 52, no. 4 (April 1990): 385.

16. Ibid., p. 387.

17. Ibid., p. 388.

18. Roger Scruton, Angela Ellis-Jones, and Dennis O'Keefe, *Education and Indoctrination* (London: Sherwood Press, 1985).

19. Marilyn R. Schuster and Susan R. Van Dyne, eds., *Women's Place in the Academy: Transforming the Liberal Arts Curriculum* (Totowa, N.J.: Rowman and Allanheld, 1985), p. 18.

20. George Orwell, *1984* (New York: Harcourt Brace Jovanovich, 1949), p. 205.

21. Thomas Sowell, *Inside American Education: The Decline, the Deception, the Dogmas* (New York: Free Press, 1993), p. 278.

22. Copies of the ground rules can be obtained through the Center for Research on Women at Memphis State University, Memphis, Tennessee.

23. Kali Tal's remarks are from the Women's Studies Network (Internet: LISTSERV@ UMDD.UMD.EDU), February 6, 1993. Her comments, and many others like it from other women's studies practitioners, can be found under the file heading "Classroom Disclosure." She used these rules in a course at George Mason University.

24. Elizabeth Fay, "Anger in the Classroom: Women, Voice, and Fear," *Radical Teacher,* Fall 1992, part 2.
25. Ibid., p. 14.
26. Ibid., p. 15.
27. Ibid., p. 16.
28. *Women's Review of Books,* in its February 1990 issue, contains several articles by women's studies professors analyzing the phenomenon of "student resistance."
29. *Minnesota Daily,* March 14, 1989.
30. Ibid., April 18, 1989.
31. Ibid., April 13, 1989.
32. Flier printed in *Vassar Spectator,* November 1990, p. 18.
33. Carol P. Christ, "Why Women Need the Goddess," in Marilyn Pearsall, ed., *Women and Values* (Belmont, Calif.: Wadsworth, 1986), p. 216.
34. Harriet Silius, Institute for Women's Studies, Akademi University, from Women's Studies Network (Internet: LISTSERV@UMDD.UMD.EDU), November 20, 1992.
35. *Proceedings of the Fourth Annual GLCA Women's Studies Conference* (Ann Arbor, Mich.: Great Lakes Colleges Association, 1978), p. 60.
36. "Women's Studies," in *Reports from the Fields* (Washington, D.C.: Association of American Colleges, 1991), p. 219.
37. *Racism and Sexism: An Integrated Study,* ed. Paula Rothenberg (New York: St. Martin's Press, 1988).
38. Vice President Harward's address was reprinted in the college alumni magazine: *Wooster* 101, no. 1 (Fall 1986): 36.
39. Schuster and Van Dyne, *Women's Place in the Academy,* p. 5.
40. For a fuller account of the defense guard episode, see the *Berkshire Eagle,* February 17, 1990.
41. *Lingua Franca* 1, no. 1 (Fall 1990): 22.
42. Amanda Martin's opinion piece appeared in the April 5, 1993, issue of the *Daily Collegian.*
43. David Margolick, "Free Speech on Campus? It's a Matter of Debate," *New York Times,* September 24, 1993, p. A26.
44. Ibid.
45. *Minnesota Daily,* August 23, 1989.
46. From Nat Hentoff, "Is This Sexual Harassment?" *Village Voice,* December 8, 1993, p. 40.
47. Schuster and Van Dyne, *Women's Place in the Academy,* p. 230.
48. *Modern Language Association Newsletter,* Summer 1991, p. 21.
49. Toni McNaron, *Women's Review of Books* 9, no. 5 (February 1992): 30.

Chapter 6: A Bureaucracy of One's Own

1. Peggy McIntosh, "Seeing Our Way Clear: Feminist Revision of the Academy," in *Proceedings of the Eighth Annual GLCA Women's Studies Conference* (Ann Arbor, Mich.: Great Lakes Colleges Association, 1982), p. 13.
2. *Transforming the Knowledge Base* (New York: National Council for Research on Women, 1990), pp. 11–12.

3. Ibid., p. 12.
4. Betty Schmitz, *Integrating Women's Studies into the Curriculum* (Old Westbury, N.Y.: Feminist Press, 1985), p. 25.
5. Betty Schmitz, "Integrating Scholarship by and about Women into the Curriculum" (Memphis, Tenn.: Memphis State University Press, 1990), pp. 18–19.
6. *Transforming the Knowledge Base*, p. 13.
7. Schmitz, *Integrating Women's Studies into the Curriculum*, pp. 26–27.
8. Ibid., p. 51.
9. Ibid., pp. 51–52.
10. Ibid., p. 52.
11. Betty Schmitz, Myra Dinnerstein, and Nancy Mairs, "Initiating a Curriculum Integration Project: Lessons from the Campus and the Region," in *Women's Place in the Academy: Transforming the Liberal Arts Curriculum*, ed. Marilyn R. Schuster and Susan R. Van Dyne (Totowa, N.J.: Rowman and Allanheld, 1985), p. 121.
12. Herman Belz, "Transforming the Curriculum," *Faculty Voice*, University of Maryland, October 1988, p. 4.
13. *Transforming the Knowledge Base*, p. 12.
14. *The Status of Women in Academe: System Summary*, Tennessee Board of Regents, 1990, p. 26.
15. "Evaluating Courses for Inclusion of Scholarship by and about Women: A Report to the Advisory Committee for Curricular Transformation," Middle Tennessee State University, 1992.
16. "Women's Studies," in *Reports from the Fields* (Washington, D.C.: Association of American Colleges, 1991), pp. 211–12.
17. *Chronicle of Higher Education*, March 17, 1993, p. A18.
18. Donna Shavlik, Judith Touchton, and Carol Pearson, "The New Agenda of Women for Higher Education on Education," in *Educating the Majority: Women Challenge Tradition in Higher Education* (New York: Macmillan, 1989), p. 448.
19. Mount Holyoke College catalogs, 1989–92.
20. *Chronicle of Higher Education*, December 7, 1988, p. A15.
21. Jim Hawkins, *California Scholar*, Winter 1992–93, p. 10.
22. Ibid., pp. 10–12.
23. From memo sent to University of Minnesota faculty by Patricia Mullen, director of the Office of Equal Opportunity, and Becky Kroll, director of the Minnesota Women's Center, August 30, 1993.
24. *Chronicle of Higher Education*, January 17, 1990, p. A15.
25. *Removing Bias: Guidelines for Student-Faculty Communication* (Annandale, Va.: Speech Communication Association, 1983), p. 45. The guide was developed with support from the Women's Educational Equity Act Program of the Department of Education.
26. Caryn McTighe Musil, ed., *The Courage to Question: Women's Studies and Student Learning* (Washington, D.C.: Association of American Colleges, 1992), p. 2.
27. Beverly Guy-Sheftall, "Consultant's Report," Ford Foundation Program on Education and Culture, March 1992, pp. 10–11.
28. Joan Didion, "The Women's Movement," in *The White Album* (New York: Simon & Schuster, 1979), p. 110.
29. Susan Sontag, "Feminism and Fascism: An Exchange," *New York Review of Books*, March 20, 1975, p. 31.

30. Doris Lessing, "Women's Quests," lecture delivered February 4, 1991. Reprinted in *Partisan Review* 59, no. 2 (1992): 190, 192.
31. Teresa Ebert, "The Politics of the Outrageous," *Women's Review of Books*, October 1991, p. 12.
32. *New York*, March 4, 1991, p. 30.
33. *PMLA* (January 1989): 78.
34. Paula Goldsmid, panel discussion, "Toward a Feminist Transformation of the Academy" (Chicago: Great Lakes Colleges Association, November 2–4, 1979), p. 54.
35. Paula Rothenberg, "Teaching 'Racism and Sexism in a Changing America,' " *Radical Teacher*, November 1984, p. 2.

Chapter 7: The Self-Esteem Study

1. *New York Times*, January 9, 1991, p. B6.
2. *Chicago Tribune*, September 29, 1991, p. 1.
3. *Boston Globe*, January 20, 1991, p. A21.
4. Testimony of Rep. Patricia Schroeder on the Gender Equity in Education Act before the House Education and Labor Committee Subcommittee on Elementary, Secondary, and Vocational Education, April 21, 1993.
5. "Summary: Shortchanging Girls, Shortchanging America" (Washington, D.C.: American Association of University Women, 1991), p. 8.
6. Looking more closely at the findings, I saw that in many areas girls were more ambitious than the boys: more high school girls than boys aspire to be high-level professionals and business executives (42 percent of girls vs. 27 percent of boys). The number-one career goal of high school girls is lawyer: 71 percent would like to be lawyers, and 53 percent think they will achieve this goal. For boys, the most popular career ambition is sports star: 70 percent aspire to it, and 49 percent think they will actually succeed. See the AAUW/Greenberg-Lake Full Data Report (Washington, D.C.: Greenberg-Lake, 1990), pp. 12–13.
7. *Shortchanging Girls, Shortchanging America*, video distributed by the American Association of University Women, Washington, D.C., 1991.
8. *New York Times Magazine*, January 7, 1990, p. 23.
9. "A Call to Action: Shortchanging Girls, Shortchanging America" (Washington, D.C.: American Association of University Women, 1991), p. 5.
10. Ibid., p. 5.
11. The original impetus for the self-esteem movement in the schools seems to come from studies done in the 1940s by Kenneth and Mamie Clark, showing that black children (ages three and seven) preferred white dolls. This was taken as a measure of their low self-esteem. The Clark studies have been challenged many times over. Adolescent psychologist Susan Harter gives seven references to recent books and articles disputing the Clark findings. Susan Harter, "Self-Identity and Development," in S. Shirley Feldman and Glen R. Elliott, eds., *At the Threshold* (Cambridge, Mass.: Harvard University Press, 1990), p. 369. Gloria Steinem is apparently unaware of the more recent findings and still cites the doll studies as authoritative. See Steinem, *Revolution from Within: A Book of Self-Esteem* (Boston: Little, Brown, 1992), p. 221.
12. "Hey, I'm Terrific," *Newsweek*, February 17, 1992.
13. "Promoting Self-Esteem in Young Women: A Manual for Teachers" (Albany, N.Y.: State Education Department, 1989), p. 3.

14. "A Call to Action," p. 24.
15. Ibid., p. 26.
16. Ibid., pp. 25–26.
17. Philip Robson, M.D., "Improving Self-Esteem," *Harvard Medical School Mental Health Letter,* June 1990, p. 3.
18. Ibid.
19. *Science News,* May 15, 1993, p. 308.
20. Harter, "Self-Identity and Development," p. 365.
21. Bruce Bower, "Tracking Teen Self-Esteem," *Science News,* March 23, 1991, p. 184.
22. His research is described in ibid., p. 186. I sent away for his studies, as well as the others mentioned in this article. They all appeared to be well designed and free of tendentiousness.
23. "A Call to Action," p. 10.
24. Roberta Simmons, quoted in Bower, "Tracking Teen Self-Esteem," p. 186.
25. Ibid., p. 185.
26. Ibid.
27. Ibid., p. 186.
28. Anne C. Petersen et al., "Depression in Adolescence," *American Psychologist,* February 1993, p. 155.
29. Bower, "Tracking Teen Self-Esteem," p. 186.
30. "A Call to Action," p. 10. The report's arithmetic is slightly off. The increase should be 9–17 points, not 7–17.
31. *NEA Today,* March 1991, p. 29.
32. *Chicago Tribune,* September 29, 1991 (story written by Mary Sue Mohnke).
33. Steinem, *Revolution from Within,* p. 121.
34. *The American Woman, 1992–93: A Status Report,* ed. Paula Ries and Anne Stone (New York: Norton, 1992).
35. Blurb on the back cover of ibid.
36. Ibid., pp. 73–76.
37. Steinem's reversed figures made it into the paperback edition.
38. *The AAUW Report: How Schools Shortchange Girls* (commonly referred to as the "Wellesley Report") (Washington, D.C.: AAUW Educational Foundation, 1992), p. 12.
39. "A Call to Action," p. 26.
40. The figures are from the Greenberg-Lake Full Data Report, "Expectations and Aspirations: Gender Roles and Self-Esteem" (Washington, D.C.: American Association of University Women, 1990).
41. Several of the questions on the survey are variants of the "Rosenberg Self-Esteem Scale"(RSE), which gives respondents the choices "strongly agree," "agree," "disagree," or "strongly disagree" to statements like "On the whole, I am satisfied with myself" and "I feel that I have a number of good qualities." The Rosenberg scale counts only the "disagree" and "strongly disagree" answers as indicative of low self-esteem responses. *See* Murray Rosenberg, *Conceiving the Self* (New York: Basic Books, 1979).
42. "Expectations and Aspirations," p. 21.
43. Ibid., p. 13.
44. See the *Digest of Education Statistics* (Washington, D.C.: U.S. Department of Education, 1993), p. 273.

45. "Expectations and Aspirations," p. 22.
46. "A Call to Action," p. 27.
47. Ibid., p. 4.
48. Harold W. Stevenson, "Children Deserve Better than Phony Self-Esteem," *Education Digest*, December 1992, pp. 12–13. See also Harold W. Stevenson and James W. Stigler, *The Learning Gap: Why Our Schools Are Failing and What We Can Learn from Japanese and Chinese Education* (New York: Summit Books, 1992).
49. *New York Times*, January 9, 1991.
50. Lawrence J. Walker, "Sex Differences in the Development of Moral Reasoning: A Critical Review," *Child Development* 55 (1984): 681.
51. Anne Colby and William Damon, "Listening to a Different Voice: A Review of Gilligan's *In a Different Voice*," *Merrill-Palmer Quarterly* 29, no. 4 (October 1983): 475.
52. Carol Tavris, *The Mismeasure of Woman: Why Women Are Not the Better Sex, the Inferior Sex, or the Opposite Sex* (New York: Simon & Schuster, 1992), p. 85.
53. Ibid., p. 63. See also Katha Pollitt's "Marooned on Gilligan's Island: Are Women Morally Superior to Men?" *The Nation*, December 28, 1992.
54. Faye J. Crosby, *Juggling: The Unexpected Advantages of Balancing Career and Home for Women and Their Families* (New York: Free Press, 1991), p. 124. This is the same Faye Crosby at that unhappy Mills College conference where the angry Rita attacked Raphael (see chapter 1).
55. Martha T. Mednick, "On the Politics of Psychological Constructs: Stop the Bandwagon, I Want to Get Off," *American Psychologist*, August 1989, p. 1120.
56. Lyn Mikel Brown and Carol Gilligan, *Meeting at the Crossroads: Women's Psychology and Girls' Development* (Cambridge, Mass.: Harvard University Press, 1992).
57. Christopher Lasch, "Gilligan's Island," *New Republic*, December 7, 1992, p. 38.
58. Carolyn G. Heilbrun, "How Girls Become Wimps," *New York Times Book Review*, October 4, 1992, p. 13.
59. "Summary: Shortchanging Girls, Shortchanging America," p. 17
60. "Teacher's Guide: Take Our Daughters to Work" (New York: Ms. Foundation for Women, 1993), p. 3.
61. Judy Mann, "My Daughter, His Griddle," *Washington Post*, April 23, 1993.
62. *Parade*, May 17, 1992, p. 20.
63. *San Francisco Chronicle*, April 16, 1993.
64. "Teacher's Guide: Take Our Daughters to Work," p. 12.
65. Ibid.

Chapter 8: The Wellesley Report: A Gender at Risk

1. "A Call to Action: Shortchanging Girls, Shortchanging America" (Washington, D.C.: American Association of University Women, 1991), p. 5.
2. *The AAUW Report: How Schools Shortchange Girls* (commonly referred to as the "Wellesley Report") (Washington, D.C.: AAUW Educational Foundation, 1992), p. vi. I am referring to the second AAUW study as the Wellesley Report to distinguish it from the first AAUW study on self-esteem.
3. *San Francisco Chronicle*, February 13, 1992, p. A22.
4. *Los Angeles Times*, February 22, 1992, p. B6.
5. Richard N. Ostling, "Is School Unfair to Girls?" *Time*, February 24, 1992, p. 62.
6. *Boston Globe*, February 2, 1992.

7. *New York Times,* February 12, 1992.

8. The Gender Equity in Education Act (H.R. 1793) is made up of nine separate bills. Two of them seem reasonable and free of gender feminist ideology (a child abuse prevention program and a nutrition and family counseling program). But the other seven appear to be based on questionable gender feminist advocacy research.

9. *Boston Globe,* September 16, 1993, p. 5.

10. Executive summary, "Testimony before the House Subcommittee on Elementary, Secondary, and Vocational Education," April 21, 1993, p. 5.

11. *Women's Research Network News* (New York: National Council for Research on Women, 1993), p. 11.

12. *The Condition of Education* (Washington D.C.: National Center for Education Statistics, U.S. Department of Education, 1991), p. 44.

13. *The Condition of Education,* 1992, pp. 42–49.

14. *Digest of Education Statistics* (Washington, D.C.: U.S. Department of Education, 1992), p. 136.

15. Wellesley Report, p. 45.

16. *Boston Globe,* January 24, 1994. The UCLA Center does a yearly study of the attitudes and goals of college freshmen. The 1993 results are based on a survey of approximately 250,000 students from 475 colleges and universities.

17. *The Condition of Education,* 1985, p. 66.

18. Ibid., pp. 50, 52.

19. Ibid., p. 206.

20. *Digest of Education Statistics* (Washington, D.C.: National Center for Education Statistics, U.S. Department of Education, 1992), p. 137.

21. Wellesley Report, p. 79.

22. *Monthly Vital Statistics Report,* "Advance Report of Final Mortality Statistics, 1990" (Washington, D.C.: U.S. Department of Health and Human Services, January 1993), p. 27.

23. The quote is from an AAUW brochure called "Executive Summary: How Schools Shortchange Girls," p. 2; the information is taken from the Wellesley Report, p. 68.

24. Testimony of Rep. Patricia Schroeder on the Gender Equity in Education Act before the House Education and Labor Committee Subcommittee on Elementary, Secondary, and Vocational Education, April 21, 1993.

25. Wellesley Report, p. 68.

26. Myra Sadker and David Sadker, "Sexism in the Classroom: From Grade School to Graduate School," *Phi Delta Kappan,* March 1986, p. 514.

27. International Assessment of Educational Progress (IAEP), (Princeton, N.J.: Educational Testing Service, 1992), p. 145. The underperformance of American boys vis à vis foreign girls is consistent with the 1988 IAEP, which showed the Korean girls similarly outperforming American boys, IAEP (Princeton, N.J.: Educational Testing Service 1989), figure 1.3.

28. IAEP, 1992, p. 21.

29. Sadker and Sadker, "Sexism in the Classroom," pp. 512–13.

30. David Sadker and Myra Sadker, "Is the O.K. Classroom O.K.?" *Phi Delta Kappan,* January 1985, p. 360.

31. Ibid., p. 361.

32. Wellesley Report, p. 68, and *Review of Research in Education* 17 (1991): 297–98.

33. David Sadker, Myra Sadker, and Dawn Thomas, "Sex Equity and Special Education," *The Pointer* 26, no. 1 (1981): 36.

34. Myra Sadker, David Sadker, and Susan Klein, "The Issue of Gender in Elementary and Secondary Education" in ed. Gerald Grant, *Review of Research in Education* 17, (1991): 297–98.

35. Myra Sadker and David Sadker, *Failing at Fairness: How America's Schools Cheat Girls* (New York: Scribners, 1994), p. 10.

36. Myra Sadker and David Sadker, *Year Three: Final Report, Promoting the Effectiveness in Classroom Instruction* (Washington, D.C.: National Institute of Education, Department of Education, March 1984), contract no. 400-80-0033, p. 2.

37. Marlaine E. Lockheed, "A Study of Sex Equity in Classroom Interaction" (Washington, D.C.: National Institute of Education, 1984).

38. Lisa A. Serbin, K. Daniel O'Leary, Ronald N. Kent, and Illene J. Tonick, "A Comparison of Teacher Response to the Preacademic and Problem Behavior of Boys and Girls," *Child Development,* 1973, p. 803.

39. M. Gail Jones, "Gender Bias in Classroom Interactions," *Contemporary Education* 60, no. 4 (Summer 1989).

40. K. Tobin and P. Garnett, "Gender-Related Differences in Science Activities," *Science Education* 71, no. 1 (1987): 91–103.

41. Jones, "Gender Bias in Classroom Interactions," p. 22.

42. Wellesley Report, p. 70.

43. Testimony submitted to the House Subcommittee on Elementary, Secondary, and Vocational Education, April 21, 1993, by Anne L. Bryant, p. 2.

44. Ibid, p. 2.

45. From summary of Gender Equity in Education Act (H.R. 1793) distributed by the Congressional Caucus on Women's Issues (1993).

46. The program was aired on January 1, 1993.

47. The article appears in *Educational Leadership* 46, no. 6 (1989): 44–47.

48. The transcript of the April 7, 1992, "Dateline" documentary (called "Failing at Fairness") is available through Burrelle's Information Services, Livingston, New Jersey. The segment was repeated on April 27, 1993.

49. "Dateline," April 7, 1992, p. 12.

50. "Dateline," April 27, 1993, p. 13.

51. Wellesley Report, p. iv.

52. Ibid., p. 65.

53. Ibid.

54. The McIntosh video was made available to me by the Brookline School Department.

55. Robert Costrell, "The Mother of All Curriculums," *Brookline Citizen,* March 15, 1991, p. 7.

56. From *The Science of Rights* (1796), reprinted in Jane English, *Sex Equality* (Englewood Cliffs, N.J.: Prentice Hall, 1977), p. 53.

57. John Leo, "Sexism in the Schoolhouse," *U.S. News & World Report,* March 9, 1992.

58. "College-Bound Seniors: 1992 Profile of SAT and Achievement Test Takers" (Princeton, N.J.: Educational Testing Service, 1992), p. iii.

59. Ibid., p. iv.

60. Wellesley Report, p. 56.

61. *Fortune,* March 23, 1992, p. 132.

62. R. McCormack and M. McLeod, "Gender Bias in the Prediction of College Course Performance," *Journal of Education Measurement* 25, no. 4 (1988): 330.
63. *Fortune,* May 18, 1992, p. 43.
64. Letters from readers, *Commentary,* October 1992, p. 2.
65. Wellesley Report, p. 86.
66. Ibid., p. 87.
67. Barry Cipra, "An Awesome Look at Japan's Math SAT," *Science,* January 1, 1993, p. 22.
68. Ibid.
69. Ibid.
70. Ibid.
71. *Science,* March 2, 1990, p. 1025.
72. Several other reports say much the same thing. See, for example, *Everybody Counts: A Report to the Nation on the Future of Mathematics Education* (Washington, D.C.: National Academy Press, 1989). According to this report:

    Average students in other countries often learn as much mathematics as the best students learn in the United States. Data from the Second International Mathematics Study show that the performance of the top 5 percent of U.S. students is matched by the top 50 percent of students in Japan. Our very best students—the top 1 percent—score lowest of the top 1 percent in all participating countries.

73. Harold W. Stevenson, Chuansheng Chen, and Shin-Ying Lee, "Mathematics Achievement of Taiwanese, Japanese, and American Children: Ten Years Later," *Science,* January 1, 1993, p. 54.
74. International Assessment of Mathematics and Science, 1992.
75. Some education watchers have tried to downplay the poor performance of American students on international tests. For example, one study, mentioned by *Time* magazine (October 25, 1993, p. 20), allegedly showed that the top 50 percent of American eighth-graders were performing just as well as their Japanese counterparts. What *Time* failed to mention is that the study showed parity only in the area of arithmetic. Our children were way behind in algebra, measurement, and geometry. Unfortunately, arithmetic is only one branch of mathematics needed to compete in a global economy. The downplayers do us no service by making light of the learning gap.
76. *Education Digest,* April 1992, p. 59.
77. The results were published in a booklet, "Secrets in Public: Sexual Harassment in Our Schools" (1993), distributed by the Wellesley College Center for Research on Women and the NOW Legal Defense and Education Fund.
78. Nan Stein, "School Harassment—An Update," *Education Week,* November 4, 1992, p. 37.
79. *Boston Globe,* March 24, 1993, p. 1.
80. Norman Bradburn, director of the National Opinion Research Center at the University of Chicago, coined the acronym SLOPS. It actually stands for "self-selected listener opinion polls," but what he says about SLOPS applies equally well to magazine polls. See "Numbers from Nowhere: The Hoax of the Call-In Polls," by Richard Morin, *Washington Post,* February 9, 1992.
81. *Boston Globe,* March 24, 1993, p. 18.

82. "Hostile Hallways: The AAUW Survey on Sexual Harassment in America's Schools" (Washington, D.C.: American Association of University Women, 1993), pp. 7–10.

83. *Boston Globe,* June 2, 1993, p. 1.

84. According to the 1992 *Digest of Educational Statistics,* p. 142, 10.6 percent of male and 7.1 percent of female eighth-graders cut classes "at least sometimes"; and 89.4 percent of boys and 92.9 percent of girls say they do it "never or almost never."

85. "Sex and School Debating Harassment," *Boston Globe,* June 6, 1993, p. 15.

86. ABC "Lifetime Magazine," aired January 2, 1994.

Chapter 9: Noble Lies

1. Gloria Steinem, *Revolution from Within: A Book of Self-Esteem* (Boston: Little, Brown, 1992), pp. 259–61.

2. A brief account of the hoax is also to be found in the preface.

3. Ken Ringle, "Wife-Beating Claims Called Out of Bounds," *Washington Post,* January 31, 1993, p. A1.

4. Reported in Jean Cobb, "A Super Bowl–Battered Women Link?" *American Journalism Review,* May 1993, p. 35.

5. *Boston Globe,* January 30, 1993, p. 13.

6. Quoted in "Football's Day of Dread," *Wall Street Journal,* February 5, 1993, p. A10.

7. Ibid.

8. Ringle, "Wife-Beating Claims."

9. Ibid.

10. Bob Hohler, "Super Bowl Gaffe," *Boston Globe,* February 2, 1993, p. 17.

11. Ringle, "Wife-Beating Claims."

12. Joann Byrd, "Violence at Home," *Washington Post,* February 28, 1993; op ed, p. C6; Jean Cobb, "A Super Bowl–Battered Woman Link?" *American Journalism Review,* May 1993, pp. 33–38.

13. Donna Jackson, *How to Make the World a Better Place for Women in Five Minutes a Day* (New York: Hyperion, 1992), p. 62. Ms. Jackson is editor-at-large for *New Woman* magazine.

14. "Female Victims of Violent Crime," by Caroline Wolf Harlow (Washington, D.C.: U.S. Department of Justice, 1991), p. 1.

15. Murray Straus, Richard Gelles, and Suzanne Steinmetz, *Behind Closed Doors: Violence in the American Family* (New York: Anchor Books, 1980).

16. *Congressional Quarterly Almanac,* 1991, p. 294.

17. Senator Joseph Biden, chairman, Senate Judiciary Committee, *Violence Against Women: A Week in the Life of America* (U.S. Government Printing Office, 1992), p. 3.

18. Cheris Kramarae and Paula A. Treichler, eds., *A Feminist Dictionary* (London: Pandora Press, 1985), p. 66.

19. Fundraising brochure sent out by the National Coalition Against Domestic Violence, Washington, D.C., 1993. The headline of the brochure is "Every 15 Seconds a Woman Is Battered in This Country." That would add up to a total of 2.1 million incidents.

20. Poster, University of Massachusetts, Amherst, advertising lecture appearance of Gail Dines, October 13, 1992: "Images of Violence Against Women."

21. Marilyn French also gives this figure, "In the United States, a man beats a woman

every twelve seconds," *The War Against Women* (New York: Simon & Schuster, 1992), p. 187.

22. The Clothesline Project is a traveling exhibit on domestic violence. It was on display at Johns Hopkins University on October 22, 1993. They did sound a gong at ten-second intervals from 10:00 A.M. to 5:00 P.M.

23. BrotherPeace is a men's antiviolence group in St. Cloud, Minnesota. The figures are from their fact sheet, called "Statistics for Men."

24. Gelles and Straus found that two-thirds of teenagers physically attack a sister or brother at least once in the course of a year, and in more than one-third of these cases, the attack involves severe forms of violence such as kicking, punching, biting, choking, and attacking with knives and guns. "These incredible rates of intrafamily violence by teenagers make the high rates of violence by their parents seem modest by comparison," in Richard Gelles and Murray Straus, *Physical Violence in American Families* (New Brunswick, N.J.: Transaction Publishers, 1990), p. 107.

25. Ibid., p. 162.

26. Ibid., chap. 5.

27. The population is aging. Men and women marry at a later age and have fewer children. Such changes might explain a drop in the percentage of women who are abused. See Gelles and Straus, *Intimate Violence: The Causes and Consequences of Abuse in the American Family* (New York: Touchstone, 1989), pp. 111 and 112.

28. Gelles and Straus, *Physical Violence in American Families,* p. 285.

29. Commonwealth Fund, survey of women's health (New York: Commonwealth Fund, July 14, 1993), p. 8.

30. Ibid. Clippings from newspapers around the country are included in the survey results.

31. This is consistent with Gelles and Straus's figure of less than 1 percent for pathological abuse. The Commonwealth sample had a margin of error of 2 percent either way. There could be other explanations: as Gelles and Straus say, the women who are most brutally and dangerously abused would probably be afraid to talk about it. But if there are several million out there, surely the Harris poll would have found at least one.

32. Incidentally, rape crisis feminist researchers like Diana Russell, author of *Rape in Marriage,* (Bloomington: Indiana University Press, 1990), have declared an epidemic of marital rape. But when the Harris poll asked, "In the past year, did your partner ever try to, or force you to, have sexual relations by using physical force, or not?" 100 percent of the more than 2,500 respondents said "not." Here again one may be sure that marital rape is out there, but this poll suggests it's rarer than Russell says. Using Russell as their source, the feminist compendium "WAC Stats: The Facts About Women" (New York: Women's Action Coalition, 1993) says that "more than one in every seven women who have ever been married have been raped in marriage" (p. 49).

33. Bias reappears in another Harris/Commonwealth finding that 40 percent of American women are severely depressed. As it happened, Harris and Associates had appointed Lois Hoeffler, a gender feminist advocate, as principal investigator in charge of the survey of women's health. For an account of her views and her participation in a poll that resulted in sensational and depressing conclusions, see chapter 11.

34. Andrew Klein, "Spousal/Partner Assault: A Protocol for the Sentencing and Supervision of Offenders" (Quincy, Mass.: Quincy Court, 1993), p. 5.

35. Ibid., p. 7.

36. See, for example, Kerry Lobel, ed., *Naming the Violence: Speaking Out about Lesbian Violence* (Seattle, Wash.: Seal Press, 1986).

37. Claire Renzetti, *Violent Betrayal: Partner Abuse in Lesbian Relationships* (Newbury Park, Calif.: Sage Press, 1992). Claudia Card, "Lesbian Battering," in the American Philosophical Association's *Newsletter on Feminism and Philosophy*, November 1988, p. 3.

38. Renzetti, *Violent Betrayal*, p. 115.

39. Gelles and Straus, in *Physical Violence in American Families*, p. 11.

40. *Mirabella*, November 1993, p. 78. In its June 1993 issue, *Mirabella* did its own SLOP survey on women's health and found that 31 percent of their respondents were beaten by their husbands or boyfriends. Eighteen percent were beaten by more than one person. The survey was cosponsored by the Center for Women's Policy Studies.

41. *Journal of the American Medical Association*, June 22–29, 1984.

42. Ibid., p. 3260.

43. According to the authors, "The study did not find a statistically significant difference between the number of male and female domestic violence victims, although a greater proportion of the victims were female (62%)." Ibid., p. 3263.

44. Stark is an associate professor of public administration at Rutgers University in Newark, New Jersey. Flitcraft is an associate professor of medicine at the Mount Sinai Hospital/University of Connecticut Health Center's Outpatient Services in Hartford, Connecticut. They run the Domestic Violence Training Project for Health Professionals in New Haven.

45. Evan Stark and Anne Flitcraft, "Spouse Abuse" (October 1985), working paper edited by the Violence Epidemiology Branch, Centers for Disease Control, Atlanta. Cited in "Violence Against Women" fact sheet from the Center for Women's Policy Center, Washington, D.C., 1993.

46. Evan Stark, Anne Flitcraft, and William Frazier, "Medicine and Patriarchal Violence," *International Journal of Health Services* 9, no. 3 (1979): 485.

47. Ibid., pp. 487–88.

48. Ibid., p. 482.

49. Carole Sheffield, "Sexual Terrorism," in Jo Freeman, ed., *Women: A Feminist Perspective* (Mountain View, Calif.: Mayfield Publishing, 1989), p. 7.

50. "Sonya Live," CNN, May 26, 1993.

51. Other references to the rule of thumb include:

Until the 19th Century, there was a charming little rule of thumb that applied to family life. A man was allowed to beat his wife as long as the stick he used was no wider than a thumb. (Ellen Goodman, *Washington Post*, April 19, 1983)

English Common Law, from which our own laws are derived, allowed a man to beat his "wayward" wife as long as the switch he used was not thicker than the size of his thumb. A female caseworker in Cleveland says she never uses the term "rule of thumb" because of what it traditionally implies. (UPS, November 9, 1986)

Today's cultures have strong historical, religious, and legal legacies that reinforce the legitimacy of wife-beating. Under English common law, for example, a husband had the legal right to discipline his wife—subject to a "rule of thumb" that barred him from using a stick broader than his thumb. Judicial decisions in

England and the United States upheld this right until well into the 19th century. (*Washington Post,* April 9, 1989)

In English common law, a man was considered to have a right to "physically chastise an errant wife." What passed for restraint was the notorious "rule of thumb" which stated that the stick he beat her with could not exceed the width of the thumb. (*Los Angeles Times,* September 4, 1989, p. 1)

Patricia Ireland said she learned the rule of thumb which, under English common law, allowed a man to beat his wife as long as he used a stick no thicker than his thumb. (*Orlando Sentinel,* December, 1991)

In state courts across the country, wife beating was legal until 1890. There was a "rule of thumb," by which courts had stated a man might beat his wife with a switch no thicker than his thumb. (*Chicago Tribune,* March 18, 1990)

52. Women's Studies Network (Internet: LISTSERV@UMDD.UMD.EDU), May 11, 1993. Many women's studies scholars know very well that the "rule of thumb" story is a myth. They talk about it freely on their network; but you will *never* see them correcting the textbooks or the news stories.
53. Sir William Blackstone, *Commentaries on the Laws of England* (New York: W. E. Dean, 1836), vol. 1, p. 36.
54. Elizabeth Pleck, "Wife Beating in Nineteenth-Century America," *Victimology: An International Journal* 4 (1979): 71.
55. Ibid., pp. 60–61.
56. Ibid.
57. Elizabeth Pleck, *Domestic Tyranny* (New York: Oxford University Press, 1987), p. 110. Pleck makes the interesting point that modern attitudes to wife battering are not that different from those in the nineteenth century—wife beaters are despised, and the public feels vindictive toward them. What has changed is that in the nineteenth century the punishment was more informal. The batterers were beaten up, whipped, and publicly shamed. Today, it is a matter for the courts: the punishment is often a restraining order, counseling, a suspended sentence, or a severe lecture from a disapproving judge or police officer. One advantage of the old system is that the batterer's punishment did not depend on the victim turning him in. As Pleck says, "Third parties were watching a husband's behavior and reporting his misdeed to a policing group." The sanctions such as whipping, shunning, and public shaming may have been the more powerful deterrents. See Pleck, "Wife Beating in Nineteenth-Century America," p. 71.
58. *Bradley v. State,* Walker 156, Miss. 1824; *State v. Oliver,* 70 N.C. 61, 1874.
59. See Pleck, "Wife Beating in Nineteenth-Century America," p. 63.
60. In 1974 an article by sociologist Robert Calvert made reference to the North Carolina and Mississippi judges. It was published in an important anthology on domestic battery edited by Murray Straus and Suzanne Steinmetz, *Violence in the Family* (Toronto: Dodd, Mead, 1975), p. 88. Martin may have learned about the two judges there.
61. Del Martin, *Battered Wives* (Volcano, Calif.: Volcano Press, 1976), p. 31.
62. Terry Davidson, "Wife Beating: A Recurring Phenomenon Throughout History,"

in Maria Roy, ed., *Battered Women* (New York: Van Nostrand Reinhold, 1977), p. 18.

63. Ibid., p. 19.

64. "Under the Rule of Thumb: Battered Women and the Administration of Justice: A Report of the United States Commission on Civil Rights," January 1982, p. 2.

65. Ibid.

66. *Time,* January 18, 1993, p. 41.

Chapter 10: Rape Research

1. Federal Bureau of Investigation, *Crime in the United States: Uniform Crime Reports* (Washington, D.C.: U.S. Department of Justice, 1990).

2. Bureau of the Census, *Statistical Abstract of the United States 1990,* (Washington, D.C.: U.S. Government Printing Office, 1992), p. 184. See also Caroline Wolf Harlow, Bureau of Justice Statistics, "Female Victims of Violent Crime" (Washington, D.C., U.S. Department of Justice, 1991), p. 7.

3. Louis Harris and Associates, "Commonwealth Fund Survey of Women's Health" (New York: Commonwealth Fund, 1993), p. 9. What the report says is that "within the last five years, 2 percent of women (1.9 million) were raped."

4. "Rape in America: A Report to the Nation" (Charleston, S.C.: Crime Victims Research and Treatment Center, 1992).

5. Catharine MacKinnon, "Sexuality, Pornography, and Method," *Ethics* 99 (January 1989): 331.

6. Mary Koss and Cheryl Oros, "Sexual Experiences Survey: A Research Instrument Investigating Sexual Aggression and Victimization," *Journal of Consulting and Clinical Psychology* 50, no. 3 (1982): 455.

7. Nara Schoenberg and Sam Roe, "The Making of an Epidemic," *Blade,* October 10, 1993, special report, p. 4.

8. The total sample was 6,159, or whom 3,187 were females. See Mary Koss, "Hidden Rape: Sexual Aggression and Victimization in a National Sample of Students in Higher Education," in Ann Wolbert Burgess, ed., *Rape and Sexual Assault,* vol. 2 (New York: Garland Publishing, 1988), p. 8.

9. Ibid., p. 10.

10. Ibid., p. 16.

11. Mary Koss, Thomas Dinero, and Cynthia Seibel, "Stranger and Acquaintance Rape," *Psychology of Women Quarterly* 12 (1988): 12. See also Neil Gilbert, "Examining the Facts: Advocacy Research Overstates the Incidence of Date and Acquaintance Rape," in *Current Controversies in Family Violence,* ed. Richard Gelles and Donileen Loseke (Newbury Park, Calif.: Sage Publications, 1993), pp. 120–32.

12. The passage is from Robin Warshaw, in her book *I Never Called It Rape* (New York: HarperPerennial, 1988), p. 2, published by the Ms. Foundation and with an afterword by Mary Koss. The book summarizes the findings of the rape study.

13. *Newsweek,* October 25, 1993.

14. Naomi Wolf, *The Beauty Myth: How Images of Beauty Are Used Against Women* (New York: Doubleday, 1992), p. 166.

15. At the University of Minnesota, for example, new students receive a booklet called "Sexual Exploitation on Campus." The booklet informs them that according to "one

study [left unnamed] 20 to 25 percent of all college women have experienced rape or attempted rape."

16. The Violence Against Women Act of 1993 was introduced to the Senate by Joseph Biden on January 21, 1993. It is sometimes referred to as the "Biden Bill." It is now making its way through the various congressional committees. Congressman Ramstad told the Minneapolis *Star Tribune* (June 19, 1991), "Studies show that as many as one in four women will be the victim of rape or attempted rape during her college career." Ramstad adds, "This may only be the tip of the iceberg, for 90 percent of all rapes are believed to go unreported."

17. Gilbert, "Examining the Facts," pp. 120–32.

18. Cited in Koss, "Hidden Rape," p. 9.

19. *Blade,* special report, p. 5.

20. Ibid.

21. Koss herself calculated the new "one in nine" figure for the *Blade,* p. 5.

22. Cathy Young, *Washington Post* (National Weekly Edition), July 29, 1992, p. 25.

23. Katha Pollitt, "Not Just Bad Sex," *New Yorker,* October 4, 1993, p. 222.

24. Koss, "Hidden Rape," p. 16.

25. *Blade,* p. 5. The *Blade* reporters explain that the number varies between one and twenty-two and one in thirty-three depending on the amount of overlap between groups.

26. "Rape in America," p. 2.

27. Ibid., p. 15.

28. The secretary of health and human services, Donna Shalala, praised the poll for avoiding a "white male" approach that has "for too long" been the norm in research about women. My own view is that the interpretation of the poll is flawed. See the discussions in chapters 9 and 11.

29. Louis Harris and Associates, "The Commonwealth Fund Survey of Women's Health," p. 20.

30. *Blade,* p. 3.

31. Ibid., p. 6.

32. Ibid.

33. Dean Kilpatrick, et al., "Mental Health Correlates of Criminal Victimization: A Random Community Survey," *Journal of Consulting and Clinical Psychology* 53, 6 (1985).

34. *Time,* May 4, 1992, p. 15.

35. *Blade,* special report, p. 3.

36. Ibid., p. 3.

37. Ibid., p. 5.

38. Ibid., p. 3.

39. Camille Paglia, "The Return of Carry Nation," *Playboy,* October 1992, p. 36.

40. Camille Paglia, "Madonna I: Anomility and Artifice," *New York Times,* December 14, 1990.

41. Reported in Peter Hellman, "Crying Rape: The Politics of Date Rape on Campus," *New York,* March 8, 1993, pp. 32–37.

42. *Washington Times,* May 7, 1993.

43. Hellman, "Crying Rape," pp. 32–37.

44. Ibid., p. 34.

45. Ibid., p. 37.

46. Katie Roiphe, *The Morning After: Sex, Fear, and Feminism* (Boston: Little, Brown, 1993), p. 45.
47. *Blade*, p. 13.
48. Andrea Parrot, *Acquaintance Rape and Sexual Assault Prevention Training Manual* (Ithaca, N.Y.: College of Human Ecology, Cornell University, 1990), p. 1.
49. *Blade*, p. 13.
50. Ibid., p. 14.
51. Alice Rossi, ed., *The Feminist Papers: From Adams to de Beauvoir* (New York: Columbia University Press, 1973), p. 414.
52. Katie Roiphe, "Date Rape's Other Victim," *New York Times Magazine*, June 13, 1993, p. 26.
53. Ibid., p. 40.
54. Women's Studies Network (Internet: LISTSERV@UMDD.UMD.EDU), June 14, 1993.
55. Ibid., June 13, 1993.
56. See Sarah Crichton, "Sexual Correctness: Has It Gone Too Far?" *Newsweek*, October 25, 1993, p. 55.
57. See Neil Gilbert, "The Phantom Epidemic of Sexual Assault," *The Public Interest*, Spring 1991, pp. 54–65; Gilbert, "The Campus Rape Scare," *Wall Street Journal*, June 27, 1991, p. 10; and Gilbert, "Examining the Facts," pp. 120–32.
58. "Stop It Bitch," distributed by the National Clearinghouse on Marital and Date Rape, Berkeley, California. (For thirty dollars they will send you "thirty-four years of research to help refute him [Gilbert].") See also the *Blade*, p. 5.
59. Sheila Kuehl, "Skeptic Needs Taste of Reality Along with Lessons About Law," *Los Angeles Daily Journal*, September 5, 1991. Ms. Kuehl, it will be remembered, was a key figure in disseminating the tidings that men's brutality to women goes up 40 percent on Super Bowl Sunday. Some readers may remember Ms. Kuehl as the adolescent girl who played the amiable Zelda on the 1960s "Dobie Gillis Show."
60. *International Crime Rates* (Washington, D.C.: Bureau of Justice Statistics, 1988), p. 1. The figures for 1983: England and Wales, 2.7 per 100,000; United States, 33.7 per 100,000 (p. 8). Consider these figures comparing Japan to other countries (rates of rape per 100,000 inhabitants):

	FORCIBLE RAPE
U.S.	38.1
U.K. (England and Wales only)	12.1
(West) Germany	8.0
France	7.8
Japan	1.3

Source: *Japan 1992: An International Comparison* (Tokyo: Japan Institute for Social and Economic Affairs, 1992), p. 93.
61. "Men, Sex, and Rape," ABC News Forum with Peter Jennings, May 5, 1992, Transcript no. ABC-34, p. 21.
62. Ibid., p. 11.
63. Ibid.
64. Senator Biden, cited by Carolyn Skorneck, Associated Press, May 27, 1993.
65. "The Violence Against Women Act of 1993," title 3, p. 87.
66. Ruth Shalit, "On the Hill: Caught in the Act," *New Republic*, July 12, 1993, p. 15.

67. See ibid., p. 14.
68. Stephen Donaldson, "The Rape Crisis Behind Bars," *New York Times*, December 29, 1993, p. A11. See also Donaldson, "Letter to the Editor" *New York Times*, August 24, 1993. See, too, Wayne Wooden and Jay Parker, *Men Behind Bars: Sexual Exploitation in Prison* (New York: Plenum Press, 1982); Anthony Sacco, ed., *Male Rape: A Casebook of Sexual Aggressions* (New York: AMS Press, 1982); and Daniel Lockwood, *Prison Sexual Violence* (New York: Elsevier, 1980).

Chapter 11: The Backlash Myth

1. Susan Faludi, *Backlash: The Undeclared War Against American Women* (New York: Crown, 1991); Naomi Wolf, *The Beauty Myth: How Images of Beauty Are Used Against Women* (New York: Doubleday, 1992).
2. Wolf, *The Beauty Myth*, p. 19.
3. Ibid., p. 99.
4. Faludi, *Backlash*, p. xxii.
5. Wolf, *The Beauty Myth*, p. 19.
6. Ibid., p. 4.
7. Ibid., p. 124.
8. According to Faludi, "Just when women's quest for equal rights seemed closest to achieving its objectives, the backlash struck it down. . . . The Republican party elevated Ronald Reagan and both political parties began to shunt women's rights off their platforms." *Backlash*, p. xix.
9. Rep. Patricia Schroeder reviewed *Backlash* for Knight-Rider Newspapers. I am quoting from the version that appeared in the *Austin American Statesmen*, Sunday, November 24, 1991, p. E6.
10. Paul Berman mentioned "Parisian determinism" during a discussion at an academic conference. He had good news for those worried about what may be coming next out of Paris: today fashionable French intellectuals are interested in liberalism and human rights, with special attention to writings of James Madison and Thomas Jefferson.
11. Richard Rorty, "Foucault and Epistemology," in David Couzens Hoy, ed., *Foucault: A Critical Reader* (Oxford: Basil Blackwell, 1986), p. 47.
12. Michael Walzer, "The Politics of Michel Foucault," in ibid., p. 51.
13. Michel Foucault, *Power/Knowledge: Selected Interviews and Other Writings, 1972–1977*, ed. Colin Gordon (New York: Random House, 1980), p. 134.
14. Sandra Lee Bartky, *Femininity and Domination: Studies in the Phenomenlogy of Oppression* (New York: Routledge, 1990), p. 75.
15. Ibid., p. 80.
16. Catharine MacKinnon, "Desire and Power: A Feminist Perspective," in Cary Nelson and Lawrence Grossberg, eds., *Marxism and the Interpretation of Culture* (Chicago: University of Illinois Press, 1988), p. 110.
17. Catharine MacKinnon, *Toward a Feminist Theory of the State* (Cambridge, Mass.: Harvard University Press, 1989), pp. 116–17.
18. Faludi, *Backlash*, p. xii.
19. Wolf, *The Beauty Myth*, p. 17
20. Faludi, *Backlash*, p. 455.

21. Wolf, *The Beauty Myth*, p. 10.
22. Thomas F. Cash, Diane Walker Cash, and Jonathan W. Butters, " 'Mirror, Mirror on the Wall . . . ?' Contrast Effects and Self-Evaluations of Physical Attractiveness," *Personality and Social Psychology Bulletin* 9, no. 3 (September 1983): 354–55.
23. Ms. Wolf did not speak to the principal author at Old Dominion, Thomas Cash, and there is some doubt that she ever saw the article she cites. She says, for example, that Cash arrived at his conclusions by studying some of his patients, who, he said, were "extremely attractive." But Cash did not study his patients. At the beginning of the article, he and his coauthors clearly state that they used "a sample of fifty-one female college students . . . recruited from introductory psychology classes." Dr. Cash told me, "I remember thinking she must be confusing my study with another. I never mentioned anything about my patients, and did not study them."
24. Wolf, *The Beauty Myth*, p. 165. There is no "American legal definition of rape." Each state has its own criteria.
25. Ellen Goodman, " 'The Man Shortage' and Other Big Lies," *New York Times Book Review*, October 27, 1991, p. 1.
26. Barbara Lovenheim, letter to the *New York Times Book Review*, February 9, 1992.
27. Faludi, *Backlash*, p. 30.
28. "Facts About Down Syndrome for Women over 35" (Washington D.C.: National Institute of Health, 1979), p. 9.
29. Lovenheim, ibid., p. 30.
30. Bureau of Census, Current Population Reports, Series P 23, no. 162, June 1989. Cited in Barbara Lovenheim, *Beating the Marriage Odds* (New York: William Morrow, 1990), p. 34.
31. Gretchen Morgenson, "A Whiner's Bible," *Forbes*, March 16, 1992, p. 153.
32. Ibid., p. 152.
33. Nancy Gibbs, "The War Against Feminism," *Time*, March 9, 1992, p. 52.
34. Ibid.
35. Cathy Young, "Phony War," *Reason*, November 1991, p. 57.
36. *Working Woman*, April 1992, p. 104.
37. Ibid.
38. Sylvia Nasar, "Women's Progress Stalled? Just Not So," *New York Times*, October 18, 1992, sec. 3, p. 1.
39. Diane Ravitch, *Youth Policy*, June–July 1992, p. 12.
40. Nasar, "Women's Progress Stalled?" The article summarizes the recent findings of three prominent women economists, *Understanding the Gender Gap*, by Claudia Goldin (Harvard University); *The Economics of Men, Women, and Work*, by Francine Blau and Marianne Ferber (University of Illinois); and June O'Neill (Baruch College), "Women and Wages," *The American Enterprise*, November/December 1990, pp. 25–33.
41. Faludi, *Backlash*, p. 364.
42. Ibid.
43. These ratios are for median earnings—i.e., the earnings of the male or female in the middle of the pack (one-half earn more, one-half earn less). Source: Bureau of Census, Current Population Reports, Consumer Income Series P60-184, *Money Income of Households, Families, and Persons in the United States: 1992*, September 1993.
44. If gender "backlash" is to be inferred from the earnings ratio, it could only have

happened back in the 1950s and early 1960s: that is the last period in which the earnings ratio fell.

45. See O'Neill, "Women and Wages," p. 29. Faludi inexplicably objects to such a straightforward correction for difference in work weeks, referring to this as "spurious data fudging" resulting in an "artificially inflated earnings" ratio.

46. June O'Neill and Solomon Polachek, "Why the Gender Gap in Wages Narrowed in the 1980s," *Journal of Labor Economics* 11, no. 1 (January 1993), part 1: 205–28. Some economists argue that the anticipation of spending less time in market activities than men leads many women to focus their education and training in less remunerative areas, both in secondary and postsecondary education, academic and vocational (see, for example, Claudia Goldin and Solomon Polachek, "Residual Differences by Sex: Perspectives on the Gender Gap in Earnings," *American Economic Review* 77, no.2 [May 1987]: 143–51).

47. This is a theme stressed by Stamford economist Victor Fuchs, *Women's Quest for Equality* (Cambridge, Mass.: Harvard University Press, 1988). A recent study of 1972–75 graduates of the University of Michigan Law School, fifteen years after graduation, found that one-quarter of the women had at some point worked part-time to care for their children, as compared to 0.5 percent of the men. It also found that this had a very large effect on subsequent earnings, even after returning to work full-time. One of the major reasons appeared to be that such women were far less likely to become partners in large law firms: "Fewer than one-fifth [of mothers] with extensive part-time work had made partner in their firms 15 years after graduation, while more than four-fifths of the mothers with little or no part-time work had made partner" (Robert G. Wood, Mary E. Corcoran, and Paul N. Courant, "Pay Differences among the Highly Paid: The Male-Female Earnings Gap in Lawyers' Salaries," *Journal of Labor Economics* 11, no. 3 (1993): 417–41.

48. O'Neill, "Women and Wages," p. 32. The 86 percent figure standardizes for age and region only; the 91 percent figure also standardizes for additional factors. This article summarizes for noneconomists such scientific work as O'Neill and Polachek, "Why the Gender Gap in Wages Narrowed in the 1980s," and Claudia Goldin, *Understanding the Gender Gap*.

49. O'Neill, "Women and Wages."

50. See Shirley M. Tilghman, "Science vs. Women—A Radical Solution," *New York Times*, January 26, 1993, p. A23.

51. There is a a good discussion of the problem of women, family, and the workplace in *Women and Work/Family Dilemma* by Deborah Swiss and Judith Walker (New York: Wiley, 1993).

52. "Does the Market for Women's Labor Need Fixing?" *Journal of Economic Perspectives*, 3, no. 1 (Winter 1989): 43–60.

53. *Chronicle of Higher Education,* December 1, 1993, p. A9.

54. American Economic Association's Committee on the Status of Women in the Economic Profession, *Newsletter,* October 1991.

55. Faludi, *Backlash,* p. 322.

56. Quoted in ibid., p. 313.

57. Sylvia Ann Hewlett, *A Lesser Life: The Myth of Women's Liberation in America* (New York: William Morrow, 1986), p. 211.

58. Faludi, *Backlash,* pp. 312–18.

59. Ibid., pp. 320–21.

60. Ibid., p. 321.
61. Wolf, *The Beauty Myth*, preface to paperback ed., p. 5.
62. Naomi Wolf, *Fire with Fire* (New York: Random House, 1993).
63. *Glamour*, November 1993, p. 224.
64. Ibid., p. 277.
65. S. Walters, Women's Studies Network (Internet: LISTSERV@UMDD.UMD.EDU.), February 2, 1994.
66. Kay Mussel, *Fantasy and Reconciliation: Contemporary Formulas of Women's Romance Fiction* (Westport, Conn.: Greenwood Press, 1984), p. 164.
67. Kathleen Gilles Seidel, "Judge Me by the Joy I Bring," in *Dangerous Men and Adventurous Women: Romance Writers on the Appeal of Romance*, ed. Jayne Ann Krentz (Philadelphia: University of Pennsylvania Press, 1992), p. 174.
68. Louis Harris and Associates, "Commonwealth Fund Survey of Women's Health" (New York: Commonwealth Fund, 1993). I discussed the fund's questionable findings on abuse in chap. 9.
69. Ibid., p. 3.
70. Ibid., p. 37.
71. Michael Posner, "Survey Shows 4 of 10 Women Depressed," Reuters, July 14, 1993.
72. *Dallas Morning Star*, July 15, 1993.
73. Ibid.
74. All the news clippings cited were included in the final report on the survey results in the Commonwealth Fund survey of women's health. See appendix: "Selected Press Clips."
75. *Gallup Poll Monthly*, March 1992.
76. *San Francisco Chronicle*, July 12, 1993, p. B3. The poll "The New Generation Gap: Boomers vs. Posties in the '90s" was carried out by pollster Mark Baldassare. He called six hundred adult residents, half men and half women, whose numbers were obtained from a computer-generated random sample.

The University of Montreal psychologist Ethel Roskies sent out a questionnaire to 1,123 "high-level professional women" in law, medicine, engineering, and accounting. She reports that "in all personal psychological measures, the married professional with children scored highest. Next was the married professional without children, and last, and least content, was the single woman with no children." She found that "single childless women are significantly more depressed, report lower self-esteem, and lower life satisfaction than married women with children." Associated Press, *Houston Post*, November 22, 1992, p. A7.
77. Questions adapted from the *Practice Guideline for Major Depressive Disorders in Adults* (Washington, D.C.: American Psychiatric Association, 1993), p. 1. The *Merck Manual of Diagnosis and Therapy* (Rahway, N.J.: Merck, Sharp, and Dohme Research Laboratories, 1982), Vol. 1, p. 957, suggests several other criteria for severe depression: have you experienced a loss of capacity to experience emotion, or a feeling that the world has become colorless, lifeless, and dead?
78. Lee Robins and Darrel Regier, eds., *Psychiatric Disorders in America: The Epidemiologic Catchment Area Study* (New York: Free Press, 1991), p. 64. The Robins and Regier study, funded by NIMH, is one of the most respected in the field of psychiatry. It is the source cited by the American Psychiatric Association in its *Practice Guideline for Major Depressive Disorders in Adults* (vol. 150, no. 4 [1993]).
79. See Karen Bourdon et al., "Estimating the Prevalence of Mental Disorders in U.S.

Adults from the Epidemiologic Catchment Area Survey," *Public Health Reports* 107, no. 6 (November–December 1992): 665. According to Robins and Regier, *Psychiatric Disorders in America,* men are at least four or five times more likely than women to become alcoholics (p. 85).

80. Faludi herself is generally distrustful of studies that claim to show that modern liberated single women are depressed. Such studies are part of the backlash. See her discussion of how the media discourage single women by suggesting that their life-styles lead to depression. Faludi, *Backlash,* p. 36.

81. Ibid., p. 37.

82. Robins and Regier, *Psychiatric Disorders in America,* p. 73.

83. Ibid., p. 72.

84. Wendy Wood, Nancy Rhodes, and Melanie Whelan, "Sex Differences in Positive Well-Being: A Consideration of Emotional Style and Marital Status," in *Psychological Bulletin* 106, no. 2 (1989): 249. Wendy Wood, in this paper and others, reports on a series of studies indicating that women and men have different styles of reporting on their emotions: "Women have . . . been found to report more extreme levels of fear, sadness, and joy than men" (p. 251).

85. *Mirabella,* November 1993, p. 38. Hyperbole on women's victimization is very much in vogue. *Mirabella* is not alone among fashion magazines in routinely publishing articles promoting incendiary feminist advocacy statistics. In the same issue, *Mirabella* called Richard Gelles and Murray Straus "pop psychologists," attacking them for their "dispassionate" (hence unfeeling) research on domestic violence and for their findings on battery, which feminists call far too low. Unfortunately, *Mirabella* and its ilk foster misandrism by introducing many a teenager to the resenter mode of male/female relationships.

86. Ms. Futter is leaving Barnard to become president of the American Museum of Natural History.

87. Secretary Reich's words are found on the first page of the paperback edition of Faludi's *Backlash.*

Chapter 12: The Gender Wardens

1. Nat Hentoff, *Free Speech for Me—But Not for Thee* (New York: HarperCollins, 1992), p. 1.

2. Jay Overocker, "Ozzie and Harriet in Hell," *Heterodoxy* 1, no. 6 (November 1992): 9.

3. Ibid.

4. "Sex, Society, and the Female Dilemma" (a dialogue between Friedan and de Beau-voir), *Saturday Review,* June 14, 1975, p. 18. As an equity feminist I find much to admire in de Beauvoir's works, but her bland tolerance for authoritarianism is not part of it. She was perhaps unduly influenced by Jean-Paul Sartre, joining him in his Maoist phase in the seventies. This may help to explain, although it would not excuse, her readiness to use state power to force people to live "correct" lives.

5. Sandra Lee Bartky, *Femininity and Domination: Studies in the Phenomenology of Oppression* (New York: Routledge, 1990), p. 5.

6. Ibid., p. 51.

7. Ibid., pp. 56, 61. Ms. Bartky is also aware that her ideas about the radical reconstruc-tion of self and society are not now popular. It does not worry her: "For it reveals the

extent to which the established order of domination has taken root within our very identities." *Femininity and Domination*, p. 5.

8. Alison Jaggar, *Feminist Politics and Human Nature* (Totowa, N.J.: Rowman and Little-field, 1983), p. 44.
9. Ibid., p. 150.
10. Marilyn Friedman, "Does Sommers Like Women? More on Liberalism, Gender Hierarchy, and Scarlett O'Hara," *Journal of Social Philosophy* 21, no. 2 (Fall–Winter 1990): 83.
11. Gloria Steinem, *Revolution from Within: A Book of Self-Esteem* (Boston: Little, Brown, 1992), p. 260.
12. Jaggar, *Feminist Politics and Human Nature*, p. 219.
13. Steinem, *Revolution from Within*, p. 309.
14. The theme of "safety" is central for gender feminism. Indeed, a favorite phrase for any place where feminists gather is "safe space." In this misogynist world, the "feminist classroom," for example, is advertised as a safe space where women can speak freely without fear of being humiliated by derisive or brutal males. On the other hand, as I tried to show in chapter 6, the feminist classroom can be very *unsafe* for those who are not true believers in gender feminism.
15. Later expanded and published in book form: Lis Harris, *Holy Days: The World of a Hasidic Family* (New York: Macmillan, 1985), p. 128.
16. Ibid., p. 129.
17. Bartky, *Femininity and Domination*, p. 58.
18. Christina Sommers, "Feminist Philosophers Are Oddly Unsympathetic to the Women They Claim to Represent," *Chronicle of Higher Education*, October 11, 1989, p. B3.
19. Marilyn Friedman, " 'They Lived Happily Ever After': Sommers on Women and Marriage," *Journal of Social Philosophy*, 21, nos. 2 and 3 (Fall–Winter 1990): 58.
20. Helen Taylor, *Scarlett's Women: "Gone with the Wind" and Its Female Fans* (New Brunswick, N.J.: Rutgers University Press, 1989).
21. Ibid., p. 130.
22. Ibid., p. 133.
23. Friedman, "Does Sommers Like Women?" p. 87.
24. *Chronicle of Higher Education*, January 15, 1992, p. A7.
25. Ibid.
26. "Men, Sex, and Rape," ABC News Forum, May 5, 1992. Transcript no. ABC-34, p. 9.
27. *Boston Globe*, July 30, 1991, p. 54.
28. Ann Ferguson, *Sexual Democracy: Women, Oppression, and Revolution* (Boulder, Colo.: Westview Press, 1991), p. 207.
29. Lindsy van Gelder, "Lipstick Liberation," *Los Angeles Times Magazine*, March 15, 1992, p. 30.
30. Friedman, "Does Sommers Like Women?" p. 87.
31. Ann Garry, "Pornography and Respect for Women," in John Arthur, ed., *Morality and Moral Controversies* (Englewood Cliffs, N.J.: Prentice Hall, 1993), p. 264.
32. Synopsis on back cover of *Seduction* by Jayne Ann Krentz. Cited in Jayne Ann Krentz, ed., *Dangerous Men and Adventurous Women: Romance Writers on the Appeal of Romance* (Philadelphia: University of Pennsylvania Press, 1992), p. 15.
33. Facts cited in Cathie Linz, "Setting the Stage: Facts and Figures," in Krentz, *Dangerous Men and Adventurous Women*, p. 11.

34. Kathleen Gilles Seidel, "Judge Me by the Joy I Bring," in ibid., p. 170.

35. Ibid., p. 171.

36. Jayne Ann Krentz, "Trying to Tame the Romance," in Krentz, *Dangerous Men and Adventurous Women,* p. 107. Ms. Krentz also writes under the names of Amanda Quick, Jane Castle, and Stephanie James. She has written for Harlequin, Silhouette, and Dell. Her books are frequently on the *New York Times* best-seller list.

37. Krentz, "Trying to Tame the Romance," p. 109.

38. Ibid., pp. 113–14.

39. *New York Times,* Sunday, July 25, 1993, p. 17.

40. Ibid., p. 17.

41. Ibid.

42. Pam Houston, "Big Sister Is Watching," *Elle,* January 1994, pp. 74–75.

43. Ibid., p. 75.

44. See John Leo, "Cultural War at the Whitney," *U.S. News & World Report,* March 22, 1993; and Carol Strickland, "Politics Dominates Whitney Biennial," *Christian Science Monitor,* March 26, 1993, p. 10.

45. *New York Times,* July 21, 1991.

46. Ibid.

47. Nancy Stumhofer, "Goya's Naked Maja and the Classroom Climate," *Democratic Culture,* (Spring 1994): 18–22. See also: transcript of NPR "Weekend Edition," November 16, 1991, "Goya Nude Removed from Penn State Classroom"; *Sunday Patriot News,* November 17, 1991; *Pottsville Republican,* November 16, 1991; *Pocono Record,* November 14, 1991; *Centre Daily Times,* November 20, 1991; *The Morning Call,* November 24, 1991; *Chronicle of Higher Education,* November 27, 1991; and *Newsweek,* November 25, 1991. Once the painting was removed from the classroom there was a storm of protest about censorship. The painting was eventually placed in a television/reading room that was carefully labeled "Gallery." "We put the sign 'Gallery' on there to forewarn people that there is art in the room," Lammie explained. Ms. Stumhofer speaks resentfully about the "chilling climate" in which she was teaching. But we may ask: In what kind of university climate do officials feel it necessary to "forewarn" students that there is art in the room?

48. Nat Hentoff, "A 'Pinup' of His Wife," *Washington Post,* June 5, 1993, p. A21.

49. This statue offended several "on the verge" campus groups. The artist had been inclusive, but that got her into hot water with some students. The black man had a basketball, thus reinforcing the stereotype that all black men are jocks; one Asian-looking figure was carrying a violin, thus reinforcing the "model minority" stereotype.

50. Liza Mundy, "The New Critics," *Lingua Franca* 3, no. 6 (September/October 1993): 27.

51. Ibid., p. 30.

Index